LAST

OF THE

LIONS

LAST

OF THE

LIONS

AN AFRICAN AMERICAN
JOURNEY IN MEMOIR

CLARENCE B. JONES
AND STUART CONNELLY

REDHAWK
PUBLICATIONS

Redhawk Publications
The Catawba Valley Community College Press
2550 U.S. Hwy 70 SE
Hickory NC 28602

ISBN: 978-1-952485-93-0

Library of Congress Number: 2022946262

Layout by Michelle Benoit

Clarence. B. Jones photo by Paul Ryan

Stuart Connelly photo by Sherry McCracken

Portions of this book have been previously published.

Printed in Canada

Redhawk Publications
redhawkpublications.com

Distributed by the University of North Carolina Press
www.uncpress.org

If surviving lions don't tell their stories, the hunters will take all the credit...

African Proverb

CONTENTS

INTRODUCTION

BLACK FEET RUNNING ON WHITE SAND

Jesus God, these boys are going to kill me. Aren't they...? **Would** *they? Why do they clench their fists, bare their teeth... why do they want to hurt me when they don't even know me?*

The son of two African American domestic servants without a roof to call their own didn't have a prayer of spending a summer right on the beach at Longport, New Jersey, but there I was anyway, staying at my parents' employer's oceanfront estate. It was wonderful for several weeks, but then the world turned inside out for me. It should've been obvious that the timeless and blind hatred that is racism seethed everywhere, but it had remarkably never boiled over for me until that day. And so, for all intents and purposes, I didn't really understand that racism existed until the bike incident in 1942.

The employer's grandson Phillip would one day become the chairman and CEO of the Scott Paper Company, but that summer he was just a kid my age, nice enough to let me use his bike when he wasn't riding it. It was on that borrowed bicycle, after a quick stop at the local candy store, that I ran into a gang of white teens who somehow decided that it was my turn to see the mask of civility this country wears pulled back and its ugly inner self revealed. Out came all the words I'd known existed but had never heard aloud before.

I knew *of* them because I'd overheard my parents and their friends occasionally discussing the weapon of words the "bad white folks" could wield. I knew *about* them but had never experienced them up close and personal. Now they rang in my ears like an echo from the Middle Passage, a shout from the plantation days, a scream from the lynch mob nights: Nigger, coon, monkey, jungle bunny, jigaboo. And I felt the power of their verbal weaponry. The hate that came out in vicious name-calling and vile threats terrified me.

I abandoned the bike and ran away, blindly seeking my parents' protection. I beat down that path so many black people before me had, wide-eyed and sweating fear. The white kids chased after me. They had no intention of letting the scare serve its purpose (To keep me in my place? To keep me from coming back the next summer?) and moving on to other activities. Perhaps they knew that if they didn't chase, I'd eventually stop running. And they couldn't have *that* now, could they? It was their world, after all, and they needed to make absolutely sure I knew that I was a stain upon it.

That was nearly eighty-two years ago. I can say from experience there has been no tipping point in America in the interim, no great hand has put down a bright line marking a "before" as distinct from the "after" on the issue of race. Rather, every African American's life is a journey along the path of one historic conceit, primarily a negotiation (if not an outright struggle) around the single absurd issue of skin color. The trip is delineated only by moments on the time-line and intensity and frequency of the incidents of racism. Sometimes, if cherry-picked for the details, some of these folks' journeys tend to look encouraging. A precious handful of Blacks that were born into American slavery lived to see the passing of the Voting Rights Bill. *That's surely some kind of upward trajectory, isn't it?* we are almost ordained to ask. And look at me: I was born into Jim Crow America and lived to see Barack Obama move from the United States Senate to his party's presidential nomination to the White House and into the waiting arms of uplifting history. If I'd died at any moment during his eight years in the Oval Office, the two zeitgeists that bracketed my life would point to a country unquestionably improving upon its racist underpinnings.

But of course, I was blessed with enough longevity to also see the next man to hold that office. To bear witness to the era of Trump and his Proud Boys. To be reminded yet again that racism is this country's original sin, and it hasn't been washed away.

The arc of history may indeed bend toward justice, but seen up close, it's a jagged sawtooth of progress and backslide. It's so hard to get on the far side of it. Jim Crow to Barack Obama is a line, while Jim Crow to Donald Trump feels more like a closed circle, perhaps even a spiral.

But not one of us ever winds up back at the starting point. Even if history seems to repeat, and it does so like an echo in the area of race relations, we're different people facing it each time.

My life story is the rope that connects the Jim Crow era to that of Black Lives Matter. Thread may be the typical metaphor here, but you need something a lot stronger than thread to hold onto during decades as convoluted as the ones in which I've lived. No, my journey feels much more like a rope, twisted and rough, knotted in many spots, but resilient. It can burn your hands if you're not careful. Lord knows it's something I easily could've been hung by. But through the grace of God and the people you'll hear about who've crossed my path, it's tethered me instead—through it all. Kept me calm and focused, and held my misery and anger in check— relatively speaking. The lyrics of Rev. James Cleveland's gospel song eloquently summarize my viewpoint of my journey so far: *Nobody told me the road would be easy, but Lord, I don't believe you brought me this far just to leave me.*

When I was able to get to the safety of the beach house, tears were streaming down my face. I ran to my mother in the kitchen and hugged her around the legs. But instead of the instant sympathy I was expecting for what I'd been through, my mother Mary spoke to me in a harsh and brusque manner: "Come here this instant."

She took me upstairs to the master bedroom. There was a full-length mirror in the corner and my mother pulled me in front of it as she knelt down, wrapping her arms around me from behind and staring at my image from over my shoulder.

"Son, what do you see in that mirror?" she asked.

I didn't understand. "Momma, I see us. I see you and me."

"That's not what you see," she barked. "Come on, what do you see?"

"I see..." I stammered. "I see our reflections, Momma..." It came out like a question.

"No!"

She sounded so annoyed with me that I started crying all over again. "Momma, don't be mad, I just see us, what do you see?" I wanted to please, but I didn't understand what she was looking for from me. Thinking back, I'm not really sure that she did, either. She was reacting, like me, to the boys' campaign of terror. Trying on the fly to come up with a way to help me shake the oppression and shame that those boys had been trying to jam into my subconscious.

She took a breath and landed on the notion she'd been searching for in front of that mirror. "Son, what you see is one of the most beautiful creatures that God has ever put on this earth."

"I do?"

"You." She turned me to face her and wiped my tear-streaked cheek. "Don't you cry just 'cause some mean white boys called you some names, tried to make you feel small. You don't see that stuff in the mirror, do you? You were made in God's image; beautiful, no matter what anyone else says. God loves you. Momma loves you, and we both think you are beautiful. You love yourself, and you love your skin."

I told her that I would, and I meant it.

"You are a good boy," she said to me. "You stay that way."

I told her that I would, and I tried to mean that, too. In a ten-minute span, I'd been shown the extremes; the power of hate and the power of love. In all its guises and complications, the rest of my life would be navigating between those two poles.

"Who's Clarence B. Jones?"

I'm told that friends who have shared bits and pieces of my story with others get that reaction all the time. The people sharing—the ones who've come to know me at some point along the way—aren't surprised. I'm not a household name. But here's the thing: By the time they've finished whatever part of my last ninety-two-year (and counting) story they've chosen to tell, the reactions have always changed. The alchemy of the information communicated has done *something* to the listener. "Who's Clarence B. Jones?" is no longer the question; it's been replaced by this:

"How have I not heard of this man?"

I say this with all modesty, and not false modesty either. For those stories don't talk about the spotlight striking me (gratefully, there never was one); they reference the powerful people in my orbit. I seek to share with you some observations and experiences I had as an African American during a nine-decade journey. And so, like my friends who tell bits and pieces of my history to the unsuspecting and uninitiated, I believe my travelogue will be of special interest because of some of the people I've met along the way, the experiences I've had, the places I've visited and worked.

Many of the people I've met were, and are, extraordinary. Some are publicly known, others less so, but no less extraordinary for the time and place where they lived when I was blessed to meet them, work with them, and often love and learn from them. And though I was often recorded secretly by the FBI, I personally didn't transcribe my own conversations. Consequently, where you see quotation marks in this book, it is not to be taken as verbatim quotes but rather to give you a sense of the substance of the interactions, which I recall quite clearly.

And of course, there are parts of my journey itself that are freighted with significance. Historically speaking, some were unique, especially within the context of the times in which they occurred; years when I was referred to as "colored," decades when I was described as a "spook," moments when I was regarded as an "uppity Negro," and those years when I was thought of as an "arrogant African American" (a point of view with which I believe I'm often still regarded to this day, although quietly and behind my back).

The question at hand: How did this Depression-era "colored" child of household servants with only grade-school educations end up making his way through the rarefied world of sports, entertainment, law, finance, investment banking, and politics—getting so far as to be honored by our first African American President—all while staying off the radar? It wasn't by accident. I did my best work in the long shadows of others.

But this is no Forrest Gump story, the tale of an unlikely man randomly popping up in the middle of pivotal and historic situations for the better part of a century. No, there was purpose and design to my work in the shadows. This is a notion that leads to the next question: Why am I telling my story now?

Because I held a backstage pass to an America most have only seen from the stands and, at ninety-two, we can't afford to have the memories I formed and the sights I witnessed go with me to the grave. They need to be preserved; there are political and social lessons here. If the surviving lions don't tell their stories, then indeed the hunters will get all the credit.

There aren't many of us left, us "lions" of the Civil Rights Movement. Of those that remain, some have said their piece, some have kept their peace. I've written here and there on specific topics, but now it's time I tell my story to those who have the wherewithal to listen, those who strive for a better tomorrow for the country and, in service of that, are willing to hear some of the uglier truths propping up the American Dream. I tend to align myself with the school of thought that Jared Sexton found himself discovering in his book *American Rule*, where he writes, "I knew American history but needed to learn the history of America." I have something to teach on that subject.

It is high time and worth the effort for this country to stand before its own kind of mirror, with all of us asking, *What do you see?*

It's worth being honest about "America the Beautiful."

I figure I can get the ball rolling by telling my story.

One evening, during the same summer that I was chased from the candy store by those white kids, I was in the kitchen watching my mother wash her employer's dishes. There wasn't a word of complaint, but I saw how hard she was working and, as would most sons in that position, I felt bad for her.

Thinking it might be kind to offer her some help, I hopped off my stool and picked up a dishtowel.

"What do you think you're doing?" my mother snapped at me.

"I'm drying," I said.

"Go sit on that chair over there." She snatched the towel right out of my hands. "The only thing I ever want to see in your hands is a pencil and a dollar bill!"

It's telling, her idea of a pencil encapsulating a rewarding life of the mind. Rewarding financially, yes, but spiritually as well. A pencil put to use meant someone whose job could be defined with a desk and a chair. A dream of sitting down while working was something indeed for a permanently exhausted cook and maid. You may need your hand to use a pencil, but people would be *paying* you to use your *mind*. That I would go on, long after my mother's death, to first write contracts and then speeches that were eventually broadcast all over the world would have made her proud. As I write this now, feeling the power of carefully chosen words weaving into ideas that can impact lives, it makes me feel as if the pencil is indeed the most powerful tool on the planet. Like some kind of telepathy machine, if done right it can let readers inside someone else's mind. Inside another's skin. With that perspective, it can perhaps change some readers' thinking.

And the dollar bill? Well, after the pencil, my mother might've thought that the dollars would just fall into place. That was the ebb and flow of my world, the finances. As an entrepreneur, as Wall Street's first "Negro" investment banking partner, and as a lawyer, I certainly saw my share of those dollars in my life, but one doesn't go into headlong battle with the most powerful government the world has ever seen for the money. My mother would've understood that. The pencil and the dollar bill gave me the freedom to fight, a luxury so many Black men could not afford, then and now. That was her gift to me. And I dedicate this memoir to her as a small token of everything she gave.

PART I

KID'S STUFF

CHAPTER 1 | PRIDE MAY NOT BE A SIN

The family my parents worked for were incredibly wealthy. The Lippincotts. A publishing family when publishing *meant* something. The Lippincotts—who had and enjoyed all the trappings of a blue blood Philadelphia Main Line empire. The Lippincotts—who held Goldsboro and Mary Jones' fate in their hands. Who held mine.

My parents were lucky to have the work at the time; domestic servants would be the job description. Indentured servitude by another name, since it was the economic realities of their country that kept them in bondage rather than an actual slave master. So it was simply called "work" for both of them, the kind of work where they lived at their place of employment and were on-call around the clock. Not a job most Americans would relish, but most Americans weren't Black in the 1920s. Goldsboro, the gardener and chauffeur, and Mary, the housekeeper and cook, were. And so, as everyone saw it, they were lucky to have such an opportunity at the time.

If they received some bad news or suffered a stroke of ill fate, that would've had to have been me—my conception. As a frame of reference, consider that while pregnancies slip into the lives of all sorts of folks not prepared for the realities of raising a child, one fundamental thing nearly every expecting married couple have in common is this: They know there is a place for their baby to sleep. Even if it's the grandparents' house. Or a studio apartment, no matter how small, there's still space for a newborn.

But, though married and both gainfully employed, Goldsboro the gardener and chauffeur and Mary the housekeeper and cook were at the mercy of outside forces when it came to their baby. Like children who've found a hurt squirrel in the yard, bring it inside, and are forced to beg their parents to allow them the time and room to nurse the thing back to health, my mother and father's ability to start a family with me was utterly dependent on the largesse of employers in the mansion where they all lived.

Not long after I was born, there was an ultimatum dropped in my parents' laps: Either baby Clarence goes or you all go. They'd felt it coming, no doubt. But still... it had to be soul-crushing. There were of course no easy options. No walking away from the work. Perhaps practicality dictates walking away from the baby.

My parents placed me with two different foster families during my earliest years, friends of theirs in Palmyra, New Jersey. Mary and Goldsboro would pick me up on their rare days off and take me along to some of their other friends' homes in Philadelphia and Atlantic City. That lasted until I was school age. By the time I turned six, they'd found a more permanent solution for me.

North of the city, in Cornwall Heights, there was... well, a boarding school, it could be called. Another word for it might be "orphanage." It was run by an order of Irish Catholic nuns, and it was specifically for Black and—because major financial support came by way of a Catholic diocese in the southwest— Navajo boys. In fact, it was called "The Blessed Sacrament School for Colored and Native American Boys," a very niche student body.

I've wondered often just what it took for my parents to entrust me to an orphanage. True, they believed I would receive the kind of education from the Catholic Church they had no way to provide for me otherwise. Still, to give up their son in this way must have taken an amazing amount of courage. To do so meant self-harm, of course: They broke their own hearts. But they also risked bearing the brunt of my permanent anger toward them. Yet they certainly acted in my best interest, and I never had any negative feelings toward them. The situation dictated their actions.

The orphanage/school was run by the head nun, Sister Mary Patricia. She spoke with a thick but warm Irish brogue. She had wonderful childhood memories of Ireland and would tell me that when I grew up, I should make a special effort to visit there. Sister Mary Patricia was stern when necessary, but her compassion and tenderness made me feel valued. I firmly believe that, throughout my life, the disproportionate affection I've maintained for white people (relative to the average Black person) stems from the feelings of care and support I received from this woman, as well as the other warm and loving nuns at the school.[1] With respect to my emotional outlook after being handed over to the orphanage, I'm proud to say that while the six-year-old me did feel disappointment, fear, and uncertainty, those feelings were mitigated and offset in no small part because Sister Mary Patricia and the other nuns weren't playing hero. While they *showed* me love, they also never stopped reminding me about the love my parents continued to have for me from afar. As they explained it, that love gave them the strength to make this hard sacrifice. I believed them, and wanted to show my love in return, love them enough to work hard, follow the rules, and make them proud.[2]

I was an exemplary student, probably because I thought that following the rules was the only way to behave. I couldn't really conceive of an alternative to doing what I was told. So, if I was ordered to study, I did. Told to make my bed, I did. I was a "good soldier," a trait that would come in handy for the first quarter of my life. At a certain point, when I began to see that there were alternatives to toeing the line, that's when my life would start to get *really* interesting.

---

1 Lately I have to say that I've had a change of heart in the matter. I've been very close to white people and have always felt as if I was one of the few Black men that really "got" that a few bad apples (white supremacists and racists) shouldn't ruin the whole barrel. But that thinking has changed. I now have a new and likely unpopular outlook after reflecting on my experiences over the last nine decades: Put bluntly, after all I've seen, I now must assume that every white person has racism inside them unless they demonstrate the alternative. It's a guilty-until-proven-innocent outlook that doesn't square with my legal training but syncs quite easily with my decades of experience.

2 Something about the Roman Catholic faith, fundamentally a kind of oxymoron, grabs you by the throat and doesn't let go. One of the Seven Deadly Sins, at least in my day, was pride. There it is: Pride is bad. Except that inside the walls of the orphanage, it seemed closer to a virtue. Not a spoken one, nothing as direct as that. But obliquely, the reinforcement was always there.

But for the time being, I was what my mother would call me years later in front of that mirror, a "good boy."

There was a fundamental problem, however; I had developed a stutter during my early years at Blessed Sacrament. It was painful and embarrassing, and hounded me during my time at the orphanage. Stammering my way through, I learned to act as an altar server, studied catechism and religious Latin to chant the church's liturgy, memorized my Catholic prayers. I was thrilled when I had my first opportunity to help serve at regular Sunday Mass. At weekly confession I found it hard to think of anything I had done that was bad or wrong. Who could? We were under the watchful eyes of the nuns around the clock.

By design, there were many Native American boys at the school. The Order of the Blessed Sacrament at that time maintained several "mission" churches and schools on Navajo reservations in Arizona and New Mexico. Those boys had names such as Little Bear and Running Deer, straight out of the Westerns. If they had other more Anglo names, they never shared them. Although we all wore the same clothes, the Native American boys wore their hair in ponytails or two pigtails. I got scolded quite severely for the transgression of taking the ponytail of a Native American boy who sat in front of me in class and dipping it in an inkwell. Yes, I'm old enough to have gone to a school with an inkwell at every desk.[3]

There were roughly twenty-five beds lined up on each side of the dorm room. At the end of each room was a section with a curtain drawn where the nun on duty for that evening would sleep and get up if any of the boys had a problem, which was usually a nightmare. My only recollection of the priests, who were much more hands-off, was confession, Mass, and Latin class.

---

3 Years later, when I was in the Army at Fort Dix, New Jersey, a young Native American man approached me in our barracks and identified himself as having lived at The Blessed Sacrament at the same time as me, and in the same dormitory. Several months later when I was working a special midnight shift at the McGuire Airbase unloading body bags from the Korean war, I recognized the name of this young man on the manifest list of those killed.

I always looked forward to working on the weekend in the school bakery where fresh bread was baked. A special treat was warm bread, butter, and molasses. We played games like capture the flag and went on hikes in the woods adjacent to the school's property.

Every class started with a school prayer and class time was focused. Students were often called individually to the English class blackboard to diagram sentences and we were taught to write cursive with the "Palmer method." (I wasn't very good with cursive and printed most of my assignments until first year of public high school.) In classes, the nuns referred to me as "Master Jones." When I was called to the front of the room either to diagram a sentence or do a math problem or conjugate a Latin word, and made a mistake, I was corrected by the forceful tap of a long pointer on my wrist or hand by the teaching nun. To this day I still write often in the style of constricted parochial school English. Writing a sentence that did not have a noun, verb, subject, and proper use of an adjective and adverb, or carried a dangling participle was the cardinal sin, subject to immediate public corporal punishment by the nuns.

It was at the orphanage, huddled around a big radio on December 7th, 1941, that I and all the other boys heard the horrible news about the bombing of Pearl Harbor. None of us had a clear understanding of exactly what war was, but the broadcast made it sound terrifying.

As far as any of us knew, I was the only boy whose parents were alive. This fact blew the minds of my classmates. Goldsboro and Mary had one day off together every other week, and on that day we'd have a visit.

Imagine the surreal nature of it; my "parents" would come to my "orphanage" in a fancy car, take me out for ice cream or a movie, and then drop me back off. All the kids would watch me leave, watch me return. Here was the question: "If they love you, why don't they take you home with them?"

I didn't have the facts or the life experience to answer. I just knew they did love me, and they didn't take me home.

My parents would often mention that soon they would be
able to take me home, but the only time ever I did leave with
them was during the summer when their work would move
to that beach house in Longport. If you think kids look forward to summer, imagine the mindset of an "orphan" whose
parents take him to the beach in July. I would stare at those
calendar pages starting in March, willing them to flip.

Once finished with eighth grade, I'd aged out of the Sisters of
The Blessed Sacrament School for Colored and Native American Boys.[4] Fortunately, my parents had been working toward
solving this problem. By the time I was ready for high school,
they had made some headway on the American Dream. Good
headway for Blacks at the time: My parents were able to buy
a home in East Riverton, New Jersey. (In an amazing coincidence, Riverton—founded in the 1800s by a group of wealthy
Quakers as one of the first planned summer communities in
America—was built on land bought from the Lippincott family.) Though across the Delaware River in another state, the
town was practically a Philadelphia suburb, and so they were
able to provide me a bedroom of my own for the first time and
still commute in to continue their work for the Lippincotts.
East Riverton sat just next to the larger town of Palmyra. It
was a Black enclave where those Negroes who didn't live in
the "colored section" of Palmyra lived. However, it was within
Palmyra's school district and so for high school I attended my
first public school.

My stutter gradually improved. A child psychologist could
probably have figured out that it was related to some aban-
donment issues or my general fear of not being a worthy
person, based on the circumstances I found myself in at the
orphanage. However, I was never diagnosed, and I had no
way of understanding for myself what created that stutter,
what powered it. I can say with certainty, however, that when
I ended up living with my parents again for high school, it

---

4 I returned to Cornwall Heights only once more, when I was twenty and
finishing up my undergraduate degree. On that visit I learned that Sister Mary
Patricia had died. This was shortly after my own mother had passed away and
the news took my grief to new depths.

receded until it disappeared forever. While I give much credit to my freshman English and speech teacher Mrs. Johnson, who worked on my stammer with me, I have to say overall the problem was overcome on an emotional level.

By count in the yearbook, my class—the Class of '49—was comprised of 175 students. Fifty-two of them were Black. Among the full student body of roughly 700, there were fewer than two hundred kids who looked like me. It was a larger representation than the national average of 11-12% of the population, and there were certainly enough of us that it didn't feel like we were from another planet. We sat together in the cafeteria. Not because of any policy or even any particular animosity from the white students, but out of a sense of comfort and familiarity.

That's not to say I didn't make friends with the white children. There was actually a group of white kids that I seemed to be at the center of, owing partially to my comfort with Caucasians instilled in me by those Irish nuns, but more due to my role as a member of the orchestra and perhaps most due to my success as an athlete.

Sports came somewhat easily to me; I was tall, flexible, decently strong and had stamina. I ran track, which garnered quite a bit of attention. I also played varsity football in my sophomore year, but my track coach discouraged me from continuing to play for fear that I would get injured and have to drop off the track team.

Friendships that I developed in the high school band and orchestra overlapped with my schoolwork. I found myself being the only Black person who studied with white students, went to their homes, and shared a social life. All my close white friends—boys as well as girls—were members of the high school Honor Society. I joined too and was eventually selected by the advising teachers and the other members to be president. Honor Society, my grade point average, and my social circle in school were the combination that positioned me to get selected by my classmates as the male student "Most Likely to Succeed" in my senior year.

"Tomorrow the World"
CLARENCE JONES — BETTY SHIPPS

My social life in high school in the Negro community where I lived was spent with the Ransoms and the Dorseys. Each family consisted of several brothers and sisters. I also spent a lot of time with and in the homes of two white classmates, Richard Burr and Everett Wills. We were in the Honor Society together. Both boys eventually went into engineering, but at school Everett was trying to get admitted to the United States Naval Academy at Annapolis. I spent so much time with Everett that he eventually asked his parents why I couldn't just live with them in their house. But I'd done enough time away from home. Everett asked me one night why I thought God made him to look the way he looked, and why I looked the way I looked.

I said, "Why don't you go ask him?"

I don't think the Blessed Sacrament nuns would have approved.

One summer, between my sophomore and junior years at Palmyra, I got a job at the Campbell's Soup plant in Camden. I worked the 7:00 a.m. to 3:00 p.m. shift, so I would get up very early every weekday morning and walk for about 10-15 minutes to catch the public bus to the factory. My job all day was loading containers of canned soup into the rolling racks of a railroad freight car. My work team consisted entirely of older Negro men, who learned that I was working so that I could go to college. These guys were veterans of the facility, and they arranged it so, somehow, I was able to "work" a double shift to make more money for school.

The second shift involved working in a railroad boxcar that had been pulled right up inside the factory for loading. This meant I was clocked-in to work from 7:00 a.m. to 3:00 p.m. working the regular shift, and then, with the help of the older men, I would clock back in for the 3:00 to 11:00 p.m. shift. I would work for a couple of hours during that shift, then the older men would provide me with a pile of burlap potato sacks to use as pillows and blankets and let me sleep in the corner of an empty freight car. When the shift was close to ending, they'd wake me up to clock out with them.

This second phantom shift enabled me to collect nearly twice as much money at my summer job as I first expected. At the time, I figured that they were proud of me, a young Black boy who planned to go to college. I assumed they wished they'd had the opportunity... or had children for whom that was a possibility. I'll never know for sure. But I'll always remember their collective paternal protection of me so I could make as much money as possible during my summer job. The fact that, technically, it was stealing from "the man" never caused me much distress.

During my time at Palmyra High, Mrs. Lippincott died. My father continued to work for her son and daughter, but my mother found another, higher paying domestic servant position several hours away from Philadelphia in Larchmont, New York. She would only come home one day and evening a week or every other week during my upper-class years of high school. I was left alone most of the time, doing my homework or practicing and performing on my clarinet and alto saxophone. My father would come home to the small house in East Riverton each day around 6:00 p.m. and fix us supper. He was a good man, and usually gentle, but I wasn't connected to him like I was to my mother. Perhaps no boy is. The only time I remember my parents having an argument, it shook me to my core. I have no idea what the fight was about, but my father went upstairs and took out a .38 pistol and threatened my mother with it. My mother was crying and the next-door neighbors came over and talked soberly to my father, who eventually put the gun away. I knew that night whose side I was on, if it ever came to that.

In the summer of 2017, I visited Palmyra High School to be honored as one of their "celebrated and famous graduates."

I was given the opportunity to speak at an assembly commemorating the opening of their Clarence B. Jones Institute for Social Advocacy. All the students were wearing white T-shirts with red lettering: *Welcome back, Clarence.*

What I had to tell them had everything to do with the value of education, particularly for African Americans. I believe what many young Black men and women have been told by their elders through the decades here in America: If you're Black, you have to work twice as hard for half as much. If you do the math, it means four times as hard for equal footing. Given nearly a century of living as a Black man in America, I can say that sounds about right. And the one fundamental element that allows you the leverage to overcome that twice- or four-fold disadvantage is education. It is the cornerstone of success for Black people, and for those in the pursuit of so-called "Black Excellence," it is of paramount importance. Yet valuing higher education is not, broadly speaking, a focal point that as a culture we African Americans foster in our youngsters through the generations. If we don't value it, praise it, and underscore it, then naturally it doesn't get the attention of our youth, and doesn't become a source of pride. So, it fails to become a goal throughout the community.

In 1949, I was not a victim of that kind of thinking. I knew I wanted to go to college. How could I be "most likely to succeed" without the right tools? I had a full grasp of the value of higher education. I'd fallen in love with learning. But was I going to graduate from high school and move right on to college? Not a chance. The reason wasn't lack of interest. The issue for me, as for so many other young Blacks, was financial. Despite the help from my Campbell Soup colleagues, I saw no way to afford university directly.

But that just made me focus more on the goal. And I did come up with an angle to play. (As you'll learn in the coming pages, a large portion of my success in life can be attributed to coming up with the right angles.)

In this case, I had an idea that the armed services could be a way forward, acting like a stepping-stone to fill in for what I imagined to be the average white American kid's college fund. I'd read of the V-12 program which, as part of your enlistment, guaranteed you a college education after you completed your service. I was good with following rules; I had no doubt I'd make a solid soldier. (Fate would allow me to prove that to myself, but not quite in the way I'd devised).

One afternoon I took the bus into Camden and went to the Naval Recruitment Center. I was a tall and solidly built high school senior and figured I could pass for eighteen. The recruiting officer looked me up and down and asked for ID. I told him I didn't have any.

"You say you're eighteen though."

"I will be by the time I graduate," I said. But I wasn't convincing, and he was onto me immediately. He called the high school's main office to verify that I'd be old enough to join up when I finished out the year. My birthday was in January; I'd be seventeen at graduation. He liked my chutzpah, and generally speaking, recruiting officers liked a warm body. But this was a no sale situation.

"Nice try, kid," he said. "Come back when you're old enough." Then he went back to the phone and arranged for someone from the school to come pick me up.

My mother was excited about my interest in education, of course. It dovetailed with her pencil-and-dollar-bill outlook. She began to speak with the school about our situation, and soon some of my favorite Palmyra teachers were asking me about my plans. They had suggestions based on my interests and their own experiences. I told them the Joneses didn't even have enough for the application fees of the universities they were telling me about, let alone the tuition. But instead of becoming deflated, they rallied to my cause.

For all the trouble I've had in my life, I know I should never underestimate the amount of kindness that has crossed my path at just the right time. Luck has a big part to play in life, no doubt about it. But the people you're lucky enough to run into must have empathy and selflessness, or the luck doesn't mean a thing. My science teacher, Mr. Lucas, my English/ Speech teacher, Mrs. Johnson, and even the school principal, Mrs. McDonald, were all upset about my trying to join the Navy, and they didn't want me to waste my potential. Collectively, those three public employees chipped in their personal funds and paid the fees to cover the cost of my college applications. They also wrote glowing letters of recommendation. Their commitment changed the trajectory of my life. It was an overwhelming gesture of their faith in me. It's hard to imagine that happening today, but, of course, teaching has always been a calling. When I hear stories of schoolteachers having to buy their own classroom supplies to be able to do their jobs, I'm pained... but I also see it as a sign that the spirit of those teachers I had at Palmyra lives on.

I was admitted to the University of Pennsylvania (where a library is named for a Lippincott), Syracuse, Yale, and Columbia. However, only Columbia offered me a scholarship and financial assistance package that covered my tuition and room. All I had to do was buy books and feed myself.

• • •

I was selected to be the class speaker at graduation and received the most awards, academic and for service, of anyone in our senior class. Both my parents attended the ceremony, which was held outside at the football stadium at Palmyra High School. I could see my parents sitting in the front row of the bleachers, beaming with pride when my name was called to receive the various awards; and, of course, giving the speech on behalf of my entire class. It wasn't as good as the speech I gave at the school 68 years later, but I acquitted myself admirably for a teen recently over a stuttering problem.

Graduation Day was a great high point; I didn't want the ceremony to end. But when it did, I wished that I could leave for New York and go to Columbia College directly from that high school football field.

I didn't have any idea of what the summer would hold for me; if I had, I wouldn't have been so eager to have those months evaporate...

CHAPTER 2 | POVERTY TURNED INSIDE-OUT

The summer after my Palmyra graduation, I worked as a counselor at a sleep-away camp. Camp Wichita was part of the Herndon County Park System in the upper Hudson River Valley of New York. Its campers and staff were predominantly Jewish. It was, among other firsts, the first time I had met and been around so many Jewish people. Camp Wichita was where I learned to understand and even speak a bit of Yiddish. However, twenty percent of its campers and a quarter of its summer staff were Negro. I later learned that it was what might be termed a "left-wing" camp, or a "Workers Children's" camp. Several of the counselors' relatives were men who had fought in the "Lincoln Brigade" against Franco during the Spanish Civil War. Paul Robeson was a hero at the camp and often performed there throughout the years.

Camp Wichita was also the first time I experienced a romantic relationship. It was with another counselor, Sandra Baer, a Sephardic Jew from Rego Park, Queens. She was 5 feet 8 inches tall with curly black hair and green eyes. To me at that time, she was the most beautiful woman I'd ever met. She was also engaged to be married that upcoming fall. Sandy and I would spend evenings together at the end of our respective workdays as counselors. We would hug, kiss, and go for walks around the campgrounds arm-in-arm.

We'd become romantically involved, but she would also share with me the letters that she received from her fiancé. She would have me read them and ask my assistance on what she should write in reply. We would then sit down and jointly write her response to his letter. (This was the first word-smithing assistance I would provide. Years later, I would do the same, if less awkwardly, as a political advisor, personal lawyer, and draft speechwriter for Dr. Martin Luther King, Jr.)

When the summer was over, Sandy had to decide if she actually wanted to marry the man to whom she was engaged. Just before the end of the season, she told me she would postpone her wedding and take some time to think about whether she wanted to go through with it after all. The man to whom I'd been writing love letters in her voice was in for a surprise.

"This is my son. He's going to college in New York City; Columbia University—one of those big old schools. Ivy League, they call them." My mother was speaking to a salesman at Wanamaker's Department Store in Philadelphia, in the middle of their Labor Day Weekend Sale. There she was, five-eight, maybe 160 pounds, shimmering black hair, a gleaming set of white teeth, a smooth complexion the color of brown sugar. She was then and always very beautiful to me, but my love and admiration for her was no match for the embarrassment I felt as she bragged on.

She had taken me with her to shop for some new clothes that I could bring along to college. When I say clothes, I'm not talking about a full wardrobe, or even several outfits, but merely the bare bones version of not wearing the same thing every day. The salesperson directed us to that section displaying clothing for young men going back to school. The average annual wage in 1949 was $2,950. My parents were domestic household servants. I am certain they made less than the prevailing annual wage; somewhere between $900 and $1,200 a year. With whatever money she somehow scraped together, my mother purchased two pairs of slacks for me—one dark brown, the other gray—along with a dark green corduroy jacket, a sweater, and a pair of leather Oxford shoes.

To anyone in earshot, employee or customer, my mother would say, "My son graduated from Palmyra High. At the top of his class. I'm so proud of him. You know his classmates, most of them white boys and girls, also chose him as the person in their class 'Most Likely to Succeed.' Isn't that nice?"

But "nice" in 1949 was circumstance dependent. Nice for whites was a different situation, no doubt. That year saw racial apartheid established by Heinrich Verwoerd in

South Africa, the Soviet Union test its first atomic weapon, and George Orwell publish his seminal and prescient tale of authoritarian rule, *1984*.

It was also probably the year that my mother's cancer began growing in her colon. Three years later she would be dead, eaten away from the inside as I started my senior year at Columbia, an event that would precipitate a strange digression in my path to adulthood.

The day I left for college on a bus from Philadelphia bound for New York, I took a shopping bag with me that held the new Wanamaker's trousers and corduroy jacket. I wore a pair of gray tweed slacks and loafers and lugged my clarinet case and a new briefcase that my high school teachers had given me. A trunk with more clothing, as limited as my wardrobe was, had been sent via UPS to Columbia ahead of time. My parents gave me fifty dollars in cash. It seemed like a small fortune at the time. My Uncle Clarence lived in New York and had assured my mother that he was there for me, the knowledge of which made the journey into the unknown a little bit easier.

Columbia University was overwhelming to me at first. The transition from the sisters of The Blessed Sacrament to Palmyra High hadn't been too difficult. Palmyra included the familiar comforts of other Negro students, some of whom I even knew before school started. The really significant difference then was the existence of white students, a sharp contrast to my previous school for "colored" and "Indian" boys.[5] Thus, the biggest shock for me in 1949 in enrolling at Columbia was that there were very few—hardly any—other Negro boys (Columbia was an all-male school at the time). Yes, there were some, but out of a combined student body of approximately 3,000 men, I don't believe there were more than nine or ten other Negro students in my freshman class. All of those seemed to have had parents who had attended

---

5 The biggest difference between the orphanage and the high school was the addition of girls in the social mix. That was a lot for a young man to process.

college themselves, or at the very least had a high school diploma. I was reasonably certain that none of the parents of those few Negro students were domestic servants. I felt like a tiny minority within a minority.

Columbia started with orientation week, ahead of the beginning of classes, set aside for incoming freshmen to learn the campus and its processes. After locating my trunk of clothes that had been sent ahead, I was assigned to a room in Hartley Hall with three other students. They were all white. Two of them were friends from the same high school in Denver and the third was a few years older than us, a veteran from Pennsylvania. The room was a large shared living space, with two bunk beds, four small tables, and four chairs. There was a shared shower and bathroom down the hall. During orientation, I saw no other Negro students among the Hartley Hall residents, but I did meet lots of other freshmen. All those I met came from other states and a few other countries. I noticed that there was always a group who seemed to be dressed in an easy, rich, and not-a-care-in-the-world style: Open-collared shirt, white pullover V-neck sweater, a blue blazer, tan slacks, white buck shoes. Was this a university or a yacht club? I would later learn this was the prep-school look, and every Ivy League school at the time was filled with boys that looked like that. Not like me.

One of my roommates had become friendly with Phil, a fellow freshman from Dallas who lived down the hall. At the end of orientation week, the four roommates and Phil went out for the evening to explore the city. It was a warm night, and on the way back to our dorm, we stopped in a bodega for ice cream. We each grabbed a disposable balsa wood spoon on our way out. Back home, we decided to share the ice cream, since we'd all bought different flavors. We ate from the various cartons scattered on the table, but soon I noticed one student had stopped eating from the containers from which I'd taken any bites. It was the Dallas boy.

The next day, one of my roommates, Wendell, told me that Phil had taken my friends aside later that night and told them that he was absolutely horrified by the get-together in the dorm, and that they should not be sharing ice cream with me.

"You could catch some disease if you eat out of the same carton as a nigger," Phil told them, adding that he was pre-med, so he knew about such things.

I listened to Wendell with growing dread. The spoon that had been in my mouth had touched some ice cream; in that white boy's eyes, it was now tainted. Welcome to Columbia. A long way from the soft arms of the Irish nuns.

But the next surprise was better. My roommates stood up for me and told Phil I was just like them.

For the first time in a while, I thought about standing in front of that mirror with my mother in Longport. I felt the strength of her belief in me. "If Phil has a problem with Negroes," I said to Wendell, "maybe he should've stayed in Texas for college."

Wendell smiled. "I told him the exact same thing."

Soon after this incident I experienced my first instance of overtly expressed Antisemitism. That Sunday, we were told to check in at the lobby of Hamilton Hall. There, we could learn which classes we'd been assigned for the start of the term. The names of the students in the freshman class were posted on a bulletin board framed behind a locked glass case. Next to each student's name was the name of their state and high school and the various classrooms for the courses we were required to take. Everyone was crowded around the board, looking for their name, classes, and room assignments.

I heard a voice behind me say, "Jonesy Boy, you are fucked now! You'd better try to get yourself assigned to a different group of students."

I turned back to see who was making this declaration. It was Dallas Phil, of course. "What are you talking about?" I asked. "What's wrong?"

"You are one unlucky man," Phil chortled. "You've been assigned to classes with all those kikes."

Based on his previous behavior, I should've known, but naively I asked, "What's a kike?"

"You might be smart but you sure are one dumb Negro boy," he told me. "A 'kike' is a Jew boy! Look at their names. And those schools: High School of Science, Fieldstone, DeWitt Clinton, Little Red Schoolhouse, Stuyvesant, Horace Mann... those are where most of the Jew boys at Columbia come from. All they want to do is study."

"So, what's wrong with that?" I demanded. I figured these kikes and I had a lot in common, since studying was all I wanted to do as well.

"You'll find out," he said. "You're going to be graded on a curve. Don't you need a B-minus average to keep your scholarship? Good luck doing that, going against—" Phil glanced at the bulletin board to grab a sample name. "– Aaron Goldstein."

I told him that the schedule was beyond my control, there was nothing I could do about it. I would simply attend my assigned classes.

"Believe me," Phil replied, "you'll be sorry."[6]

I never was. On the contrary, some of those so-called "Jew boy" friendships I developed in New York would remain a part of my life for many years. One such friend was Robert Barron Nemiroff. Two years older than me and a Phi Beta Kappa student at NYU, Bobby was truly "a man for all seasons." His family owned a celebrated Israeli restaurant and supper club in Midtown Manhattan called Habib.[7] As a boy who always had a big appetite and limited access to food or cash, I would often accompany Bobby to eat at his parents' restaurant on the weekends. That was my first introduction to Jewish cui-

---

6 After these two events, Phil remained distant with me at school until our second year, when he saw how good a student I was in the classes we shared and began to ask me if we could study together. That might've been my first lesson in situational ethics.

7 Bobby introduced me to Lorraine Hansberry, who he would eventually marry. She went on to become a celebrated playwright ("Raisin in the Sun" was the first play ever produced on Broadway written by an African American woman). Lorraine was very disappointed I was unable to come down from Boston for the Broadway opening in April of 1959. But as the play was garnering rave reviews, I was hunkered down studying for my law school final exams.

sine. His mother Mae effectively spoke no English. She'd take two of her fingers and pinch my waist, saying "There's no meat on your bones" in Yiddish. She wanted to fatten me up; I was happy to let her try. I was like a hungry puppy dog to her. She piled the food on a plate at the table in the back of the nightclub dining room, near the kitchen where Bobby and I would sit. Our conversation would be robust, with Bobby acting as a Yiddish-English translator good enough for the U.N. Mae spoke to me so often that I began picking up and even starting to use a bit of Yiddish, which just endeared me to her even more.

My experience with Bobby went beyond having a nosh and chatting with his mom at the club. One of my proudest moments came in the spring of 1950. Around midnight, several of us helped Bobby climb the main flagpole on the NYU campus so he could hang a large "Ban the Bomb" banner as public declaration of our opposition to the Cold War's Sword of Damocles, the hydrogen bomb.

Those experiences, and the attitude about Jews expressed by Phil in that lobby, gave me an early awareness of what Antisemitism entailed and how similar it felt to racism.[8]

Another incident involved a young man named Norman Frankel, with whom I had become very friendly. He and his sister Audrey lived with their parents in a lovely home on the Grand Concourse, which is the main thoroughfare running through the Bronx (though at the time that meant nothing to a "country boy" from Palmyra, New Jersey).

My on-campus friendship with Norman was such that he invited me to spend a Saturday and Sunday with him and his family. The genuine spontaneous warmth between Norman and me must have been infectious. His parents and sister embraced me with equal affection. Norman's parents made it clear I was always welcome to come to visit at their home on the weekends rather than stay in my stuffy dorm room.

---

8 Of course, Hitler's program depended heavily upon delineating Jewishness as a racial distinction, not merely a religious one. So perhaps "similar to racism" is gilding the lily; Antisemitism is the precise equivalent of racism.

Norman did so well academically that he became a Phi Beta Kappa Scholar in his junior year. One day, I encountered Norman on the quad. He wore horn-rimmed glasses, but I could see through them that his eyes were rimmed red from crying. My first reaction was that something terrible had happened in Norman's family—to his parents or to his sister. No, he had just received word that his application for admission to Columbia's prestigious Physicians and Surgeons Medical School had been rejected.

I thought, how could this be possible: A junior Phi Beta Kappa student *at* Columbia College is rejected for admission to Columbia's graduate School of Medicine?

I immediately went to see Mr. Coleman, who was the Dean of Admissions. Dean Coleman seemed almost like he'd anticipated my arrival. He said, "Clarence, I know that you and he are very close friends. Before you get yourself all worked up over this, notwithstanding Norman's good grades and Phi Beta Kappa status, he applied for admission to P&S later than he should have. By the time his application for admission was received, P&S had already reached its quota of Jewish students."

He said this in a matter-of-fact tone. I didn't know what a quota was, so I asked.

Dean Coleman explained that the Medical School had a percentage limit of Jewish students they would accept in a given year.

"You mean to tell me that the school will accept a non-Jewish football player from Iowa with a B-minus average over Norman Frankel because of his religion?" I asked.

Dean Coleman said yes. I hope he said it with regret, but I can't be sure.

The school's response was of course crushing to Norman and his family. Norman was inconsolable and embittered. He decided to attend Medical School in Italy, eventually becoming Minister of Health in the Italian Communist Party Coalition Government of Pamir Togliatti.

. . .

In early October of my freshman year, Sandy, the engaged girl from camp, called and asked to come and see me. On one beautiful fall afternoon, we strolled over to Riverside Drive and sat on a bench. As we looked out beyond the cars on the Westside Highway to the Hudson River, Sandy told me she had been doing a lot of thinking about us; about her affection for me and our time together earlier that summer at Camp Wichita. She said she had decided to marry her fiancé, but she wanted to come speak to me in person about why.

She confided that during the course of our summer together, she had quickly fallen in love with me. She'd even considered the thought of the two of us getting married. She realized, however, that my education was a very important opportunity, and she didn't want my relationship with her to interfere with it in any way. She reminded me about how I had shared with her information about my childhood struggles and how proud my parents, especially my mother, were of my acceptance to Columbia. She'd taken that very seriously. Prophetically, Sandy told me she'd decided that the most important thing for me at that stage in my life, as a young Negro, was to continue my college education. She said the opportunity of a first-class Columbia education as a scholarship student should be my number one priority.

She felt any relationship with her would hinder and distract me from that goal. She tearfully said this is not what she felt in her heart, but what her head told her was right. She said she felt certain that our marriage would break my mother's heart, making her forever angry at Sandy. Without mentioning our skin color, she suggested that not even our love for one another could overcome adverse consequences our marriage could cause to me. She dismissed or minimized any discussion about what effect it might have on her family and friends. She only spoke about me and my parents. If we were to marry, she was fearful that it would endanger this once in a lifetime opportunity for me.

Despite my initial devastation, I came around to seeing things from Sandy's viewpoint. It's amazing how much more mature than I was than Sandy was at that time.

"You may not believe it," she said, "but the Clarence Jones I have come to know and love will someday be a great man and make a great contribution to this country." She said she knew deep in her heart, that one day my people, the Negroes, would be even more proud of me than my beloved mother was right then. The same mother who bothered every Wannamaker's shopper to tell them about her son.

I suppose I agreed with Sandy, though her words seemed impossibly grand to me. I had no idea what I was doing. I was only eighteen at the time; little did I know what my future would entail.[9]

Bobby Nemiroff was one of the people I knew off-campus; he attended New York University. We met in the second half of our sophomore year. On the weekends, if I was not attending a Columbia football game (or playing, starting in my second year), I would leave campus and go downtown and meet students from other colleges who were politically active in their respective schools. This was one of the high points of political discourse at the time. Student activity on college campuses skyrocketed after the tumultuous presidential election of 1948, in which Henry Wallace had run a third-party campaign for president on the Progressive Party ticket. Many students on campuses worked nationwide for his candidacy, calling themselves the Young Progressives of America.

Bobby was an active member of the NYU chapter of the YPA. I'd joined the Student NAACP, which led me to an interest in the YPA. Soon I became active in Columbia's chapter, eventually taking on the role of the club's president. The

---

9 I could never imagine that years later I'd be a guest speaker at Farleigh Dickinson College in Teaneck, New Jersey, and Sandy, by then a professor of English Literature, would be in the audience. I was single at the time, but she was married to her fiancé from the camp. That didn't stop us from resuming our romance. During this brief period, lying in bed next to one another and talking, Sandy would say, "Remember what I said to you as we sat on that park bench. See, I was right."

Young Progressive Party would eventually become one of the organizations that Joe McCarthy would tie to his (mostly fictional) communist conspiracy during his Cold War witch hunt. But the context of the young communist movement at that time had a very different tone in popular culture and particularly at universities.

Anti-communist propaganda was not yet in the zeitgeist. Joseph McCarthy hadn't stood for anything in particular and wasn't yet on the political map, and the word *communist* didn't yet have the red-hot brand of traitorous connotations attached to it. It was a political philosophy, plain and simple—one that focused on the poor and the powerless. It was a reasonable area of political attention for the disenfranchised: Blacks, the working class, Jews.

My friends in the intellectual circles were frustrated with me at Columbia; they wanted me out on the streets proselytizing, passing out pamphlets and converting people. Yes, I was a progressive, maybe even a radical, but I was also a student athlete. The football coach, Lou Little, had seen me running track one day and asked me if I'd ever played football. I told him about my short season in high school. Coach Little suggested I come to junior varsity football practice. I was interested. Even with tuition and board paid for, I had to struggle to pull together enough money to eat. Certain days I worked in the dining room, clearing tables to earn money for food, but that was a band-aid at best. The most immediate benefit of being on the football team was that it entitled me to eat at the football training table, guaranteeing one free meal a day during football season.

I played left halfback. It turned out that I enjoyed football much more than track, and I realized in college that I should've made football my sport in high school. Instead, I had listened to my track coach. I wasn't about to make the same mistake by listening to my friends who were giving me a hard time about playing.

But I was able to do a bit of both. I'd become active in campus politics during the second half of my freshman year. Student political activities often took place on Saturdays, with the primary activity comprised of handing out leaflets in connection with various social causes and talking up the strangers who would take them. Because of the football schedule, I wasn't available to participate in the fall; consequently, I was criticized by some of my political friends as not being "committed." I felt the pressure—a pull in mutually exclusive directions. Until a chance meeting with the right man set me straight.

That man was Paul Robeson. An icon. I'd missed him at Camp Wichita (he didn't visit my summer there), but his shadow loomed large over my life. Until I met Martin Luther King, Jr., I can say without a trace of uncertainty that Robeson was the most impressive and accomplished Negro with whom I'd ever crossed paths. Depressingly, he's not as well known today as he deserves to be. His legacy has faded. But if it were up to me, every man, woman, and child in America would think of Robeson with reverence. The quick breakdown: He was an actor, opera singer, professional athlete, Columbia graduate, lawyer, scholar, and Civil Rights leader.

I met Robeson at the Riverside Drive apartment of Charles and Fran White. Charles was a renowned artist whose work reflected the Black experience in America. He and his wife had taken me under their wing when I first arrived in New York. I told Robeson that I admired his athleticism as well as his intellect. I mentioned the pressure I'd been feeling from my politically active friends. "They want me handing out pamphlets on game day," I complained. "But I can't let the team down."

"Forget the team," Robeson boomed in his famous baritone. "You can't let those people in the *stands* down!" He advised me to remind my Columbia friends about priorities. "These are your friends? Trying to make you feel bad about who you are? You need to *educate* them. I know from experience: America's a celebrity culture." He put his massive arm around my shoulders and looked deep in my eyes. "Listen to me," he growled. "You tell your friends that *any* Saturday afternoon, a single touchdown by a Negro like you in front of a full, mostly white stadium will have more impact on the mindset of white people about Negroes than anything contained in all the leaflets they'll try to hand out all day long. In those two seconds, you'll *show* them instead of trying to tell them."

Robeson raised his glass in a toast and offered me a wry smile. "Of course, the great ones do it all. The end zone and 116th Street. And everything in between."

Isn't that the truth?

During my sophomore year, I attended a student political conference in Chicago; it was the first time I'd ever flown on an airplane, and it didn't go well.

The conference was on a weekend. I left the hotel early on Sunday morning to return to Columbia. At Midway Airport, I realized I had lost my wallet, including whatever money I had *and* my return ticket. It being a Sunday, the travelers' aid desk was closed. At the ticket counter, they told me I could fill out some form and maybe I would get credit for another one-way trip from Chicago to New York, but in the meantime, I had to buy a new ticket. But I had no cash, and even if I did have my wallet, a credit card was out of the question for someone of my station at that time.

A Negro skycap standing nearby overheard my dilemma. He pulled me aside and asked what happened. I explained I was a student trying to return to Columbia University. He told my story to the other skycaps and quickly a collection was taken up—enough for me to purchase a one-way ticket back.

Like the Campbell Soup factory workers, here was another situation of Black men looking out for their own, and I saw it as an important lesson. In fact, I was as grateful for the lesson as I was for the rescue. When I had my first break in my Monday classes, I went to the post office and sent a money order to repay the cash those working men had collected. I doubt they thought they'd ever see a dime.[10]

---

10 I actually invited the two skycaps who took up the collection to my college graduation. Much to my surprise, they both attended!

CHAPTER 3 | RHYTHM AND BLUES

Music was important to my life. It is in many Black homes, with roots in Negro spirituals, work songs, and field hollers. Listening to music was a salve for Black people, singing along together a form of communion. Music education, on the other hand, was often out of reach for the lower class. Lessons cost money, instrument rentals even more. Music education is a form of luxury. Now, we see that in public school, it's one of the first areas hacked away during school budget cuts, as if music's ethereal nature equates to unimportance.

Around about the age of eight or nine, my mother and father, who liked Benny Goodman's music, sprung for a cheap clarinet in the hopes that I could teach myself those Goodman hits. I practiced sporadically at the orphanage (whenever I was allowed and the sound didn't drive the nuns crazy, which was rarely), and for hours in our small house in Riverton.

I don't know how they managed it, but my parents arranged for me to take lessons with the first clarinetist of the Philadelphia Orchestra. His studio was in the Presser Building downtown, and my mother would take me there for weekly lessons. Initially, I had my nickel-plated instrument, but when I started improving, my parents found a second-hand wooden clarinet for me. As an only child, the many hours I spent practicing and pretending to play like Goodman, Sidney Bechet, Artie Shaw, Woody Herman and Barney "Albany" Bigard (the clarinetist in Duke Ellington's band) were a form of companionship. I connected with the ones who wrote and recorded those songs and escaped into my own world of music. But my clarinet teacher frowned on jazz. He said the clarinet was an instrument loved by Mozart, Paganini, Brahmans, von Weber, and the like. So, I would practice endless Paganini caprices, Mozart, Brahms concertos, and other classical pieces in between my jazz jams.

The Earl Theatre on Market Street (Philadelphia's version of the Apollo Theatre in Harlem) used to feature a weekly "amateur night" talent competition. When I was almost fifteen, I entered the competition to play a clarinet solo of "Pennies from Heaven." I thought I had the win in the bag, but onto the stage came a sixteen-year-old Italian boy from South Philadelphia by the name of Buddy DeFranco. He blew everyone away with his rendition of "Back Home Again in Indiana," and when he followed it up with a sultry "Sunny Side of the Street" encore, I could actually *feel* the gold medal slipping out of my hands. It was okay; I didn't mind being beaten by the best.[11]

When I was sixteen years old, I competed to become the first clarinetist in the New Jersey All-State Orchestra. (As I recall, this was 1946, and I was the only Negro in the company.) I won the position by playing "Flight of the Bumble Bee," a song that radio station WKYW in Philadelphia later requested I perform on the air. The show aired live, and though I was nervous at first, I relaxed into it. Around halfway through, as I played, I wondered if Buddy DeFranco was tuning in. It was my first time in a radio station. Soon enough I'd become very familiar with them.

When I was sixteen, at the suggestion of my clarinet teacher, I had auditioned for the Julliard School of Music's summer intensive program and was accepted.[12] I moved in with my mother's brother Clarence Wesley Toliver, after whom I was named. I took a bus to New York City's Port Authority where Clarence picked me up and took me to Mount Vernon, the suburb where he and his wife Charlotte lived. At Julliard, it

---

11 Fast-forward: Fifty years later, in the 2010s, I saw Buddy DeFranco playing at a nightclub in downtown Manhattan. During intermission, I went backstage to introduce myself. He remembered the talent show well. He had another clarinet and mouthpiece and invited me to sit in with him on the next set. Discretion being the better part of valor, I passed on this opportunity.

12 The audition intimidated me; I was in a room with nearly fifty other clarinet players all being evaluated. I believe they only accepted about ten percent of that group.

was eight weeks, five days a week of learning music. For the first week, Clarence rode the bus and subway into Manhattan with me, which allowed me to get my bearings.

I attended this program two summers in a row, in '47 and again the next year. I continued my study of the clarinet and took other courses, such as ear training, harmonics, music theory, and elementary piano. It was during this time that I learned to improvise jazz alongside other musicians.

In the afternoons during the week, I'd practice my clarinet in the backyard of my uncle's home. He and his wife occupied a large area on the first floor of a townhouse. There was a woman who lived in the apartment above my aunt and uncle. Often when I would practice, she'd sit on her balcony overlooking the yard. When I wasn't practicing some classical piece, she would shout down, asking me to play various popular songs of the time. I did my best to honor the requests. This eventually led to our having conversations while she would watch my practices from above.

One day, this woman invited me to come up and visit with her. She was in her late twenties or early thirties. She had a golden olive complexion and identified herself as Portuguese. She appeared to live alone, although on more than one occasion during the summer, I heard other voices coming from the apartment. The afternoon she invited me to see her, she answered the door wearing only a sheer housecoat. She had prepared iced tea and poured two glasses. I sat down and took a drink. I could hear myself swallowing. The woman played several songs on her record player, then just turned on the radio. She sat down next to me, asking nothing questions about life as she started unbuttoning my shirt with a magician's grace. Then she opened her gown, exposing her chest, and drew me to her to kiss me. I experienced a rush of fear and anxiety. The woman asked me if I had ever been with a woman before.

"No," I stammered. I wouldn't know about real love until Sandy a year later, but I was definitely feeling *something*. Among other things, looking back I realize I was sensing a true loss of innocence.

"You're a handsome young man; all the girls should love you," she said. "I'll teach you." And she was as good as her word.

Is it any wonder I believe so strongly in the power of music?

I've never told anyone about that incident before. In fact, I'd kept it close to me, as if sharing it with anyone would dilute its power. When I think back on it, the tangle of emotion always reminds me of the Sarah Teasdale poem *The Coin*:

> Into my heart's treasury
> I slipped a coin
> That time cannot take
> Nor a thief purloin,
> Oh better than the minting
> Of a gold-crowned king
> Is the safe-kept memory
> Of a lovely thing

At the time, Manny's Music on 48th Street in Manhattan was the spot where a lot of working musicians went to purchase instruments, sheet music, and supplies. Mostly it was anonymous studio players, but occasionally a big name would show up, particularly from the jazz world. Manny loved jazz, and upstairs on the second floor of the store he'd built out a gathering place where late in the afternoon, musicians would hang out and improvise with one another. Periodically, Charlie "Bird" Parker would stop by, play his sax, and encourage young musicians to play with him.

Once I swung past Manny's and he came out from behind the counter. "Kid, come with me," he barked.

Manny insisted on taking me upstairs to meet Mr. Parker. I was nervous and uncomfortable. I heard no music as we went up the steps; Parker and his group had taken a break from playing.

Manny went over and said, "Bird, this is the young man I've been telling you about, the talented clarinetist from Juilliard."

Bird told me to take out my clarinet. I said, "No, no. I... Mr. Parker, I just want to watch and listen."

"I don't think so."

Bird and the others were warm in their encouragement, but forceful. He insisted that I put my clarinet together and join in with him and the band.

Reluctantly (in terror, actually), I agreed to play a set with them. They were kind and asked me if I knew various common jazz standards, pelting me with titles. I did know several, and Bird asked me what my favorite was.

I told him *Stardust* and instantly the other members of the band started playing the tune.

The tempo scared the hell out of me. "I can't play it that fast!" I said.

Kindly, they began again, at maybe eighty percent speed. I slipped in and started playing, and I caught Charlie Parker looking at Manny with approval.

It would've been hard for me to imagine then that not too many years later, I would become involved with music on a business basis, working in the recording and radio broadcasting industries. I would come to learn of the profound impact that radio stations serving a Black audience would have on American culture. I knew then that music was an important part of my life, but I didn't understand it would play an important part in my career.

Jamming with Bird was my first brush with fame, and it set the tone for my attitude toward that sort of thing. Those working musicians brought what they brought to the table, and I brought what I brought. Not notoriety, but expertise. It set me clear for how to work with those in the spotlight, whose number one problem, it turns out, is finding people to treat them as equals while they work together. This is the magic that Hollywood agents and managers have mastered; the art of honestly treating the fame and glory as a sideshow, a distraction from the real work. It was a realization that would serve me well going forward. Getting starstruck was for amateurs.

But that would all come later. Being a Black man in 1940s and '50s America, there were going to be a few hurdles on my way to Hollywood and Vine.

CHAPTER 4 | DIVIDED, I STOOD

You don't need to be a lawyer to understand the fundamental concept of the "spirit" of the law standing in some kind of opposition to its "letter." In fact, any schoolyard kid can tell it to you. There's fair, and then there's *fair*. So much of what goes wrong in our society—the Enron scandal, the Covid-19 relief fraud, the January 6th insurrection—can be traced to the idea that most of us have an inherent understanding of a law's intention, while the few determined to take advantage can study that law at such a microscopic level that they can essentially construct a legalized version of theft. Some may call that kind of precision free enterprise, but personally I would label it soulless and cowardly greed.

For a considerable part of my life, I was a lawyer by trade. During those years, although I respected both the legal system's letter and its spirit, Martin Luther King, Jr. would remind me that there were "just" and "unjust" laws and that, sometimes, application of or adherence to the "letter of the law" resulted in genuine *injustice*. Racial segregation was the "letter of the law" for many years in substantial swaths of our country. Was this "just" or "fair?" Of course not. Yet legal.

But before I had even met Dr. King, I'd a personal experience which, in retrospect, was perhaps my earliest lesson in dealing with letter-of-the-law people, and my conflict with them didn't end well. In fact, it resulted in my being drafted into the United States Army.

As the Christmas season of 1951 wound down, the Korean War, which had erupted in June 1950, continued to rage. At the time, by law, full-time students at accredited universities were granted "student deferment" status and didn't have to serve in the military until after graduation. This deferment

continued beyond undergraduate college if you were accepted
to commence graduate school prior to your college graduation.
And there I was, halfway through my junior year at Columbia
College, with every intention of going on to graduate school.
To be clear, this was not a plan to avoid armed service, per se;
I would've been picking out a course of study for an advanced
degree in peacetime too, because my mindset ran in that
direction; that pencil and the dollar bill my mother had referenced remained the target. Yet of course I was aware that
my next planned move would also keep me out of harm's way
overseas. That didn't hurt the plan.

But we all know man plans and God laughs. I'd had a
pretty good run through high school and college—popular,
happy, maybe even admired—but I was about to be given a
lesson that would hammer itself into my psyche for the rest
of my life: The good times never last forever.

Bad news rained down on January 8th, my twenty-first
birthday, extinguishing all the joy I'd ever felt. I was in the
middle of a midterm exam when the proctor tapped me on
my shoulder and asked if I was Clarence Jones. I identified
myself and he said there had been an emergency call for me
from a hospital in Camden, New Jersey. He told me to go to
the Dean's office at the college and get the details.

My mother, at age 52, had been diagnosed with a very
aggressive form of cancer. My immediate thought was to be
by her side and help her. The new semester had started, but
I quickly moved out of my dorm and back to Riverton. I was
able, through the good graces of my professors, to arrange a
kind of correspondence school situation with Columbia. Each
teacher was actually willing to mail me my course assignments individually, in order, and in advance of the classwork
so I could not only remain enrolled but also remain in step
with my cohort. I would submit the assignments the same
way, while literally staying by my mother's bedside.[13] It went
that way the first four months of my final semester. Near the
end, it was torture assisting my mother to get to the bath-

---

13 I'd pushed a table up against the bottom of my mother's bed and used it
as a desk so I could react to any request or issue she had immediately.

room. For all my life she'd weighed about 160 pounds, but by then she was down to around 90 pounds, all bone.

Mary Jones fought hard, but she lost the battle. I was there at the foot of her bed when she died on May 4th, 1952. When men from the coroner's department were carrying her body out of the bedroom, I noticed there was a scrap of paper, jammed down between the pillow and mattress.

She had left a letter, working on it when I was out of the room so I wouldn't know, anticipate, or have to confront the fate she'd already processed. She wanted me to find it after she was gone. In it, she told me again how I was the best thing that had ever happened to her and that her pride at watching me grow knew no bounds.

During that time, at first consumed with funeral arrangements, then through a summer of crippling grief, I couldn't bring myself to go back to campus for senior year. I managed, with the help of the administration, to continue my "correspondence school" relationship and stay with Goldsboro, who was the only person in the world having as much trouble processing my mother's death as I was.

Throughout this tortured battle to keep my life on track while it seemed to be unraveling, I made one crucial misstep. In all the misery, I hadn't had time, or, more accurately, I hadn't *made* the time, to focus on choosing a graduate school. As a result, I wound up without any applications submitted by the deadline. It was a chink in my armor, one that Uncle Sam could easily exploit. Unless, of course, the Army looked at the law about student deferments in terms of its *intention*. No. It was, of course, a letter of the law problem. It was an early lesson that emotional turmoil can foster intellectual distraction and wind up creating disastrous consequences in my personal life. The Selective Service draft board had caught me between my plans for graduate school and the actual submission of the required applications, the way a basketball referee catches that micro-second of double dribbling. The whistle was blown.

I was ordered to report for active duty.

Americans had been fighting in Korea for two and a half years by that point. It was a serious situation. Canada? Out of the question. I needed to be close to my father. A former dorm-mate suggested that Korea wasn't exactly South Jersey-adjacent, but I was a principled young man. I wanted to take this thing head-on. The more I confronted the possibility I could be sent overseas to fight in the Korean War, the angrier I became. My country was asking me to put my ass on the line, to possibly get killed. I thought to myself, for what? Only three years earlier the armed services had been racially segregated. Even after President Truman's executive order desegregating the military, Negroes like me in civilian life were still treated like "second class" citizens. This led to an idea, and the night before I was scheduled to appear for service, I worked very late, trying to write my way out of a tight spot.

In 1953, *everyone* joining the U.S. Armed Services was required to sign, among the various papers, a "loyalty oath." It was an attestation of one's love of country and a declaration that one hadn't been a member of some 400 or more organizations deemed "subversive" or a "communist front" by the Attorney General of the United States. I reported to the Induction Center on Whitehall Street in lower Manhattan, where they tried to get me to sign a big pile of papers, including the loyalty oath. The oath was a problem, because as a student I had in fact occasionally attended meetings of some of those organizations, but full and honest disclosure was beside the point. *My* point, anyway, was more foundational. I pushed the papers aside and slapped down a sheet of paper for the master sergeant to read: The letter I'd written the previous night. A manifesto, really. I had distilled all my anger at the system (and truthfully, my anger at God for taking my mother as well) into a diatribe focusing on one critical passage in our so-called mighty Constitution. The "Three-Fifths Compromise" from the Constitutional Convention of 1787 which said, in effect, that as a Negro I was not in fact a full citizen of the United States.

If this was going to be a letter of the law problem, then by all means, let's make it a letter of the law problem.

I told the master sergeant that I'd be happy to fight their war, so long as they could guarantee me all the rights and privileges a white man received as a "first class" citizen. I believe my exact quote was, "If you people can figure out how to send three-fifths of me to Korea, that fraction of me would be happy to fight."

"What's with the word games, boy?" he demanded. "Are you some kind of lawyer?"

"No, sir. But I can read."

"Listen here. Are you looking for trouble, son?"

"No sir, I'm looking for reason. Maybe I'm looking in the wrong place."

They had no idea what to do with me. Was I serious or just trying to be another smart-mouthed jokester? Was I some kind of nut? Maybe a Commie? A conscientious objector or some wise-ass trying to show off his "college boy education?"

No, I was a young Black man angry at any and everything. And with nothing to lose.

Their first step was trying to talk me—bully me, really— into signing the loyalty oath. Not a chance. The master sergeant first assured me that he was trying to keep me from getting in trouble; when that didn't work, he tried to make me feel like I'd get *him* in trouble.

He gave up and turned me over to his superior officer. We went through a few levels of that, with me continuing to politely but firmly hold my ground: The Constitution plainly states that the U.S. Army is not entitled to my entire person. These men were not legal scholars and they were not used to having their chain of command challenged, but they also knew without signed paperwork they couldn't continue to process me in the traditional manner. At some point, it became clear to them that the most efficient way forward for this group was for them to make my objection somebody else's problem. They may have been concerned that my philosophical outlook would spread throughout the induction center, which held a large number of African American draftees.

After all the recruitment officials who had talked to me conferred among themselves, I was eventually told that, regardless of the paperwork, I would be put on a bus to Fort Dix with all the other draftees. Fort Dix was the site of basic training for the draftees from the Northeast, the last stop in America before new soldiers were shipped overseas to see combat. This suited me fine; I had no idea where my protest would lead, but as angry as I was, it just felt good to continue the fight.

At Fort Dix, the commanding officer seemed to have received advanced warning about my outlook on being drafted. He met the bus and pulled me aside. He tried a different tack with me than his induction center colleagues. Flipping through the sheaf of paperwork with my name on the pages, he stopped at one.

In a low and conspiratorial voice, he said, "Jones, I understand your issues, I get where you're coming from, but I'd advise you to sign at least this one."

"What is it?" I asked.

"It's the income tax form, for withholding. If you don't sign that, you don't get your paycheck." He smiled, inviting. "Near as I can tell, you're going to be a guest of the Army until this thing gets straightened out. It's going to be your full-time job, so you might as well make sure we pay you."

I looked around the grounds of the base; the low Quonset huts, the sprawl of pavement, the endless puke green of uniformed men. And I knew there was nothing here on which to spend money. What, the PX? Magazines, sodas, decks of cards? I'd have a roof and hot meals; I didn't need a government paycheck. If I signed one sheet, whatever the reason, it might open the door to an argument that I was agreeing on all the terms and conditions. It wasn't worth the risk. "I'm not signing, sir. It might set a bad precedent."

With a *well-I-tried* shrug, he walked away, clutching the unsigned papers.

And so began my nearly two years of semi-involuntary semi-imprisonment. I was in limbo, neither in the military nor out of the military. I was on what they called "holdover status." I was "Schrodinger's Private." Here's how it worked: I was in basic training, which for the other traditionally drafted and recruited soldiers, lasted sixteen weeks. I, however, lived through a repeating sixteen weeks at Fort Dix like it was some kind of government purgatory. A new group of green recruits would come in, and I'd be among them. I marched in formation with them, my sixty-pound pack on my back. I fired rifle rounds at targets, bayoneted dummies, dug foxholes, mastered camouflage face makeup, and shined my boots with them. Then the company would ship off to their "second sixteen" before getting posted in theater, but it would start all over again for me. I was a member of all of those companies for almost two years, and a member of none.

I remained respectful and followed orders the entire time, while never acknowledging the legality of the Army drafting me. Since I was well versed in all the aspects of my *Groundhog Day*-like training, I was often asked to assist in the mentoring of draftees. These were jobs I took on without complaint. I won the "soldier of the month" citation twice, as well as some marksmanship awards. I was getting training as a signal phone communications technician. All the while refusing to sign any documentation. And all the while, unbeknownst to me, the government was trying to pry into what would motivate me to behave the way I had.

There were some people at Fort Dix who didn't come and go with the tide of new companies, and I became friends with a few of them. Two were especially memorable, for being on opposite sides of the spectrum. Herbie Fields was a Black master poker player, and he made it his singular goal in life to separate every soldier, whatever his color, from his money. He did it with a combination of smarts, experience, a distractingly killer sense of humor, and the deployment of a word I'd never heard until I met him:

Motherfucker.

Herbie Fields used that word the way a chef uses butter—motherfuckin' this, motherfucker that. It was a noun, an adjective, a damn adverb. I learned a lot about poker from Herbie, and a lot about keeping your opponents off-balance.

Once Herbie pulled me aside to tell me that the word was being circulated that my "Commie ass" needed to have a whipping. Herbie said, "Now don't pay that motherfuckin' shit no mind, because I sent motherfuckin' word back through the motherfuckin' grapevine that any motherfucker that touches a hair on your motherfucking head was going to have to answer to my buddy motherfucking Leroy."

"Who's Leroy?" I asked.

Herbie said, "Jonesy boy, this here is motherfucking Leroy." He pulled a folded straight razor from inside his shirt and hooked the little barb on the end with his thumb. "Leroy," the gleaming steel blade, slid out. "See, Leroy loves motherfucking Private Jones."

The other friend I made I don't look back upon so fondly. I've decided not to use his real name here, but let's call him Ray Miller. We were housed in old barracks from World War II, where there were bunk beds. My bunkmate was replaced one day by Ray, who would eventually be stationed at Fort Dix to work in the Cryptography Unit. He was incredibly nice to me. I spent a lot of time reading, and other barracks-mates used to give me a hard time about it, calling me "professor" and that sort of thing. But not Ray; he always took an interest in what I was reading. Once on a trip off-base he came across a copy of Paul Robeson's book *Here I Stand* and bought it for me, because he remembered I'd been talking about Robeson a week prior. He wouldn't even let me pay him back; he wanted it to be a gift.

Ray and I became best friends, almost like brothers. He did most of the talking, always asking me questions and trying to get to know me better. He loved my Induction Center story. I'd find out why early New Year's Day. On leave for New Year's Eve, I'd taken Ray to Harlem to show him around. We had a great time, danced with some beautiful woman, and by the time we returned to base we were loaded and exhausted. I climbed into my bunk and just as I was drifting off, Ray shook my mattress.

"Clarence, I got to talk to you."

"Ray? Go to sleep, man. We'll talk at chow."

"No. I have to say this while I got the nerve up." Ray started crying.

This was serious. I sat up.

"What is it, buddy?"

"I know you've been nothing but good to me all this time."

I figured it was just the liquor talking. "Same goes for you," I said.

Ray was indignant. "No, no, don't say that... All this time, this palling around. They told me to do it. They *made* me."

The phrase sent a cold spike down my back. "Slow down," I said. "What exactly are you talking about?"

"The brass sent me here to spy on you. I report on everything: Who you see, what you do, who you call on the phone..."

The implications washed over me. The devastating feeling of betrayal. "Why...?"

Ray didn't sound drunk to me now. "They think you're up to something. My job was to get close enough to find out what. But there's nothing. I keep telling them. You're a decent guy, a loyal guy, and they say get more. I've felt like shit all this time, the lying..."

I stared at my friend like I'd never seen him before. I suppose I really hadn't.

"Can you forgive me, Clarence?" Ray begged.

I told him I didn't know. I rolled over and tried to go to sleep, the revelation ringing in my brain, the betrayal stinging my eyes. I did eventually fall asleep, and when I startled awake to Reveille, Ray's bunk was empty. I never saw him again.

But now I was onto the Army, and they knew it. They only took one more run at me. One day when we were lined up in morning formation, a young and attractive female military attaché joined us on the drill field. I was pulled out of line and told I'd be joining her for dinner in the officer's club.

That night we had a wonderful bottle of wine and a succulent seafood dinner. I'm sure it looked for all the world like a date.

"What is it you want?" she asked me. "You're no communist, no conscientious objector. What exactly are you?"

"You spy on me, dig around in my past. You find nothing," I said. "Have you considered there's nothing to find?"

"No. Because you won't cash the paychecks. It's un-American, it makes people uneasy. If you can explain your angle, we can work something out. Without that... we're at an impasse."

I made my point plain. "I refuse to fight for a country that won't fight for me. My angle is: I got pulled out of school on a technicality, I'm pissed off, I don't care."

The attaché stared at me in raw surprise. But it was true. I had been to the summit of pain, I had watched my mother die right in front of me, and it truly didn't matter what this woman or her bosses did to me.

Somehow, that made all the difference. A few days later, before Reveille, as the entire company slept, two military policemen made their way down the rows of bunks to mine.

"Jones! Attention!" one barked in a hushed tone.

I was on my feet in a heartbeat, still a model soldier. "Sir, yes sir!"

"You are Clarence B. Jones? Duty uniform, Private. On the double."

I scurried to get dressed. Out of a nearly two-year habit, I turned to make up my bunk, but the silent MP grabbed my arm to stop me.

"Now, Private."

The other MP slipped a folded sheet of paper into my hand. I opened it. It was a filled-out summons with that day's date that read "Field Board of Inquiry." The technical term for Court Martial.

"On what grounds?" I demanded.

In the words of Herbie Fields, the MPs didn't say another motherfuckin' word.

They escorted me to building I had never been to before, and I stood quietly before a sort of tribunal made of up high-ranking men. This was the Field Board of Inquiry. The Board read the charges: They had labeled me as a National Security Risk and this meeting was to determine whether I should be dismissed from the Army as such. The charges spelled out in no uncertain terms that I was a troubled soldier not up to military muster and unbefitting of an Honorable Discharge.

There were several witnesses called who testified that in fact I was a model solider, but it all sounded thin and uninspired. My commanding officer seemed to be avoiding eye contact, like this was an embarrassment to him. But he stood up for me and echoed what the enlisted men had said.

Nevertheless, all the testimony seemed to fall on deaf ears. It was a foregone conclusion; the Field Board of Inquiry was a kind of show trial. During my twenty-one months at Fort Dix, before being discharged from the 47th Infantry Regiment, this "security risk" was assigned and trained and armed, given the good conduct medal, and chosen as "soldier of the month" multiple times. But somehow, I was now a risk to national security. The powers that be wanted me gone, and when the gavel came down a few hours later, it was with the proclamation: *Undesirable Discharge.*

I was summarily dismissed. A new MP, armed this time, escorted me to the main gate. As we traveled across the grounds, I felt conflicted. Part of me felt free, another part felt like I was getting marched to the gallows.

The MP stood me on the far side of a white line painted on the blacktop. "Bus to the Port Authority will be by at 0-10:30," he said as he signaled the gatehouse with the hand that wasn't resting on the grip of his sidearm. The mesh gate slid closed between us with a rumble. The MP turned without another word and walked away into the shadows of the Quonset huts.

And just like that, I was a U.S. Army veteran.

But I knew as well as the Field Board that an Undesirable Discharge meant I couldn't take advantage of the G.I. Bill, which would foot the bill for graduate school. This was the Army's payback for the game I'd been playing with them. They knew they pulled me out right before I was to attend law school, and they had no intention of helping me get there now.

You'd think by this point they'd have realized I don't take no for an answer. Before the bus pulled up in front of me, I'd started formulating my plan of attack...

PART II

OUT IN THE REAL WORLD

CHAPTER 5 | THE WASP NEST

There was a lot to be done after my discharge—step one, preparing my lawsuit against the U.S. Army.

My reason was pragmatic, not principled. Or at least not particularly principled. At issue was the G.I. Bill—a bit of legislation that had the government pay the college tuition of recently discharged soldiers. Get that education, get that pencil and a dollar bill.

Getting sidelined with an Undesirable Discharge had blocked that route for me. Thanks to the commanding ranks at Fort Dix, when I was let go from the Army, I was up the creek without a paddle. There was no way for me to afford to go to graduate school and, quite frankly this seemed wrong to me. While I'd performed my military service honorably, they sent someone to spy on me. Though I'd been awarded medals and commendations, they shamelessly called me a security risk. I had been escorted from the base under armed guard like a criminal following the hearing, and this public treatment of me in front of other soldiers, many whom I considered friends, further stoked my anger.

The only way to correct the record was with force. As Frederick Douglass taught us, "power concedes nothing without a demand." It never has and it never will. Those words rang true when spoken in 1847, and they rang true to me more than a hundred years later.

Those Irish Catholic nuns had taught me to stand up for what was right. I had become even more thoughtful about our society and the world around me, and more committed to my own ability to fix things. The foundation of my bitterness toward the Army was the genuine belief that I'd done nothing wrong. What I had done was merely to challenge the basis of the government's alleged right to induct me. In my written statement submitted at the time of my induction, I recited constitutional protections which I believed continued in the United States military. Subjecting myself to being killed in the defense of my country was unfair when I genuinely believed, as a civilian, that my country treated me as a second-class citizen. Wouldn't the nuns be proud of me...

Well, my Uncle Sam wasn't. The court-martial category, defining me as a "National Security Risk" only highlighted the irony: A democratic government, through its drafting of me, had decided for me and others what were acceptable organizations for us to be associated with in *civilian life*. That is, *prior* to my induction. I felt adrift in Kafka territory. My view was that the list of over four hundred groups on the Attorney General's list of "subversive organizations," attached to the documents soldiers were requested to sign as part of their induction process, was moot. Mere membership in one or more of these perfectly legal organizations was none of the government's business with regard to non-military personnel, and for the United States military to use its power and authority to determine what organizations were acceptable for their free citizens to join was undemocratic and actually anti-American.

I was able to interest the American Civil Liberties Union in taking my case, and I so wanted to be a part of it that I was willing to do some research on my own into case law. I went to the New York Public Library on Fifth Avenue in midtown Manhattan to research my options and find any angle I could on the art of suing the federal government. While I was there, in walked someone I knew. I recognized the ash blond hair and piercing blue eyes immediately across the lobby, though I hadn't seen her in several years. Anne Aston Warder Norton had attended Sarah Lawrence in Bronxville at the same time I'd been in college. As an all-women's school at the time, her school would have mixers with Columbia's male students. We'd been to a lot of the same parties.

Anne approached, beaming. "Clarence!" She asked what I'd been doing since we'd seen each other.

I told her, "Figuring out how to sue the Army." That got her attention.

She said she was working at the American National Theatre Academy and that the organization was having a benefit performance of the Broadway show *Damn Yankees* with Gwen Verdon that night. She asked whether I would like to attend as her guest. I said yes—thus began my relationship with Anne Aston Warder Norton.

If her three surnames haven't already made it clear, I should point out that Anne came from privilege. New York Upper East Side privilege. Her father was a self-made man from Ohio who, with his wife Mary, founded the W.W. Norton & Company publishing venture in 1932. (It occurs to me that, between the Lippincotts and the Nortons, publishing families have played an outsized role in my path.) Anne was four when W.W. Norton started, but it succeeded quickly, and so the Nortons' only child grew up in an incredibly wealthy and influential household. Anne was destined for high society, but William and Mary were dedicated to the working class on many levels, and Anne had a deep streak of social consciousness woven into her from an early age. She cared about the poor, the dispossessed, the downtrodden, in that particular way that only the rich can. But Anne was no dilettante, and she had the courage of her convictions. When she heard about my time at Fort Dix, she understood why I felt the need to fight back. She decided to help me research my options for overturning my discharge. We'd flirted and danced at various mixers back in college, and dating each other now seemed like the natural progression of our grown-up study sessions at the New York Public Library.

In the time after my discharge in fall of 1955, while my appeal process was pending, I worked as a counselor in a YMCA youth program for a public housing unit in the Southeast Bronx. I worked with teenagers aged 14 to 17. My job was to be a physical presence in the housing project recreation room and "rap" (in the old school, non-musical sense of the term) with Black and Puerto Rican boys. Sometimes we discussed nothing more important than New York sports, other times we'd talk over various problems they were experiencing in school and at home. And while I didn't have any siblings growing up, the other boys at the boarding school run by the Sisters of the Blessed Sacrament had become my "brothers," so I was pretty good at listening and offering advice.

During this time, I also had several meetings and discussions with Mr. Stanley Faulkner, the lawyer who was appealing my discharge. And, of course frequent meetings and time spent with Anne, as well as with her friend Phyllis Lewis, who was working with Anne on the typewritten transcription of the proceedings of my court-martial from Fort Dix.

Working as a youth counselor, along with the back-and-forth process of appealing my discharge, and Anne's encouragement[14] that I read books like *White Collar*, *The Power Elite*, and *The Lonely Crowd* all led me to the conclusion that, in order for me to be more effective at fighting "The System," legal training should be part of my arsenal.

People seeking admission to law schools for September 1956 had already decided where they wanted to apply. My first instinct was to go back to Columbia, so I visited the Law School Admissions Office there. I told them about myself, including that my court martial was on appeal for an Honorable Discharge and that I needed the benefits of the Korean G.I. Bill for tuition, should I be admitted.

The admissions officer told me it was too late to apply for the fall of '56. Yes, I could go on a wait list, and since I was a graduate of the college I could even be positioned at the top of that list. In the remote possibility that someone dropped out before September, I'd get the slot. Practically speaking though, I was looking at September of '57. But in either case, with an Undesirable Discharge hanging over my head, the

---

14 Anne was a prolific reader. We would discuss various books that had been discussed in the media, on college campuses, and in educated households across America. For example, Sloan Wilson's *The Man in the Gray Flannel Suit* and W. Wright Mills' *The In Crowd* became part of our discussion about what career paths going forward were most meaningful to me after my Army experience.

question of payment would need to be answered. Without payment, acceptance to law school meant nothing.

At the time I was twenty-three years old. I didn't want to wait a year on the mere "possibility" that I might be admitted. In that case, when I graduated I would be twenty-seven. For reasons unclear to me from the perspective of someone in their nineties, at the time I thought that I'd be too old if I waited on an admission slot the following September. This and the suggestion at the time of my application that candidates deemed "undesirable" by the Army would be looked at the same way by the Admissions Board made me rethink Columbia, even as Anne indicated that she was thinking of returning there to get a master's in social work. She even encouraged me to consider getting the same degree with her *ahead* of getting my law degree. She believed that the combined diplomas would provide me with a skill-set more in keeping with my social justice "state of mind."

My "challenge the system" mindset had perhaps started to solidify at that induction center on Whitehall, but it had been building ever since and did not exist in a vacuum. No, it was all part of my perspective on the national and international events on race at the time. In particular, the 1954 landmark decision in *Brown v. The Board of Education of Topeka, Kansas* came down while I was in my Fort Dix purgatory. I discussed the court's verdict with other Negroes on the base. The common denominators of these discussions were skepticism and cynicism. I had developed a distant admiration for the lawyers of the NAACP, especially Thurgood Marshall, who had successfully argued the case. This had a profound impact on my views about going to law school, even before the advent of Dr. King as a figure on the national stage the following year.

My thinking at the time aligned closely with David Halberstam who, in his book of *The Fifties,* wrote that the *Brown* ruling was:

> ...the first important break between the old order, staider America that existed at the start of the era and

the new, fast-paced tumultuous America that saw the decade's end. The decision not only legally ended segregation, it deprived segregationist practices of the moral legitimacy as well. It was therefore perhaps the single most important moment in the decade, the moment that separated the old order from the new and helped create the era just arriving. It instantaneously broadened the concept of freedom, and by and large it placed the court on a path that tilted it to establish rights to outsiders; it granted them not only greater rights and freedoms, but also moral legitimacy, which they had previously lacked.

But I just couldn't imagine holding off on law school while I waded through getting a master's. I'd lost crucial time at Fort Dix, and I was trying to play catch-up.

So—ignoring the tuition issue for the time being—I began looking for law schools that could take me that fall. On the recommendation of Stanley Faulkner, I considered NYU and Boston University. After a visit to the Dean's Office at BU Law School, I felt they were more open to my admission than either Columbia or NYU, the Undesirable Discharge notwithstanding. It was this sense of confidence in admission in 1956 that prompted my application to Boston University. I was soon accepted, but this happy news, of course, came with a bitter reality: It would mean me leaving New York. The move to Boston would precipitate another major change in the direction of my life: The question of whether Anne and I were a permanent couple became an urgent one.

I didn't want to leave her.

I proposed, she accepted, and we were soon engaged.

Anne's father had died, and her mother Mary had remarried, so by the time I met her she was Mrs. David Crena de Iongh. The widow of the founder of W.W. Norton publishing had, when Anne was a teenager, married a banker from the Netherlands. David was Treasurer of the World Bank and a close business and personal confidante of Henrik Verwold, former Prime Minister of South Africa and, perhaps more telling, the architect of Apartheid. Though Mary was steeped in Gilded Age Upper East Side snobbery, the stepfather made Anne's patrician mother look like a bleeding-heart liberal by comparison. Yet neither of them seemed thrilled when Anne brought me home to meet them for the first time.

Mary Crena de Iongh was smart as a whip. She knew publishing and theater and banking inside-out. She had studied poetry and German. My relationship with my mother-in-law was frosty at first, but it warmed a bit as we came to respect each other's intelligence.

What helped even more was music. Mary's one true passion was the violin. She had written *The Art of String Quartet Playing* and performed with various orchestras. So, I further endeared myself to her one afternoon when I brought over my trusty clarinet and suggested we try out Heinrich Kayser's *Grand Duo Concertant* together. I held my own, and she began to act a little nicer toward me. Though I'm sure Mary would've preferred her daughter marry almost any blue blood walking along Lexington Avenue, she eventually welcomed me as a part of her family. Anne and I were married in June 1956 at Church of the Master on Morningside Avenue in Harlem.

Anne would often joke afterward that she imagined friends of her mother and stepfather seeing photos from the wedding and asking how the waiter got into a framed picture with the bride.

Just because America treated Black people terribly didn't mean you couldn't have a sense of humor sometimes.

Once I had been accepted for admission at BU, Anne and I traveled to Boston to look for an apartment near the school. We drove to Massachusetts in mid-August 1956 and started house hunting, using a motel as our base of operations. Because we were both political junkies, we listened to some of the proceedings of the Democratic Party National Convention in Chicago on the radio during the drive. Adlai Stevenson was chosen as the Democratic Party's nominee for President, Senator Estes Kefauver from Tennessee for Vice President. Less than a week later, the Republican Party National Convention was held in the Cow Palace in San Francisco. Dwight

Eisenhower was selected as the GOP's nominee, sharing the ticket with Richard Nixon. Anne and I talked about Nixon's notorious past as an anti-communist "red baiter." His Senate race against the Democratic opponent, Helen Gahagan Douglas, was noteworthy as one of the dirtiest campaigns in U.S. political history. Good thing he isn't running for president, I remember thinking.

In the attempt to find an apartment in Boston, Anne and I first tried responding to ads in the local papers. In a couple of instances, we went together to local real estate offices seeking assistance in finding a place to live. It soon became apparent that we were being given the runaround because we were an interracial couple. With the September start of the semester looming, we decided that the reality of the racism we were experiencing wasn't going to change, and we came up with a strategy to circumvent it. To avoid being shut out of any rental possibilities, Anne—blonde and blue eyed, wearing her most white, Anglo Saxon protestant attire—would hunt for options alone. She would tell the broker or potential landlord that I was a U.S. Army Veteran planning on attending the BU School of Law and that I was in transit from New York to join her for the weekend to review the possible places she'd found. She also told them we'd agreed that if she found the perfect apartment, she would sign the lease and put down the deposit.

Anne hit the jackpot with the top floor apartment on Beacon Street: Magnificent view of the area, near Kenmore Square and transit for my law school commute. When I showed my brown face in the office, the realtor, having already arranged for us to meet the superintendent of the building to show us the apartment, now seemed unsure if it had already been rented. We insisted on going through with the scheduled appointment.

The building's superintendent turned out to be an Irishman with a thick brogue. He seemed a little taken aback by us as a couple, but he took an immediate liking to Anne.

Intuitive and sensing an opening, she turned to me and said, "Honey, I'll bet you haven't heard that Irish accent since you were with the nuns in boarding school!"

Grabbing the opening, I smiled. "That lilt, it takes me back. It's soothing. Those nuns were wonderful."

Curious, the super asked me about the school. I gave him some background about Blessed Sacrament and then he cut to the chase. "Can you say your Hail Mary?"

I demonstrated happily, adding that I'd been an altar boy.

This seemed to seal the deal. Black or not, I was Catholic enough for him. "Do you drink beer?" he asked, and before we knew it, we were downstairs in his basement flat, meeting his wife. Handing me a bottle of beer, the super started talking baseball. After two or three beers, he asked, out of the blue, "When would you two like to move in?"

When I asked if we could expect any complications with the two of us as an interracial couple, he said that he made the decisions on the "suitability" of his tenants and, if the land-lord or the rental office had any problems about me and Anne, they could take it up with him. It was concessions like these by white people that gave me a little bit of hope, even to this day.

During our time at the building, we became close friends. His wife would often babysit for us. On weekends, we'd some-times watch baseball on TV and drink beers together.

My initial BU tuition bill was one of the first pieces of mail to arrive at our new Beacon Street apartment. It was an amount that Anne and I didn't have, but the plan all along had been for the G.I. Bill to cover the cost. However, the court case in prog-ress to overturn my Undesirable Discharge had hit a snag. The Army had agreed to amend their court martial decision to a General Discharge, apparently thinking the compromise would make me go away. I'd refused, and told Stanley Faulk-ner, the ACLU lawyer, to keep pushing. A General Discharge wasn't what I needed to cover my law school costs.

I headed into the Bursar's Office at BU to update them on the situation. While they were sympathetic, there was a limit to their kindness. A time limit, actually. I had to be paid up before classes started. No money, no classroom, no fucking exceptions.

It was a long and sweaty August worrying about everything lining up. Amazingly, I was back in the Bursar's Office the week before the semester started to register for my classes with my tuition still unpaid when the secretary's phone rang. It was for me.

Anne was on the other end of the line. My first thought was that something terrible must have happened. "Clarence, there's a special delivery letter here for you. It's from Stanley Faulkner."

I told her to open it and read it to me over the phone. I could hear the rustling of the papers. My heart started beating faster.

"He says the Army upgraded your Discharge to Honorable! It's taken care of!"

Stanley wrote that he was checking with the Boston Veteran's Administration office to find out where this information should be sent so that I would immediately qualify for G.I. Bill benefits.

I hung up and went immediately to the Dean's Office to share the news. Neither of us knew when the G.I. Bill was going to compensate the university, but the dean didn't care. He said, "Okay. Write out a check for the first semester's tuition so we can process everything. I'll make sure the Bursar's Office doesn't cash it. Get your lawyer to get us that money as soon as he can." The dean stood up and shook my hand. "Welcome to Boston University, Clarence."

And with that bad check, I was on my way to the start of my legal career.

During my first year in law school, I became part of a study group with three other students, all white and Jewish. We became good friends and would sometimes socialize on the weekends. Having these white Jewish members of my study group was reminiscent of those similar early friendships I had forged with Jewish students in my classes as a freshman at Columbia. For the most part, we met in my apartment. It became clear to me that the size of the rooms and location of my place with Anne had made it the favored choice of the other members of our group. Although I made many other friends, Black students and white, the men in my study group—Oscar Wasserman, Lewis Whitman, Mortimer Aaronson—became my closest companions in law school.[15]

Barbara Jordan from Texas was in my class. We would often talk in the law library and study hall. Neither of us could foresee at the time how, independent of one another, after graduation we would each play some role in the history of our country. Barbara gained national prominence as the very eloquent spokesperson for the House Judiciary Committee investigating President Richard Nixon for impeachment.

In June 1957, at the end of my first year at BU, my first child Christine was born at the Boston Lying-In Hospital. With Anne in labor, her mother and I waited downstairs in the family lounge. When the doctor came to tell us that Anne had given birth to a healthy baby girl and took us to see my daughter for the first time, Anne's mother burst into tears. She hugged me and told me how proud she was of me. (I would learn later that she rarely had complimented Anne on anything she ever did or accomplished).

At the end of June, Anne, baby Christine, and I all moved to New York City to stay in Anne's Aunt Kitty's townhouse on Gramercy Park while I took an internship as a law clerk and research assistant to Thurgood Marshall at the NAACP Legal and Education Fund. Anne was closer to her Aunt Kitty than to her mother. Kitty was Christine Herter Kendall, married to William Sargent Kendall, an artist. His paintings were on display in several rooms of the townhouse where we stayed that summer. Our daughter was named Christine after Aunt Kitty at Anne's insistence.

Working as an intern for Thurgood Marshall would have a lifelong impact on me. Mr. Marshall had asked me to search for case law that would support a particular argument he was planning to incorporate in a brief that he was writing. His offices in Manhattan were not too far from the New York Bar

---

15 I could not know that in 2006, forty-seven years later, they would nominate me on behalf of our class of 1959 to receive the Law School Alumna's Silver Shingle Award, its highest award for Public Service. It was presented to me in Boston at a special dinner in my honor attended by the University's Board of Trustees following a more private dinner at the Law School hosted by the dean.

Association Building and its library, so I headed over there for the morning. I don't remember the issue or the legal area in question. What I do remember, however, was returning to Mr. Marshall to tell him that I couldn't find any case in the law library to support the point of argument he'd described. When told this, he leaned back in his chair, looked over his glasses, and asked me: "Are you telling me that you looked in the entire library and found no case among all those books to support my argument? Is *this* really what you're telling me?"

Sheepishly, I went back. With more meticulous and thorough research, I found several cases with apparent precedent to support Mr. Marshall's argument.[16] That experience would stick, and it would serve me well during my time working with Arthur Kinoy, a brilliant lawyer who would become my mentor and shape the way I analyze legal matters, especially those pertaining to the U.S. Constitution. The lesson remains: There is no substitute for shoe-leather, elbow grease, putting in the time and grinding.

Throughout my time in law school, Anne was earning her master's in social work. She began to work part-time in her chosen field of community organizing for senior citizens at a social services agency in the Roxbury section of Boston.

The decision I made in my final year in law school that would significantly influence and impact my life was enrolling in a class called Copyright Law and Trademark and Patent Protection. My professor was named Donald Schapiro, and during the course I became fascinated with the issue of copyright protection of literary and musical works. I wrote a term paper entitled *Judicial Criteria Employed to Determine Musical Copyright Infringement.* About two weeks after I'd handed it in, my professor called me to his office.

---

16 Years later I would win the Thurgood Marshall Award from the American Bar Association, and the celebration would be hosted by Barack Obama. Unfortunately, because of the Covid-19 pandemic, we were unable to have the gala in person. The upside is that I was given a memento for the ages; a personalized video introduction by the former president himself, from which came the quote on the cover of the book you're reading right now.

"Your paper was top notch," Professor Schapiro told me. "Intellectual property, it's at the vanguard of law. What do you know about music, Clarence?"

I told him about the clarinet work at Julliard, playing in the Army, my encounter with Charlie Parker.

Learning about this background, he encouraged me to pursue a career in entertainment law. He told me that most people are impressed by the footlights and the applause. "God knows, plenty of Negroes are in the field," he said. "On stage, on camera, behind the mic. Entertainers. But few work at the studios and record companies, where business decisions are made. Where the money is." The real power, he said, resided in the recording and motion picture production businesses. Offstage, beyond the footlights.

Professor Schapiro told me about his close friend Leslie Charlow, who was general counsel of a Hollywood company called Revue Productions, at the time the music arm of Universal Studios. Then he dropped the bomb: Without my permission, he'd sent along a copy of my term paper to Mr. Charlow. Just that morning, Charlow had called my professor to share his high opinion of me as a writer and a student of copyright law. I had previously told him that Anne and I were thinking of going to California after graduation, because our then-best friends, the Whites, had recently moved to Pasadena.

Professor Schapiro said, "Leslie told me to let you know if you want to move to Los Angeles, there's a job waiting for you. No questions asked."

That sounded great to me, but California was a decision for the family, and Anne had other plans. One of her closest friends, Francis Damon, was the daughter of the owner of Dole, the massive international fruit company. Part of the reason Hawaii became a U.S. territory was to allow Dole to send its produce to America without having to pay import taxes. Hawaii had only recently become a state, and its culture was, at that point in time, still quite colonial. Francis was heading back to work with her father, and she was very committed to having her best friend along for the ride. Like

Leslie Charlow, she too was offering jobs where there weren't necessarily openings.

When I asked "What would I do in Hawaii?" she had an answer.

"You pick out a spot on the beach where you like the view, my father builds you a brand-new house there, and you go be a lawyer for Dole."

I told her it wasn't as easy as it sounded.

She leaned in and whispered, "Yes, it is. We're Dole, we goddamn *own* Hawaii."

I had no idea what life would be like there, but I figured I'd be even more of a minority than I was at white bread Columbia. And that was saying something. As a Black man, working for a company made up entirely of *plantations* didn't feel like a great step forward.

In the end, Anne and I decided the mainland was the place for us.

Anne had given me a powder blue 1959 Chevrolet Impala convertible as a law school graduation gift. It was a stunning car. I could imagine the family driving across the country together. But Anne didn't want to subject the baby to the days on the road. She and Christine flew out ahead, leaving me to make the 3,000-mile drive to California.

I had advertised in the local college papers for students who were planning to go to Southern California that summer who would be interested in sharing the driving duties to Pasadena. Numerous students replied to the ad, but only two of them seemed suitable to me after meeting with them. One needed to get to Bakersfield, and the other, like me, was LA-bound.

The new car was small for a drive across the country, especially with two strangers on board. But Anne and I weren't bringing much from our Boston apartment life with us. It was going to be a fresh start. So, the little convertible felt like freedom, and so did California. We decided on the northern route, driving from Boston to New York, then along the Pennsylvania

Turnpike into Ohio, Indiana, Illinois, South Dakota, Wyoming, and through the Sierra Nevada Mountains. And, of course, with foolish feelings of youth and invincibility, we drove across the Bonneville Salt Flats with the top down at 100 miles an hour. Everything Anne and I owned was in the trunk of that car, so it was a good thing we didn't roll it in Utah.

During the cross-country journey, we stayed in cheap motels, sharing rooms with double-beds and a cot. We drove between twelve and fifteen hours a day and entered my new home state early in the morning, after passing through the high-altitude road of the Donner Pass where we were required to buy chains for the tires because of the snow. The snow-capped mountains glittering in the sunrise were so beautiful that the vista brought tears to my eyes. It would be the last snow I would see for a while.

After dropping off my two passengers, I arrived in Pasadena at the home of Charlie and Fran White a few days after Anne and Christine. Anne had already discussed with them our need to find a place to live, and fast. I had a job to get to, a life to start. It was 1959 in Los Angeles. I was educated, married to a blonde heiress, driving a convertible, and living white collar by the blue ocean.

If there was trouble for people who looked like me, people in places like Louisiana and Georgia and Mississippi and Alabama, my concern for it—for *them*—was starting to fade in the rearview mirror like the Bonneville Salt Flats.

CHAPTER 6 | THE LIVING ROOM WITH THE TREE

It didn't take long for the shift of coasts to completely transform me. If there was an African American Don Draper, I might've fit the bill. Though not Madison Avenue, the music business world of '50s-era Sunset Strip had its *Mad Men*-esque excesses; I indulged, all right? And I jumped at the chance.

Leslie Charlow, as good as his word, had me at Revue working directly for him as *de facto* Assistant General Counsel. It was the kind of law work I was eager to do, and I dove in.

We found a house in Altadena on Highview Avenue that my wife fell in love with. It was not too far from Fran and Charlie White, and we settled in quickly. These days that house would be thought of as "mid-century modern," but at the time— mid-century—it was simply new, notable for its sleek lines and enormous panes of glass. Oh, and the palm tree that grew out of the terracotta floor of the living room (along with the retractable skylight directly above it). Notable from our neighbors' standpoint for the number of parties we hosted.

There was serious consumption of martinis on a frequent basis, just like my Uncle Clarence used to mix them. Friday and Saturdays I had more, sometimes drinking so much I passed out. Anne kept up with me. As it would turn out, she not only kept up but surpassed me. Surpassing in this sense would not be considered a victory.

The office was a strange and exciting place. Drinks at lunch in places like the Polo Lounge, The Brown Derby, and the Ivy. Recording sessions in the Capitol Records building, which had been designed to look like LPs stacked on a turntable and remains an LA skyline icon. Deals made and lost, participation percentage points argued over, fortunes rising and falling with the ring of the pre-caller ID phone or the spin of some disc jockey's hand in a major market.

Popular stars like Nat "King" Cole, Johnny Mercer, and Sidney Poitier would pop in while I was working. Bobby Darin had a provocative sense of humor. One day, he and Sandi Dennis were in my office and out of the blue Bobby asked where I came from. And he did it in his particular style:

"Universal doesn't have a single Negro on the lot," he said. "They don't even have any Negroes sweeping their soundstages, so how in the fuck did you manage to be the lawyer working for Leslie Charlow?"

I wasn't offended. The question made me feel special. "Listen, the only color Leslie sees is green, you dig?"

Bobby practically did a spit take.

Actually, everything about my life made me feel special. A vodka martini in my living room with feet up, the skylight open, and a silk Pierre Balmain tie loosened around my collar. Like that picture in my yearbook, I had the world in my goddamn hands.

Anne was always in my corner, even as I began to act like a person who was a hundred and eighty degrees off from the one she'd married. The truth is, I wouldn't have ended up working with Martin Luther King, Jr. if it weren't for her insistence that I meet with him when he first reached out to me.

Late one evening in February 1960, I received a call from New York. It was Judge Hubert Delaney, a mentor of mine, telling me he was calling in his capacity as chief defense counsel for Dr. King. King, I'd read, had recently been indicted by the State of Alabama for tax evasion and perjury in connection with the filing of his state income tax returns. He needed some help; *pro bono* help, I assumed. "I spoke with Professor Shapiro up in Boston," the Judge said. "I asked him to recommend a research coordinator for the defense team. He mentioned you first."

As in the hero's journey, this was my refusal of the call. As I talked to Judge Delaney, who had already recommended me to Dr. King, I indicated that while I was flattered, I felt I wasn't the right man for the job. What I *meant* was that I had no interest in it. I thanked the judge but told him I wouldn't be able to help. I was squeezing everything I could out of the material world—new cars and custom-tailored suits—and enjoying it. To my embarrassment, I have to say that I couldn't have cared less about the Civil Rights struggle at that time.

Anne read me the riot act when I got off the phone. How could I say no to Martin Luther King, Jr.? Easy. I turned to her and spat out, "Just because some Negro preacher got his hand caught in the cookie jar doesn't make it *my* problem. 'The Movement.' I've read about it. But I don't see what tax evasion has to do with Civil Rights."

"They say it's a conspiracy," Anne told me.

"I don't care how many speeches he's made, how many magazine covers," I said, feeling put out. "It's no conspiracy, it's the same old story."

"After the way the Army treated you, are you really saying our government couldn't possibly—"

"And are you saying men don't lie on their returns? Point's moot since I don't practice tax law, but even if I did, I have no sympathy for some famous Negro careless enough to get himself in trouble with the IRS."

Anne's hands slowly slipped off my back. "You don't believe that for a minute.

I held my ground. "Wouldn't say it if I didn't."

Anne stepped back, taking honest, critical measure of me. I didn't like the bug-under-the-microscope feeling. Her eyes spoke volumes: Is this really the man I married?

"Look," I said, "I've got a career cooking. It's not a good time to get involved."

"Rev. King worries more about what's right than what's convenient." Something I could learn. And would. The hard way. Anne looked at me like I was a stranger to her. She was disappointed in me, but I wasn't going to back down. Bobby Darin had noticed that Negroes didn't exactly dominate the business world, but I was paving my own way to the top. My time, my talents—I used them the way that best served me and my family. Not some stranger. Not some headline-grab-bing *preacher*. I had no intention of changing that. Even if it meant sleeping on the couch that evening.

But one thing about Dr. King, he didn't take "no" for an answer very often. The next day I received a call from his steadfast assistant, Dora McDonald. She said that Martin had forgotten to mention his upcoming trip to Los Angeles to Judge Delaney. "He'd love to call on you and your wife."

Anne wasn't going to let me stop that. The next Friday, Dr. Martin Luther King, Jr. was at my door with two unfamiliar men[17] to ask for my help in person. But I wasn't the type to get star-struck easily. I invited them in.

His eyes took the place in, landing on the palm that hung over the living room. "This sure is a nice house you have here," he said with a smile. We made small talk for a while, with him taking an interest in my background, education, marriage and me answering his questions like I was talking to a salesman.

Eventually, the conversation turned to the tax case, as I expected.

"I thought a personal plea might make a difference," Dr. King confided.

I begged off, politely telling him my career needed attention, I had bills, I had responsibilities. I had a family to support. "Dr. King, you have plenty of lawyers to mount a top-notch defense," I told him, squirming out of the work as politely as I could.

King agreed he indeed had plenty of white volunteer lawyers, but Negro lawyers... *that* was the problem. Maybe, but it wasn't *my* problem. He'd repeated the word *volunteer* enough times to make it clear: He was asking for the gift of my time. As a man with a career just starting to simmer, donating the precious resource of my time was the last thing I was interested in.

---

17   I would come to know and love Wyatt Tee Walker and Ralph Abernathy, but at the time they might as well have been Dr. King's bodyguards for all I knew or cared.

He finally got the message. Although he respected my decision, on his way out the door Dr. King turned back. "I'm guest pastor at Baldwin Hills Baptist this coming Sunday. I would be privileged if you'd come to see me speak."

I indicated I wasn't much of a churchgoer, but King had woven his spell on Anne. "We'd be the honored ones." She looked at me with a smile every bit as arm-twisting as any of her words could be.

"Like she said, we'd be delighted," I told Dr. King as I shook his hand, not even sure if I meant it.

But when I closed the front door and turned back to Anne, the look on her face told me everything I needed to know.

"You may have wriggled out of going to Alabama for that great man," she shouted, "but you sure as hell are going to that Sunday service!"

It would turn out to be quite a service. In fact, that church sermon would change the trajectory of my life.

CHAPTER 7 | THE COME-TO-JESUS MOMENT

Anne wasn't feeling well that Sunday morning, so I went alone to the Baptist church up in Baldwin Hills, a section of Los Angeles about a half-hour drive up the freeway. It was and is known as the Black Beverly Hills and has been home to many well-to-do Black businesspeople. As I pulled in, looking at all the fancy cars in the church parking lot, I saw the Cadillacs, the Rolls Royces, the Lincolns. Driving a car named after the Great Emancipator, I thought. These were *my* people. Good for you, getting a taste of the high life. And then I thought, not a bad place to do your fundraising, Dr. King. Bravo.

I was escorted to my seat close to the front row, just behind the church trustees, deacons, and other important guests. Every other seat was filled. There must have been 2,000 people in attendance, many who surely hadn't been to church since Easter Sunday and had now shown up just to hear the great man speak.

I felt unnerved. I didn't like going through the motions, and while I was and remain a devout believer, and though I'd been raised by Catholic nuns, the rituals of the Christian faith don't mean much to me. But at least a Black church has some soul. I clapped along with the music and tried to get onto the wavelength. But all the readings and songs were just the appetizer. When the church's pastor, Rev. H. B. Charles, turned over the proceedings to Dr. King, we all knew the main course had just been served, and no one missed a syllable for the next hour.

"Brothers and sisters," he began, "the text of my sermon today concerns the role and responsibility of the Negro professional to the masses of our brothers and sisters who are struggling for Civil Rights in the South."

With a natural storyteller's ease, he related how the Montgomery Bus Boycott Supreme Court decision had galvanized tens of thousands of ordinary southern Negroes to begin to think of themselves as human beings—and how, if you were to visit the South now, you could just sense a new day was coming.

I leaned forward in the pew, eager to hear whatever it was that came out of this man's mouth. With just these few words (witnessed in person instead of caught over the radio or quoted in the newspaper), I realized that I'd never heard anyone so thoroughly capable of transforming a listener. It was like the magic Frank Sinatra was renowned for having with his singing voice. That same quality was something that somehow Rev. Martin Luther King, Jr. alone had in his speaking voice. His phrasing was immaculate, the inflections and rhythms giving you half the story even if you couldn't understand the words. But what words they were, adding to the tapestry. The hairs on the back of my neck stood up.

I was glad Anne hadn't come. Because she would've been elbowing me in the ribs as she figured out way ahead of me what the point of the sermon was.

King moved from the broad to the more specific. He spoke of those Negroes who had become doctors and lawyers and accountants and performing artists all with a moral obligation to those Black adults, especially in the Jim Crow South, who never had the chance to do what they did and those Black children who could never by themselves rise out of poverty and indignity.

I felt like he was speaking to his audience here in the rich church.

It was powerful stuff, made poignant when he noted the hundreds of offers from white northern professionals, particularly lawyers, to help in the Civil Rights struggle. What a shame it was, he said, that the kindness, generosity, and goodwill of those whites—while dearly appreciated—was not dwarfed by the kindness, generosity, and goodwill of those Negroes most in position to offer it to their own people, "Negroes in a position of financial security." At the lectern,

King made up in fiery rhetoric what he lacked in physicality. There was almost a stillness to him, but a rock-star vibe undulated through the air as he preached. "Nothing wrong with it. But don't you feel, brothers and sisters, getting along as well as you are, that perhaps there's an extra burden on you to look back, reach out a helping hand to the less fortunate?"

I thought I knew where the sermon was going, but it took a sharply unexpected turn.

"There's a young man here today, a spit-and-polish professional my associates in New York tell me could do wonders for the cause of racial justice. A man who can find things in a law library no one else can. They tell me this man's brain has been touched by God. They tell me that when this young man writes down language in support of a legal argument his words are so compelling and persuasive that they all but jump off the page."

For just a fraction of a moment I wondered whether this young lawyer he was talking about was me. But it couldn't have been. The lawyer King described obviously had skills far beyond mine. To be honest, I started thinking I should try to meet whoever this guy was after the service.

But then, the fatal blow:

"This gentleman lives in a fine home," he continued. "In fact, it has a *tree* in the middle of the living room—"

Uh-oh.

"– and a ceiling that opens up to the sky!"

Dr. King never looked directly at me, though he ended up making eye contact with everyone else there—or so it seemed. They reacted to the words the way only Black folk in church know how to, with *oohs* and *aahs* and amens and hallelujahs and calls to "tell it!"

"Now this man, his parents struggled as impoverished domestic servants. Struggled and suffered under the tyranny of racial inequality and wanted to give him a better life."

Dr. King's speeches have changed many lives over the years, but the one that changed my life was about *me*. Not by name, mind you, but he used bits of my past he'd picked up in our conversation at my home two nights earlier to set me up as a straw man for the uncaring successful Negro.

"A better life, indeed. The man has it all, a beautiful wife and child, a convertible car..."

Come on, I thought. What did I do to deserve this? But of course, the question was what *didn't I do*?

The Reverend continued, "This man puts his talents to work chasing after record royalties instead of justice. He shows no compassion for his brothers who aren't so fortunate. I'm afraid this man has forgotten from whence he came."

I listened with growing misery. With his palette of words, Dr. King poignantly painted a picture of my mother selflessly scrubbing floors and hoping for better things for her son, while he—me—ended up self-centered and thoughtless. I sat in the pew tense, feeling like I'd been pierced in the heart with an arrow. Was I the son she deserved?

Now I could hear hundreds *tsk-tsking* and women muttering *mmm mmm mmm* in a way that means "for shame." I tried to sink down in the pew. I felt like I was in a white-hot spotlight but, of course, no one but the two of us knew who Dr. King was talking about.

"So here was this Negro woman working in a white woman's house. She had to send her boy away to live with others telling him, 'Life ain't easy son, but you can't give up. I'm doing this for you.'"

I could feel tears start to well. Unreeling like a movie before my eyes were the moments I knew of in my mother's hard journey, her short life.

Dr. King kept the pressure on. "I can't help but wonder if this man's mother could speak to him right now, might she share the immortal words of Langston Hughes?"

Before long the tears came. They rolled down my cheeks as Dr. King recited Hughes' poem *Life Ain't No Crystal Stair*:

Well son, I'll tell you, life for me ain't been no crystal stair

But all the time I'se been a-climbin' on
So, boy, don't turn your back
Don't you set down on the steps

Dr. King's withering criticism hit home. Maybe it was his oratorical skills, but I didn't take offense. I simply looked inward. I imagined my mother and what she might think of me today. Pencils and dollar bills notwithstanding, was I doing what was *right*?

It was time to reconsider the earthly pursuits of this post-law school career. It felt like I was shedding my skin right there in the pew, molting and transforming.

After the service, I found Dr. King on the steps, shaking hands as people spilled out of the church. As I approached, he offered a calm smile, his expression hard to read. Parishioners continued parading past in awe with kind words, handshakes, pats on the back.

"Mr. Jones, I'd like to point out that I didn't use your name. You noticed?"

"You don't need another lawsuit," I joked. I told him I considered myself quite verbally dexterous, but his way with words... I was simply blown away.

"I try to get through to people," he said.

"Indeed." I offered my hand with a sincere smile. "Dr. King, when do you want me in Montgomery?" And from that point on, I was a Martin Luther King, Jr. disciple. From that moment until the assassination on April 4th, 1968, I served as Dr. King's personal lawyer, political advisor, and draft speechwriter. It was the most important relationship I've ever had. Martin's shadow looms not over my entire life, but those of my wives and children as well. I cannot say that fact is an entirely positive thing, but it is unique, and I certainly can't imagine it being any other way. My relationship with Martin King, like the color of my skin, is the defining aspect of my time here.

• • •

I joined Martin down south and gleefully helped Judge Delaney and his superb team of defense lawyers (including Robert Ming and Bob Leighton from Chicago). Say what you will about Martin Luther King, Jr., but one thing for certain is that he cared little for the creature comforts money can bring. He was probably the last person who'd cheat on his taxes. I didn't know that at the time he visited me in Altadena, but I knew it by the time the trial was through.

At first Martin tried to explain his tax situation to me, but I was a good soldier, eyes only on the target. "You don't owe an explanation to anyone," I reminded him. "Innocent 'til proven guilty. That's the American Way, my brother." But I couldn't help wondering, *Even Black and in Alabama?*

On March 29th, 1960, "The Committee to Defend Martin Luther King, Jr." ran a full-page ad in the *New York Times* featuring the headline "Heed Their Rising Voices." The letterhead of the Committee had the names of Harry Belafonte, Marlon Brando, Nat King Cole, Eartha Kitt, Van Heflin, Sidney Poitier, Eleanor Roosevelt, Lorraine Hansberry, Langston Hughes, Hope Lange, Mahalia Jackson, Howard University's Mordecai Johnson, Shelly Winters, and others.

The ad was run as a fundraising appeal; money was needed to defend the tax case brought by the State of Alabama. But this wasn't really about taxes, of course. The ad described the vicious actions of the police in Montgomery and Birmingham, many of whom were on horseback, and the peaceful protest of Civil Rights demonstrators. The two demonstrations were part of the effort to desegregate lunch counters, department stores, and other public facilities in the deep South.

The ad had the intended result. It spiked a significant flow of contributions to the Southern Christian Leadership Conference. It was the subject of commentary by other media outlets, which widened the audience hearing the message. But it would lead to further complications down the line.

• • •

In the end we destroyed the government's obviously trumped-up tax evasion charges. The judge had no choice; Martin was acquitted on all counts. It was a victory, not the only one in our eight-year relationship, but the first. At that point, I was batting 1.000 for the Movement.

Of course, even Hank Aaron would tell you that you can't keep up an average like that forever...

PART III

BOOTS ON THE GROUND

CHAPTER 8 | BACKSTAGE AT THE MOVEMENT

We were dead tired, put up for the night in a cramped room—two tiny beds side-by-side beneath the sloped gables of the roof. It looked like a scene from a sitcom, but the situation in the Albany, Georgia, of 1962 of course, was deadly serious. Shoes off, ties loosened, after a long day of fighting and threats, we settled in at Dr. William G. Anderson's attic for another less-than-glamorous night on the road. Just so we could get up and do it all over again. Looking back, it's hard to believe the stamina we had, and in some ways, it's hard to believe one of those stubborn, committed-to-the-core young "Movement" guys was actually me.

Martin seemed lost in thought. And then, out of nowhere, he turned to me, and in that remarkable, passionate voice of his, said, "Clarence, I really have to thank you, because I've been watching you closely and I can see, just like Stanley Levison, you're one of those wintertime soldiers."

I craned around to look at Martin directly. I knew how highly he thought of Stanley, and it wasn't the first time I'd had the honor of being compared to him.

"Anyone can stand with you in the bright warm summer sunlight of August, but only a wintertime soldier can stand with you at midnight in the Alpine chill of winter."

I flushed with embarrassment. I thought the idea surely applied to Stanley, but at that time, I knew I wasn't worthy of this compliment; I wouldn't accept it for another decade. So, it felt fraudulent, accepting praise like that, particularly from a man whom I admired so deeply, a man whose capacity for giving of himself was without limit.

I said the only thing I could to try to turn that heat down. "That's a little much, don't you think?"

We both laughed, but I never forgot those words, or that experience of sharing a room with Martin in Albany. More than fifty years later, the term would be thrown away as the title of a film in the Marvel Cinematic Universe. That's the kind of world we live in.

After meeting and assisting Martin's defense team in Montgomery, I began to travel from Los Angeles on Southern Christian Leadership Conference (SCLC) matters frequently. Often to New York or sometimes Georgia. I had two areas of focus for the SCLC: Assisting lawyers working on Civil Rights cases and raising money to support the cause. Martin had put me to my best use. He was a theologian; I was a (nonviolent) pugilist. So, I fought for court wins and I fought for dollars. New York was where the money was, the South was where the cases were. Often, I'd catch up to Martin on the road and travel with him a few days.

I spent less and less time in the house with the tree in the living room. I had left Revue Productions soon after the tax case to travel for the Movement and spent so much of my time on the East Coast that eventually Anne and I realized it would make more sense to live back in New York. In 1961, my family moved to Riverdale, a suburban community in the West Bronx. Our choice of location was influenced by the availability of good schools, public and private, and proximity to the residence of one of my legal mentors, Arthur Kinoy. Anne and I had rented a spacious five-bedroom house while we awaited the construction of our new home on a piece of land we'd purchased nearby. The rental sat next to the Arturo Toscanini estate and was an easy four-block walk from the town's Metro North Railroad stop that headed into Grand Central Station.

Stanley Levison was one of the first people I met in New York. A Manhattan real estate and business owner, Stanley was a whip-smart proponent of liberal causes. He was also a communist. He had met Martin four years before I did. In 1956, the two men introduced in Baltimore. Stanley was forty-four at the time, Martin a baby-faced twenty-seven. Stanley fell under Martin's spell upon seeing him speak not unlike my own conversion in that Baldwin Hills church. Eventually, Stanley and I would become two of Martin's closest confidants.

Stanley became and remained devoted to Martin while he was alive and passionate about protecting Martin's legacy until his own death in 1979. It is not an exaggeration to say that Stanley was *critical* to the operational survival of the SCLC. He wrote most of the fundraising appeals that went out with Martin's personal signature or under the SCLC letterhead. As a well-educated Caucasian who had plenty of other options to pursue in his life, I've always considered Stanley's work in support of Dr. King the highest level of patriotism and public service.

Judge Hubert Delany and the brilliant lawyer Arthur Kinoy, whom I subsequently worked for and developed a warm friendship with, strongly recommended me to Stanley. Eventually, Stanley and his wife Beatrice became quite close to me and Anne. It registered with Stanley, as it had with Martin, that unlike many associated with the Movement, I had varied choices on how to spend my life. I did not involve myself with Martin and the SCLC out of necessity. I was not seeking a job, publicity, glory, or money. Martin's confidence in me was buttressed by his knowledge of how Stanley described me as his closest confidant and advisor in New York on SCLC and Civil Rights matters.

Everyone who has written about Dr. King during the years from 1956 to his murder in early 1968 agrees that Stanley became perhaps Martin's most trusted advisor. Much has been written—both for publication and throughout internal FBI documents no one ever intended to see the light of day— about the "influence" that Stanley had or was alleged to have had on Dr. King. Little, if anything, has been noted about the profound influence that Martin had on Stanley Levison. I could plainly see that working with Dr. King was *the* transformative experience in Stanley's life. The price for that transformation was steep, however. Stanley Levison became a target: For those who wanted to take King down, for those who wanted to change King's mind, for those who wanted power for themselves, and for those who were afraid of the growing power of American Blacks.

In New York, Stanley and I teamed up with Harry Belafonte, who used his fame to open avenues to deep-pocketed
white people. We used every tactic we could think of to shake
donations loose. A good friend once told me, "It seems like you
were the bagman of the Civil Rights Movement." He meant
it as a compliment, I'm sure, but either way, he was exactly
right. Along with Stanley, my role in the SCLC was to make
it rain.

Eventually, another task was handed off to me: Drafting
speeches. Martin Luther King, Jr. loved to write, but as his
fame and the demands on his time increased, he found he
had fewer and fewer hours to write to the high standards to
which he held himself. It's telling that he did some of his best
writing in a prison cell, where the distractions of his hectic
life were held at bay.

But without the time to properly prepare the kinds of
speeches he wanted to deliver, Martin was in the fortunate
position of having other people willing and eager to write for
him. He came to rely on Stanley and me as his draft speechwriters primarily because a) he trusted us to keep the facts
about an issue straight, and b) with our legal training, we
had a way of presenting an argument with a slant that went
straight for the jugular. Our writing style worked within a
careful structure and was designed specifically to sway opinions. However, it was not without its shortcomings. Martin
used to kid me after he'd read a draft I'd offered, saying,
"Clarence, it's as tight an argument as I can imagine, but
where's the humanity?" When it came to my speech drafts, he
often acted like a decorator: I'd deliver four strong walls and
he would use his God-given abilities to furnish the place so it
felt like home.

There was fallout from Dr. King's victory in the income tax
case within the year. The ad, which had been so useful in
raising awareness and funds, turned out to be a problem. The
text of the ad hadn't been focused on the tax case but rather
the sit-ins in the South. The *Times'* fact-checker found that:

- Where the ad had said that students from Alabama State had sung "The Star Spangled Banner" on the Capitol steps, the students had actually sung "My Country 'Tis of Thee;'" and

- Where the ad had said police armed with shotguns and teargas "ringed" the campus, the police had merely repulsed the students who were leaving it; and

- Where the ad had said the Alabama State dining hall had been padlocked "to starve the students into submission," no such padlock had been put on the doors.

The *Times* ran a correction, but lawyers for the City of Montgomery decided that the ad, and by extension the *Times*, had defamed Public Safety Commissioner L. B. Sullivan. Sullivan filed suit against both the newspaper and the named leaders of the Southern Christian Leadership Conference.

While the *Times* as a media organization was facing a potentially major damage award payment, the reputation of the paper would undoubtedly be unharmed. They were concerned solely with financial exposure.

Money was on the minds of Dr. King and his SCLC team as well. Martin, Stanley, and others in the leadership of the SCLC debated the financial threat to the individuals in the Movement. But there was more to it. Several of us stepped back to appraise the political implications of the libel action. At the time, nothing else was regarded as a serious threat to Dr. King or the leadership of the Civil Rights struggle. But this was different. Martin, Stanley, and the rest of the SCLC leadership decided that this lawsuit was *the most serious threat* to the survival of the organizations and the Civil Rights Movement itself.

We concluded that the political objective of the lawsuit was to bankrupt and decapitate the SCLC. The individual named defendants had few assets to satisfy any potential libel judgment; the SCLC leaders were all ministers, with the exception of Joseph Lowery, a dentist. These people did not have deep pockets. Even to go to trial and win would stretch the financial resources of the SCLC.

Counsel for the *Times*, Lord, Day & Lord, had requested an urgent meeting in New York. Stanley Levison and I attended on behalf of Martin and the other SCLC defendants. The *Times* thought a statement of retraction by the SCLC would help mitigate Sullivan's claim for damages. Under extensive questioning by the *Times'* lawyers, Stanley and I held firm that the events described in the fundraising appeal were accurate or substantially accurate reflections of the acts of brutality committed by the police in Birmingham and Montgomery against the demonstrators. Moreover, we had ample evidence from photos, both in the *Times* and other media, and statements of witnesses who either took part in or observed the demonstration, to support the description of events recited in the ad. A retraction would be our admission that the events described in the ad were untrue. They were not. Therefore, an SCLC retraction was out of the question.

Stanley Levison and I concluded the suit would be costly beyond the resources of SCLC. Therefore, my principal responsibility would be to mobilize support from the legal professionals from New York. The first people I discussed the matter with were two neighbors of mine in Riverdale, Anne and Theodore Kheel. As a result, Ted and I jointly worked to bring the seriousness of the case to the attention of several other prominent members of the New York Bar. Ted organized an interim defense committee of lawyers to assist Dr. King and the other Movement defendants. Martin traveled to New York to speak to the committee and to express his gratitude for their assistance.

Ted had a professional relationship and friendship with former Secretary of State William P. Rogers of the law firm Rogers & Wells. They had elegant offices on the top floors of the then-Pan Am building. Rogers & Wells agreed to take the case on a *pro bono* basis and rallied several other law firms to work with them as *amicus curiae*—friends of the court.

The defense of the case by Rogers & Wells for the SCLC and Lord Day & Lord for the *New York Times* wound its way all the way up to the United States Supreme Court. In March 1964, the Court ruled in favor of the defendants in what has become the landmark decision in the law of libel and First Amendment rights: *The New York Times vs Sullivan.*

In the opinion by Justice William Brennan, the Court noted, in part:

> *The publication here was not a "commercial" advertisement... It communicated information, expressed opinion, recited grievances, protested claimed abuses, and sought financial support on behalf of a movement whose existence and objectives are matters of the highest public interest and concern.*

> *That the Times was paid for publishing the advertisement is as immaterial in this connection as is the fact that newspapers and books are sold. Any other conclusion would discourage newspapers from carrying "editorial advertisements" of this type, and so might shut off an important outlet for the promulgation of information and ideas by persons who do not themselves have access to publishing facilities—who wish to exercise their freedom of speech even though they are not members of the press. The effect would be to shackle the First Amendment in its attempt to secure "the widest possible dissemination of information from diverse and antagonistic sources. To avoid placing such a handicap upon the freedoms of expression, we hold that, if the allegedly libelous statements would otherwise be constitutionally protected from the present judgment, they do not forfeit that protection because they were published in the form of a paid advertisement.*

> *Thus, we consider this case against the background of a profound national commitment to the principle that debate on public issues should be uninhibited, robust, and wide-open, and that it may well include vehement, caustic, and sometimes unpleasantly sharp attacks on government and public officials. The present advertisement, as an expression of grievance and protest on one of the major public issues of our time, would seem clearly to qualify for the constitutional protection. The*

question is whether it forfeits that protection by the falsity of some of its factual statements and by its alleged defamation of respondent.

Authoritative interpretations of the First Amendment guarantees have consistently refused to recognize an exception for any test of truth—whether administered by judges, juries, or administrative officials—and especially one that puts the burden of proving truth on the speaker. The constitutional protection does not turn upon "the truth, popularity, or social utility of the ideas and beliefs which are offered." As Madison said, "Some degree of abuse is inseparable from the proper use of every thing; and in no instance is this more true than in that of the press."

To persuade others to his own point of view, the pleader, as we know, at times, resorts to exaggeration, to vilification of men who have been, or are, prominent in church or state, and even to false statement. But the people of this nation have ordained in the light of history, that, in spite of the probability of excesses and abuses, these liberties are, in the long view, essential to enlightened opinion and right conduct on the part of the citizens of a democracy.

If neither factual error nor defamatory content suffices to remove the constitutional shield from criticism of official conduct, the combination of the two elements is no less inadequate... Erroneous statement is inevitable in free debate, and it must be protected if the freedoms of expression to have the "breathing space" that they need . . . to survive.

It often happens in important historical moments that those who were at the center of a struggle are not fully known or do not have the significance of their efforts recognized. Theodore W. Kheel, Rogers & Wells, and the lawyers who came together in defense of Dr. King and the others are truly unsung heroes of the Civil Rights Movement They prevented the political decapitation of Dr. King's leadership at a crucial juncture.

After the victory in the Supreme Court, the then-publisher of the *Times*, Arthur Sulzberger, had a party at his apartment on Park Avenue. Dr. King was there, along with Bayard Rustin and lawyers for the *Times*. During the course of the celebration, Sulzberger raised a glass and told those gathered, "I'm glad we listened to this young man, Clarence Jones, and didn't give in."

It was a proud moment, and I thought this profoundly important constitutional protection would be enduring. Perhaps it will be. But until recently, we thought the Supreme Court decision in *Roe v. Wade* was the "settled law" on the controversial issue of a woman's right to choose to have a safe, legal, and medically supervised abortion. Now that *Roe* has been overturned, how can I feel true assurance about the continued longevity of *Sullivan v. The New York Times*?

Those early years we all worked hard, not knowing the work would get more intense as the decade wore on. I was on the road all the time. When, in 1962, I received word that my father died, I was working in Atlanta. For some reason, the news didn't come with the same kind of despair that visited me at the death of my mother. It was a blow, but I was in the midst of important work, and I hesitated about dealing with the funeral arrangements.

Martin put his hand on my shoulder and said, "You have to go and do this. This is important."

He was right. I had to see the larger framework of responsibilities in this world—it isn't all about the work. So, I dropped everything to get back up north and handle the burial arrangements. What's more, I wasn't the only one who dropped everything.

At the little church in Southern New Jersey two days later, the funeral service began. Unannounced and unplanned, at least by me, Martin showed up. I hadn't presumed to put him on the spot by inviting him to the funeral—he'd never even met my father. Yet, he wanted to say a few words at the service. *Another* lesson in selflessness I could learn from him.

"I did not know the deceased," Martin began before the small, amazed crowd, "but I know his son." He went on to commend my father and enumerate the qualities Martin was *sure* were part of his character. He used me as the linchpin of his touching remarks, an echo of his sermon in Baldwin Hills. He led a celebration of my father's life by tying my work in the Movement as my father's "gift" of me to a greater cause. My father getting credit for all I'd done because he had me! Fair enough.

In my estimation, the turning point in the Civil Rights struggle came from the advancements in the sharing of visual information. If a picture is worth a thousand words, imagine the value of a *moving* picture. Of course, you have to think back before the time when everyone had a high-definition television studio in their pocket. Television news was different from radio or newspapers. The power of the moving image cannot be overestimated. Television coverage of the struggle had a powerful effect on people who were not directly affected by Jim Crow, racism, and segregation.

One example: In early 1963, Martin called to tell me that Libby Holman Reynolds had reached out to his SCLC office in Atlanta. Ms. Reynolds, a former actress, was the widow of the heir of the R.J. Reynolds Tobacco Company. As a result of the call, she indicated she would like to help support his work and wanted to meet Dr. King at her home in New York. When he shared the information with me and Stanley, we concluded that I should go visit Ms. Reynolds to explain to her that Dr. King was unavailable to meet with her at that time.

Dora MacDonald spoke to Ms. Reynolds and advised her that since I lived and worked in New York, Dr. King had requested me to pay her a visit.

Her townhouse was on the Upper East Side, naturally. There was a white male butler who answered the door. Ms. Reynolds was dressed in a white blouse and elegant flowing trousers. She sat on a chaise lounge with both legs and feet extended, smoking a cigarette (naturally) in a long, elegant ivory holder.

She told me she had come to admire the courage of Dr. King. She then went on to describe how it was only a matter of time before racial segregation would end in the South. She was proud that her father and she had financially supported education with endowments. She was especially proud that Reynolds had supported and was continuing to support Black colleges in North Carolina. Ms. Reynolds asked me lots of questions about Dr. King, his Southern Christian Leadership Conference, and about myself.

After an hour and a half of discussion about the South, the United States, the legacy of slavery, tobacco farming and the issues of the day, she opened her purse and took out her checkbook. She handed me a check made out to Dr. King for $25,000. (The equivalent of nearly a quarter of a million dollars in 2023.)

I told her I could not accept a check made out to Dr. King. I suggested that she could make out donation to the SCLC. She did not want to do that.

We then concluded that she would make it out to me "in trust" for Southern Leadership Conference. Over the next few years, she would continue to make similar donations in support of Dr. King's work.

The key here is that an heiress like Ms. Reynolds needed to see the action to feel its importance. That was the power of the images of the struggle that NBC, ABC, and CBS were pouring into Americans' living rooms on a nightly basis.

This connected us to the other key: Financing was a constant issue for the Movement, and white people had a lot more money than Black people did.

It was the whites that bailed us out, sometimes quite literally.

Six months after that Upper East Side meeting, I had an encounter with Nelson Rockefeller that made Ms. Reynolds' donation look like chump change. It was during the Birmingham campaign and concerned the effort by the SCLC to raise bail money for the youngest jailed protesters, whose parents were putting a lot of pressure on us to get them out.

The Rockefeller family's concern for minorities' rights was well known. In fact, Spelman College was funded by his family and christened with Nelson's mother's maiden name as a thank-you. Despite this kind of "advertising," they were quiet about their participation in the Movement. Whether that was a kind of humble, just-doing-what's-right kind of attitude or something a little bit more unsavory (some of the people the family did business with did not want to deal with a bunch of bleeding hearts) I cannot say. But I respected their sense of propriety and justice. Nelson Rockefeller's attitude back then was the very soul of the well-worn yet misappropriated phrase "compassionate conservatism."

Even the most casual student of American history knows that Martin King ended up imprisoned in the Birmingham city jail in the spring of 1963, and the "hows" and "whys" are recounted in numerous books. But what's been missed in the ongoing historical excavation is a fascinating issue of economics. Just how was the SCLC able to make good on its promise to bail out the schoolchildren when we didn't have enough money to cover even a fraction of the unanticipated number of protesters locked up by "Bull" Connor? That question hasn't really been explored until now.

Still, we must grapple, as all the Birmingham stories do, with the letter. So, as my mother might have put it, we will cover both the pencil and the dollar bill.

Martin famously spent several gut-wrenching days in solitary confinement, but by the time I got in to see him, he'd been allowed back into the large holding cell. (A call from the President's brother accomplished a change in circumstance that all the saber rattling from me—Martin's attorney—could not.) Solitary had been an intense experience. Martin King may have been a man whose very personality was forged by the discipline of Christian faith, but he was not unafraid in that cell. Fear is something so primal it can't be willed away by sheer discipline. The tendrils of fear touched Martin because he loved life, and he knew how tenuous its continuation might be for a person in his position. Solitary confinement slowed him down to focus on these things in a way his everyday life didn't allow. But though it was unnerving to Martin, solitary confinement fed the flame of his spirituality and nourished— emboldened—his soul.

While in jail Martin had been given a copy of *The Birmingham News*, the paper that ran the now-infamous so-called "open letter" signed by eight white Alabama clergymen. It was a full-page paid advertisement, one harshly critical of Martin's techniques for trying to effect change in the South. An attempt at appeasement by the city's white religious establishment. The ad read, in part:

> *In Birmingham, recent public events have given indication that we all have opportunity for a new constructive and realistic approach to racial problems. However, we are now confronted by a series of demonstrations by some of our Negro citizens, directed and led in part by outsiders. We recognize the natural impatience of people who feel that their hopes are slow in being realized. But we are convinced that these demonstrations are unwise and untimely.*

Martin was this outsider. While he was in jail, I was the only one from the SCLC allowed to see him (other than those fellow protesters who'd been hauled in alongside their leader—Ralph Abernathy and Fred Shuttlesworth—who were likewise cooling their heels in the packed cell).

When I finally reached him, he pushed the newspaper at me, agitated. "Have you seen this?" he demanded.

I told him I hadn't. "I've been tied up raising funds, Martin," I said. I looked over the ad there in the jail cell. When I finished, I pointed out it was cowardly bullshit. But I had to agree if the statements went unanswered, they had the potential to adversely influence white people of good will throughout the country. So, yes, a timely response to the white clergyman's ad was a good idea. But you have to put out the fire closest to you first. I shared with Martin my concern (as well as Stanley's) regarding the potential impact on his leadership if we could not provide sufficient bail money for many of the child demonstrators who had joined him in incarceration. Mothers were screaming for us to get their kids out of jail and back to school, and we didn't have the money to honor our promise.

Martin acknowledged the seriousness of the bail issue, but he seemed far more concerned about—almost distracted by—the newspaper ad. He was stuck tight to this thing they'd published about him. "I have to answer this," he said.

Now I noticed what Martin had done to his copy of the newspaper. The margins were black with his scribblings, and it was accompanied by some equally marked-up toilet paper. His manifesto. I knew what it was like, that feverish rush of ideology coming out the point of a pen. Or in this case, the broken nub of a pencil. The eight white clergymen had gotten under Martin's skin, and this was a man who'd been nothing but forgiving when he'd faced down fire hoses and police dogs or been stabbed in the chest.

"Take this out of here," Martin whispered. "Have Dora type it up, okay?"

I thought it was crazy, but I *was* his lawyer. I opened my suit jacket and pulled up my shirt and stuffed the pages into my waistband.

This mishmash of words and arrows connecting them was destined to become the *Letter from A Birmingham Jail*, a document that ranks in American social history up there with the Gettysburg Address. But I didn't know that then. All I knew: There was newsprint and toilet paper stuffed under my shirt and down my pants, and Martin wasn't going to solve the bail money problem from inside a cell. It was up to me.

"See if you can smuggle some paper in for me tomorrow," Martin said.

I handed in the first scraps of what would turn out to be several days of Martin's writings to Dora and Wyatt Walker, the SCLC's Chief of Staff at the time.

"What am I supposed to do with this?" Dora asked.

"Treat it like anything else he writes out and asks you to type," I said.

"Yeah, but he gives me those on lined paper. In *order*."

I offered a shrug. She knew exactly what to do. "Decode it," I said. "We'll see what it looks like in the morning."

From my room in the Gaston Motel, I called Harry Belafonte. It was the same call some of us have made a hundred times in our lives. We have a money problem; we need someone to complain to about it. I wasn't asking for a solution, just a friend to support me while I worried aloud. I needed a sounding board while I kicked around what our options were for raising funds.

But Harry surprised me. "I have an idea," he said. "I think I can stir the pot. Let me do a little leg work. I'll get back to you."

The next day I returned to Birmingham jail and was able to slip to Martin a legal pad, a pen, and the typed-up draft material he'd handed to me the previous day. It wasn't exactly a file baked in a cake, but I have to admit I did some sweating as the guards debated whether it was proper procedure to frisk a prisoner's attorney.

With paper and pen, Martin was able to make much better progress on his answer to the clergymen. Now, even I could see the power of what he had in mind. No wonder he couldn't be bothered to worry about mundane bail issues. What amazed me was there was absolutely no reference material for Martin to draw upon. Here he is, pulling quote after quote from thin air. The Bible, yes, as might be expected from a Baptist minister, but also William Gladstone, Mahatma Gandhi, William Shakespeare, and St. Augustine.

Two days later, on Friday afternoon, I spoke to Harry again. He said he had been talking to Hugh Morrow, Governor Rockefeller's speechwriter, and there was an opportunity. He asked me to return to New York as soon as I could. When I arrived later that night, he instructed me to call Morrow at his home on Sutton Place, "no matter what time your plane lands, Clarence."

It was late by the time I got off the plane, sometime after midnight. From the gate at LaGuardia, I called the number Harry had given to me. Hugh Morrow answered and said he'd been waiting for my call. If he'd been asleep or wanted to be, I couldn't sense it. It might as well have been two in the afternoon. "Mr. Belafonte tells me you and Dr. King have some difficulties down there. The governor and his family would like to be of help."

Be of help was—if you're a Carnegie, a Vanderbilt, a Rockefeller—a kind of coded phrase interchangeable with this never-to-be-uttered-aloud sentiment: "How much do you need?" I hadn't asked Harry for money, but he'd gone and asked someone else on my behalf. I suppose I have my coded phrases too.

"Mr. Rockefeller and I would like for you to meet us tomorrow morning at the headquarters of the Chase Manhattan Bank on Sixth Avenue and 47th Street," Morrow told me.

I started to remind him that tomorrow was Saturday. This was 1963, and bankers' hours meant something very specific. No bank in the country was open for business on a Saturday. Then I remembered who I was talking to. The Rockefeller Family owned this particular bank. He could probably walk in at midnight on Christmas Eve if the desire struck him. I didn't quite know what to say. "Thank you," was as far as I got. It was a start.

Morrow waved off the thanks. "Save that for Mr. Rockefeller," he said.

Saturday there was a skeleton crew in the main branch of Chase Manhattan: A security guard, a banker, me, Hugh Morrow, and Nelson Rockefeller. Everyone would play his part; Rockefeller as the somewhat detached philanthropist, Morrow as careful mouthpiece, the banker as the one making sure all the i's were dotted and t's were crossed, the Brinks agent with the gun making sure nothing went haywire. And me, the hat-in-hand Negro trying hard not to appear as though this was the strangest situation I'd ever encountered.

It was more money than I'd ever seen in one place before. Come to think of it, it was more stainless steel, too. The thickness of that vault door was in perfect proportion to what it was guarding. Money stacked floor to ceiling. Literally. I was smart enough to know it was just paper, just a representation of something, not really the wealth itself, but still I had an almost primordial reaction to seeing all that currency. Some genetic memory that tells you money is freedom flushed adrenaline into my system. I stood there jittery with it as a banker counted banded stacks of bills into a brand-new briefcase. I was just starting to feel like I was going to get out of this in one piece and that I'd return to Alabama a hero of the Movement, when the confusion arose. As the security guard locked the briefcase the banker handed me a single sheet of paper.

"Please sign this, Mr. Jones."

It was filigreed, and stamped with official-looking seals. In bold letters along the top it read: "DEMAND PROMISSORY NOTE."

The banker saw the concern in my eyes. "Banking regulations, sir. It's... required."

I didn't have to be a banker to know what the paper meant. If I signed it, I became responsible for paying the money back. One hundred thousand 1963 dollars, equal to well over a million today.

"I can't personally promise this will be paid back."

"There are legal conditions that apply here," the banker said. "We need a signature or we can't release the funds."

I looked over at Rockefeller. "I don't have this kind of money, and neither does the SCLC."

"Just sign for it, Mr. Jones," Rockefeller said to me. "You don't need to worry about it."

Worried or not, I was out of choices. I thought of Martin, of all those kids in the jail missing school, and I scrawled out my name.

Remarkably, though Rockefeller never said so aloud, he'd given his word and would stick by it. He would never make the demand for repayment. Quite the opposite, in fact. After everything was sorted out with the bail money in Birmingham over the weekend, I returned to my downtown Manhattan law office. The following Tuesday our receptionist buzzed to let me know a messenger was at our reception desk with something requiring my signature. He handed me an envelope from Chase Manhattan Bank marked "Personal And Confidential." Inside I found the one hundred thousand dollar Demand Promissory Note I'd signed on Saturday morning. Across its face was one red rubber-stamped word:

PAID

My office and home phones were tapped by the federal government. I wouldn't know about these recordings for almost twenty years, but it didn't surprise me greatly when I learned of their existence. Martin always thought my caution bordered on the paranoid, but I'd had some experience with the people who make the rules, and I knew they didn't play by them. And though the wiretaps may have been illegal, I can imagine, times as they were, permission to set them was not hard to come by in Robert Kennedy's Justice Department. We were square in the middle of the deepest part of the Cold War, and if any government organization, particularly an investigatory agency like the FBI, slapped a communist label on you regardless of the facts, it meant all the rules were off. Rightly or wrongly, when J. Edgar Hoover decided to play the "red card" with the Civil Rights Movement, our privacy was merely another casualty in the struggle against the Soviet Union. It's not too different from the post-9/11 hysteria in 2001, some inverted version of the PATRIOT Act that said America must invade the privacy of men and women peacefully striving to achieve freedom and equality for all. As if spying on citizens is clearly underscored in our Declaration of Independence, our national anthem, and other etched-in-stone sites where we crow to the world about how open and compassionate we are as a nation.[18]

Well, Martin Luther King, Jr., Stanley Levison, and I had nothing to hide but our strategy. Part of that strategy,

---

18 Lerone A. Martin's *The Gospel of J. Edgar Hoover—How the FBI Aided and Abetted the Rise of White Christian Nationalism* outlines Hoover's mindset toward my race: "J. Edgar Hoover was a white Christian nationalist. He believed America had divine origins. Throughout his career, Hoover reminded the public that 'The American ideal has its roots in religion. The nation was conceived by God and thus chosen for a special purpose. God revealed the sacred plan to the white Founding Fathers.'"

predictably, was to make the government nervous. So, as it turned out, the wiretaps served some of *our* purposes as well, though unbeknownst to us in the moment.

The March on Washington was not actually the brainchild of the Civil Rights Movement, nor even an idea borne of the 1960s. More than a generation earlier, in 1941, the president of the Brotherhood of Sleeping Car Porters, A. Philip Randolph, had conceived of the original "March on Washington" as a way to pressure President Franklin D. Roosevelt to guarantee jobs for black men and women in the World War II armament industries. This demonstration was canceled at the last moment when Roosevelt capitulated to Randolph's demands and issued the first Presidential Executive Order protecting African American rights since the Emancipation Proclamation.

Randolph had been carefully following Martin's unsuccessful campaign to desegregate public accommodations and facilities in Albany, Georgia, twenty-one years later. Bayard Rustin was one of Martin's close advisors, and Randolph had mentored him years earlier. Randolph called Bayard and talked to him about the possibility of staging a large demonstration in Washington, D.C. as an "updated" version of his idea. It was a notion that he had never let go of throughout the intervening years. Together Bayard and Randolph conceived of two days of rallying and lobbying, linking Civil Rights to the national economic demands of working-class people. They planned to create a coalition of both labor unions and unorganized workers. They contemplated a massive protest gathering, accompanied by direct-action campaigns, such as sit-ins in congressional offices. Bayard was excited and agreed to suggest the concept to the SCLC.

Following the successful campaign that led to the desegregation of public facilities and department stores in Birmingham in the spring of 1963, Martin and other Civil Rights leaders began informal discussions to consider the next strategic move in their campaign. When Bayard presented Martin with the March as an option, I was honored to be part of a kind of strategic brain trust to consider the pros and cons. Together with Stanley Levison and some of Martin's other advisors, Harry Wachtel, Cleveland Robinson, Professor Lawrence Reddick, and the Reverends Thomas Kilgore, Walter Fauntroy, Wyatt Tee Walker, Andy Young and Ralph Abernathy, we formed Dr. King's inner circle. The FBI turned out to be a silent partner in that inner circle as well.

As we talked, they listened. As we moved closer to an understanding of just what needed to be done, they worried. And when the Movement came up with a plan to stage the March effectively, the FBI shuddered at what it could mean for race relations in America.

We speculated that if the idea for our demonstration were to get to those in authority, it might be regarded as a threat to the stability of our government. What we didn't know was that our plans were already being discussed at the highest levels of government. During the midsummer days of 1963, hundreds of FBI internal memos—many featuring pages of wiretap transcript—were piling up detailing the conversations we were having about the March:

...Martin Luther King, Jr., had also been thinking about some new and larger form of demonstration. He said to his aides, "We are on a breakthrough... We need a mass protest," and told them that offers of help had come from certain trade unions and from Paul Newman and Marlon Brando —both "Kennedy men..."

...King asked the aides to contact Randolph to see if they could all work together...

...Jones called an unwoman [unknown woman] and told her that Dr. Martin L. King was coming to town today, and would be staying at his house. He said that Ralph Abernathy and his wife and children were coming with him, and wondered if she knew of a place they could stay in Croton. The woman said no...

...Reverend King stated that he planned to attend a conference soon with leaders of other organizations in order to discuss the march on Washington with them. Levison suggested to King that King take advantage of the two public appearances he will make in New York City, during the coming week, to announce his plans for the March on Washington and the demonstrations that will go along with it...

Yes, the government had a direct line into all our planning and strategy. The question that information brought to the door of the Kennedy White House was what—if anything— was the government going to do about it?

A meeting was held at New York's Roosevelt Hotel on July 2nd, 1963, attended by nearly two dozen desegregation activists, including the "Big Six" Civil Rights Movement leaders: King, Randolph, Roy Wilkins, James Farmer, John Lewis, and Whitney Young, Jr. There, a March organization was established. Soon a vote was planned to determine who would take on the vital role of Chief Coordinator. Bayard Rustin, one of the March's principal organizers, wanted the job. Unfortunately, he was met by a bit of skittish opposition from some of the other leaders. There was Bayard's earlier membership in the Young Communist League to consider, some argued. And even those closest to him had to acknowledge his prior conviction in 1953 on morals charges as a homosexual could cause some problems. The vote was taken, and Bayard wound up Deputy Director. I loved him all the more for not backing down in the face of such harsh but practical considerations for that era.

There was little time to lose, and Bayard went into high gear in Randolph's West 130th Street office in Harlem. Within two weeks, he had distributed two thousand copies of his *Organizing Manual No. 1* to Movement leaders at centers throughout the country. The idea was to create a coordinated

system that would allow us to pull off the demonstration on
an extremely short timetable.

> * *
>
> ## MARCH ON WASHINGTON
> ## FOR JOBS AND FREEDOM
>
> August 28, 1963
>
> Organizing Manual No. 1
>
> This manual is designed to give you information you
> will need regarding the March for Jobs and Freedom,
> and to help you prepare for this event.
> The time to organize your delegation for the March is
> NOW. The time is short – start as soon as you have
> received and read this manual.
> A Second Edition of the manual will appear before
> August 28 and will provide final and detailed informa-
> tion as it becomes available.
>
> *National Office*
> *March on Washington*
> *for Jobs and Freedom*
>
> **170 WEST 130th STREET**
> **NEW YORK 27, NEW YORK**
> FIlmore 8-1900
>
> **Cleveland Robinson**   **Bayard Rustin**
> *Chairman, Administrative Committee*   *Deputy Director*

Martin had been of two minds regarding the entire enterprise. He knew that the March was the right idea, that Randolph's old concept had an energy that fit with the times. But
Birmingham had taken a lot out of him. In the aftermath, he
had wanted nothing more than to take Coretta and his four children away for a vacation and forget—forget his looming book
deadline, forget the office politics of running the ever-growing
SCLC, forget the constant need to raise funds to sustain the
staff and support the various Civil Rights programs, and forget
the demands for speaking appearances from all over the country that he had a difficult time turning down (these appearances were an essential part of our fundraising program).

Martin had gone on record with his advisors, saying he
didn't believe he could pull off the planning of such a massive
undertaking while working under the conditions in which he

usually conducted his affairs. No, if this March was going to come together on such a tight time frame, he would have to get away from all the distractions. Get away to where very few people knew how to reach him.

The logistics of the March on Washington preparations and planning dictated that Martin needed to be available to talk by phone and possibly meet in person while he was on this working "vacation." Of course, what was a perfectly reasonable bit of strategy for Dr. King turned into a bit of a problem for me. One afternoon in early June, I called Anne from my office to notify her what train I would be taking home from Grand Central. That's when I learned that she, Stanley Levison, and a neighbor in Riverdale, Cora Weiss, had decided that the Joneses would be vacating their house to enable Martin and his family to move into it. Cora and her husband Peter also had a home on Martha's Vineyard, so the plan was that Anne, the children and I would move into the Weiss's house while they were on the island. This would enable Martin, Coretta, and their children to spend that time in our house, where Martin felt comfortable working.[19] Bayard Rustin, the deputy director of the March, was living in New York at the time, and our residence provided him with a way to work with Martin in person. This act of generosity by the Weisses in support of Martin was singularly important to the strategic advance organization of the March on Washington.

The house in Riverdale had an enormous sunken living room as well as a recreation room, but as we packed up to make the place ready for Martin and his family, I realized quickly what I would be missing most that summer: The deck overlooking the Hudson River.

Compounding matters, Ralph and Juanita Abernathy asked us to also find a vacation home for them in Riverdale. We had our hands full. But all this shuffling around was done quietly. We knew that no one from the outside world could be permitted to penetrate Martin's refuge.

---

19 Years later, Martin Luther King, III would share with me that the six-week stint in my home with his mom and dad was one of the most memorable times of his life.

We managed to pull that off. Sort of. According to a memo from the Atlanta field office of the FBI to J. Edgar Hoover:

Jones states that only four individuals will know where King will be staying.

Well, four individuals and the entire Justice Department. On July 22ⁿᵈ, 1963, J. Edgar Hoover sent a memorandum to Attorney General Robert Kennedy that read in part:

Pursuant to your request that in view of the possible communist influence in the racial situation consideration be given to placing a technical surveillance on Jones, it is requested that authority be granted to place a technical surveillance on Jones at his current residence, 5505 Independence Avenue, Bronx, New York; at his law office, 165 Broadway, New York City; and at the Ghandi [sic] Society for Human Rights, 15 East 40ᵗʰ Street, New York City.

According to the now declassified record, in late July the FBI installed electronic eavesdropping devices and telephone wiretaps at my home on orders of Robert Kennedy. Once again, what we thought we were doing in secret was, for the most part, broadcast to the Kennedy Administration.

Authority for electronic surveillance of Clarence Benjamin Jones at his residence, 5505 Independence Avenue, Bronx, New York, was obtained on July 23, 1963. This surveillance was requested in order to develop information regarding the plans of the Communist Party, USA, (CPUSA), relating to influence in racial matters.

Martin's "vacation" residence at my house was, while he was there, SCLC's de facto command and control center. Away from the hectic day-to-day activity in Atlanta, he was able to fully concentrate on the work at hand.

During the weekends that the Kings stayed at our home, Anne would go with our children to her mother's house in Wilton, Connecticut, and I would remain behind in Riverdale to be available to Martin. Stanley would make his way over from Manhattan, and we would discuss the details of how the March might eventually occur. The three of us started to see this would be a logistical operation on a scale we'd never attempted. The churches, always playing a pivotal role, were critical here. They were the way to focus the "ground troops," those people that wanted to change the world, but who didn't feel empowered to take an individual public stand. Naturally, there was an enormous difference between a focused and goal-oriented endeavor like a local bus boycott and a drive across the country to illustrate an overarching point about segregation and racial inequality. Travel operations were going to play a major role. People might be willing to march from the Washington Monument to the Lincoln Memorial, but someone had to get them to the Washington Monument first.

Meanwhile, while we were laying out the blueprint of how to bring the masses into the nation's capital in a show of faith, hope, and solidarity, those in power continued to listen and were also considering their options very, very carefully.

Nowadays, people know all about the concept of political "spin." But in 1963, there was no pocket-sized word for it. Still, methods of attempting to control events by controlling perception have existed at least since Machiavelli, and there were many people on Capitol Hill who knew how to deploy those methods with vicious efficiency.

There were so many parties interested in a preemptive downplaying of our venture that it sometimes seemed we were wildly outnumbered. The halls of Congress rang with this attitude. We were at war with the status quo, as we'd always known.

And we knew it had always been a war of public opinion. But the March was different—if those in power had their way, the battle over the nation's perception of the March would be a cold war, a clandestine war. It was a clash for which the winner, it struck me, would be decided before the first performer appeared in the dawn light on the Washington Mall.

The history books may tell us John F. Kennedy supported the March on Washington, but the truth is a bit murkier. In fact, the President's initial strategy was simply to try to persuade the leadership to cancel the March. "We want success in Congress, not just a big show at the Capitol," came the President's message. "Some of these people are looking for an excuse to be against us, and I don't want to give any of them a chance to say 'Yes, I'm for the bill, but I am damned if I will vote for it at the point of a gun.'"

His arguments fell on deaf ears, of course. And political animal that Kennedy was, after failing to stop the March, he decided to embrace it.

But behind the scenes, Attorney General Robert Kennedy's enforcer, J. Edgar Hoover, repeatedly tried to scuttle our attempts at pulling off a cohesive demonstration. In the weeks leading up to the March, he intensified his already passionate campaign to defame Martin. Hoover tried to persuade the Kennedys that Communists were influencing Martin, and his specious denunciations of some of Martin's associates were taken much more seriously by the Kennedys than was warranted. Hoover's baseless suspicions about Dr. King, his virulent attacks on him, and his repeated attempts to destroy his reputation with the Kennedys were spurred by racist delusions and pathological animosities. Hoover tried, unsuccessfully, to exploit wiretap information about Martin's sexual indiscretions and Bayard's homosexual liaisons that had nothing to do with the Movement.

Those who opposed us were desperate to find that leverage point that would deflate the number of marchers. If they could cut our attendance down, the effect would be devastating. It wasn't a proportional issue—half as many marchers means half as much impact—but a binary one. If the supporter turnout appeared anemic, everything in the media coverage (and hence the general world opinion) would focus on our disappointment and paint a picture of the March as a failure.

But the flip side of that strategy existed too. If a significant number of marchers turned out, they were going to say we brought the government to its knees. The media, as I'm sure

I'm not the first to point out, works on the poles of the human experience, not the middle ground.

So, it was all about perception. If the March seemed likely to be a washout, people wouldn't come, and it would indeed become a washout. When you get into the fine grain, action is based on decision—should I or shouldn't I—and it is attended with all manner of conscious and subliminal cues. Second guessing, flip-flopping, fear. Something takes off like a rocket only when it seems inevitable. A marketer's job is to take all that doubt away so whatever they're hawking seems inevitable. *It's a bestseller, everyone's reading it. Eventually you'll read it, might as well buy it now.* Our March needed to do that, too. But it was less like an advertising campaign than a political campaign: We had an opponent just as dedicated to the opposite result. Both tactics were valid: No one wants to be the only guest to a party (their inevitable failure campaign) and no one wants to miss the party everyone's going to be talking about (our inescapable and transcendent success angle). History would judge the better PR effort.

Ted Brown, one of Mr. Randolph's organizers out of the March Committee's Washington, D.C. office called Martin at my house on August 10th. He reported that Washington was "running from fear; everybody's scared stiff around here. Leaves have been canceled for hospital personnel, police, and all long-distance telephone operators."

This gave us a nice boost of confidence. Ted went on to say that Burke Marshall (Robert Kennedy's Deputy Attorney General on Civil Rights) was terrified as well. "They are all afraid in Washington because of the possibility of violence," he reported with a certain amount of glee. Ted also let us know that Robert V. Murray, the District of Columbia's Chief of Police, had put the entire department on the highest level of alert. Officers were scheduled for 18-hour shifts instead of the typical eight hours.

The "fear" in the nation's capital Ted referenced in his conversation with Martin was a fairly accurate characterization of prevailing state of mind among political leaders and the media at the time. Jack Eisen, one of the columnists for *The Washington Post*, wrote several pieces in advance of the March that raised all sorts of dire possibilities and predictions of violence and disorder that would likely take place if the March occurred. In an August 18th piece, he rhetorically asked these questions: "Will Washington Negroes accept the leadership that has brought them this far or will they turn to the extremists? Will future historians record that Washington made a successful transition with peace and pride, or will they record a failure that was marked by turmoil and violence?"

The opposition fanned the flames of fear on both sides of the racial divide, a well-worn but useful political tactic. Even if we Negroes were peaceable, what about those virulent racists who would come looking to extract payment for our audacity with clubs and knives?

Martin believed that the people opposed to our show of solidarity were those who most frequently raised the issue of possible violence and disorder during or from the March. His sense of humor was somewhat dry but always up and running. Martin wondered aloud, "Why would people travel all that distance to a peaceful demonstration for the principal purpose of engaging in violence and disorder? It seems like a long way to go."

Indeed it does.

One weapon of choice for people within and outside of government who opposed the March was a time-honored method in Washington: Spreading untraceable information. The off-the-record quote. The press leak. The whisper campaign. As we'd half-expected, disinformation about Bayard's socialist leanings, homosexuality, and prior criminal convictions was first out of the gate. The March organization took a few knocks, but it was nothing we couldn't handle. In the end, taking down Bayard was a non-starter, and his personal life dropped away from the news cycle quickly.

Another early issue fueling the fear of disorder in the minds of those in power was our initial plan to have the marchers assemble on the steps of the U.S. Capitol Building. The Kennedy Administration came out against this idea. Strongly against it. But we were determined. Martin Luther King would speak from the very top step. Nothing would dissuade us, we thought.

In 1963, Martin Luther King and his SCLC may have commanded national attention in a way no other Civil Rights group did, but the organization had no intention of tackling the massive undertaking of the March alone. Nor did the many other players in the Civil Rights arena look to defer to us. Both the ideology of the Movement and the logistics of the March dictated that the undertaking would be a team effort. CORE (the Congress of Racial Equality), the NAACP (the National Association for the Advancement of Colored People), the National Urban League, the Student Nonviolent Coordinating Committee, the National Council of Negro Women, and labor unions under the leadership of A. Philip Randolph and Walter Reuther all had skin in this particular game.

The trick was to balance all the various agendas. We were working side-by-side with many noble-minded groups and though in general they all had the same vision for improving the Negroes' condition in America, the truth was more subtle than that. Each organization had different strategies for achieving the goals they saw for Blacks. As different as each of the groups' leaders were, it's hardly surprising that every organization looked at the struggle through a slightly different pair of eyes. And this was how the March itself was viewed.

Roy Wilkins (head of the NAACP), for example, fought to focus the March almost exclusively on legislative reform. That mirrored his (and his constituents') belief that changing the law was the key to racial equality. The Kennedy Civil Rights Bill was in play in the House at the time, and there were those among the organizing Committee who saw the March as a rallying cry in support of the bill's passage. On the other hand, there were some who saw that same bill as watered down and ineffectual. Some, for example, despised the bill's component making educational institutions fulfill racial quotas. Others viewed our demonstration as a condemnation of the Kennedy

Administration, a way of sending a message of our disenchantment and frustration with the White House's "foot dragging"
procrastination of getting a true Civil Rights bill signed into
law.

There were disputes beyond the legislation as well. Some
factions were more concerned with issues of poverty among
Blacks. Others supported the March primarily as a vehicle to
focus the attention of the Movement and the country on over-
coming educational barriers, which seemed to connect directly
with poverty issues. (Statistics subsequently released in 1964
appear to vindicate this concern: Even after the unanimous
Supreme Court decision in *Brown v. The Board of Education*
in 1954, only 1.18% of black children attended integrated
schools.) And, of course, there were members of the March
Committee who, along with their supporters, saw the demonstration as principally focusing on the need for jobs and our
continuing struggle against Black poverty.

John Lewis wanted to stir the Negroes themselves to
immediate action, while others wanted to thrust the burden
of change into the laps of those in power. Each organization
participating had their own take on which direction to set the
public posture and perception of the March.

Against this background, Martin and those of us who represented him were confronted with the exact same office politics
he found in the halls of Atlanta's SCLC headquarters. The
same politics that Martin had to "vacation" to escape from.
They'd followed him to New York, and they were magnified
dramatically as a result of the growing sense of the March's
importance. What became clear very quickly in those early
weeks of August was that we had a lot of chiefs and very few
foot soldiers. Among the more contentious issues was the
order of the speakers from the various groups comprising
the umbrella organizations of the March and how much time
would be allotted for each organizational representative to
speak. This not only involved the obvious logistics of time,
but it also required delicate maneuvering among the mine-
field of the egos of the respective participants. Now, I'm the
first to admit that Martin King had an ego. But I can also say

the man truly let the circumstances before him pave the way for his response. In contrast, many of the other organizers seemed at least as concerned with how they personally came across as with how the March itself worked. We were blessed to have the over-arching presence, wisdom, and stature of A. Philip Randolph, "Chairman" of our March, to serve as a steady compass in an otherwise stormy sea of participants' egos.

Nowhere was this easier to see than in the discussions about the speaker schedule at the March. One of the wiretap transcripts of that time reads:

> *On August 21, 1963, a confidential source, who has furnished reliable information in the past, advised that on that date, CLARENCE JONES held a discussion with an unidentified individual regarding the March on Washington. According to this source... JONES indicated that he was unhappy about the time limitation which had been placed on the March on Washington speakers, limiting everyone alike to five minutes. JONES states that his proposal was that Dr. King be introduced by Randoph [sic], that he be the last speaker and be allotted the most time to speak.*

As planning progressed, people were pushing for a uniform time limit of five minutes for every speech. Martin didn't agree with that but could not say so personally. He remained concerned throughout August about the time allotted for the speakers. He felt there were too many speakers and that time reserved for him was not enough. Martin wondered aloud whether "they are trying to throttle me. Maybe they're determined that I not be in a position of making a speech that will get a great response from the people." Now, this may sound like a man with a large ego. But everything we'd been hearing suggested that a large percentage of the potential crowd was coming to Washington to hear Martin Luther King, Jr. speak. The reality we were facing was this: Is it better to placate other leaders of the Civil Rights Movement or to give the crowd what it was expecting?

The sad truth is that I saw firsthand that there *was* some jealousy of Martin's national stature among the Civil Rights leadership. It wasn't hard for people toiling in the Movement to watch Martin's rise to prominence and say to themselves, "Why isn't that me?" I understand that instinct. That doesn't, however, make it right.

It fell to me to have some frank conversations. I talked the situation over with Cleveland Robinson. Affectionately known as "Cleve," he was an international vice-president of the District 65 Retail Wholesale Workers Union, whose headquarters at the time was located in downtown Manhattan at Astor Place on the Lower Eastside. "District 65," as Martin called them, was one of the most consistent sources of financial support and "foot soldiers" to him and his SCLC. Six-foot four and partially blind, Cleve had a booming baritone voice with a signature Jamaican accent. His presence emanated a "take no prisoners" aura. Together Cleve, Stanley and I came up with a game plan.

The plan was simple: Get the people on our side who the other committee members could not possibly argue with. Bayard was the Chief Coordinator, but he wasn't enough. We knew just from the push back during the original vote for that position that people were not going to demure if they disagreed with Bayard. No, Cleve and I knew the silver bullet in all this was A. Philip Randolph. This was a man who had said, "Nothing counts but pressure, pressure, more pressure." He was revered. He was the elder statesman of the March. We knew if he agreed that Martin should be the de facto keynote speaker, it would be so. Then we would be honoring what we believed was the overwhelming sentiment of the people coming to the March, based upon our pre-March intelligence and political analysis.

I presented our case to Bayard and Mr. Randolph, insisting that it was the right thing for the March (not Martin, mind you, but the *March*) that Martin be the last and longest speaker. They agreed with my reasoning. It was then decided that either Cleve or I would be the "heavies" in conversations with Roy Wilkins, Jim Farmer, Whitney Young (or their designees), and other March organizers to explain our reasons why we strongly believed Martin should be the last speaker with the most time allotted.

As Martin's lawyer I was used to tough negotiating on his behalf. Several of the March leaders, however, had never seen me in this role, up close and personal. But I honestly didn't mind, nor was I reluctant to be the "heavy." And I wasn't shy about pulling out my ace in the hole line: "Believe me, my brothers, nobody here will want to follow Martin as a public speaker." How true that turned out to be.

In the end the other organizers made the exception for Martin's speech, and in doing so paved the way to a singular chapter in American history.

To be fair, we may have had differences of opinion, but every tension was compounded by the continuing pressure of the looming deadline. An endless stream of reports were pouring into my Riverdale home (now converted by Martin into his "command post north" for the March), with every bit of good news canceled out by some nugget of worrisome information. Everyone was working overtime to bring the event together. The phone was ringing off the hook with reports from the field.

Ted Brown called again, this time to fill us in on attendance projections. He told Martin that the best-guess estimate was 150,000 people, which was not bad, but it wasn't the stellar number we were hoping for either. Ted said he was quite worried about support for the March from residents in the D.C. area: "I don't think we will get as much as five thousand Negroes out of Washington."

To me, it was nothing short of bizarre to think that Blacks coming from as far away as California would be spending days to get to the March and all the while a large percentage of those who were having the party thrown in their backyard might not bother to attend.

Ted's answer was a simple one: "Not too many Negro ministers are involved from here."

It wasn't a publicity or public relations misstep; it was more straightforward than that. People do what their leaders ask them to do. We would need to make a fast, concerted effort to get the leaders of Washington's Black churches on track with the demonstration.

Ted also shared his concern about March access to the majority of SCLC's constituency—people living in Alabama, Georgia, Mississippi, and the rest of the southern states. He suggested the only way to get a significant number of attendees from the South was to rent trains. We weren't even sure that renting trains was possible, but the suggestion went on our list just the same. There were almost no ideas too far afield for the coordinating committee to consider.

The transportation issue continued. Steven Courier, a respected and influential New York philanthropist, had pledged a contribution to the March of fifty-one charter buses to help with the estimated 30,000 people that would be coming to Washington from New York City. And we were able to charter three private planes coming out of California in addition to the "celebrities plane" we'd already planned.

There was some good news. We heard that Detroit participation should be high, primarily because of the United Auto Workers association with the Movement. The Protestant and Catholic churches were going all out to try and get their members to attend. In fact, Catholic churches in Washington were encouraging all their parochial students to attend the March.

Still, A. Philip Randolph continued to be very concerned with the apparent overall lethargy of Negroes in Washington. *The Afro-American*, a leading black newspaper in the D.C. area, had reported there was complete apathy in Baltimore and Washington regarding the March.

It was a refrain we heard again and again. Reverend Thomas Kilgore, a close friend of Martin's and then pastor of the Friendship Baptist Church in Harlem, told him in a mid-August phone call, "It looks like there may be more white people than Negroes."

This struck Martin hard. "We can't afford to have under 100,000 people and there has to be more Negroes than Whites," he told Tom. This was always a tough issue to navigate. We all knew Negroes needed to be seen as handling their affairs themselves. And yet part of the struggle was to show the white world that there were plenty of white people who didn't engage in racism, who supported our struggle for equal treatment, who condemned segregation. In fact, one of the key reasons Malcolm X and some other militant community leaders decried the March was because it wasn't a Black-only show of strength.

Tom told Martin he was trying to get 150,000 people in Washington. This seems like a large number, but I wondered how it would look in a long television shot of the entire Washington Mall.

Martin inquired about Tom's opinion of the Washington-area clergy's responsibility in pulling together a big crowd. Both men agreed they had to contact ministers in the area in an effort to encourage them to boost March support.

Tom told Martin after he preached Sunday morning he was going to Washington. "We're going to put six men in Washington and Baltimore," he said, meaning our agents of the March assigned to drum up participation from those communities. "We already have three guys in Philadelphia, and they've estimated there will be fifteen thousand coming from there."

There were other "givens" that Tom reported, all in an effort to assuage our nerves. (I put quotes around the word because if we'd learned one thing in our Civil Rights work, it was not to count your chickens before they hatched.) There were at least seven buses coming from Norfolk, Virginia. Martin's brother A.D. was working to charter a train out of Birmingham. We contemplated trying to book twelve trains to carry a thousand marchers each directly from New York City and sixty buses that could come out of Long Island carrying another three thousand people.

"The whole Eastern Seaboard is aflame with this," Tom told Martin. "You can't find a bus to rent in New York now."

Martin asked for a guess at the number of people they could expect from New York. Tom told him a conservative estimate was thirty-five thousand.

The phone call ended on a note of foreboding. Tom asked if we should consider stopping marchers that were arriving in their cars on the outskirts of town, having them park and shuttling them in to avoid horrific gridlock.

Martin thought for a moment. Then he responded, his low voice caught for eternity, snagged in the FBI wiretap dragnet: "Tom, I don't think they ought to block people from driving into Washington. If it's necessary to paralyze the city for the whole day, then it's necessary."

The budget for the March organization was put at $120,000—a huge sum in its time. Funds came in through donations both large and small. Official March on Washington buttons were sold for a quarter each, with nearly two hundred thousand sold by August 17th and more on order. All the profit went into the coffers of the March organization.

The official mementos of the March were five red, white, blue, and black prints that incorporated *Life Magazine* photographs of the police dog and fire hose attacks, a human chain of hand-holding, and other Movement iconography. The type— We Shall Overcome—appeared ripped from somewhere else and attached collage-style, so that each poster transmitted that sense of hope and urgency. Forty thousand of each poster was printed and they sold in advance for a dollar a piece. The beauty of this approach as a fundraiser was that, since we presented them not as a choice among several posters but as a unified portfolio, many people ordered all five. The finances were coming together, and in addition to raising capital for the March organizers, these presold items gave us something perhaps even more valuable than money: They gave us a sense that the *zeitgeist* was on our side. We did whatever we could to raise the March's profile, and encouraged others to do the same. For example, in France (a country that has always taken great interest in America's racial problem), Josephine Baker, James Baldwin, and Burt Lancaster led a small march to call attention to the upcoming one in Washington.

As the date of the March approached, I began turning more of my attention to coordinating with Harry Belafonte on the logistics of arrival and participation of the so-called "Celebrity Delegation." Martin was not particularly enamored with the Hollywood lifestyle of consumption and superficiality, but he was a realist. The power of the celebrity contingent was quite simply to attract eyeballs, they knew it and we knew it. The actors and musicians could (and still do) capture the attention of what might potentially be an otherwise inattentive or distracted TV audience.

The irony was that Martin had slowly but surely been building up his own form of international celebrity. He might have found that embarrassing, but he was not above using it to the Movement's advantage. In fact, that star power was, in our estimation, what would finally drive the attendance of our March. It was why we insisted Martin have the position of last speaker. That, my friends, is show business.

And so, as the March needed Martin, Martin needed celebrities. Luckily, despite the narcissistic tendencies of many in the entertainment business, many stars either have or need to believe they have open humanistic hearts and liberal-leaning politics to match. Either way, they could help us, and we were taking them up on their offer.

Harry, artist that he is, preferred to think of the group as the "cultural" delegation. He went throughout Los Angeles rattling cages in film studio suites and recording studio booths to try to get the hottest talent in America to participate. He advised me that the "chairman" of the delegation, Charlton Heston, would be arriving by private charter plane from Los Angeles with the other members of his delegation. Among the celebrities that would be traveling with him were Marlon Brando, Shelly Winters, Steve McQueen, James Garner, Anthony Franciosa, Judy Balaban, Sidney Poitier, Sammy Davis, Jr., Diahann Carroll, Burt Lancaster, Josephine Baker, Paul Newman and his wife Joanne Woodward.

In August 1963, these celebrities were at the top of their popularity and their attitudes and opinions carried real weight in America. But just what would they do to improve race relations? They'd wave, they'd pose for pictures. They would grant interviews to select media outlets and go over our talking points. Some would perform, some would even speak at the podium. In general, they'd mingle and create a surging sense of importance on top of the already intense philosophical issues we'd brought to the foreground.

And though not as difficult then as it is these days, getting in touch with celebrities and wrangling them, pinning them down to a particular day and date wasn't so easy. At Harry's direction, I spent endless mornings rushing into Manhattan meetings with New York-based agents or the occasional star him- or herself. Afternoons meant calling talent agencies on the West Coast from my home. In the end, the celebrities responded to Harry Belafonte's appeal for them to join him at the March and try to change America. That was too juicy a role to turn down. It was also a testament to Harry's stature in the entertainment industry at the time and the industry's acknowledgment of just how close he had become to Martin Luther King, Jr.

One of the last musicians Harry was able to line up (after already getting commitments from Joan Baez, Josh White, and Bob Dylan) was Pete Seeger, who would actually end up performing Dylan's song "Blowin' in The Wind" at the March. Other versions of the song were at the top of the Billboard charts and played in heavy rotation on radio stations across the country. (Dylan's original, of course, and don't forget the cover version by Peter, Paul and Mary. But I will always have a soft spot for Seeger's sultry rendition.) As a type—an activist barely disguised as an artist—Seeger always showed support for social justice in all forms. His dedication was legendary then and remained so to the day he died.

Once the composition, travel and arrival of the Celebrity Delegation fell into place, I was free to travel to Washington and catch up with the other organizers. It was now Monday, August 26th and time was turning into the enemy.

Anne wanted to join me on the trip and we discussed it at length, but I insisted I didn't have the time to be worrying about my wife and young children in the middle of this unknown and unknowable undertaking. Of course, I wanted her there, but who knew for sure? Fights could break out on Constitution Avenue. National guardsmen could start launching tear gas. A Ku Klux Klansman could start firing from the top of the Washington Monument. Maybe the idea of violence wasn't merely (or only) a public relations tool. It was likely to be safer for her in New York.

Anne certainly deserved to be there in person. I wouldn't have been working with Martin if it weren't for her insistence that I meet with him when he first reached out to me. So yes, perhaps we should've made arrangements for someone to look after the children and gone to the March together. But that wasn't the entire breadth of my reasoning at the time, though. There was something else, something I kept to myself. A part of me needed to go off on this adventure by myself for reasons I couldn't exactly explain then. I loved my family very much, and these marchers for whom I was turning my back on Anne were strangers. But they needed salvation, I believed they needed my help and that there was something I could do for them. It never occurred to me that I might be depriving Anne and my children of the opportunity for their own salvation as well. The March wasn't only for the downtrodden and impoverished, it was a kind of baptism for everyone who attended. In the end, we decided it was better for her to remain behind and she missed out on that. The decision lives on with me—a true regret.

An enormous and dynamic fundraiser was planned to light up Harlem's Apollo Theatre on the Friday night before the March. William "Cozy" Cole, Herbie Mann, Quincy Jones, Tony Bennett, Thelonious Monk, Carmen McRae, and Billy Eckstine were among those donating performances. I loved those artists, but I would be unable to attend. The evening before that amazing concert, I boarded the train at Riverdale Station all alone.

It was crammed with people heading to Grand Central Station, some of whom would then switch trains with me to catch the D.C.-bound Afternoon Congressional.

The others, I could only assume, were heading to the fundraiser at the Apollo.

As the train slowed alongside the platform in Washington D.C.'s Union Station, I began to experience conflicting emotions, a mingled sense of both anxiety *and* exhilaration. What we were planning to do in a few short days could be like the work we'd achieved in Birmingham multiplied by a factor of ten or more, both in terms of its power but also in terms of the potential for police or agitator violence. It was a rush of a feeling, that sense of being on the edge of something vast.

As I gathered my valise and suitcase, I reflected on how many times I'd had to leave Anne and our children to go meet Martin for one reason or another. I stood on the station platform as people brushed by me. But I wasn't quite ready to move. I asked myself, "I wonder how many of these people getting off the train might also attend our March on Saturday?"

I took a deep breath. It seemed to me this "thing" we had built, this March, was either going to work spectacularly or fail on the same level. Maybe we are about to build an unforgettable pyramid in the sands of American history; maybe the whole effort would be a big bust, a failure that would result in a substantial setback for our Movement and a blow to Martin's national non-violent civil disobedience leadership. There was no middle ground and no turning back. We'd gone all in and now we would see if our bets paid off.

As I moved through Union Station, I thought back on that day in the Baldwin Hills Baptist church outside of Los Angeles. From the willfully blind comfort of my living room in Southern California only three years earlier to the sticky air of the District of Columbia. I couldn't help picturing my mother again, smiling at me this time, and saying "Clarence, you've come a long way baby!"

I stepped out of the train station and into the muggy summer night. There was no one in the cab line. I took a Checker about a mile and a half to the Willard Hotel at the corner of 14th Street and Pennsylvania. This was where generations of D.C. power brokers plied their trade, two blocks from the White House. President Grant coined the term "lobbyist" to describe those who would approach him for favors in that very hotel's atrium. This is where we would work on the final touch: Martin's speech to the assembled marchers.

I began to think of the March as a symbolic validation—even a *celebration*—of Martin's leadership of the Civil Rights Movement. If it would turn out that a significant number of people attended, especially people whose racial identity differed from Martin's, it would be a further and definitive statement that Civil Rights was not a Negro issue but an *American* issue.

Tuesday afternoon, on the eve of the March, I received a call from Rev. Walter Fauntroy, the SCLC's representative in D.C. He told me that some of Martin's closest advisors were coming to meet with him. He suggested the lobby at the Willard. In addition to Fauntroy, the group included Andrew Young, Rev. Ralph Abernathy, Wyatt Tee Walker, Prof. Lawrence Reddick from Morgan State University, and Cleve Robinson of the Retail Wholesale Workers Union.

When I passed the request on to Martin, his initial reaction was to resist meeting with them. I persuaded him that he could not tell those people that he was too tired or too busy to meet without consequences. Finally, he agreed,

So, I went downstairs and talked to a couple of the Negro bellhops, who arranged a special area for us. It was near the bar but secluded behind the greenery provided by large decorative planters.

We all gathered shortly thereafter. Rev. Abernathy was the first to speak: "You know Martin, these people tomorrow who have come from all over the country, are coming because they want to hear you preach about our progress."

Prof. Reddick disagreed. "No, Martin. Many of these people have heard you preach before. They won't be looking for another sermon, but some overall direction and leadership. From you they want to know 'Where do we go from here?'"

Everyone else started throwing out ideas. Martin had intended this to be a session of thoughtful questions and the ideas those questions bring forth. But it seemed everyone had a stake in this speech, a predetermined angle.

Martin looked over at me and said, "Clarence, would you mind taking some notes?"

Hours of clashing ideas (and personalities) later, Martin asked me to head upstairs and try my hand at folding in the group's key ideas into some kind of a cohesive draft.

With a smile, he added, "And try to do this without too many martinis."

There was no such thing as a personal computer, but it seemed as if a typewriter wouldn't have been too much to ask for. But there wasn't a Smith-Corona in sight. Fortunately, my style then (as it is often today) was to write my thoughts in parochial school long hand on a yellow legal pad. I sat at the desk in my hotel room, flipping through the sheets of paper on one legal pad after another, trying to find my "in," my way to clarify the heart of our struggle. Mindful of what Martin has asked me to do, I tried to summarize the various points made by all of his supporters in the lobby. It wasn't easy; voices from every compass point were ringing in my head. Abernathy's conservative stance, Bayard and Cleve's take-no-prisoners call to arms, all of them with their tiny slice of a way to look at a large problem. There was justice, there was religion, there was compassion, there was self-determination. I wrestled internally to find some way to nail down the right balance of celebration of achievements and goals yet to achieve.

Earlier in the month, Stanley and I had prepared some material for a speech, and I reexamined it now. I thought about coming here not just with complaints but with demands. I toyed with the entire concept of making a demand of someone else, of the legal aspects, the personal aspects, and the vast gulf between the two.

As an example of a possible opening, I crafted an analogy of the people marching to Washington to redeem a promissory note or a check for justice and freedom that had been handed back to us, marked "insufficient funds."

I also compared those points to the direction of the text which Stanley and I had suggested that Martin consider and tried to blend the two sets of ideas and information together. Something worked its way up from the depths of my subconscious.

It wasn't a purely academic exercise in analogy.

Ninety minutes after I went up to my hotel suite, I finally felt like the work was in order. Though I harbored no illusions about my ability to get the emotion of the issue across, I knew that I'd gotten to the roots of the ideas, which was a difficult task considering all the differing opinions downstairs. I collected those papers that weren't crumpled up in the corner by the overflowing trashcan and returned to the lobby. The participants were now more animated in their discussions than when I'd left, but I think it was that giddiness that comes with exhaustion. Their voices were shrill and worn out. Martin looked tired to me. More tired than usual, and I saw him tired often.

I returned to my place in the loose arrangement of lounge chairs opposite Martin and waited to present the material. Martin asked everyone to be quiet and give their attention to what I was about to report. I had the floor. As requested, I spoke and gave a summary of what, in good faith, I truly believed to have been the essential points from the earlier discussion with Martin and the group. They let me go on for maybe three minutes, no more, when the group began to interrupt me—

"What about—"

"No, no, no, no—"

"Why didn't you—"

"I thought we AGREED—"

One man after another claimed that either I had left out an important concept that had been made during the earlier discussion or had inaccurately summarized what had been said about any of a dozen particular points. And given the fact that most of the men there were Southern Baptist preachers, there was no small amount of grandstanding and finger-wagging.

This reaction took me off guard. I began to defend my work and respond to those who challenged the accuracy of my summary.

But I didn't get very far. Martin intervened. "Okay, brothers," he said, "thank you so much everybody for your suggestions and input." He singled me out as I handed him my handwritten sheets of paper. "Clarence, I want to thank you for your efforts."

I nodded my appreciation as Martin stood up. He'd been there in that chair for nearly six straight hours.

"I am now going upstairs to my room to counsel with my Lord," he announced. "I will see you all tomorrow." He turned to me one last time. "Clarence, Dora will be in touch with you in the morning to share my completed speech."

And then he walked quietly out of the room and made his way to the elevators, leaving the rest of us to look at each other for just a moment. "Tomorrow, then," someone said, and we dispersed.

I took a breath. Pictured the bed waiting for me upstairs. Then retreated to the lobby bar alone, ordered an ice-cold gin martini, just a small signal to myself that the work was done. I held the glass, its inverted construction an insult to gravity and the order of things. Just like our Movement, from the outside the balance of power seems all wrong. But hold a martini glass in your hand and you know instinctively that it's just right.

The drink went down gloriously. I signed the check and then went upstairs to my room to try and get what little rest I could realistically hope for.

Early, about 7:00 a.m., my hotel room phone rang. I had to drag myself out of a deep sleep to answer. It was Martin's secretary Dora MacDonald on the line. She told me Martin's speech had been completed. If I'd been more awake, I would've felt surprised, because it hadn't been that many hours since I'd handed in the outlined approach and like me, Martin had to be exhausted. But apparently the speech had been finished. I told Dora that it was great news.

"It's being mimeographed now," Dora said to me, explaining that the March organizer in charge of the press was going to insert a copy in each of the journalists' press kits. This was a standard practice at lectures and speeches. It allowed newspaper writers to get a significant portion of their coverage to their editor in advance of the event, which in turn helped the speaker ensure the timeliness and accuracy of his press coverage. Excellent, I thought, we're moving along. But as I hung up, I realized something was nagging at me. I couldn't put my finger on what it was exactly, and I was exhausted and had a long list of tasks to handle. So, for the time being, I simply had to let it go. I showered and dressed and prepared myself to face the day.

When I stepped outside and discovered the sun and clear skies, I became energized. It looks as though the weather will cooperate with us, I thought. But my attention was soon off the sun-kissed morning and onto the crowds of marchers I saw assembling on the Mall at the base of the Washington Monument across Pennsylvania Avenue. The crowd was increasing even as I watched it. People were joining, some holding placards I couldn't read from my distance. I knew the soul of their messages, though. We were all here in support of the same ideals. It was heartening. We were giving a party, and people were actually showing up. Soon they would begin to march—not east to the Capitol steps as we'd originally envisioned, but west to the Lincoln Memorial. There had been a change of plans.

Our March was being organized under the administration of President John F. Kennedy and his Attorney General brother Robert.[20] Though we knew and accepted that pressure was the instrument of change, not presidential empathy, we still would have enjoyed an indication that JFK and his brother would welcome our March as an opportunity for us "to make them" act to forthrightly and immediately address those issues of Civil Rights and work opportunities of foremost concern to Negroes in 1963. There was no such indication. In fact, our original planned site for the March's finish line, the Capitol Building, which would have put us on the "making him" footing, was met with utter disregard from the White House. The President said his lawmakers would perceive this as "putting a gun" to the collective head of the leadership of the Congress.

---

20 They weren't quite the astute politicians Roosevelt had been when discussing government policy in racial matters with A. Philip Randolph. Roosevelt told him, "I agree with everything you said. Now go out and *make me* do it!"

We thought about this long and hard in the weeks leading up to the March. Holding a gun to the head of the government. Is this the image a Civil Rights Movement based on non-violent disobedience to evil and injustice wanted to project? In the end, the offensiveness of this idea persuaded the organizers of the March to change the venue of the demonstration. In Bayard's update to his March Organizing Manual, the finish line for the marchers was changed to the foot of the Lincoln Memorial. With its Mall and reflecting pool, its 180 acres of lawn and its enormous reminder of the emancipation of the nation's slaves, it would prove to be a brilliant move.

But looking across at the Washington Monument, I felt a darker sensation running through me as well. My first glimpse of Washington's crowd control troops made me feel as if there was real trouble in store. They were moving along Pennsylvania Avenue, wedged between the early marchers and me like a fence.

On the day of the March, Washington, D.C. seemed virtually under martial law. President Kennedy had ordered federal troops to duty and combat readiness on standby at nearby military bases. That very morning, J. Edgar Hoover had assigned several agents to telephone celebrity participants in a futile last-ditch attempt to get them to withdraw their support.

The District's police force was approaching the March like an army approaches a battle. In Nan Robertson's front page *New York Times* piece on city planning for the March that ran Wednesday, August 25th, the operation is described as "military in its precision and detail." The area around the Mall had been divided into five "police commands." Two-thirds of the police force had been assigned to the March. An internal police department memo was quoted in *The Washington Post*, calling Saturday, "the most important day in the history of the metropolitan police." And that's not just any old city police force, we're talking about an organization that routinely has to deal with inaugurations, visiting royalty, and demonstrations of all stripes.

Why the high tension? Fears of a possible riot were intense, even though the Washington authorities were determined to ensure a peaceful day and the March organizers had called a press conference mainly to underscore the ideals embraced by the marchers. At that press conference, the Washington leadership of the SCLC and other Movement leaders pledged that the marchers would be:

> *Orderly, but not subservient*
>
> *Proud, but not arrogant*
>
> *Nonviolent, but not timid*
>
> *Outspoken, but not raucous*

Regardless of our intent, the authorities were gearing up for the worst. As a result of this martial thinking, all District police units had their leaves canceled; neighboring suburban forces were given special riot-control training. Liquor sales were banned for a day—for the first time since the repeal of Prohibition. Two Washington Senators' baseball games were postponed. The Justice Department and the Army coordinated preparations for emergency troop deployments; at the Pentagon, seventy different potential emergency scenarios were studied. A crew of lawyers was convened to prepare in advance proclamations authorizing military deployments. Fifteen thousand paratroopers were put on alert.

On the other hand, the administration also dreaded the potential for any bad press that would follow one of these hypothetical riots. For example, because of the worldwide reaction to images of German Shepherds attacking demonstrators in Birmingham months earlier, the Attorney General expressly forbade the presence of police dogs.

The government put on a show of acting helpful. The Justice Department and the police had worked hand-in-hand with the March committee to develop a state-of-the-art public-address system; what the March coordinators wouldn't learn until after the event had ended was that the police had rigged the system so that they could take control of it if trouble arose.

· · ·

The main rally would be at the Lincoln Memorial. For us, the organizers, that site had powerful symbolism, particularly on the centennial of the Emancipation Proclamation. The police liked the site because, with water on three sides, the demonstrators could be easily contained. The irony of a Gandhi-influenced Christian leader of a non-violent ethos needing to be contained seemed lost on D.C.'s finest.

Looking around at all the activity, I made a decision. I had celebrities to meet, but I headed for the press area. I'd just figured out what was bothering me about the organization's plan to distribute copies of the speech to all the attending members of the press.

CHAPTER 11 | INTELLECTUAL PROPERTY

In the past I had witnessed so many instances of images of Martin or excerpts from his work being used to promote all manner of commercial or political agendas. From which, naturally, neither he nor the SCLC received any benefit. I started to fear it could happen to him again.

Suppose Martin and I were walking down the street in Cincinnati. Or Baltimore. Or any decently large city. Suddenly, a man would run up to us—"Dr. King, Dr. King, your work means so much to me!" he'd say, beaming. All very nice, handshakes and flattery, big smiles. But before you know it the man is standing next to Martin, walking alongside him while he's elbowing me out of the way. In that same instant he waves to someone standing nearby. Up comes the friend with a camera and click, a chance meeting with a famous public figure is captured for posterity.

Except it was no accident. Often, many in the Negro communities of each city we visited knew where Martin was scheduled to be, and there were always those who wanted their pound of flesh. This was a planned ambush.

I can imagine someone who wasn't there having a hard time understanding this. A planned ambush, merely to take a photograph?

But now, imagine three months later I'm back in that same city, I go in for a shoeshine at the local barbershop. Wouldn't you know it? I look up at all the pictures of the establishment's many famous so-called customers. That guy who pushed me out of the way, the owner of the place, is in all of them. He's standing next to Sammy Davis, Jr., Nat "King" Cole and, naturally, Martin. If the barber's relationship with Martin is any indication, not one of these other renowned men was among the shop's clientele, either. But you wouldn't know that from the pictures.

As far as a man considering a haircut here, just one glance at Martin Luther King, Jr. will make up his mind. So now we have the voice of morality in America shilling for some two-bit barber without his permission and without any compensation.

This kind of incident may sound insignificant. As a one-off event I would tend to agree. But the number of times I saw things like this happen is astounding. His image and his voice were like logos companies could stamp on their products. Everyone wanted a piece of Martin, and the irony is he held the stature he had by acting selflessly, and this stature was being used for selfish personal gain. Martin was a man of great patience, of course, and he put up with this time and time again.

I'd make it as clear as I could, constantly telling him, "They're using you, you know."

And though he saw, he didn't particularly mind. I think he saw it as his way of helping businessmen who could use every break they could get. But I saw it as a hustle, and it rubbed me the wrong way every time.

Martin and I were opposites in many ways. The discipline of patience was one of those ways. I had no patience at all for this kind of misappropriation of his name, likeness, and work. And one of the things I've always been very good at is speaking out on behalf of my friends.

It may not be so easy to stop a sneaky business owner from taking Martin's picture, but I could protect him in other ways.

I've come to think of law school as a kind of cerebral analog to the physical process a recruit goes through in the basic training portion of the armed services. For better or for worse, I've gone through both experiences. And the parallel is simple. In the military, the people in charge do not want individuals, they want to make every soldier into the ideal. They physically melt you down and they recast you at the absolute limits of your strength and endurance. The exact same process happens in legal training, but it happens to your mind. You have to make it through a grueling educational process, but once you do, you're primed to view the world through a lawyer's eyes. You are not emotional; you are not afraid. Still, you cannot help but see the potential pitfalls and downsides in every interaction. It is a cautionary mindset they hand you on graduation day, and you couldn't get rid of it if you wanted to.

I looked at the mimeographing of the speech in just this way—what do we stand to lose here? It was from this viewpoint I decided to act on Martin's behalf.

One of the limited areas of specialty I had as a lawyer at that time was copyright law. I knew well the clear distinction and legal consequences between common law and statutory copyright protection. At that time, everyone had a proprietary right, under common law in most states, for all their intellectual creation embodied in words they had written in a speech or manuscript to a book. Retention of common law copyright would qualify an author to apply for subsequent statutory copyright protection under the United States Copyright Act for an initial term (in 1963) of 26 years, with the opportunity to renew for a second term of statutory protection. However, if the owner of a common law copyright in and to his writing widely disseminates his writing without notice of common law copyright protection, that dissemination is deemed to have effected a "publication," extinguishing the common law copyright and disqualifying the author of the right to register his writing for legally enforceable copyright protection.

I didn't want that to happen to whatever Martin planned on saying at the closing of the March on Washington. I truly neither want nor take any real credit for the value of the intellectual property the copyright provided. Like many of both my best and worst decisions over the years, the decision to copyright Martin's speech was fueled mostly by a sense of frustration and vague anger with just a dash of paranoia thrown in. (And as a man who had experienced around-the-clock illegal government surveillance, I think I have a right to my paranoia.)

I wasn't thinking about upside, I was thinking defensively. And when I did finally get around to considering the upside, it's almost embarrassing how off-target I was. The urge was to protect, not to profit, and it was the culmination of various feelings that I couldn't subsume no matter how hard I tried. I was sick and tired of watching people take advantage of Martin's easygoing nature. His open heart. I had a strong feeling it could happen again here. He was going to give his ideas away, and somehow it felt like people were going to make money off those ideas.

It's not that the speech itself seemed so all-fired important. I'd be lying to myself if I claimed that kind of foresight. I hadn't read it, for one thing. It was more the sense that the March felt like it would have a reverberating impact, and Martin Luther King, Jr.'s speech would be a tangible by-product. It would be recorded and reproducible. In essence, it was something concrete to which he could lay claim.

It was under this belief that I decided I had to make my way to the March Committee's "News Headquarters," a gigantic tent near the Lincoln Memorial we'd put up to make sure reporters received all the information they needed about the day. I found some March volunteers there working. The speech was being mimeographed, stapled, and inserted in large envelopes comprising the "press kits" for the journalists at the March. I picked up one of the copies of Martin's speech lying in a pile on a table. I realized that they did not contain a notice of copyright protection. This didn't surprise me, of course. We'd never before affixed that little circled "c" on any press copies of his previous speeches. What surprised me was that I was suddenly thinking about it.

Press coverage for the March was more extensive than for any previous political demonstration in U.S. history. The Committee issued no fewer than 1,655 special press passes, augmenting the 1,220 members of the regular Washington press corps. News agencies sent large crews of reporters and photographers—some were assigned to celebrities, others to workaday marchers, still others to aerial coverage. Forget for a moment the newspapers that would be running at least parts of the speech, the mere distribution of the work to this many members of the press could potentially be deemed to constitute a publication, thereby extinguishing Martin's common law copyright protection.

Traditionally, how it worked in the public-speaking-and-press game was that an individual making a speech, if they even understood the ownership value of intellectual property at all, traded that value away on the assumption that the usefulness of the press coverage for his appearance was of greater value than potential copyright profits. But in legal reality, it was not an either/or proposition. Preempting the newspapers' first publication rights didn't mean that a newspaper could not run the speech. It only meant that the rights were still retained. All it would take is a focused effort. Why not be sure that the seventy-five or one hundred mimeographed copies of his speech in the press kits contained a common law notice of copyright? The smart move would be to retrieve the copies of the speech from the press kits and handwrite a symbol of a small circle with a "C" inside on each page of each copy. Accordingly, I introduced myself to the people who seemed to be in charge of assembling and distributing the press kits and told them exactly what I wanted.

They told me what I could do with my idea.

But the sheer determination in my face got through to them, and my raised voice alerted others with a little more authority that were on the other side of the tent. Someone came over and recognized me. He mentioned to the people I was arguing with that I was "Dr. King's New York lawyer." That changed everything. My request suddenly didn't seem so intrusive, and my instructions were followed. Several young women and men volunteers used ballpoint pens at my direction to render a handwritten version of the appropriate copyright notice.

I did my share of the work as well. As I flipped through page after page of the mimeographed speeches, it was as if I was on autopilot. My attention was divided. I was distracted by the need to reconnect with Harry Belafonte to find out the logistics of the arrival of the Celebrity Delegation. Harry had asked me to assume responsibility for meeting the delegation at the March, directing them to their designated reserved section in the stands near the podium. Thus, thinking about how I was going to be able to reach Harry (by phone, I supposed, going through his personal secretary Gloria Kantor and hoping she knew how to find him) had a higher priority in my mind during that Saturday morning than the actual text of Martin's address to the March. The upshot of this is as I worked the rote strokes of the letter c and the circle on all those pages, I still didn't think to read the "final" text of what Martin had written for his speech for the March on Washington. It just wasn't my principal concern, and it's not as if someone was tapping me on the shoulder to tell me I was in the middle of anything more historic than my work with the Movement in general.

I gave no further thought to Martin's speech that morning. I turned my attention to coordinating with Harry to do what he had asked of me with respect to the celebrity delegation. The next time I saw a copy of that speech it would be on the lectern in front of Martin Luther King, Jr.

Little did I realize the value of that copyright over the years would amount to more than fifty million dollars for the King family.[21] I didn't know this was "I Have a Dream."

---

21 Some of the most enduring sadness I still carry to this day stems from the fact that no one from the "King Estate" or King family has ever thanked me privately or publicly or "commemorated" my efforts to protect and assure the copyright of the "I Have A Dream" speech. I now better understand Harry Belafonte's hurt and disappointment with the King children for the way they treated him for everything he did for them as kids.

The demonstrators gathered at the Washington Monument, where a stage had been set up for the morning's entertainment. Joan Baez opened the program with "Oh Freedom" and followed that up by leading a rendition of "We Shall Overcome." Other performers included Odetta, the Albany Freedom Singers, Bob Dylan, and Peter, Paul and Mary, whose version of Dylan's Civil Rights anthem "Blowin' in the Wind" was number two on the Billboard charts (after Martha and the Vandellas' "Heat Wave"). Josh White performed as well, a touching moment since Bayard had been his sideman thirty years earlier, when he was performing not only under his own name but also using stage names like "Pinewood Tom."

For many of the marchers, the trip to Washington was a festive affair, enlivened with freedom songs and the excitement of participating in what they knew to be a historic action. Most demonstrators came in buses chartered by local branches of the Movement; another thirty thousand or so arrived on twenty-one chartered trains.

On August 28th, the day of the March, New York's Penn Station reported the largest early morning crowd since the end of World War II. Members of CORE's Brooklyn chapter actually *walked* the 230 miles to the March; it took them thirteen days. Three of the first arrivals were Robert Thomas, age eighteen; Robert Avery, age seventeen; and James F. Smith, age sixteen—all veterans of the Gadsden Student Movement out of Alabama. Arriving almost a week ahead of time after a 700-mile walk and hitchhike, they were housed and put to work by Rev. Walter Fauntroy, head of the Washington branch of the SCLC. Surveys indicate that about fifteen percent of the participants were students, about twenty percent were white, and a majority of the Black participants were middle class, northern, and urban. Estimates of the crowd size range from 200,000 (too low, in most people's opinion) to 400,000 (too high). It was unquestionably the largest political demonstration in the United States to that date.

As I'd predicted, the demonstrators' signs and slogans ranged from the mass-produced to the unique. Both editions of Bayard's March Organizing Manual let people know they were not allowed to make their own placards, but there was no way some pamphlet was going to tell this crowd how to express themselves. The United Auto Workers union, one of the March's biggest sponsors, printed hundreds of signs with slogans such as "UAW Says Jobs and Freedom for Every American." A young Black man in a white shirt and tie wrote on his sign:

> *There Would Be More of Us Here*
> *But So Many of Us Are in Jail*
> *Freedom Now*

A young white woman painted "Stop Legal Murders" on her sign. On the day before the March, Robert Moses picketed the Justice Department with a sign reading, "When There Is No Justice, What Is the State But a Robber Band Enlarged?" One elderly Black man ingeniously covered twenty-one slats of a five-foot-wide Venetian blind with his poem "Martyr Medgar Evers," one stanza of which read:

> *Ole Glory's tarnished with his blood*
> *for having shabbily allowed*
> *a noble son to be downtrod*
> *because he was both black and proud*

I saw a young Black woman in a paisley dress carrying an utterly prescient sign reading, "Not 'Negroes' But AfroAmericans! We Must Be Accorded Full Rights as Americans Not in the Future but Now." (Debates over appropriate labels were heating up in the summer of 1963. "Negro" was used almost exclusively in the March speeches; only John Lewis referred to "Black people" and "the Black masses.")

The music was gratefully absorbed by the crowd for some time, but as the hours moved on, impatience began to take a hold of some of the marchers. Just before noon (which was ahead of schedule), some demonstrators took matters into their own hands and began to march up Independence and Constitution Avenues toward the Lincoln Memorial. The March leaders got word of this surprise development while lobbying on Capitol Hill, and they rushed to join the advancing throng. Some enterprising March marshals opened a passageway for them so that they could be photographed arm-in-arm "leading" the March.

The March was also one of the first events to be broadcast live around the world, via the newly launched communications satellite Telstar. The three major television networks spent over three hundred thousand dollars (more than twice the March committee's budget) to broadcast the event. CBS covered the rally "gavel to gavel," from 1:30 p.m. to 4:30 p.m., canceling *As the World Turns*, *Password*, *Art Linkletter's House Party*, *To Tell the Truth*, *The Edge of Night*, and *Secret Storm*.

Using the time-honored political tactic of pressure, we had cordoned off an area right by the main stage reserved for key government officials. Reserved by *name*. Best seats in the house, as the saying goes. We made it clear that the world would know whose name was on any empty seats. I'm proud to say every one of those folding chairs were filled, though in some cases it's likely they were filled not by the officials they were intended for but by one of their staffers. No one knows for sure. Politics can be an amazingly subtle game.

The huge audience heard many speakers and singers, both scheduled and unscheduled. One of the first, reading a speech written by James Baldwin, was Charlton Heston, representing an "arts contingent" that included Ossie Davis, Ruby Dee, Marlon Brando, Sammy Davis, Jr., James Garner, Tony Franciosa, Sidney Poitier, Steve McQueen, Shelley Winters, Lena Horne, Diahann Carroll, Paul Newman, Joanne Woodward, Tony Bennett, and Harry Belafonte. Josephine Baker, wearing her Free French uniform with her Legion of Honor decoration, was the only woman to speak at the rally. The exclusion of women speakers had been debated, with the all-male leadership opting for only a "Tribute to Women," a decision that didn't mean much to me at the time, but looking back feels very much like a slight to the concept of "equality for everyone," which was the true theme of our demonstration.

Bayard introduced to the roaring crowd Rosa Parks, Daisy Bates, Diane Nash, Gloria Richardson (a leader from Cambridge, Maryland), and Prince Melson Lee (widow of the slain Mississippi activist Herbert Lee), as well as citing Myrlie Evers in absentia. Marian Anderson, the great contralto, made it to the platform too late to lead the national anthem as planned; instead, she later sang "He's Got the Whole World in His Hands."

Finally, John Lewis got his licks in. Though we had toned-down Lewis' speech, you wouldn't know it by the audience reaction. His words were received with unmatched enthusiasm; it was interrupted by applause fourteen times. When he finished, Lewis walked past the other leaders on the platform. Every Black hand reached out for his, while every white speaker sat uncomfortably still, staring straight ahead.

As the afternoon of the March program was winding down, after all the artists performed and the other speakers from the major participating organizations finished delivering their remarks, there came that moment everyone assembled anticipated what they had been waiting for. The sun was shining brightly. The lawn around the Lincoln Memorial and the giant rectangular reflecting pool shot glints of light in every direction. From my vantage point near the dais, I could see thousands and thousands of people standing and clapping as they watched and listened to various speakers and performing artists. Others were still walking onto the grounds where the stage was located.

Following John Lewis, Mahalia Jackson stepped up to warm up the crowd in advance of the final scheduled speaker, Martin Luther King, Jr. Mahalia had a lovely, moving voice, a talent that made her career seem inevitable. But more than her vocal ability, she was a consummate entertainer because she understood audiences. She could take temperatures from the stage; she could make the right artistic choices because she understood the dynamics of performer-audience intimately. It was a skill that was about to come in extremely useful to America.

Mahalia sang the gospel classic, "I've Been 'Buked and I've Been Scorned," a spiritual of woe and hope like many others. At first glance. But consider this lyric:

Children, I've been 'buked and I've been scorned
Tryin' to make this journey all alone

Here was the key—in oppression everyone feels alone, or at least vastly outnumbered. It was a musical and social counterpoint, an emotional reminder of just how important the crowd was—not simply the ideas and actions, but the people—and it was beautiful.

In his 1963 book *The Day They Marched*, author Lerone Bennett eloquently described the response to Mahalia's performance that day: "The button-down men in front and the old women in back came to their feet screaming and shouting. They had not known that this thing was in them, and that they wanted it touched. From different places and different ways, with different dreams they had come, and now, hearing this sung, they were one."

Mr. Bennett hit the nail right on the head. Mahalia galvanized a crowd that was already unified in their purpose. No more making the journey all alone, not when there's a quarter of a million of your brothers and sisters ready to stand with you.

Mahalia had struck a spark and ignited something. And she wasn't done helping yet.

At the end of a long procession of speech and song, protest and prayer, the time was now at hand.[22] A. Philip Randolph moved

---

22 I would be remiss if I didn't mention the speaker ahead of Martin, Rabbi Joachim Prinz, President of the American Jewish Congress: "When I was the rabbi of the Jewish community in Berlin under the Hitler regime, I learned many things. The most important thing that I learned under those tragic circumstances was that bigotry and hatred are not the most urgent problem. The most urgent, the most disgraceful, the most shameful and the most tragic problem is silence."

slowly to the podium. He seemed serious, yet he was beaming as his eyes swept the glistening, apprehensive faces of the marchers. Looking back, I can see exactly why Mr. Randolph looked so thrilled. In a sense, he had had a dream as well, his own dream. And at that moment, in front of the endless wave of hopeful people, his dream had come true. He introduced Rev. Martin Luther King, Jr. I could feel the tension and an air of anticipation as I watched the crowd springing to life, moving into some kind of spiritual equivalent of DefCon 1. During his introduction, Mr. Randolph referred to Martin as "the moral leader of our nation." I was in complete agreement. In fact, he was talking about my personal moral leader, the man who saved me from my destiny as just another hard-headed man in pursuit of status and the almighty dollar.

When Martin stood up to make his way to the front of the stage, the crowd applauded. Then Martin replaced Mr. Randolph at the podium to deliver the March's closing address. The polite hum of excitement died down. A hush draped over the crowd. I was standing perhaps fifteen yards behind Martin. It seemed that this precise moment was exactly what the people who made the sojourn to the March were waiting for. They knew he would say something that would give them direction. I didn't know what he was going to say; I still hadn't had a chance to review exactly what he'd turned my notes into. I silently wondered if some of my ideas might've remained, but I didn't have much to hang my hopes on.

Martin offered a traditional ad hoc greeting to the people assembled. Then, glancing at the written text he had placed on the podium before him, Martin began to speak.

I listened carefully to his words. For the first time, I learned what was typed on the papers before him. A pleasant shock came over me as I realized that Martin was reciting verbatim those suggested opening paragraphs I'd scrawled down in the summary of points the night before. I repeated the words in my head as Martin spoke the first seven paragraphs, and I shouted a quiet *hallelujah* when he arrived at the section that references the promissory note drawn on the bank of justice that's been returned unpaid due to insufficient funds.

I can't reproduce the speech here; it's copyrighted. But when he came to the section that said, "We cannot turn back," I noticed that Martin paused. It was as if, for a split-second, he was wondering if the content of his speech was appropriate for that time and place. In that moment of silence, Mahalia shouted to him from the Speakers and Organizers stand, "Tell 'em about the 'Dream,' Martin, tell 'em about the 'Dream!'" Not many people had heard it.

But I did.

And so did Martin.

He clutched the speaker's podium, a hand on each side, leaned back, looked at the throng of two-hundred-and-fifty thousand people or more assembled in front of the Lincoln Memorial.

What's this? I thought.

Then I watched Martin turn the text of his prepared remarks face down. Observing this from my perch, back and raised above the podium, I leaned over and said to the person standing next to me. "These people out there today don't know it yet, but they're about ready to go to church." I said this because, having seen his body language and heard the tone in his voice, I knew Martin was about to become the superb Baptist preacher he was. Like three generations of Baptist preachers before him in his family.

He was about to utterly transform himself for a time, about to transport himself to a place of oratorical elegance few living beings have ever reached. Even those few that do can only stay there so long.

Then, honoring Mahalia's request, Martin spoke those words which have become memorialized in our history:

"I have a dream..."

My Lord, what could possibly motivate a man standing before a crowd of hundreds of thousands, with television cameras beaming his every move to a watching nation and a cluster of microphones tracing his every word, to abandon the prepared text of his speech and begin an *ad hoc* riffing on a theme that he had used on more than one occasion without much of an enthusiastic reaction?

The answer is twofold: Trust and instinct. Martin's trust was not easily won. A scant few, really, had Martin's undiluted trust. Stanley had it, as did I. Why? Because Martin was an astute observer of politics, both at the national and the office level. Office politics exist in every organization, from the brutally secular to the charitable and compassionate. The Southern Christian Leadership Conference was no different, and Martin knew that all too well. Those who would discount him as a simple do-gooder or a scholar of only the Bible do a disservice to his powerfully nimble and logical mind. He was quite aware that his staff at the SCLC and many of the people he associated with had ambitions and designs. They all wanted his ear, because they all wanted power, praise, promotions, authority, bragging rights, the list goes on. And that affected the way Martin looked at their advice on many important matters. They were damaging their own credibility in the act of trying to strengthen it. But for the most part they couldn't see the unintended consequences.

Imagine the kind of connection you have when you're in a hospital bed, doped up, terrified and confused, looking up at the tubes and leads. All the while knowing your loved one is taking all the information down and is going to make all the right decisions for you. No questions asked. No agendas, no conflicting appointments, nothing but your safety in mind.

This was the ground you occupied when you had Martin King's trust.

And this was how it was when you were not just Martin's favorite gospel singer, but practically his *muse*. When Martin would get low (and considering all the fronts he was battling on, this wasn't an infrequent situation) he would track down Mahalia Jackson on the phone wherever she was. He would say, "I sure could use some cheering up, Mahalia." And she would sing him his favorite hymns. Over the scratchy long-distance phone, without question or complaint. Even if he'd just woken her up. She would start singing *Amazing*

Grace to Martin *a capella*, or *The Old Rugged Cross*, or *Great Is Thy Faithfulness*. And he would close his eyes and lean back in his chair, barely the strength to hold the receiver to his ear, releasing his tension. Letting his uncertainty slip away into the music.

This is the kind of trust Martin shared with Mahalia Jackson. It is why she could shout to him "Tell 'em about the 'Dream,'" on the steps of the Lincoln Memorial, and he would instantly take the suggestion, calculate the benefits, and run with it.

And so, in an instant, Martin saw the opportunity in front of him through Mahalia's eyes. Even, I think, in the midst of deciding its value versus its risk, he'd already begun to continue his remarks. And they were beyond the borders of the now face-down pages in front of him. Martin was moving into the uncharted territory of extemporaneous speech, but then he'd spent time in that territory before.

I've often said the sheer processing power of Martin's mind left me awestruck. His dexterity with memory and words ran along the lines of the cut-and-paste function in today's computer programs. The *Letter from a Birmingham Jail* showed me his recall for the written material of others, his grueling schedule of speeches illuminated his ability to do the same for his own words. Martin could remember exact phrases from several of his unrelated speeches and discover a new way of linking them together as if they were organic to one another. And he could do it on the fly. Like the finest stage performers, he could live in the moment of his words with his entire being and yet reside in that future tense at the same time, building the structure of his verbal bridge ahead of the words, moving everything in the right direction invisibly.

The balance of the speech departs drastically from the metaphor I had set up regarding the promissory note that has not been paid, and today no one is happier about that than I am. I see the speech as a graph-line, moving along an up-swinging curve. We started with a solid foundation, but as I've mentioned, I'd fully expected a Martin Luther King, Jr. rewrite on my material.

I eventually received that rewrite, only it was halfway through the speech and in real time.

Most of all, I'm happy because I know anyone could have delivered the speech I'd written—Roy Wilkins or Cleve Robinson or Ralph Abernathy. Even A. Philip Randolph. But a different man could not have delivered "I Have A Dream," this meditation on freedom.

So much for providing advance material for the March reporters to feed their editors. I could picture irritable type composers in newspaper press rooms all over the country ripping up their carefully typeset printing plates and starting from scratch.

As Martin had gone along his improvisational way, people in the crowd had been shouting "Amen," "Preach Dr. King, preach," "Tell it like it is Dr. King, tell it like it is," offering every version of the encouragements you'd hear in a Baptist church multiplied by a hundred thousand or so. The effect was nothing short of soul-stirring.

A shudder went through me as Martin finished. Whatever I thought was going to happen, I now knew that I had witnessed something beyond my wildest expectations. In truth, I know they were far beyond Martin's expectations as well. Everyone on the Mall and a whole lot of people watching on their tiny television sets were aware they had just witnessed something transcendent. The "I Have A Dream" speech was less than a minute old, yet it already felt timeless. Martin had reached deep and, with a loving prod in the right direction from the angelic Mahalia Jackson, come up with a way to paint a portrait of how it felt to be black in America. He had riffed like a masterful jazz soloist. During the second half of his speech, he was like Charlie Parker, Freddie Hubbard, John Coltrane, Sony Stitt, and Lionel Hampton, rolled into one. Martin's words seem to ignite the spark Mahalia has struck. The pure joy and hope in the air that day burned white hot.

Whenever I'm asked to speak to groups, whether they are students, historians, bankers, or religious leaders, the question always comes up. Who today is most like Martin Luther King, Jr.? My answer is always straight out, "No one." And,

I continue by asking a question of them: "Who today is like Michelangelo, Mozart, Galileo, Shakespeare, Beethoven?"

I'll tell with utter conviction to whoever will listen that Martin Luther King, Jr. was *sui generis*. That is, singularly of his own kind. A once-in-a-lifetime (or, more likely, a once-in-a-millennium) figure. And this isn't coming from someone who's made a worship-filled career studying him from afar, I'm speaking as a friend who shared meals and conversation with him. His intellect, his passion, his patience, his faith, his fearlessness... Martin, it sometimes seemed, was not of this earth. The "I Have a Dream" speech was the oratory equivalent of a *sui generis* experience. The concept that's most significant about Martin Luther King Jr.'s appearance at the March on Washington (and what I would implore you to keep in mind whenever the subject of comes up) is this: We caught lightning in a bottle because the right man spoke the right words to the right people at the right time. No part of this formula should be undervalued. And though one or two components *could* gel together, the entire is not likely to be replicated ever again.

Of course, it couldn't have happened with another orator. Martin's choice of words were a perfectly balanced outcry of reason and emotion, of anger and hope. His tone of pained indignation in turn matched that note for note.

But neither could "The Dream" have happened in another location. Not simply the nation's capital, but at the foot of the Lincoln Memorial. For those too far away to see Martin speaking at the lectern, it's not too hard to imagine with a little squinting it could've easily seemed like the nineteen-foot marble statue of Lincoln was the one speaking the words.

And it all played out at just the right moment, and in front of a vast freedom-starved crowd right on the verge of getting to the end of its collective patience. We'd marched in 1963, the hundredth anniversary of the issuance of the Emancipation Proclamation, and everyone at the demonstration knew that if Abraham Lincoln could look down and see where the Negro stood in America on that day, his heart would be riddled with conflict. Yes, there would be pride at seeing the men and women he'd freed stand up for themselves and for justice, of course. But could that pride possibly overshadow the shame he would have to feel that one hundred years after the abolition of slavery his country would be the kind of place that would make these Negroes have to protest for the right to be treated like ordinary citizens?

By some miracle I don't claim to understand, each of these elements—person, place, time, and audience—were firing on all cylinders. Then into the equation comes the literally hundreds of cameras and microphones blasting Martin's message out into the wide world. What came through to anyone watching was nothing short of a revelation. Martin had a dream, but it was America's wake-up call. Its likes will never come this way again.

The next day I covered Washington's best newsstands and collected Sunday edition newspapers from all over the east coast. *The Boston Globe, The New York Times, The Hartford Courant*; they all ran the March story on their front pages. All above the fold, as the newspapermen used to say.

As we moved into the week the Sunday papers started arriving from the west and international editions arrived as well. Again, papers from Edinburgh, Mexico City, Rome, Cairo, they all ran Martin's picture and many had the complete text of the speech in a big sidebar. The March was covered, of course, but only somehow it was all a subset of the speech. Like a fireworks display, no one notices the guys on the ground running around with the electrical wires, cardboard tubes and walkie-talkies. People just remember the thrilling explosions across the sky.

More than forty years later, in the spring of 2005, I was given an amazing invitation. Stanford University in Palo Alto, California, runs one of the world's leading scholarly departments in the field of Civil Rights study, the Martin Luther King, Jr. Research Education Institute. In April of that year, I was invited to visit from New York City as a candidate for the position of the Institute's first Scholar in Residence.

It was a significant honor for me. I truly believe that education is the single most important focus to allow young African Americans to pull themselves out of the traps of poverty, menial work, drugs, and crime. As a result, I feel fortunate to be well educated. But to be lecturing at a venerable institution like Stanford? That was something else altogether.

First up was a get-to-know-you meeting with the Institute's then-director, Dr. Clayborne Carson (the man who told me he came to think of the March as sanitized and middle-class). I knew Clay was a good man upon meeting him, because in essence he trying to "sell" me on coming to the Institute for my own good. I had just started work on a new book about Martin and Clay knew there was no better place to write that book than the King Institute, with its wealth of research materials.

Going through the features and benefits of the opportunity they were offering me, Clay explained to me the resources of the Institute and the breadth and depth of its database. But talk is cheap, Clay acknowledged. So, he asked me to choose a date during those years I worked with Dr. King and he would line up something from that time accordingly. I spontaneously offered up the date August 28th, 1963. In retrospect, it was perhaps one of the least useful for the purposes of Dr. Carson's demonstration. We both knew that was the date of the March on Washington. They might have had more individual pieces of information on that day than nearly any other of King's life, short of the date of the assassination. August 28th wasn't exactly a stress test for the Institute's system.

But it was the day I chose.

One of the staff people in the Institute's Research Department went off to retrieve the material. A little while later he brought in a cardboard box with some papers related to that day. Among the documents retrieved from the box was a photocopy of the simple folded program that had been distributed by hand at the March. At the time, neither Dr. Carson nor the Institute staff could possibly understand the emotional impact seeing this had on me. It was merely the March program, except in one corner it had a handwritten note to Dr. King. From me.

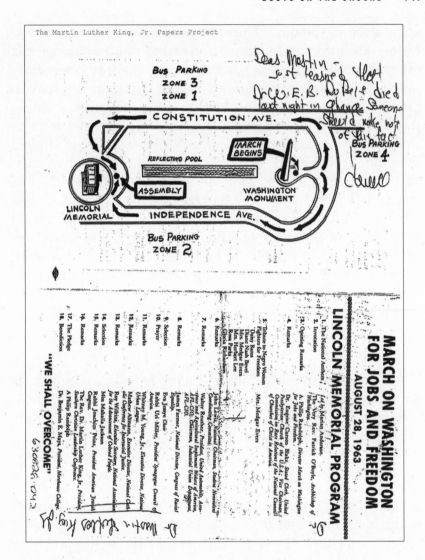

I was looking at *my own* program from the March, something I'd urgently written on and passed along to Martin.

Tears welled up in my eyes as I immediately began trying to mentally reconstruct the long journey it must have taken from my hand to the King Institute files...

Sometime in the middle of the afternoon on the day of the March, someone tapped me on the shoulder. I was standing where I had been for most of the day, on the Lincoln Memorial steps close to the dais. The stranger had seen a man waving for my attention and pointed him out to me. I motioned him over. The man squeezed his way to me. He was a reporter I didn't know (the media credentials hanging on the lanyard around his neck identified him as a representative for the Associated Press), but he'd recognized me. He told me that they had just received word on the wire services that Dr. William Edgar Burkhart Du Bois, the legendary and eminent Negro historian and scholar, had just died. W.E.B. Du Bois was ninety at the time, and had been living in Accra, Ghana, after essentially turning his back on the United States. In 1903, he was the man who had tried to tell the world that the "color line" would be the foremost issue in the twentieth century. And he'd been right. Even at Du Bois' advanced age, I found the news shocking. Perhaps it was the coincidence of timing that struck me.

The reporter offered his opinion: "That's a pretty important thing, isn't it?"

I nodded. "Especially today," I said, looking around at the crowd. A Black icon had fallen. News of Dr. Du Bois' death would be of more importance to these people than almost any other group on earth I could imagine.

"You should get word to Dr. King," the reporter said. "So they can make an announcement."

It was true, I was in receipt of some information important to the March and the attendees. I looked around for the nearest sheet of paper. It was the copy of the March program I was holding in my hand.

I clicked my ball point pen and wrote:

Dear Martin—

Just learned that W.E.B. Du Bois died last night in Ghana. Someone should make note of this fact.

I folded the program lengthwise with my note facing in so it couldn't be read casually. Then I asked the man in front of me, a stranger in the crowd, to pass it along. "To Martin Luther King," I said. He nodded and tapped the person next to him on the shoulder. "This is for Dr. King," I heard him say. With a hand-waving gesture that said, "Pass it along," I watched the note make its way closer and closer to Dr. King. So, by a daisy chain of nameless people at the March standing between the dais and me, my note was passed from person to person, unopened, until it was handed by a March "marshal" to Martin. Upon receipt of the note, Martin opened and read it, stood up halfway, turned around and waved to me with a sorrowful expression, acknowledging that he'd received it. Within a few minutes Roy Wilkins, President of the NAACP, approached the lectern and made the announcement to the crowd assembled about W.E.B. Du Bois' passing.

Martin had placed the folded program with my note into a pocket of the suit he had worn on that day.

Following the March, Dr. King and other March organizers were invited by President John F. Kennedy to the White House for a post-March conversation and evaluation of the March. Presumably, Martin continued to carry my note on his person.

Martin had a habit of pocketing the things throughout his day he felt might have potential lasting importance. At the day's end he would lay these items out on his bureau—maybe ten or twelve business cards, notes, phone numbers and the like—and reevaluate them. Most would be discarded. A few, he would keep.

After the March, I could picture Martin returning to his home in Atlanta. He empties the personal contents of papers and other miscellaneous items from the clothing he wore to the March or from the briefcase he'd carried with him. My March program with its note is among these items. The ones he wants to keep he turns over to Coretta for storage. She places these personal items in several boxes in the basement, along with other treasures including handwritten copies of some of Martin's sermons.

After his death, Coretta donates many of the materials to various scholarly organizations. A photocopy of my handwritten note on the program of the March is turned over to Dr. Carson and the Institute, filed as part of relevant King material from that date.

Until I was standing in the King Institute in Stanford, I had completely forgotten about this incident at the March. I remember W.E.B. Du Bois' death, of course, but I didn't remember passing the note that let all the other attendees at the March know. It made its way from my hand to Martin's, then made its way through all these years and across this great country back into my hand.

I looked at my copy of the program, blood racing, running the emotional spectrum from love to loss and hitting every sharp feeling in between. This was more than instruction on the way history reaches out to us. I felt Martin King, my friend, reaching out. His soft hand waving back toward me one more time.

Keep passing the messages on, Clarence, he seemed to be saying.

CHAPTER 13 | SPEAKING TRUTH TO POWER

There was and is a kind of spell cast on this country that has smeared on the Camelot mythology so thick it's hard to remember back to a time when the Kennedy brothers were simply considered politicians. Good ones, maybe, and attractive ones, but politicians nonetheless. Pragmatic, Machiavellian flesh-and-blood people.

But I remember it. I had never fallen under that star-struck spell with anyone. Particularly not in the White House. So, I have never had trouble telling people the unpleasant if not ugly truth they needed to hear. Some who knew me back then said I relished holding an irreverent position toward the political establishment. There is probably something to that. More accurately, though, I had no reluctance and not an ounce of fear in speaking truth to power.

I can assure you there was no jolt of pleasure, for example, that day at the Justice Department when I told Bobby Kennedy that he was full of shit.

Robert Kennedy had been a central government figure in the Civil Rights struggle while serving as Attorney General under his brother, President John F. Kennedy.[23] However, there appeared to be a vast difference between Robert Kennedy the Attorney General and Robert Kennedy the Democratic presidential candidate who was assassinated on June 6th, 1968.

My first discussion with Martin about Robert Kennedy and the Civil Rights Movement occurred in 1961. Stanley Levison and I told him how important we felt it was for him to seek out a meeting with the President in the early part of his term

---

23 And, of course, Robert Kennedy's role in relationship to Martin during those years must be considered in light of the role of J. Edgar Hoover and the Federal Bureau of Investigation.

in office to raise several Civil Rights concerns. Martin was friends with Harris Wofford, an advisor to President Kennedy, and we suggested Harris as a conduit.

By March 1961, the Attorney General and the President were preoccupied with the escalating tensions with the Soviet Union over the Berlin Wall and the failed Bay of Pigs invasion of Cuba to overthrow Fidel Castro. Martin received word back from Wofford that President Kennedy was not available, but the Attorney General would see him in April. They met in a private dining room at the Mayflower Hotel in Washington. When I asked why it was held at a hotel, Martin said he was told by Louis Martin, a Black political operative in the White House, that the Attorney General feared that if word leaked out that he had met Martin at the White House it would jeopardize his political relationship with the Southern Democrat leaders in Congress.

I wondered, upon hearing of the hotel meeting, whether the reluctance to publicly disclose a meeting at the White House was limited to Martin only, or was the Attorney General fearful of creating an opening for other Civil Rights leaders to also demand meetings?

Ironically, the day following the meeting at the Mayflower I learned from Martin that Harris Wofford had nevertheless invited Martin over to his office in the White House to continue their discussion that had taken place at the hotel. I asked myself, was Wofford acting on his own in bringing Martin into the White House, based on their long-standing personal friendship? Martin indicated that when the President learned that he was in the building he came to Wofford's office to say hello. It was a meet and greet, and nothing of substance occurred other than some reference by the President that the Attorney General was keeping him up to date about Martin and SCLC's plans regarding voter registration.

Earlier that year, James Farmer had assumed the national leadership of the Congress of Racial Equality (CORE). One of his first initiatives was to test compliance by several of the southern states to the recent Supreme Court decision outlawing segregation in interstate bus travel and terminals.

In May 1962, CORE started a campaign of "Freedom Rides" from Washington, D.C. to New Orleans, traveling through Virginia, North and South Carolina, Georgia, and Alabama. The Freedom Rides posed an opportunity for Martin and the SCLC. Our continuing concern at the time was fundraising to sustain the daily operations of the SCLC and supporting the defense of Martin and the other individual defendants in the libel cases that had been filed against them the previous year. The Freedom Rides presented an ideal opportunity to send out a fundraising appeal to help us pressure the Attorney General to provide federal protection for the riders. A fundraising letter from Martin to SCLC's donor base would enable us to achieve those two objectives.

Martin's request to Robert Kennedy required the involvement of the FBI. Our pressure on the Department of Justice precipitated the first of several disputes between the Kennedys and J. Edgar Hoover over the role of the FBI in Civil Rights issues.

When Robert Kennedy took over the Department of Justice, the FBI was not only all-white (with the exception of Hoover's servants), it was *defiantly* all-white. Some agents would parody Kennedy's Boston accent: "Boys, if you don't work with vigah, you'll be replaced by a niggah."

Robert Kennedy's response to our request for federal protection for the Freedom Rides was that no federal laws had been broken when mobs violently assaulted the riders at various stops along their route. Rather, these were violations of local laws. Robert Kennedy reflected Hoover's position that the FBI was strictly an investigative agency and not a police force with peace-keeping responsibilities. This fueled the cynicism of those of us around Martin, who would say that the main role of the FBI under Hoover and Kennedy was to take notes and pictures for use at the funerals of Civil Rights workers whose lives were taken by mob violence.

The next major crossroad in Martin's relationship with Robert Kennedy was during Martin's unsuccessful efforts the following year to desegregate Albany, Georgia. The idea I tried to drive home during my several calls and meetings with Martin during 1961-62 was the necessity for him to persuade

Robert Kennedy to be proactive rather than reactive to Civil Rights events and issues. I urged him to *insist* on the active engagement of DOJ lawyers and federal marshals in protecting the rights and lives of the Freedom Riders.

The Freedom Riders and the racist mob reaction to their peaceful efforts to use interstate bus transportation and terminal facilities stirred the conscience of America. On May 29th, Robert Kennedy filed a petition to the Interstate Commerce Commission to end segregation in interstate travel and eating and drinking facilities used by interstate motor travelers. The following month, on June 26th, the DOJ filed suit in U.S. District Court in New Orleans to bar segregation in airport facilities, and on September 22nd, Kennedy requested the Interstate Commerce Commission issue rules prohibiting segregation in interstate bus facilities.

Beyond the federal enforcement measures, this period also saw some indication of good will from white people in the South. Martin was deeply proud of the voluntary desegregation of many restaurants and lunch counters in Georgia. On September 28th, 1961, some 300 Negroes in 177 restaurants in Atlanta were served for the first time.

In addition to their work on public access, Martin and SCLC also dedicated their attention to voter registration. SCLC already had a Voter Education Program, spearheaded by Dorothy Cotton. Dorothy worked closely with Jack O'Dell, who had been the director of the New York office of the SCLC, to implement a systemic campaign of voter registration in the South. This was incredibly dangerous work. In almost every instance, the efforts by local community organizers to register eligible Negro voters were met with intimidation and harassment by police, sheriffs, or Klansmen, meaning this SCLC program urgently needed the protection of DOJ. Again, I urged Martin to reach out to Robert Kennedy for assistance. In order to "make a record" of our appeal for protection, I proposed to Martin that he do it in writing. On March 26th, 1962, Martin sent Kennedy a telegram requesting that he meet with him and other leaders in early April.

The meeting took place on April 11th. To demonstrate to our fundraising base of supporters and to publicly commit the attorney general to follow through, I recommended that Martin issue a press release detailing Kennedy's oral commitment to pursue irregularities in voter registration. Martin did on April 25th, including the information that the home of a Louisiana Civil Rights leader was destroyed because of his voter registration efforts.

Later that year, prominent artists and celebrities began to speak out in support of the Civil Rights Movement. James Baldwin published his essay, "The Fire Next Time," in the *New Yorker*, addressing his nephew on the centennial of President Lincoln signing the Emancipation Proclamation in 1863. Baldwin wrote:

> *If we do not now dare everything, the fulfillment of that prophecy, re-created from the Bible in song by a slave, is upon us: "God gave Noah the rainbow sign. No more water, the fire next time!"*

One day I got a call from Jimmy (I had come to know Baldwin since my law firm represented him), telling me that Robert Kennedy had asked him to assemble a group of Negro intellectuals to meet with him—unpublicized and off the record—to discuss the Civil Rights Movement. Jimmy said that he wanted me to join the group.

We all met on May 24th in the New York apartment of Stephen Smith, Robert Kennedy's brother-in-law. Kennedy brought along only one other person with him: Burke Marshall, the head of the Justice Department's Civil Rights Division. On our side, it was a who's-who of the early '60s Black experience: My old college friend (and Pulitzer-winner) Lorraine Hansberry, psychologist Kenneth Clark, Harry Belafonte, Lena Horne, writer John Killens, Jerome Smith from the Student Non-Violent Coordinating Committee. Rip Torn, a white actor who was a vocal proponent of Civil Rights and close friend of Baldwin's, was also there. He'd go on to portray a vicious racist in Baldwin's second play, which was based on the Emmett Till lynching.

I believe, going in, that Kennedy thought this would be a genial affair. Otherwise, it probably wouldn't have gotten on the calendar. But he was surprised. The discussion was acerbic and confrontational. In one form or another, the African American participants expressed their frustration, impatience, and skepticism as to the genuineness of the Attorney General's commitment to furthering Civil Rights, including protecting young civil rights workers in the South.

He was taken aback by the sharp tone of the questions and anger he heard about the government dragging its feet and responding with too little, too late. He was defensive, noting how the Justice Department had tried to protect Civil Rights workers in the South. He said, "I could see the country electing an African American president in the next forty years," which was eerily prescient considering Barack Obama was elected 46 years after the meeting.

The question arose about African Americans fighting for the country overseas.

Jerome Smith, the SNCC leader who Lorraine Hansberry told Kennedy was the most important person in the room to listen to, responded with tears streaming down his face. He said he would not serve in the Army overseas, triggering a sharp exchange with Kennedy and a loss of temper on both sides. "I've seen you guys do nothing more than stand around taking notes while we're being beaten," Jerome spat at Kennedy. "Just being in the same room with you makes me want to vomit!"

Burke Marshall snapped at Jerome, saying he couldn't speak to the Attorney General that way, but of course he already had. Kennedy, normally composed and confident, looked like a deer in the headlights. He left the meeting shaken and angry.

Harris Wofford, a special advisor on Civil Rights in the White House during the first two years of the Kennedy administration, later wrote that RFK had told him he had been verbally attacked for nearly three hours and said:

> *You couldn't talk to them as you can to Roy Wilkins or Martin Luther King... It was all emotion, hysteria.*

They stood up and orated. They cursed. Some of them
wept and walked out of the room.

Days later, details of the meeting were leaked to the press.
James Reston, a *New York Times* columnist (and close friend
of the Kennedys), singled me out for criticism, writing that I
had sat silent, not coming to Kennedy's defense in describing
some of DOJ's efforts in the South. My guess is that Reston
got this from the still-ruffled Kennedy, who seemed to take
issue with my unwillingness to defend him and his brother.
Dr. King hadn't sent me there to play the "good Negro" and I
didn't, but the Attorney General took that personally.

Reston's column conveyed that, as Martin's lawyer, I should
have spoken up. But I *had* spoken up at the meeting, which I
noted in a *New York Times* Letter to the Editor, published on
June 10th, 1963, in rebuttal to Reston's column:

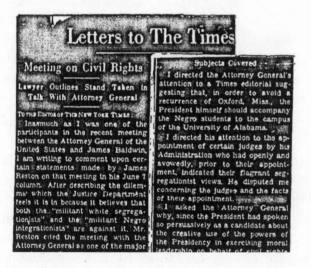

Inasmuch as I was one of the participants in the
recent meeting between the Attorney General of the
United States and James Baldwin, I am writing to com-
ment upon certain statements made by James Reston
on that meeting in his June 7 column. After describing
the dilemma which the Justice Department feels it is in
because it believes that both the "militant white segre-
gationists" and the "militant Negro integrationists" are

against it, Mr. Reston cited the meeting with the Attorney General as one of the major events contributing to this feeling.

Specifically he reported:

"After the meeting, an attorney for the Negro leader, Dr. Martin Luther King, came up to thank Attorney General Kennedy for his efforts to settle the Birmingham case, but he did not speak up for the Justice Department in the meeting itself.

"Robert Kennedy asked the attorney why he had remained silent, and noted that other Negro leaders who had written to thank him for his help on the Civil Rights question had also sat silent while militant Negroes in a meeting condemned his administration.

"The reply given to these questions was that militants in the Movement for Negro leadership were now in the ascendency, that "moderation" or gradualism" or "token integration" were now offensive words to the Negro and that sympathy by a Negro leader for the Administration's moderate approach was regarded as the work of collaborationists."

I was invited to the meeting as one of the attorneys for Mr. James Baldwin. I am also counsel to Dr. Martin Luther King, Jr., and general counsel for the Gandhi Society for Human Rights. In this connection, I assisted Dr. King and Reverend Shuttleworth, at their request, in raising bail for persons participating in the demonstration in Birmingham, Alabama. Thus, the reference to an attorney for Dr. Martin Luther King in Mr. Reston's column is obviously intended to refer to me. Consequently, I would like to bring the following matters to Mr. Reston's attention. Contrary to Mr. Reston and other stories which have emanated out of Washington to the effect that a lawyer for Dr. King remained silent throughout the meeting, the implication being as a moderate such a lawyer was intimidated from speaking, I participated in four specific areas of discussion with the Attorney Gen-

eral, two of which were initiated by my questions and or comments.

1. I directed the Attorney General's attention to a Times editorial suggesting that in order to avoid the reoccurrence of Oxford, Mississippi in connection with the entrance of the two students to the University of Alabama the President himself should accompany the Negro students to the campus and see that they are enrolled. The Attorney General's reply was that this had already been reported.

2. I directed his attention to the appointment of certain judges by his administration who had openly and avowedly prior to their appointment indicated their flagrant segregationist views. He disputed me concerning the judges and the facts of their appointment.

3. I asked the Attorney General why, since the President had spoken so persuasively as a candidate about the creative use of the powers of the presidency and exercising moral leadership on behalf of Civil Rights (see for example the President's speech of September 9th 1960 in Los Angeles), the President could not reinstitute the procedure initiated by Franklin D. Roosevelt in his famous fireside chats to the American people about pressing national problems the suggestion was made that the President make a series of television speeches specifically addressed to the elimination of segregation and discrimination in America.

4. I participated in a discussion on the role of the FBI in Civil Rights cases making the point that there was a crisis in the confidence that Negros had in the FBI insofar as their efficacy on behalf of Civil Rights concerned that some of the crisis of confidence was due to the fact that many members of the FBI were white Southerners themselves (a fact which the Attorney General also disputed).

After the meeting was over, the participants went up to shake the Attorney General's hand, some commenting to him at the time, others merely shaking his hand and leaving. I similarly shook the Attorney General's hand, and in the process acknowledged that I had been aware of some of the efforts of the Department of Justice in Birmingham. The Attorney General replied to the effect that "I wish you had spoken up and said something about that." I further commented as I was leaving that without federal troops in or near Birmingham (while Eugene O'Connor and Mayor Hanes were in office), the accord reached between the Negro and white leaders of that community would be scuttled by the segregationists.

The reply ascribed to me partially by paraphrase and partially by quote in Mr. Reston's column is factually inaccurate. No such statement or reply was made by me or anyone authorized to speak for me to the Attorney General during or after the meeting on Central Park South.

I mention this not so much in terms of what I personally did or did not do at the Attorney General's meeting but lest there be some derivative implications that because of my association with Dr. King, actions or inactions which have been ascribed to me are a reflection of the "moderate" movement being "intimidated" by the "militants."

The important point, however, is that the Attorney General would be compounding errors made if he and his department regarded the feelings expressed, the questions asked, and the statements made by Mr. Baldwin and those persons associated with him in the meeting as reflecting only some "extremist" militant integrationist point of view. And to equate such a point of view politically with the militant white segregationists can only lead to national disaster. Sentiments expressed by all persons in the meeting reflected the grassroots feeling prevailing throughout the Negro communities in the North and the South. Contrary to Mr. Reston's statements and the implications therefrom, Dr. King and his nonviolent Movement have been pointing to the national crisis in race relations prior to the meeting and do not *dissent from the indictment of segregation and discrimination in America expressed by those persons assembled with the Attorney General.*

And, of course, it is sheer nonsense to state directly, indirectly or by implication that as an attorney for Dr. King I have been or am personally intimidated by any militant integrationists. In this connection an attorney friend, knowing my Civil Rights position, humorously reminded me that describing me as a moderate in the context of Mr. Reston's article could conceivably be "libelous per se."

Though the discussion with the Attorney General was very frank and sharp, such a meeting was, in my judgment, most constructive and should be regarded as such by the Administration. The Attorney General and Mr. Burke Marshall have been more vigorous in their prosecution of actions on behalf of Civil Rights than any previous administration. Our complaint, however, is that this admittedly increased vigorous activity is incommensurate with the enormity of the racial crisis confronting our country. When the chief legal officer of the United States displays a certain shock over the sentiments expressed by the participants at that meeting, the fact in and of itself is frightening, because it is indicative of how the Administration underestimates the explosive ingredients inherent in the continued existence of racial discrimination and segregation.

Although Martin wasn't at the May 24th meeting, I was acting partly as a surrogate for him. Robert Kennedy and Martin had butted heads over Civil Rights tactics as early as the spring of 1961, when several Freedom Riders were jailed in Jackson, Mississippi. These riders had refused bail and threatened a hunger strike. Kennedy called Martin to find out if he knew how long they intended to stay in jail. Martin replied that they planned to remain until the aims of their protest were met.

According to Martin, Kennedy responded by saying, "That is not going to have the slightest effect on what the government is going to do in this field or any other. The fact that they stay in jail is not going to have the slightest effect on me."

Martin responded that it might make a difference if students came down to Jackson by the hundreds or thousands to protest in support of the Freedom Riders. He told me he didn't intend that as a threat, but Robert Kennedy took it differently.

"That's not the way to deal with us," he said. Which is another way of saying, "Be patient, Negro."

Similarly, during the course of Martin and SCLC's campaign to desegregate Albany, Georgia, Martin was seriously considering disobeying an injunction from the federal court prohibiting further demonstrations. In December 1961, Robert Kennedy telephoned Martin to persuade him to abide by the court's order. This conversation also resulted in a heated exchange between them, Martin told me.

Our expectations and consistent efforts to get the Justice Department to be proactive in support of Martin's Civil Rights leadership were fueled in part by statements made by JFK when he was campaigning for president. Mindful that President Kennedy's margin of victory in the popular vote was only 120,000 votes nationwide and 9,000 in Cook County—a Democratic stronghold that includes Chicago—we still believed that his Justice Department would be more sympathetic to Civil Rights law enforcement. I would sometimes remind Martin that the hallmark of his leadership was his ability to arouse the conscience of white America, and an aroused national conscience would support the Kennedy brothers on Civil Rights. Martin liked me to repeat what Lincoln said during even more turbulent times 100 years earlier:

"In this and like communities, public sentiment is everything. With public sentiment, nothing can fail; without it, nothing can succeed. Consequently, he who molds public sentiment goes deeper than he who enacts statutes or pronounces decisions. He makes statutes and decisions possible to be executed."

• • •

Thus, we were always in the position of appealing, pleading, or seeking to persuade the Attorney General to be more proactive and supportive of Civil Rights workers. It became clear to me, although Martin did not always agree, that Robert Kennedy was more of a political pragmatist than someone interested in setting an example of moral leadership. Every potential decision was seen through his prism of how it would affect their political base of white Southern Democratic Party leaders.

As for the time when I told the Attorney General that he was full of shit... that was a moment of clarity that came to me when I was analyzing a problem with which we had been struggling. We had noticed an alarming pattern of violence at the locations for Martin's speeches throughout the South. In an effort to avoid such dangers, we were extremely secretive in our travel plans, especially our lodging itineraries. Yet somehow, inexplicably, nearly every time we showed up at the private houses where Martin would be staying, there would be a segregationist protest presence. This almost always included hooded KKK members. There was shouting, there were burning torches. It was not the Welcome Wagon.

Now, the Justice Department had presented itself as concerned for our safety over the years, and that made a pragmatic kind of sense to me. We were on the national stage, and it wouldn't be good for the country if something truly horrible happened to the Movement's leader.[24] Robert Kennedy had specifically asked the SCLC to keep him updated on Martin's travel plans so that, at each location, his office and the FBI could alert local police ahead of time so they could prepare and be on alert for signs of trouble.

It hit me that the answer to the leak was staring me right in the face. The KKK and other segregationists were getting the information from the police. Obviously, throughout the

---

24 More horrible than the norm, I mean. Firehoses, teargas, rubber bullets, dogs. That was business as usual, of course, nothing to get excited about.

South, many members of the local police forces were against the Movement. Some were undoubtedly members of the Klan.

I made an appointment to see the Attorney General and headed to Washington. There in Kennedy's office overlooking Pennsylvania Avenue, I laid out my theory. "This 'advanced notice' that's supposed to protect him only acted as a tip-off to the same people who want him dead!" I shouted.

Political animal that he was, Kennedy denied it all. But we both knew I was right. "You're so full of shit, Bobby," I said as I stormed out of the office. Okay, maybe there was a *tiny* jolt of pleasure in saying that.

I still would've rather he'd taken responsibility and offered a solution, though.

On October 30th, 1963, President Kennedy issued the following statement regarding the bill to end racial discrimination in public accommodations, which was then pending in the House Judiciary Committee:

> *The House Committee on the Judiciary, in approving a bipartisan Civil Rights bill today, has significantly improved the prospects for enactment of effective civil rights legislation in Congress this year. The bill is a comprehensive and fair bill.*
>
> *It will provide effective legal remedies for racial discrimination in voting, education, public accommodations, employment, and federal programs. It will provide the basis for men of good will in every city in our land to work together to resolve their racial problems within a framework of law and justice.*
>
> *The bill must now pass through the House Rules Committee, be approved by the House, then by the Senate. I am hopeful this can be done as rapidly as possible.*
>
> *From the very beginning, enactment of an effective Civil Rights bill has required that sectional and political differences be set aside in the interest of meeting an urgent national crisis.*

Less than a month later, this hopeful Civil Rights moment was obliterated. President Kennedy has been assassinated.

That night, I was at a neighbor's dinner party when the host, Charles Wechsler, came over to me and said that I had a telephone call. The operator told me that she had "an emergency call" from Atlanta, from Dr. Martin Luther King Jr. (He'd gotten the Wechslers' phone number from our live-in housekeeper who was at home with our children.)

Martin had been besieged with calls to his home and office for his reaction or "official statement" on the assassination. He said he did not want to have any discussions with the press or issue any statement without consultation with me.

We decided the only way this could logistically be done within the limited constraints of time was for him to fly up the next morning, Saturday, and meet with me in LaGuardia Airport to draft the statement.

When Martin walked into the Eastern Airlines lounge, the first thing he said to me was, "You see, they got to the President, killed him. We have to stop this foolishness of thinking that the Kennedy Administration or anybody can protect me. When they want to get me, they will kill me too. It's not a question of whether they can do it, it's only a question of when."

I did not argue; I merely said, "Well, as you have told all of us so many times, only our Lord Jesus Christ can protect you. You're here with us now, so how about we get to work?"

Initially, we spent some time discussing the possibilities of who or what was really behind the assassination of President Kennedy. We didn't believe it could be the work of one person acting alone. Why in Dallas? Was it Cuban exiles angry with JFK for, in their mind, abandoning their abortive attempt to overthrow Fidel Castro during the Bay of Pigs invasion in Cuba? Was it some racist white supremacist Klan member or some hired gun engaged by wealthy Southern segregationist businessmen?

They were the same questions almost everyone was asking.

Thereafter, we began to discuss the effect President Kennedy's assassination would have on Dr. King's leadership efforts to end racial segregation in America. Was this, like the bombing of the 16th Street Baptist Church in Birmingham (where four young girls were murdered 17 days after the I Have a Dream speech), a response to the March and JFK's efforts to get a Civil Rights bill through Congress?

Most important of all, what were the prospects for Civil Rights under the new President Lyndon Baines Johnson, a white Southerner from Texas?

We decided that Martin must start by acknowledging the great loss to the nation and the Kennedy family. Thus, the first paragraph of Dr. King's eventual public statement:

> *In a period of change, the nation has lost a leader who was unafraid of change.... It is a sad commentary on our time that it took a brave man to be a leader for human realities.*

We spent some time discussing whether we should go so far in Martin's statement to say "a brave man to be a leader for *Civil Rights.*" But based on the Kennedy Administration's response to the Freedom Riders, Dr. King's campaign in Birmingham earlier that year, and the more recent March on Washington, we concluded that we had to strike a more measured description of the deceased President's "leadership" on Civil Rights:

> *The unmistakable cause of sincere grief expressed by so many millions was more than simple emotion. It disclosed that President Kennedy had become a symbol of people's aspirations and yearning for justice, economic well-being, and peace, as well as the importance of the commitment to moral values.*

This enabled us to segue to the words that President Kennedy had used in his address to the nation following his federalization of the Alabama National Guard to protect the admission of two Negro students at the University of Alabama that previous June:

> *We are confronted primarily with a moral issue. It is as old as the Scriptures and dear as the American*

Constitution. The heart of the question is whether all Americans are to be afforded equal rights and equal opportunities and whether we are going to treat our fellow Americans as we want to be treated.

Reference to this part of the assassinated President's address during that civil rights crisis was deliberate. Not knowing what was behind the assassination, Dr. King wanted to focus on religious and moral imperatives of Civil Rights. We felt we had to say unequivocally that *"The murder of the President, regardless of the precise identity of the assailant, occurred in a context of violence and hatred that has been building up in our nation for the past several years."*

We felt it was essential to call the nation and the world's attention to the fact that *"We have seen children murdered in church, men shot down in ambush in a manner so similar to the assassination of President Kennedy*[25] *that we must face the fact that we are dealing with a social disease that can be neglected or avoided as we have done only to our deadly peril."*

We then debated quite a bit over the content of the conclusionary characterization of the forces behind the President's assassination before we felt comfortable enough to say: *"We must face the tragic fact that President Kennedy was the victim of developments that have made violence and hatred a popular pastime in all too many quarters of our nation."*

After resolving how to strike the right balance between acknowledging the terrible personal tragedy experienced by the Kennedy family, commending the slain President for what he had done (as opposed to what we had asked and he had *not* done), we thought that it was extremely important that Dr. King provide some benchmark or historical background to the struggle for Civil Rights when other momentous events had occurred:

Many will raise the question of whether President Kennedy's assassination will mean an inevitable setback for the cause of civil rights. When Abraham Lincoln was assassinated, he was succeeded by a Vice Pres-

---

25   This was in reference to that June's murder of Medgar Evers, an NAACP leader, in Jackson, Mississippi.

ident of Southern origin. His successor neither had the experience or the passion of Lincoln. The Reconstruction Movement was unified and the release from chattel slavery was carried through because the forces that had generated that change were too powerful to be turned back. Later, Negroes suffered a setback in being denied full freedom and equality, but different elements were responsible.

It was not the assassination of the President that stopped the clock of progress. When President Roosevelt, a friend of Negro rights, died, the Civil Rights Movement did not diminish but accelerated because it had a momentum and logic of its own.

It was during our discussion concerning the prospects of our future relationship with the new President Johnson that we developed the political thesis that would constitute the core of our strategic approach to the Johnson presidency. Ironically, we viewed LBJ's ascendency as an opportunity. It seemed unlikely that any transformative change to race relations in the United States or major opportunities for equal political and economic justice for Negroes would happen unless they occurred under a white Southern leader.

This was clear from the history of the United States on issues of race. The Civil War, Reconstruction and its failure, and the Hayes-Tilden compromise of 1877 (which led to the withdrawal of federal troops from the South in exchange for the Southern congressional Democratic support for the Republican presidential candidate Rutherford B. Hayes) all suggested the country would respond best to the leadership of a white Southern politician on issues of race.

Dr. King wrote in the statement that he'd had "*several meetings with President Johnson when he served as Vice-President. I felt that he had a statesmanlike grasp of the problem and great political sagacity. I think he will realize that civil rights are not one of several issues but are the dominant domestic issue. Guided by a clear appraisal of reality he is equipped to be affirmative in getting Congressional results.*"

We also wanted to make sure that the new President Johnson and the country at large knew that *"Negroes found that non-violent direct action was a powerful weapon for successfully effectuating social change. They have become immeasurably stronger this year, in self-confidence, determination, and in the acquisition of white allies. They will not pause or turn back. The time is past when Negro protest was a momentary emotional phenomenon and could be dismissed to peter out, whether or not it was satisfied. Because it has hardened into a social force at the root of American society and now possesses dynamic strength, it will move inexorably until its demands are fulfilled.*

We decided it would be most appropriate for Dr. King to conclude by saying:

As we mourn the death of John Fitzgerald Kennedy, I am mindful of the words of Lincoln in his Gettysburg Address: "It is for us the living, rather to be dedicated to the unfinished work which they who fought here so nobly advanced. It is rather for us to be here dedicated to the great task remaining before us."

The political metamorphosis of Robert Kennedy may have started with the assassination of his brother. Or maybe it was his decision to resign from the Johnson Administration and run for Senate. RFK personally invited Martin to attend the state funeral services for his brother. From an insider's perspective[26], a genuine shift seemed to have occurred for Robert Kennedy by the time he ran for president in 1968.

He was at a campaign stop in the predominately African American city of Gary, Indiana on April 4th when he received word that Martin had been assassinated. To a hushed crowd, Kennedy gave a moving impromptu speech:

Ladies and Gentlemen—I'm only going to talk to you just for a minute or so this evening. Because...I have some very sad news for all of you, and I think sad news

---

26   That is to say, from the point of view of someone like *me*, who has never bought into any of the public relations machinations coming out of the Kennedy family.

for all of our fellow citizens, and people who love peace all over the world, and that is that Martin Luther King was shot and was killed tonight in Memphis, Tennessee.

Martin Luther King dedicated his life to love and to justice between fellow human beings. He died in the cause of that effort. In this difficult day, in this difficult time for the United States, it's perhaps well to ask what kind of a nation we are and what direction we want to move in.

For those of you who are Black—considering the evidence evidently is that there were white people who were responsible—you can be filled with bitterness, and with hatred, and a desire for revenge.

We can move in that direction as a country, in greater polarization—Black people amongst Blacks, and white amongst whites, filled with hatred toward one another. Or we can make an effort, as Martin Luther King did, to understand and to comprehend, and replace that violence, that stain of bloodshed that has spread across our land, with an effort to understand, compassion and love.

What we need in the United States is not division; what we need in the United States is not hatred; what we need in the United States is not violence and lawlessness, but is love and wisdom, and compassion toward one another, and a feeling of justice toward those who still suffer within our country, whether they be white or whether they be Black.

My favorite poet was Aeschylus. He wrote: "In our sleep, pain which cannot forget falls drop by drop upon the heart until, in our own despair, against our will, comes wisdom through the awful grace of God."

It's difficult to pinpoint the origin of Robert Kennedy's personal change on the issue of race. Something must have touched him deeply at a certain point. Coming from a background growing up, then going to college and law school surrounded almost exclusively by white people (except for servants), he viewed race the way other rich Bostonians of the day did. But in the later part of his life, he began to show concern and compassion for the poor, the least of these, and Black and Brown people. Maybe it was following Marian Wright Edelman in 1967 to witness up close the Black poverty in the Mississippi Delta. Perhaps it was when he federalized the Mississippi National Guard to protect James Meredith after he was shot during his voting rights march through that state.

Whatever the origin, critics like me of Robert Kennedy's political opportunism and deference to the political power of the white segregationists in the South must acknowledge what appeared to be a genuine change in attitude. The bullet fired by Sirhan Sirhan's in the kitchen of the Ambassador Hotel in Los Angeles in the summer of 1968 deprived us of the opportunity to see the ultimate course of this new concern. He might have turned out to be something more than merely a politician. He might've been a true leader.

Violence, as always, leaves us with unanswered questions.

PART IV

STRADDLING TWO WORLDS

During those early years with Martin, I continued to be focused, if not obsessed, with advancing my own professional life. I felt that, with effort, dedication, and sacrifice, I could advance both causes in tandem.

Part of that sacrifice was the relocation from California to New York. From this new base in the Bronx, I was able to improve my service to the Movement, at least in a fundraising capacity, while simultaneously exploring my commercial options.

Notwithstanding my commitment and love for Dr. King, when I was not directly involved in serving his needs for my legal advice and draft speech writing to satisfy a speaking commitment for which he did not have time to prepare, I continued to try and create business opportunities for myself.

In late 1963 I met Bertram Hartnett, a lawyer and entrepreneur in the insurance business. He had been a co-founder of Beneficial National Life Insurance, and we became friendly. I visited his home in Great Neck and he and his wife reciprocated, coming to Riverdale. I'd also become good friends with D. P. Park Gibson, who published a monthly research report called *The Negro Market*, providing economic and financial information on the buying power of Negroes in America. For example, his report showed that while Blacks constituted less than twelve percent of the population, we purchased forty percent of the Scotch whiskey in the United States. He provided similar economic statistics on soft drinks, clothing, electronics, and more. Park provided Bert and me a window into the expanding Negro life insurance needs and purchases.

On the basis of this market research and our general reading of the political mood of the country at that time, in 1964 we decided to form a financial and life insurance enterprise that would be directed toward the growing economic power in the Negro market. We organized Intramerica Life Corporation as a holding company and had a target of raising four million dollars to capitalize it. As a first step, we set out to raise a million dollars from a select group of private investors. We would then create a board of directors whose business affiliations and personal connections could instill in other potential private investors confidence that the company was a serious undertaking. The plan, after raising the private equity, would be to seek a Wall Street investment banking firm to take Interamerica Life Corp. public.

Bernard Fishman, a friend and early investor, told me and my law partners, David and Jonathan Lubell, that he had colleagues at an investment firm who might be interested in taking us public. So, we met Arthur Carter, Roger Berlind, Sanford Weill, and Arthur Levitt, Jr. Several of us then made a presentation to the firm which included a list of those who had agreed to serve on our board of directors. Among them were the then-chairman of Xerox, the then-chairman of Pitney Bowes, Harry Belafonte, Sidney Cohen (a partner in the entertainment and labor law firm of Cohen & Glickstein), and the president of the San Juan Racing Association, a track in Puerto Rico. We also enlisted the commitment of Robert Randall, the only certified Negro actuary in the life insurance business in the United States, and Leon Burney, one of the top-selling insurance agents in the United States at the time.

Carter, Berlind & Weill was impressed enough to sign an underwriting agreement in early 1964 to take Intramerica public with an initial offering of $4 million. A proposed public offering was filed with the Securities and Exchange Commission, and all was on track—briefly.

To our dismay, a "downturn" in the market cancelled the public offering, with Carter, Berlind & Weill using its "market out" clause in our agreement. They suggested we wait a couple of months, in the expectation that the market for public offerings of small and medium-size companies would improve. We were devastated by the changed circumstances delaying our starting operations. We had begun to look for office space in midtown Manhattan and had started to staff up. We'd also initiated discussions with insurance agents who would agree to sell the company's life insurance products. We didn't want to lose the momentum.

There was another way forward; however, it was a riskier one. We could make the public offering ourselves, while still paying Carter, Berlind & Weill their underwriting fee. The difference was that in this scenario they could not guarantee we would be able to raise the capital needed.

In my briefcase I kept a yellow legal pad with the names of people over the previous year who had indicated an interest in possibly purchasing stock in Intramerica Life. Bert Harnett asked me how confident I was that most of those people would in fact purchase shares when the company went public. I said I obviously couldn't guarantee anything, but I had a strong belief that, assuming for example the stock was offered at twenty dollars a share, several of them would purchase stock in amounts of $1,000, $2,500, $5,000, and $10,000.

Bert said he was prepared to "roll the dice" if I was. We talked with a Bernard Fishman and a couple of the other investors to let them know what we were doing. Bernard suggested we file solicitation with the SEC, which we submitted. We rented office space near my law office and hired a group of "Kelly Girls" to begin making calls to the list of 1,300 potential investors I'd been carrying around.

In three weeks, instead of our targeted goal of four million dollars, we raised five. The partners at Carter, Berlind & Weill were astounded by our success. One of them reportedly said, "Either Clarence Jones is too dumb to know you can't sell stock in a down market or he may be one of the greatest salesmen on Wall Street."

While working at Intramerica, I met Leonard Davis, a founder of Colonial Penn Life Insurance Co. He had wanted Colonial Penn to do business in New York but had been unable to get the company affiliated as licensed insurance carrier in the state. He wanted a way in, and of course, Intramerica was licensed to operate in New York. Colonial Penn made an offer to purchase Intramerica. As an owner of 25,000 Intramerica shares, I would be able to buy Colonial Penn shares at ten dollars each, as would other Intramerica shareholders. I knew the deal would be personally lucrative, but I didn't know that Colonial Penn shares were selling for about $100 each on the open market. When the deal closed, I was given a check for $750,000, my biggest payday by far. Carrying around that list of potential shareholders in my briefcase proved to be enormously beneficial to all of us.

Shortly after the sale of Intramerica, I was invited to join Carter, Berlind & Weill as a partner and vice president. I had to take examinations to qualify as a registered representative and National Association of Securities Dealers to serve as a partner in a Wall Street investment-banking firm that had a seat on the New York Stock Exchange, but compared to the bar exam it felt like a cinch.

I was not the first Negro to work on Wall Street. Others worked in the mailrooms or as messengers, while a few worked as stockbrokers at firms such as Goldman Sachs, Merrill Lynch, or PaineWebber. But in 1966, I became the first Negro to join a Wall Street investment banking firm as partner and principal. The *New York Times* carried the story in its Business Section:

Negro Named To High Position In Financial Firm
Clarence B. Jones, a 36-year-old legal and financial whiz kid from New York City, is believed to be the first Negro appointed as an allied member of the New York Stock Exchange. He became a vice president and a stockholder of Carter, Berlind and Weill, Inc., an investment and banking firm which belongs to the Exchange. Before joining New York's financial community he was a partner in the law firm of Lubell, Lubell and Jones.

Jones

This rarity soon became evident: When I attended meetings at Carter, Berlind & Weill or other investment banking firms, conferences held with clients, or with potential new businesses, there was *never* even one other Black person present.

Yet there was a flipside to being the first and only Negro partner in a Wall Street investment-banking firm. I met so many Negro entrepreneurs and dealmakers because those few would seek me out for a meeting to enable them to make a presentation to my firm. These included people in music, construction, and cosmetics, along with those seeking potential acquisition of radio or television stations. Rare was the chance for me to interact at the executive level with another man of my race. But it did happen.

I worked with some extraordinary young African American entrepreneurs. They included Joe Glazer, the owner and operator of the Associated Booking Company. Glaser was a feared and powerful person in his business, which was setting up tours for musical acts. ABC had represented Duke Ellington, Benny Goodman, Billie Holliday, and T. Rex, to name just a few.

Once, when my firm was considering making a proposal to the recently formed Metropolitan Washington Transportation Authority to create and sell bonds to finance construction of the Metro, the subway system in Washington, D.C., the chairman of the Authority turned out to be Rev. Walter Fauntroy, a longtime associate and colleague of Martin and his SCLC.

One of the challenges I confronted with many Negro entrepreneurs was that they would seek me out as a financing partner. I would have to explain that our firm did not engage in venture or start-up financing. The threshold issue was always their providing me with a set of certified financial statements indicating the financial history of their own or a proposed acquisition.[27]

. . .

27 All members and representatives of the firm were bound by the foundational element of Rule 405 of the New York Stock Exchange: "Know your customer." If they couldn't paint a clear picture of the financial landscape, our hands were tied.

Shortly after I joined Carter, Berlind & Weill, I interviewed several candidates to serve as my personal secretary. The young woman I selected, Diane Boylan, was very capable and supportive. She became invaluable to me in short order. She would share with me office gossip about me, gleaned from other secretaries or clerks. We had conversations in my office about the pitfalls of being the only Negro of note on Wall Street and a partner in a prestigious firm. She warned me to be careful of certain women in the firm who were seeking to get me involved in a comprising personal relationship. Although I had enormous respect for Diane, I thought that she might be exaggerating and being unnecessarily protective of me—until the company had a Christmas party. After a lot of drinking and merriment, a very attractive woman surreptitiously dropped a note into my suit jacket pocket, along with a key to her hotel room. It went unused. I let Diane know she was right on the money, though.

There were other such temptations along the way, all ignored. Bemusedly, I remembered the title of a book by Sam Greenlee, *The Spook Who Sat by the Door*. It was a reference to the CIA seating their one token Black recruit near the entrance like a trophy, so anyone coming in could see they were "changing with the times." Often, I felt like Greenlee's character on Wall Street.[28]

As a counterbalance to this, there were several memorable experiences in relationships with white people, colleagues in my firm and others, that felt like a bridge to the relationships with white people I had developed at Columbia University. Principally, of course, were the partners of the firm that had invited me in: Arthur Carter, Roger Berlind, Sandy Weill, and Arthur Levitt, Jr. I was assigned an office next to a small lounge area. On the other side of was a larger shared office space for the principal partners, and we spent a lot of time together in that no-man's-land between our respective offices.

---

28 Sam Greenlee once came to ask me to help finance the film version of *The Spook Who Sat by the Door*. I was able to convince the Algerian government to foot the bill and they in turn convinced Costa Garvas to direct. However, Sam tanked the deal because he wanted to direct the movie himself! Of course, he never would get that choice; eventually it was shot by *Hogan's Heroes* actor Ivan Dixon. And though I applaud having a Black director for the project, it certainly would have been a better film done by Garvas.

Although I did not know the details, I was at the firm less than a year when a dispute between Arthur Carter and his other senior partners arose. Arthur left the firm. The name was changed to Cogan Berlind Weill and Levitt, Jr. This was an especially uncomfortable time for me, initially, because I had had a good relationship with Arthur and had also developed a growing friendship with Sandy. Sandy was another Jewish man in my life who felt like a kindred spirit.[29] Indeed, it was my friendship and relationship with Sandy Weill that has endured the longest and remains so today.

Through a series of mergers and acquisitions, the firm which I had originally joined as a partner evolved into CBW— L. Hayden Stone joined, and then subsequently left to become an affiliate associated with the American Express Company. Soon, through his relationship with Hayden, Sandy became the president of American Express. Shortly thereafter, we had lunch together in a private executive dining room.

We spoke warmly with one another, old friends now. I shared with them that AMEX seemed to be a business culture that was different and a little out of sync with the one he'd been a part of the past several years. "Candidly, Sandy," I said, "this doesn't feel like the right place for you."

He smiled, smoking a cigar with a slight twinkle in his eye that said, in effect, "We'll see."

That was on a Friday afternoon. Monday morning, I read an article in the *Wall Street Journal* that indicated that Sandy had resigned from American Express and was now in Baltimore working with Jamie Dimon and Chuck Prince on a transaction involving the acquisition of the Commercial Credit Corporation. This would become Sandy's empire: Citibank.

One of the areas in which I remained active was the music and artist performing rights business. One of the legendary "deans" of lawyers in the music business was attorney

---

29 When Sandy's oldest son Mark was thrown his bar mitzvah, my wife and I were invited. It was the first bar mitzvah I'd ever attended.

Paul Marshall. I had become friendly with Paul and his wife, Betty, often visiting with them at their New York apartment and home in the country. One of Paul's clients was Bob Crew, the talented songwriter for many of the hits of the '60s, '70s, and '80s, including "Lady Marmalade," "Silhouettes," "Walk Like A Man," "Twistin' All Night Long," "Rag Doll," "Sun Ain't Gonna Shine," "Sock It to Me Baby," "Heaven Above Me," and more. His songs were performed by Roberta Flack, The Four Seasons, and many other well-known artists.

Bob Crew and I became friends. At the top of his game Bob had a triplex apartment on Fifth Avenue and 79th Street and filled it with the furniture and artifacts that had been displayed at the Philippine Pavilion at the 1964 New York City World's Fair. Bob seemed to like me and my wife, Anne very much. He frequently invited the two of us to his social events.

Bob also had a full-time resident astrologist on hand. He would not sign any important business contracts or make any sort of binding commitment unless it aligned with the stars. Naturally, this held up deals and used to drive his lawyer absolutely crazy.

At one point Bob moved from the Fifth Avenue triplex to a duplex on West 72nd Street and Central Park West. This is the (in)famous Dakota building, Ira Levin's model for the Bramford building in *Rosemary's Baby* and site of John Lennon's last home (and murder).

One evening in 1967, Bob invited Anne and me to a dinner party he was having at his new apartment at the Dakota. After a great night the guests began to thin out. By around 2:00 a.m., Anne and I were the only ones left. We tried to make our excuses and get on the road; it was an hour's drive to our place in Riverdale. But Bob sat down at the piano in his apartment. He encouraged me to come and sit next to him on the bench while he played and composed.

He kept playing around with a melody and then started to scribble down some accompanying lyrics. I was impressed— blown away, actually—by the originality and spontaneity of his songwriting abilities. Yes, of course, I knew he had written many hits. However, there was something immediately special about "Can't Take My Eyes Off of You." Or maybe it was just the fact that I was in the room when he wrote it. When Frankie Valli recorded it later in the year, it reached number two on the Billboard Hot 100.

CHAPTER 15 | RED MENACE

On the basis of years of up-close observation, I can definitively say there was no white person in Martin Luther King Jr.'s life that he was closer to, or on whom he relied and depended upon more, than Stanley Levison.

Of course, there were other white people that Martin developed close working relationships and friendships with—religious leaders like Rabbi Abraham Joshua Heschel, businessmen like Harry Wachtel, and labor leaders like Leon Foner, David Livingston, Ralph Helstein, and Walter Reuther. But none of them ever earned the level unequivocal trust, love and respect that Stanley Levison did. Trust, love, and respect he deeply deserved.

And yet, Stanley had an Achilles heel that had the potential to bring Martin Luther King, Jr. down...

Stanley knew and had great respect for Arthur Kinoy, one of my legal mentors, former student editor of the Columbia Law Review, and a brilliant left-wing constitutional lawyer. When I first moved from Los Angeles to New York in 1961, prior to Anne and our children coming east, I stayed at the Kinoy house. During that time, I tried to give Arthur as much space as I could, so I would often eat out with Stanley and his twin brother, Roy Bennett, or we'd cook together at Stanley's apartment on West 88th Street in Manhattan. During one of those dinners, the brothers disclosed to me how two events in 1956 (before they met me but in the same year Stanley met Martin) precipitated their break with the Communist Party of the United States.

Initially it was Soviet leader Nikita Khrushchev's disclosure of the "crimes" of Joseph Stalin, especially allegations of anti-Semitism against Jewish leaders in the Soviet Communist Party. Then, later that same year, the Soviet Union invaded Hungary to crush a burgeoning Hungarian Revolution. Taken together, these were the straws that broke the ideological camel's back of Stanley and Roy's loyalty to the Communist Party of the USA and to the Soviet Union. Having in my youth occasionally attended Communist Party USA meetings, read the *Daily Worker*, and worked at Camp Wichita, I understood the state of mind that would make some of the more compassionate communist ideologies attractive. It made sense to me both what might draw these brothers to and repel them from the Party.

I thought little of the matter after that dinner-time discussion. Until two years later.

In the summer of 1963 Martin's "kitchen cabinet" was sweating bullets trying to plan the March on Washington. Stanley and I were in the thick of it, along with Jack O'Dell. On June 21st, slightly more than two months ahead of the March, President Kennedy asked to meet with a group of the major civil rights leaders in the Oval Office to discuss the event. From all reports, the meeting was cordial enough, though perhaps a bit toothless. However, near the end of the afternoon, Kennedy asked Martin to join him for a walk in the Rose Garden. Nothing in his tone or demeaner indicated the blow that was about to be delivered.

As the two men strolled, the President disclosed to Martin a startling piece of intelligence: J. Edgar Hoover had told him directly that "Stanley Levison and Jack O'Dell are communist agents of Moscow." Kennedy "recommended" that Martin sever all ties to both of these long-time supporters. He made it crystal clear that the Movement couldn't afford to have Martin dragged down by a "Soviet conspiracy."

To my knowledge, the only person who has reported on this accurately is author Nick Bryant in his book *The Bystander— John F. Kennedy and the Struggle for Black Equality*. What Bryant wrote aligned completely with what Martin told me shortly after the walk:

>   *Kennedy ushered King into the Rose Garden and*
>   *spoke in a conspiratorial tone... Kennedy did not*
>   *mince his words. 'I assume you know that you're under*
>   *very close surveillance' he said, adding that the FBI*
>   *had incontrovertible evidence incriminating Levison*
>   *and Jack O'Dell. "Get rid of them," he said, "they're*
>   *communist."*

To make his point, the President compared Martin's continued association with the two advisors to the failure of
England's then-Prime Minister Harold MacMillan to dismiss
Lord Profumo, a member of his cabinet, following disclosure
of his affair with Kristine Keeler, a call girl simultaneously
involved with a Soviet naval attaché linked to the KGB.

"MacMillan is likely to lose his government simply because
he's been loyal to a friend," the President said.[30] "You must
be careful not to lose your cause for the same reason. If they
shoot you down, they'll shoot us down, too."

No less a figure than the President of the United States
was telling Martin who his friends should and should not
be. According to the President, the FBI had determined from
their investigation of Stanley and Roy Bennett that for several years they had businesses which they used to finance the
operations of the United States Communist Party. Jack was
described as the "fifth ranking member of the Communist
Party in the United States."

Fortunately, Martin had been previously informed of Stanley's old ties to communism, so he wasn't blindsided with that
accusation. The O'Dell situation, however, was another matter. This was the first Martin had heard of it, and though he
didn't tip his hand to Kennedy, the news upset him.

But despite the surprise revelation about O'Dell, the real
problem involved Stanley, because only a year prior he'd been
subpoenaed to appear before the Senate Internal Security
Subcommittee, which was chaired by Mississippi plantation

---

30 The MacMillan administration indeed collapsed within four months of
the Rose Garden discussion.

owner and proud segregationist James Eastland. The topic of communist infiltration in the U.S. was hot at the time, and it seemed likely that Stanley had been targeted at least in part to be questioned on that topic.

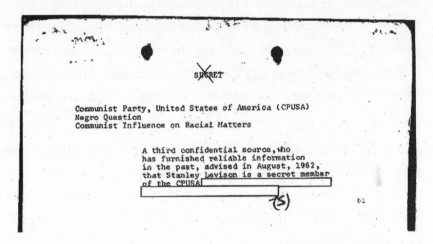

As soon as he received the subpoena, Stanley contacted me. We met alone at his apartment on West 88th Street. The first question we discussed was who should be selected to represent him before the subcommittee. Stanley asked me to act as his counsel. I felt strongly that I wasn't the right choice, and that his affection and respect for me was blinding him to picking the best man for the job. After consideration of various lawyers, I strongly recommended William Kunstler, a former adjutant general in the U.S. military and experienced New York-based civil liberties trial lawyer. Stanley agreed, and I told him that I'd call Kunstler for him.

We then discussed how best to "handle" with Martin the issue of his required appearance before the committee. We considered the possibility of keeping news of the subpoena from Martin to insulate him, but we both immediately concluded that this would undermine the cornerstone of our relationships with him. Additionally, there was the possibility that Martin would be blindsided with this information from some third-party source before we had a chance to disclose it.

• • •

I arranged to meet Martin to break the news and advise him about what he might say in response to any questions from the press. We settled on a low-profile strategy, hoping (perhaps praying) that there wouldn't be any blowback to the Movement. If questions did come up, he'd deflect, making the situation about Eastland and his hatred of any civil rights legislation. In other words, he'd focus on the witch hunter, not the hunted.

At that first meeting with Kunstler that I attended, the main question involved what, if anything, Stanley would say at his appearance. Asserting his Fifth Amendment rights against self-incrimination was the clearest course of action, but Stanley wasn't so sure.

So, no one except perhaps Kunstler had any advance knowledge of what other statement Stanley might make in connection with his appearance. Stanley wisely kept that quiet. Shortly after being ushered into the committee chamber with his lawyer on April 30th, 1962, Stanley stared down Senator Eastland and Chief Counsel Jay Sourwine.

Writing on the hearing in *The Atlantic*, journalist David Garrow claimed:

> Before the segregationist James O. Eastland's Senate Internal Security Subcommittee, Levison testified under oath, "I am a loyal American and I am not now and never have been a member of the Communist Party," but he invoked the Fifth Amendment in response to all questions about the CPUSA and its financial affairs.

The historical record can get blurry, however, and Garrow's account wasn't precise. At least, according to the FBI:

NY 100-129302

In 1962, STANLEY LEVISON appeared before the Senate
Internal Security Sub-Committee and refused to answer questions,
however, he did introduce an unsworn statement denying past CP
membership. The Bureau is requested to advise whether it is
able to have this released since it would have a damaging
effect on LEVISON, which in turn would become publicly
knowledgeable to MARTIN LUTHER KING and the civil rights
movement.

The key is that it was an *unsworn* statement. Technically,
Stanley had not lied to Congress *under oath*.

Someone as practiced as Kunstler wouldn't have made such
an unforced error and would have had Stanley plead the Fifth
on *every* question. Stanley also had his law degree, so it's not
the kind of thing that would slip through. This was important
because, while it may be a commonplace occurrence,[31] lying to
Congress is nevertheless a crime, one that carries stiff penalties if those in power decide to prosecute.

Something Garrow got right, in any event, was this:

> *To Levison's surprise, King's name was never raised
> at the committee session.*

Sometimes prayers do get answered. Martin Luther King,
Jr's. name, in fact, did not come up during Eastland's hearing.

But a year later, we knew the highest levels of government
were somehow aware that Stanley had misled them. And
while it wasn't a crime, it did seem like great ammunition to
deploy against Martin.

After the Rose Garden meeting, Martin flew back to New York.
He didn't want to discuss the Levison/O'Dell matter over the
phone. He met with me alone, which was rare; when he came
to Stanley Levison's hometown, Stanley was almost always
by his side. I soon understood this exception. These threats

---

31   For example, Brent Kavanaugh's recent Supreme Court confirmation
hearing was riddled with transparent lies and obvious dodges, and in a less
polarized political landscape he would've been held accountable. Instead, he's
now one of the most powerful people on earth.

disguised as warnings from the White House were troubling. He told me about his conversation with the President.

"You've known Stanley longer than I have," I reminded him. "He told me that he and his brother had been members of the Communist Party early on, before he met you. And I was under the impression that he also told you that, too."

Martin confirmed this was true, but the question now was whether he had secretly resumed his Party membership.

"Do you think he *rejoined* the Party?" Martin asked.

I replied that nothing I had seen, heard, or spoken with Stanley about provided any evidence or suggestion of that.

Nevertheless, to satisfy the President, Martin wanted me to revisit the issue. "I want you to serve as a kind of one-man 'independent investigative panel,'" Martin requested. "Find out as much as you can about Stanley and Jack through friends and associates and meet with the two of them separately." He let me know about a scheduled SCLC retreat in Asheville, North Carolina, less than a month away. He wanted a report ready for the SCLC Board then.

I said that was fine, I'd do my best.

"Exercise your independent judgment," he told me.

In late June of 1963, as Stanley was planning his annual visit to Ecuador to check up on a coin-operated laundromat he owned there, I met with him one-on-one, as Martin requested.

We met in a restaurant near his apartment. It may have even been the same restaurant where he had told me about leaving the Communist Party in the fifties.

Stanley and I were close friends, and I needed to be straightforward with him. I told him about Martin's walk with the President in the Rose Garden and the question Martin had posed about Stanley afterwards.

"Have you rejoined the Communist Party?" I asked.

Stanley claimed he didn't have time. "You come to meet me at my office, my home; sometimes on the weekends I would come and visit you in Riverdale to talk about Martin and the SCLC. Aside from my employees, my family, and you, the only other persons I occasionally see are my brother and our business partner."

Of course, the President had said Stanley and Roy funded the Party, which didn't really require a lot of face time. I actually didn't know if Stanley was an active Party member or not, but I did know that his sympathies for the masses were in line with some of the better aspects of communist ideology. Once, in response to Martin's repetitive attempts to pay Stanley for everything he did for the cause—all refused—Stanley sent a written reply:

> *My skills were acquired not only in a cloistered academic environment, but also in the commercial jungle ... Although our culture approves, and even honors these practices, to me they were always abhorrent. Hence, I looked forward to the time when I could use these skills not for myself but for socially constructive ends. The liberation struggle is the most positive and rewarding area of work anyone could experience.*

Those aren't the words of a foreign agent, but they are the words of someone who wants to change the status quo of his own country. That might be threatening enough.

Stanley ran down his entire communist résumé for me: Shortly after graduating from St. John's Law School in New York, Stanley and Roy joined the Party. Like many young idealists of their generation, they were attracted to the progressive Party ideas, like seeking to eliminate segregation, racism, and worldwide colonialism. During their time in the Party, they became a source of funding for several of its domestic political initiatives.

Stanley reiterated that he had become disillusioned in 1956 after the Soviet invasion of Hungary and that he gave up on the Party after the revelations by Khrushchev about Stalin's anti-Semitic repression and execution of several Party leaders. Stanley said that when he and his brother left the Party, they'd severed all organizational and personal ties with those who remained active. He never looked back.

This left the nagging question: Where did the Kennedys' intelligence about Stanley's loyalties come from? It was a riddle for which I'd have to wait patiently before I'd learn the answer.

In North Carolina, I reported to the SCLC Executive Committee on my conversations with Stanley. The March on Washington was coming up fast, and all assembled felt Stanley would be very helpful there. The question we wrestled with was whether his presence around Martin would provide Hoover and the FBI with a basis to attack and discredit the March as "commie led" or "influenced."

We jointly decided to terminate all direct contacts between Martin and Stanley. Martin initially objected to this course of action, principally because of his great respect and affection for Stanley and because he knew that Stanley's "disassociation" would deprive us of an invaluable asset. In addition, he bristled at the idea of the government essentially telling us whom *they* regarded as "acceptable" for Martin's organization. That was downright un-American.

I strongly agreed with Martin's reasoning, but I also knew that in the end we needed to deprive Hoover of a clear opportunity to discredit us.

Stanley didn't make any fuss. In fact, he insisted that Martin immediately cease all direct contact with him. Martin was loyal, and I'm sure he would've stood by him if Stanley had pushed back, but Stanley was smart enough to see the big picture.

It wasn't a personal decision. Stanley's position was simple: Martin, his leadership, and the Movement were too important to have potential support from the Kennedy Administration compromised or undermined because of their relationship. That's what made him great. Stanley Levison always thought about the greater good. That was rare, even in the seemingly selfless world of the Civil Rights Movement. He was at the forefront of those many unsung heroes of our cause.

STRADDLING TWO WORLDS   193

We made a plan to best protect Martin and maintain his credibility with President Kennedy: If either he or Stanley needed to get a message to the other, I would act as the middleman, conveying the information without ever mentioning Stanley's name. And that's how it would go for the rest of Martin's life. In the meantime, Stanley wanted me to be sure that I spoke to Martin directly to tell him that Martin's leadership and the Movement was far more important than their friendship. While Stanley promised he would continue to work in support of SCLC, he insisted that I make Martin understand any public acknowledgment of their friendship would be a major mistake. In Stanley's estimation, Martin was going to shoot himself in the foot, and he didn't want to be the reason. Stanley insisted that I advise Martin to contact the Attorney General and tell him and President Kennedy that he had followed their advice and had severed all direct contact, public and private, with him.

I watched the man fall on his sword...

President Kennedy had said his underlying concern about Levison and O'Dell was that Martin's relationship with them would provide ammunition for conservative Southern Democrats and Senator Everett McKinley Dirksen, (R—Illinois), the conservative leader of the opposition to the President's proposed Civil Rights Bill. Therefore, Martin and Stanley felt that it was important that I personally go to the Justice Department and meet with Robert Kennedy and Burke Marshall to advise them that Martin was executing President Kennedy's recommendations.

I've never had a disproportionate respect for institutional authority. I always knew the "authority figure" men in government or private enterprise still put their trousers on one leg at a time. I was ornery when I went to the Justice Department, and I couldn't let the meeting pass without getting some kind of dig in. In his book *Bobby and J. Edgar*, Burton Hersh wrote of my attitude and the response it garnered:

> *Robert Kennedy's determination to hound King and his cronies (about Levison and O'Dell) continued to shadow his judgment. When Clarence Jones dropped*

*by the Justice Department to alert Burke Marshall that
Dr. King was not prepared to get along totally without
Stanley Levison's good office, but intended to stay in
touch with Levison through Jones, and would be grat-
ified were the leadership of the Civil Rights Division to
let him know which telephones around the SCLC circuit
might not be tapped, Robert Kennedy blew up. Already
under pressure from Hoover over the Ellen Rometsch
incident (a German woman, suspected of being an East
German spy, with whom President Kennedy had had a
sexual liaison as a senator), the whole idea that Jones
seemed to be leaning on him to collaborate with this
perverse preacher to deceive the FBI was so infuriat-
ing to Kennedy that on that same day Kennedy passed
word to the FBI that he had decided to augment the
Levison surveillance with wiretaps on Clarence Jones
and Martin Luther King.*

Ah, well. You win some, you lose some. It still felt good to say.

To tie the whole mess in a bow, I turned my attention to Jack
O'Dell. I first met Jack in Los Angeles in 1960, where he
worked for SCLC's West Coast office. He was a former union
organizer, and he knew a thing or two about mob mentality.
I learned a lot from Jack and had deep respect for him. Jack,
though, was not nearly as close to Martin as Stanley. Though
quite skillful and as dedicated to our work as anyone, Jack
was simply not as *personally* valuable to Martin.

In the intervening weeks between Martin's conversation
with the President and this meeting, I'd managed to catch up
with Jack. He told me the truth: He had been a Communist
Party organizer in the National Maritime Union in New Orleans. He insisted to me that he had "severed" his ties with the
Party when he came to work for the SCLC, but it was too late.
He'd lied about a compromising political situation from his
past, and it had caught up with him.

The decision was made even easier by Jack himself, who,
when I discussed the issue with him directly, fought back
fiercely. When I told him it might be necessary for him to

STRADDLING TWO WORLDS 195

be formally off the payroll of the New York SCLC office, he invoked the ideas of oppressive governments and free politics and was correct in his political analysis of some of the possible consequences of, as he put it, "Caving in to Hoover."

But caving in might still be the smartest decision for us. We had to make a strategic judgment about the consequences to Martin's leadership and influence with the government should the relationship with Jack continue.

I met with Jack, Wyatt Walker (then Executive Director and SCLC Chief of Staff), and Martin in a hotel room in Manhattan. Had Jack been straight with Martin about the communist association, there's a chance that it would've textured his thinking on the issue. There was no denying the pangs of mistrust, understandable though they were in those "red-baiting" times. We told Jack he'd have to step down. He said that "Hoover could kiss my Black ass" and the Kennedys with their "dirty compromising hands in Civil Rights" should not dictate who a private Civil Rights organization could hire and fire.

"I agree with you in principle," I said, "but look at Stanley's position. He sees the bigger picture here, Jack. I think you should follow his example."

In the end, we let him go. I don't believe he ever forgave Martin or ever saw the political leverage we would lose if we did not sever our organizational ties with him.

Martin fired Jack and sent Attorney General Kennedy a copy of Jack's notice of termination to forward on to his brother. The Kennedys had won at least a partial victory in their attempt to put a controlling hand on the Movement's throttle.

But there were other players in the picture.

CHAPTER 16 | THIS MEANS WAR

To repurpose Dr. King's words to me, it was clear to him that there were Negro leaders who were "wintertime soldiers" and, and there were those who, in terms of what would have been in the best interests the Negro community at the time, could be considered merely "summertime soldiers."

My beloved friend was a member of the exclusive Negro men's fraternity Alpha Phi Alpha, and had a doctorate degree, but he was not an "establishment" Negro leader. He didn't go along to get along. In hindsight, the leaders of many other Civil Rights groups seemed to be establishment-oriented Negroes trying to cozy up to the Kennedy and Johnson administrations. Leaders of the National Urban League and other such groups were given government appointments. They served on the boards of foundations and universities, and in a few cases, on the boards of corporations.

By contrast, despite the generational and lifestyle divide between the student-aged members of SNCC and Martin, whom they sometimes derisively called "Da Lawd," they never questioned the integrity of his commitment to the struggle against injustice or the courage of his leadership.

Nothing better illustrates the chasm that developed between Martin and the establishment Negro leadership than the debate over the Vietnam War. That there were differences of opinion is not surprising. Martin's advisors were divided over how he should approach the war. But Martin did not believe Johnson's support of Civil Rights gave the President immunity from criticism about his escalation of the war in Vietnam. Accordingly, when Martin was publicly critical of the President's conduct of the war, Johnson would use establishment "Negro Leaders" to publicly attack him as being "misguided" and outside of his competence as a Civil Rights leader, and that he was "hurting the Civil Rights Movement."

The cascade of criticism he received after his statements on the war was a reminder of what Martin said to me about the Johnson Administration and establishment Negro leadership trying to isolate Martin and cut him off from his base of support.

In addition to the "traditional" war, Martin was becoming especially disillusioned with Johnson's so-called War on Poverty. Though Johnson's White House worked to pass Medicaid and created food stamps, overall our impression was that the poor continued to suffer in the same manner they had for a century, even under LBJ.

Throughout the mid-sixties, the war in Vietnam continued to divide the country.

Muhammad Ali, recently converted to the Muslim faith, was stripped of his boxing championship for refusing, on religious grounds, to report for induction into the U.S. Army. "I ain't got no quarrel with them Viet Cong," he famously told the press in February of '66. Ali may have also said, "No Viet Cong ever called me a nigger," but the historical record on this is a little hazy.

President Johnson increased the troop presence there to nearly a half million of our young men in 1967. In his book *1968, The Year that Rocked the World*, Mark Kurlansky wrote about American demographics, citing:

> *Only 11 percent of the population was black while 23 percent of the combat soldiers in Vietnam were.*

He was right on that statistic, although when it came to the Black casualties, he—and every writer—would underreport the totals... because the government lied to them.

Martin had been contacted by a Negro at the Pentagon, Brigadier General Walters,[32] who wanted to share some information about racial and ethnic demographics of those killed and wounded in Vietnam. Walters asked Martin to send one

---

32 Not his real name, which I will keep to myself to honor the promises I made both to him and Martin. It is the man's real rank, however.

of his most "trusted advisors" to meet with him and discuss the statistics in person, and I was chosen for the job.

This was the second time I'd ever visited the Pentagon— the first, of course, being during my Army discharge review appeal. When I entered the general's office, he turned on the radio which played some jazz in the background; he then handed me a yellow legal pad. We spoke pleasantries, but he'd written on that pad that what he was going to show me and discuss was confidential and he did not want me to say anything in the office about what he was going to share with me. Clearly, he was concerned about the office being bugged. So, we spoke about the weather, my trip from New York, my earlier military service, and family while he quietly brought files to the table and indicated for me to read what he presented to me.

His papers made clear that the public racial and demographic information on the casualties in Vietnam was wrong. Through the first quarter of 1967, the percentages of those killed and wounded ranged from 25-35%. Many of the Negro casualties came from states in the South and cities like Detroit, Newark, Chicago, LA, Philadelphia, Oakland, and Boston.

He jotted a message: I could study the data carefully and take notes, but I could not take anything, even those notes, with me from his office. He was going to shred them the second I left. *Hope you have a good memory*, the last line read.

I did. After I left his office, I took a taxi to the nearest coffee shop, sat down in a booth, and wrote as quickly as I could as much as I could remember from the meeting. I called Martin on the pay phone and told him that I needed to see him in person immediately. I didn't want to discuss the general's meeting with Martin over the phone. I was in possession of information very few people had, and I'd been increasingly concerned about the possibility of others listening in.

When I provided the data on the racial mix of casualties to Martin, it underscored his determination to speak out against the war. However, even with this information in hand and his belief that his earlier receipt of the Nobel Peace Prize imposed a moral responsibility upon him, he had to consider whether it was still politically appropriate for him to publicly criticize President Johnson. After all, with his leadership and the enactments of the Civil Rights Bill of 1964 and the Voting Rights Act of 1965, this Texas tough guy was regarded as the greatest Civil Rights president since Abraham Lincoln. Therefore, was it smart for Dr. King, America's preeminent Civil Rights leader, to publicly criticize Johnson's conduct of the war?

Martin had been invited to be the keynote speaker at an event hosted by the Committee of Concerned Laymen and Clergy at the Riverside Church in Manhattan set for on April 4th, 1967. Beforehand, he convened a special meeting of his team of advisers to discuss the pros and cons of making the speech and its content. Martin's advisors all agreed that the war was bad for the country. But there was a divide between those who questioned the wisdom of Martin attacking LBJ and those who thought that, regardless of the President's track record, Martin had moral duty to oppose the violence and killing going on in the name of America.

Something was nagging in the back of my mind. I remembered from law school something about a federal statute prohibiting citizens from interfering directly or indirectly in the conduct of U.S. foreign policy. What was it? That's right... the Logan Act. I described it briefly to those gathered.

The question: Was Martin putting himself at risk, giving the government an excuse for another trumped-up indictment like the tax evasion charge that had brought the two of us together? Fiery debate commenced. The entire meeting was a risk vs. reward analysis. But it was clear that Martin was leaning towards speaking against the war, with morality pulling ahead of politics or pragmatism, as it always did with him.

He asked me to propose some remarks for him, and within a couple days I had a draft. My version had some equivocation—*on the one hand, but on the other hand* stuff. I would set up a fact about the conflict, following up with a criticism from one side and then a way of looking at the same fact from more of a war-supporter standpoint. My reasoning was driven by my function in the SCLC to consider the ramifications of each move as it related to our task of building a broad base of support for Dr. King's work. I had one eye on the Logan Act as well.

What I had missed, missed by a mile, were the deep moral roots which had always guided Martin's actions. I failed to see the forest for the trees, and my friend was the first to point this out.

His major speech opposing the war in Vietnam would become forever known as "Breaking the Silence." I find this one of its more compelling points:

> As I have walked among the desperate, rejected, and angry young men, I've told them that Molotov cocktails and rifles would not solve their problems. I've tried to offer them my deepest compassion while maintaining my conviction that social change comes most meaningfully through nonviolent action. But they ask—and rightly so—what about Vietnam? They ask if our own nation wasn't using massive doses of violence to solve its problems, to bring about the changes it wanted.
>
> Their questions hit home, and I knew I could never again raise my voice against the violence of the oppressed in the ghettos without having first spoken clearly to the greatest purveyor of violence in the world today: my own government.

Damning words indeed. And the Johnson Administration didn't like hearing any of them.

What became most personally hurtful to Martin following his public criticism of the United States' involvement in the Vietnam War was that shortly thereafter, fellow members of the Alphas who had also become ministers, and, in several cases, were pastors of churches with substantial membership, began to disinvite Martin to speak at their churches.

I know in my heart that it was this speaking out against the war, coupled with Martin's continued push against poverty regardless of skin color (The Poor People's Campaign) that really scared the government to the core. At the end of the day, these were the issues—and not equality for Negroes—that got

STRADDLING TWO WORLDS   201

Martin killed. If he'd just stayed on the Black cause, the governmental forces opposing him probably would have just let him go and hope the spotlight would eventually move away from him. But that wasn't how Martin Luther King, Jr., worked.

If that strikes you as an unhinged conspiracy theory, just read on.

Uncovering the lengths to which our own government will go to control the thinking of the masses is a full-time job. A position I'd argue is currently unfilled. It used to be the job of investigative reporters like Carl Bernstein and Bob Woodward, back when major metropolitan newspapers were, for the most part, rock-solid pillars of objective reality. These days, of course, the news business is an entirely different landscape.

In my life, I've been far too busy to focus my time on the kind of digging and legwork one would have to undertake for an investigation into the misdeeds of the FBI. But I know a lot about it anyway, because the government gave me a gift one day. Until you've been handed boxes of documents where transcripts of your private phone calls have been pawed over by government agents, you are living under a myth about American freedom. I no longer have the luxury of being in the dark on such matters.

On the memo line of the hundreds and hundreds of FBI documents about my time working with Martin King, two lines appear over and over:

Communist Infiltration In Racial Matters and
The Negro Question

This really does shine a spotlight on the fact that racism is a tacit government policy. It's not a bug, it's a *feature*. You don't need to take my word that the FBI was on the warpath to discredit Martin Luther King, Jr. You can see it on the memo line of half the reports in my voluminous FBI file.

It was also more generally illuminated in the 1976 U.S. Senate Report on Government Intelligence Operations, the report from the so-called Church Committee. In reviewing the documents in the FBI files, the Committee noted:

Many of the techniques used would be intolerable in a democratic society even if all of the targets had been involved in violent activity, but COINTELPRO went far beyond that....The Bureau conducted a sophisticated vigilante operation aimed squarely at preventing the exercise of First Amendment rights of speech and association, on the theory that preventing the growth of dangerous groups and the propagation of dangerous ideas would protect the national security and deter violence.

It's a matter of public record. I'll say it again:

Not a bug.

A fucking feature.

It's no coincidence that the so-called Negro Question[33] and Communist paranoia were locked hand-in-hand. William T. Sullivan, Hoover's Assistant Director for Domestic Intelligence, wrote a memo to his boss on August 30th, 1963, two days after the March on Washington. It's worth reading in the actual memo format:

> I do think that much of the difficulty relating to the memoranr dum rightly questioned by the Director is to be found centered in the word "influence." We do not have, and no Government agency or private organization has, any yardstick which can accurately measure "influence" in this particular context, even when we know it does exist such as in the case of the obvious influence of
> over Martin Luther King and King's influence over other Negro leaders. Personally, I believe in the light of King's powerful demagogic speech yesterday he stands head and shoulders over all other Negro leaders put together when it comes to influencing great masses of Negroes. We must mark him now, if we have not done so before, as the most dangerous Negro of the future in this Nation from the standpoint of communism, the Negro and national security.

Notice that he suggests Dr. King is the most dangerous Black man for the future of America from a standpoint of communism first. Sullivan went on to write that the FBI must concern itself

---

33 The Negro Question could most accurately be summarized the way I tried to make clear at the induction center in '55: "All these American citizens are upset because they don't have the same rights as the other citizens. The question is: How can we get them to shut up without changing anything?"

with "the many Negroes who are fellow travelers, sympathizers or who aid the Party, knowingly or unknowingly."

The point is that communism at that time was the boogeyman, and anything that could be tied to it was given the draconian mark of needing to be dealt with by any means necessary. Including means that were extralegal.

The Bay of Pigs mission was wholly illegal, but it was a government operation. Stopping Martin Luther King, the man who wouldn't stop asking those irritating "Negro Questions," was deemed as threatening to the safety of the United States as Fidel Castro.

Inasmuch as the organizations we entrust to protect us let us down frequently, they rarely do the exact opposite. Sadly, in the case of race relations in America, that is exactly what the government—and specifically law enforcement—have done.

While I have no doubt that James Earl Ray pulled the trigger on the gun that killed my friend, I know that the entire system enabled the killer, and I place the blame for Martin's death squarely on them. The system was at fault.

Regrettably, with few exceptions, this is the same system, the same moral near-sightedness, that has continued to dominate the actions (or inactions) of America's media, corporate, and political elite during the last seventy years. Social and political pressures and efforts for women's equality, environmental protections, gay and lesbian rights, and ending gun violence have all suffered setbacks. We're not interested in right, we're interested in safe, convenient, familiar, and, if you're at the top of the social and economic order, keeping change at arm's length.

Perhaps a better question for the FBI to ask would've been: What kind of Negro was Dr. King? It isn't a one-size fits all situation; there are all different types of Black people, and so long as you're tapping his phone and following him around it only makes sense to try to understand your opponent. Hoover never did, though. He wasn't that smart.

Just as Martin's description of how my family background during his California sermon had shaped my beliefs, his own family also played a foundational role in the development of his role as a Civil Rights leader. Martin was preceded by three generations of Baptist preachers. I could clearly see that this grounding in ministry, combined with his formal theological education, provided both the religious and intellectual base of his approach to Civil Rights. This grounding was further shaped by the experiences he gained early, with the Montgomery Bus Boycott and his subsequent organization of the Southern Christian Leadership Conference.

He entered the ministry during the summer of 1947. More than ten years later he wrote about the decision:

> *My call to the ministry was neither dramatic nor spectacular. It came neither by some miraculous vision nor by some blinding light of experience on the road to life. Moreover, it did not come as a sudden realization. Rather it was a response to an inner urge that gradually came upon me. This urge expressed itself in a desire to serve God and humanity, and the feeling that my talent and my commitment could be expressed through the ministry. During my senior year in college...I came to see that God had placed a responsibility on my shoulders...*

After graduation from Morehouse College in Atlanta, he enrolled in Crozier Seminary in Pennsylvania. During his years at Morehouse, his mentors were Benjamin E. Mays, the college president, and his religion professor, George D. Kelsey. His subsequent graduation from Boston University's School of Theology with a PhD would provide him with additional academic experience and credentials that would help cement his stature within the African American community.

Although he was the founder and president of the SCLC, it was evident that Martin was not the most experienced preacher among its members. However, the man had the clearest vision for the movement. Regrettably, I can now better see in hindsight that Martin's transformational leadership was not enough to shield him from some of the petty rivalries and ego-driven jealousies he frequently encountered.

James Baldwin was an astute observer. He described Martin in a February 1961 *Harper's Magazine* article, saying:

> *He is the first Negro leader in my experience, or the first in many generations, who says to Negroes the same thing he says to whites and what he says to whites, he will say to Negroes...most of his predecessors were in the extraordinary position of saying to white men, hurry, while saying to black men, wait. Martin Luther King, Jr., by the power of his personality and force of his beliefs, injected a new dimension into our ferocious struggle. He has succeeded, in a way no Negro before him has managed to do, to carry the battle into the individual heart and make its resolution the providence of the individual will. He has made it a matter, on both sides of the racial fence, of self-examination; and has incurred, therefore, the grave responsibility to continuing to lead in the path that he has encouraged so many people to follow.*

Baldwin's description of Martin in 1961 was like a still frame in a film of the man: Frozen at that point in time. Baldwin's article ran after the Montgomery Bus Boycott and his acquittal in the Alabama criminal case for perjury and tax evasion. But it came before the subpoena in 1963 to appear before the conscience of America in the court of public morality: Before Birmingham, the March on Washington, Selma, and the Voting Rights Act, The Poor Peoples Campaign, and Martin's role in the debate over the war in Vietnam.

Like so many others who were blessed to work closely with him, I came to view Martin as *the* moral commanding general of an army of non-violent soldiers. The signature feature that defined his leadership was that he never asked others to undertake any endeavor that he himself was not prepared to personally lead. His willingness to subject himself to the risks associated with what he believed to be unjust is what endeared Martin to the masses of the Negro community and earned him the respect of a cross-section of leaders from all walks of life. And, of course, he influenced a large number of white Americans. Although they may not have agreed with everything he said or did, he was widely admired for the integrity of his leadership and his courageous and brilliant efforts to shine a spotlight on the evil of racism.

In a 1965 speech in Montgomery, Martin said:

Another thing that we must do in speeding up the coming of the new age is to develop intelligent, courageous, and dedicated leadership. This is one of the pressing needs of the hour. In this period of transition and growing social change, there is as dire need for leaders who are calm and yet positive, leaders who avoid the extremes of "hot-headedness" and "Uncle Tomism." The urgency of the hour calls for leaders of wise judgment and sound integrity—leaders not in love with money, but in love with justice; leaders not in love with publicity, but in love with humanity; leaders who can subject their particular egos to the greatness of the cause.

I was mindful of how successful the government had been in isolating Paul Robeson years earlier. They revoked his passport so that he couldn't travel abroad to speak, sing, make a living really. Martin and I discussed Robeson, and we were determined that neither President Johnson nor his surrogates among the Negro establishment would isolate or alienate Martin from his base of support within the Civil Rights Movement and the country at large.

But the threats to Martin's leadership were not only coming from the top. Negro and white political figures would try to use him for their own political benefit. One instance: In the summer of 1964 New York City Mayor Robert Wagner was under considerable pressure to establish a Civilian Police Review Board following several high-profile instances of police brutality against members of the Negro community. The NYPD and the Catholic Archdiocese were opposed to the creation of such a board. But since much of Wagner's electoral support had come from the Black community, the mayor was between a rock and hard place. Wagner sought to do an end-run around local leaders by inviting Martin, unofficially, as an outside voice, to mediate.

When Martin called me for advice on July 25th, I replied, according to the FBI wiretap: "There is a very—well let's put it this way—there is an almost total absence of confidence on the part of broadest cross-section of people in Harlem and Bedford-Stuyvesant in the police department. The mayor is being stupid, because to have an independent civilian review board is not a big concession. It's just to let a significant section of the population have greater confidence that their complaints will be heard."

Within few days, Martin had grown very concerned about riots that had occurred in Rochester, far upstate, and he told me, "While I am organizationally linked to the South, so many people in other sections look to me for national leadership," he said. He then called Bayard Rustin. Again captured on FBI wiretaps, Bayard, who had little interest in a review board, advised Martin not to meet with Wagner unless it was an on-the-record discussion which Martin could report publicly afterward. He suggested that Martin urge Mayor Wagner to move vigorously to address the underlying issues of jobs, housing, and schools. "Nothing short of that could do anything but spoil your image," Rustin told Martin.

Still, the next day Rustin and other Negro leaders publicly criticized Martin for meeting with Wagner, although Rustin, in a private telephone conversation to an unknown party, said Martin "acted properly."

Rustin and the Negro leadership clearly were attempting to use Martin's prestige to get Mayor Wagner to agree to their demands. Martin later commented more broadly on the tensions between African American leaders and police departments across the country:

> *Whether it is true or not, the Negro of the ghetto is convinced that his dealings with the police deny him the dignity and respect to which he is entitled as a citi-*

zen and a human being. This produces a sullen, hostile attitude that results in a spiral of hatred on the part of both the officer and the Negro. This whole reaction complex is often coupled with fear on the part of both parties and every encounter between a Negro and the police in the hovering hostility of the ghetto is a potential outburst, where either party may initiate an action which sets in motion the whole sordid, steaming cauldron of psychic and social forces. This is the reason that Negro leaders have so often centered their grievances in a civilian police review board and in increased human relations training for the entire police force.

Eventually, Mayor Wagner listened to Martin's wise counsel. We orchestrated a political scenario that enabled the mayor to retain the support of the police leadership, the Catholic Church and the Negro community. The result was the creation of an independent civilian police review board to look into instances of alleged police brutality. The new review board required police officers to inform people they are asserting their constitutional rights to legal counsel and not answer questions without counsel present, years before the Supreme Court enshrined that as a constitutional right.

This experience of being manipulated by Black leaders, and the attitudes of most establishment Black organization heads towards Martin's criticism of Johnson's approach to the war, was reflected in Martin's 1967 book, *Where Do We Go From Here? Chaos or Community,* which touches on code-switching and moves to more insidious areas:

> *Negroes are capable of becoming competitive, carping and, in an expression of self-hate, suspicious and intolerant of each other. A glaring weakness in Negro life is a lack of sufficient mutual confidence and trust...*
>
> *Negro leaders suffer from this interplay of solidarity and divisiveness, being either exalted excessively or grossly abused. Some of these leaders suffer from an aloofness and absence of faith in their people. The white establishment is skilled at flattering and cultivating*

emerging leaders. It presses its own image on them and finally from imitation of manners, dress and style of living, a deeper strain of corruption develops. This kind of Negro leader acquires the white man's contempt for the ordinary Negro. He is often more at home with the middle-class white than he is among his own people. His language changes, his location changes, his income changes, and he changes from the representative of the Negro to the white man into the white man's representative to the Negro. The tragedy is that too often he does not recognize what has happened to him.

Our other alliances were no less complicated. The Civil Rights Movement had close philosophical ties to organized labor, which was still a political force to be reckoned with in the 1960s. The SCLC was a clergy-based organization operating in anti-union states of the South, so union support was critical. The "godfather" of African American labor union leadership, A. Philip Randolph, was President of the Brotherhood of Sleeping Car Porters, representing railroad personnel throughout the United States. Randolph, with his imposing physical stature, deep ideology, and resonant baritone voice, had a great influence on Martin.

Randolph told Martin and others that "Negroes have no permanent friends or permanent enemies, only permanent interests. Your friend today may become our enemy tomorrow. The only thing we should be concerned about is our permanent interests."

Randolph held a life-long belief in the importance of organized political action. This was the touchstone of his advice to Dr. King. I would remind Martin that this was reminiscent of the political belief of the abolitionist Frederick Douglass, who in 1848, said, "Power concedes nothing without a demand; it never has and never will."

It was against this political background that Martin courted the support and participation of labor unions. The "big three" were the Hospital Workers Local 1099 in New York, the United Packinghouse Workers out of Chicago, and Dis-

STRADDLING TWO WORLDS   211

trict 65 Retail Wholesale Workers Union. Leon Foner of 1099, Cleveland Robinson and David Livingston of District 65, and Ralph Helstein of the Packinghouse Workers, together with Randolph, were, in Martin's mind, his labor family. We felt we could share with these leaders our most intimate organizational and financial details as well as seek their guidance.

This is not to say that support from other labor unions was unimportant. It was. The work of Walter Reuther and William Lucy from the automobile workers in Detroit, Al Shankar from the United Federation of Teachers, and Victor Gotbaum from District Council 37 Municipal Workers, to name just a few, was invaluable.

Of course, communism has deep roots in workers' causes and unions were in some ways as threatening to the powers that be as the existential "red menace" of Communist Party membership. The two went hand-in-hand.

Another problem was the Mob. We frequently talked about the importance of gaining the support from the International Brotherhood of Teamsters. At the time, the Teamsters were the largest labor union in the United States and perhaps more importantly, it had more Negro members than the NAACP. But there were frequent allegations of corruption against the Teamsters, and their leader, Jimmy Hoffa, had an ongoing feud with Attorney General Robert Kennedy around Hoffa's alleged association with organized crime.

The Mafia had a way of creating problems even for people who didn't have any dealings with them.

Well, that was true about Martin, not so much with me. I'd had my direct run-ins with Cosa Nostra...

During my New York law practice throughout the '60s, I did not regularly see other Negro lawyers in the federal court- house. This was in sharp contrast to the District Courts in the states of Alabama, Georgia, Mississippi, Louisiana; in those states, Negro lawyers were frequently in federal court, almost exclusively involved in Civil Rights matters. Up north, segre- gation wasn't really the problem. Crime was.

One of the earliest cases I remember distinctly in New York federal court involved a Black narcotics dealer. The mother of the young man came into our firm and asked me to repre- sent her son. He had been arrested and was being held on a number of counts in connection with his alleged drug dealing, with the most serious accusing him of distributing and selling cocaine.

This young man was about nineteen. He'd attended an elite academic New York City public high school. When I first went in to meet with him, I told him that the government didn't appear to have a slam-dunk case. On the other hand, I could not assure him that if he went to trial he would be acquitted. There was always a risk that he could be convicted and face a stiffer punishment than if he agreed to a plea bargain.

He told me that he'd heard that our law firm was top notch but insisted he didn't want to go to trial. He said he appreci- ated all the efforts his mother was making to assist him, but he only wanted me as his lawyer if I agreed to represent him to negotiate the best plea deal I could without a trial.

"How much do you make a year as a lawyer?" he asked

I told him it fluctuated, depending upon the cases we had.

"A hundred thousand? Two?"

"We're managing to get along," I said. Ours was a young law firm, and we weren't quite yet making that amount of take-home money for each partner.

The kid said, "Mr. Jones, I made over one million dollars last year."

"But you're behind bars right now. I can go anywhere I please." I told him I wasn't there to discuss how much money he made with criminal behavior versus the straight and narrow path, but to discuss a defense strategy to pursue based upon our analysis of the case against him.

He listened thoughtfully. Our conversation was free flowing. He told me his life of crime started when he was a high school student and acted as a "numbers runner" for the Mob.

I knew what he was talking about. The "numbers" was, quite simply, an illegal (i.e., non-government) lottery. Players wagered on a random number event—at the time I believe it was the last three digits including to the right of the decimal point of the closing Dow Jones Average—and the winner or winners got a big chunk of the pot while the people who run the game kept the rest. Number runners were the salesmen and errand boys who took the bets and money and handed it all into the organizing "bank," so there was a record of who bet how much on what numbers. In New York at that time, for police to get a conviction on an arrest for running numbers, they needed evidence in the form of "policy slips;" paper receipts on which was written the amount of money and the number bet as well as the name and address of the bettor.

In this case, however, the young prisoner had been extremely valuable to his numbers banker because he never wrote anything down. He had the capacity to keep everything in his head. If he had collected bets from twenty people playing the numbers, he could retain the names, addresses, numbers, size of bets. If he was stopped on the street by New York's finest, he'd only be guilty of having a lot of cash, which is never a crime in America.

When he told me this, I thought, what a waste of talent... This young black man had a photographic memory, and the only option he could see was running numbers. Which of course led to dealing drugs. Which led to jail.

Numbers was the tip of the iceberg. Like anyone else who did business in New York in those years, I saw the Mob's fingerprints and footprints pretty much everywhere. In fact, I'd contend that you can't be my age, race, and profession in the second half of the twentieth century and not have had a personal, Mafia-centered story or two.

It would be like spending considerable time in Harlem and not having any stories about Sammy Davis, Jr. Just not possible.

Hell, sometimes you had both in the same story.

Sammy was a showman, a dancer, a member of Sinatra's famed Rat Pack, a consummate talk show guest. He was also a gambler, though probably not as good at that as he was at the other stuff he did.

It was the mid-sixties, and I was getting a trim at Sugar Ray's Golden Gloves Barber Shop in Harlem when the phone rang. A barber answered and brought the phone over to me.

"Harry's looking for you, Clarence," he told me.

Harry Belafonte, who also got his hair cut at Golden Gloves, knew to try tracking me down there on a Saturday. I took the call.

"Sammy needs help," Harry told me. He sounded uncharacteristically panicky.

"What's up?" I asked.

"He needs twenty-five grand by Monday or they're going to break his legs."

I didn't need to ask who. "That's a lot of money, Harry."

"He can't dance with broken legs," Harry said, not really trying to be funny about it. "I'm in for ten, I've got some feelers out for another ten. If you can stake him five, we should be okay."

I don't have that kind of money! I thought, but I stayed cool. "Let me get back to you."

Harry said, "Wait there. I'm coming to the barber shop."

I discussed the situation with my barber friends. The head man who ran the place for Sugar Ray told me, "Look, if I have to, I can cover you for five thousand, but I can't get it today." He told me I could use the place as a marker to borrow from a more nimble source.

I thought about who I knew who had real cash on hand. After a moment, I landed on Art D'Lugoff. He was the owner and empresario of The Village Gate, which was a thriving jazz and comedy nightclub in Greenwich Village. Art cared about performers and, just as importantly, ran an-all cash business that sold liquor. It wouldn't have surprised me if he had five thousand-dollar bills wedged under a table leg to keep it steady. I made the phone call.

When Harry got to the barbershop about fifteen minutes later, we jumped in a cab and headed a hundred and thirty blocks south. Harry held the taxi while I went to the door of the Village Gate. The place wasn't even open yet, but the money was waiting in a bag that the bouncer there was holding for me.

Back in the cab, we raced over to Sammy's place on Central Park West, just minutes ahead of the muscle who was out to collect.

Sammy made it safe and sound to his gig that night. And, eventually, everyone got paid back.

Sammy kept on dancing until his death in 1990, at 68. Way too young. But if there's a heaven, you *know* he's keeping them all entertained.

There was a judge in the Southern District of New York (the federal district that includes Manhattan) by the name of Irving Ben Cooper. He had a reputation of being tough on counsel and parties appearing before him. He was an equal-opportunity misanthrope, doling out for the prosecution and the defense alike. And he was a hanging judge. The rumor was, if you were found guilty in a Judge Cooper case, when you came before him for sentencing you should bring your toothbrush.

You were probably going to be sent away for the maximum... or close to it.

One day, I had an appearance before Judge Cooper. I don't remember the details of the case, but the Judge and I got into quite a verbal back and forth about the finer points of the rules of the criminal code and the issue of the bench's fairness to my defendant. I was polite and respectful, but very forceful and firm in my position. This type of professional argument had occurred between me and most of the other federal judges in the Southern District. I didn't think much of it on that day, but because of Cooper's strict reputation, other people noticed.

Not long afterward, as I returned to my office, one of my law partners pulled me aside in the reception area. Putting his finger up to bend his nose—the classic silent indicator of Mob connection—and told me that two well-dressed Italian men asked our receptionist if they could visit with me.

I said I didn't know the gentlemen, but if they wanted to speak with me, they could. I asked the partner to sit in on the initial meeting.

The two men—I don't feel I should identify them, but for the purposes of this story I'll refer to them as the Infante brothers—told me that they and some of their friends had observed me over a long period of time in federal court. They watched not only my appearance before Judge Cooper but also my interaction with other judges, including Winzer B. Wyatt, the judge who had provided a favorable ruling on protecting the copyright to Dr. King's "I Have a Dream" speech from infringement by the recording industry. The Infante brothers told me one of their companies had matters pending before the federal courts, and they anticipated an indictment. They asked if I might be interested in representing them.

I asked for details, and they went on to describe their various businesses activities. One of their more legitimate enterprises was as the owners/operators of Infante's Italian Restaurant on Desbrosses Street on the Lower West Side. I was familiar with it; it was one of the best Italian seafood places at the time, and one where wise guys were known to hang out after a long day of strongarming.

The brothers were also involved in commercial carting—the business of collecting trash and hauling it away for incineration. This, and not the seafood restaurant, was the purpose of the meeting. At the time, a young man from the Brownsville section of Brooklyn named Al Sharpton had been making a lot of noise about how carting companies shouldn't be allowed to come and pick up trash in Brooklyn unless they did it in partnership with a Black-owned company. In terms of racial equity it was an unfair business practice, Sharpton said, and he claimed that the citizens of the neighborhood weren't going to put up with it any longer. These white people couldn't just continue to come into Brooklyn and have it be business as usual.

The Infante brothers' reaction to this demand was less than enthusiastic. Unsaid in the clamor was the salient fact that Sharpton had formed a carting business of his own and was trying to carve out territory. The Infantes felt that they were being bullied and put on notice in the public eye. Mobsters believed that men settled their differences quietly.

"Al Sharpton is just using the only leverage he's got," I told them. He was using the press as a weapon because it was the only weapon within his reach.

They interpreted Sharpton as using a public bully pulpit to take a bite out of the carting business that had been theirs for years as theft. They saw no reason to have to do a joint venture with a new Black-owned carting company. Merely being Black did not make Sharpton and his partners "entitled parties" for doing business in Brooklyn.

"Mr. Jones?" the older Infante asked. "Can you talk some sense into him?"

It was an offer, as they say, I couldn't refuse.

But I told them it was better business to work with Sharpton. "I know it doesn't feel right to have to split profits with some upstart when you had them all to yourself yesterday," I said. "But there is such a thing as having the right public face on an issue, the right social stance. They are bringing something to the table." The brothers considered my perspective and said it made a kind of sense.

I was able to broker "a sit-down" later that week between the managers of the carting company and Sharpton, along with a couple of his colleagues. Before we started, I pulled Sharpton aside and told him that while I wasn't certain I could be helpful, the Infante brothers believed that I could be. "They said they didn't want to have any discussions with you without my being present, so if I walk, the meeting's over."

Sharpton asked what would keep me from walking?

I said, "A straight-up deal." I told him I agreed with his outlook on the situation in Brooklyn and, even if he was doing it for selfish reasons, the logic held. I agreed to try to persuade the Infante brothers to do a joint venture in carting work, but it had to be on the level—no bullshit, runarounds, scheming, stealing, skimming, or any games at all. Because the Infantes were serious people.

Sharpton told me *he* was serious, too. Time would prove just how serious Al Sharpton was. But I'd said it with a slightly different meaning—seriously dangerous.

"Aside from that, Al, my word is my reputation. If I say this is going to work, it's gotta work."

As a result of that a discussion, a joint venture accommodation was created to enable a Black-owned company to work the commercial carting route along with the Infante brothers in Brooklyn. I am proud to have played a role in the Mafia negotiating this accommodation with Sharpton.

Can I say that Al Sharpton is currently alive as a result? Not necessarily, but if the following Copacabana story offers a glimpse into what the Mob considers "minor infractions," imagine how they'd react to someone trying to steal their very profitable garbage route?

Over time I represented the Infantes in a handful of matters, and they eventually introduced me to Johnny Giovanone[34] who

---

34 Also not his real name.

was higher up the ladder and in need of some legal advice. Mr. Giovanone was alleged to "control" the workers in the retail, hotel, and restaurant industry unions as well as in some various independent manufacturing plants that made low-end trinkets and jewelry and some high-end leather goods and clothing.

One rainy evening, I was advised that there was going to be a celebration dinner honoring Giovanone's birthday at Infante's restaurant and that I had been invited. (My Mafia friends loved ending their days there.) I attended the birthday party, but hadn't been told that part of the evening's celebration also involved going to the Copacabana to see Sammy Davis, Jr.

The nightclub was in Midtown East, nowhere near Infante's. I loved Sammy, but Anne was expecting me home after dinner. The moved to the Copa came as a surprise to me, so I said to Mr. Giovanone and his associates that, regretfully, my wife was expecting me home and she would not be happy if I did not arrive as anticipated. He insisted that I call home from a phone booth at the restaurant.

So, I phoned Anne. Mr. Giovanone asked if he could speak to her. He explained how much he respected the work that I had done for him, how much he valued our friendship. That I did not know in advance of this planned celebration of his birthday at the Copacabana. So... would she *please,* in this *one* instance, permit me to join him at the Copa to celebrate his birthday?

Mr. Giovanone hung up the phone. "She wants you to have a good time, Clarence!" he told me. I doubted she'd said that, but it seemed she was okay with the plan. I was told that when I got to the Copa I should go in and ask for Carmine, who was the maître-d'.

It was still raining as I parked in the open lot and walked towards the nightclub. There was a long line of people stretching along East 60th Street rounding the block at Madison Avenue. As usual, Sammy Davis, Jr. was drawing a big crowd.

Per Mr. Giovanone's instructions, instead of getting in line I walked to the front doors of the restaurant. In the foyer, I shook off my raincoat and asked to speak to Carmine. The maître-d' identified himself and said he'd indeed been alerted that I'd be coming.

Carmine asked me to follow him to the coat check and took the raincoat off my hands. There was another long line for the coatroom, but Carmine took me directly to the coat check girl.

As he handed me my receipt and started leading me into the club, we heard someone shout: "Who does that nigger think he is that he can just jump to the head of the line?"

I ignored it, but Carmine was visibly embarrassed. His face turned red, and he ushered me quickly to my seat at Johnny Giovanone's table, which was front and center, directly by the stage.

Two of Mr. Giovanone's associates were there, but we were waiting for the man of the hour to arrive. Suddenly, I heard a bloodcurdling scream and an accompanying clattering ruckus coming from behind the swinging saloon doors that led to the kitchen. Now, this didn't sound like your ordinary scuffle; it sounded like somebody getting the living shit beaten out of them.

Which it was.

Then all went quiet.

Moments later, Johnny Giovanone arrived with a few more big guys and sat down. He leaned over to me and said, "This is *my* birthday celebration, and you are *my* guest." He grabbed my hand affectionately. "Clarence, you may be a nigger, but you're *our* nigger. And *nobody* talks to our nigger like that man in the coat check line."

They had found the guy, dragged him into the kitchen, pounded on him and threw him out in the alley behind the nightclub. I felt a bit uncomfortable… but not too bad. After all, that racist stuck his nose into a situation he had no idea about. It was definitely a lesson he only needed to learn once.

Several months later, I came into my office the day after my own birthday. There was a messenger waiting with a box from one of Mr. Giovanone's companies called Joy Manufacturing.

The box was gift wrapped. When I peeled away the colorful paper, I discovered a glittering gold Piaget watch inside.

It probably hadn't "fallen off a truck," but I doubt Johnny Giovanone paid full retail for it, either.

The next time I saw Sammy Davis, Jr. he flashed that famous grin at me and quoted Mr. Giovanone: "You may be a nigger, baby, but you're my nigger!"

My baptism-by-fire in the world of print journalism in the early '70s was also my first up-close view of the New York Mob control over the city's labor unions. Shortly after becoming publisher of the *New York Amsterdam News* (more on how that happened coming up), I examined the distribution routes showing the locations throughout the five boroughs where our paper was delivered to newsstands. In addition to having the paper in traditional "Negro" neighborhoods, I wanted distribution in select areas outside of those communities. I especially wanted to reach the *Village Voice* readership on the West Side and in Greenwich Village.

To get the lay of the land, I drove up to the facility in Westchester County where the *Amsterdam News* was printed and loaded onto trucks for delivery to various newsstands in Westchester, Bronx, Manhattan, Brooklyn, Queens and Staten Island. One of the first things I noticed when examining the records was that we were paying some deliverymen who never actually showed up for work. I knew a classic Mafia no-show job when I saw it.

I asked to meet personally with the president of the Newspaper Deliverers Union. When I tried to discuss the no-shows, he simply explained, "This is the way the delivery's been handled for years. The previous owner had no problem with it." It was clear after some discussion that I was treading in waters that I didn't really know and in dangerous currents.

I decided to leave well enough alone and focus on addressing the issues of wider distribution in the communities I wanted to reach. A friend arranged for me to meet with the owner of the vast majority of the newsstands in the city. The company was part of the S.I. Newhouse newspaper publishing group. He took a personal liking to me and told me someone he greatly respected said I was a "nice, clean-cut Negro."[35]

He intervened on my behalf with the Newspaper Deliverers Union, and suddenly two of the no show jobs were eliminated. It wasn't perfect, but it was a move in the right direction. And two birds with one stone, because he also helped get the *Amsterdam News* on more stands throughout the five boroughs.

Every summer in those years, I would spend several weekends fishing out in Sag Harbor, often staying at the Sea Spray Inn.[36] One July weekend, my sons and I were enjoying the ocean from beach chairs at the Inn. We were sitting near an elderly white woman, who was alone at the beach looking concerned. The beach attendants were so busy they could not respond to her. Noticing this, I got up and asked if I could bring her an umbrella or some towels. She was very gracious and thankful for our attention and assistance. My boys and I would see her around the Inn for the rest of our stay and say hello.

When I returned to Harlem to resume work at the newspaper the following week, I received a call from the law office of Roy Cohn, the well-known and often feared lawyer. I returned his call, somewhat anxious as to why he would be calling me. He told me I had met his "favorite aunt," whom he adored, at the Sea Spray. Apparently, she could not stop talking about how kind we had been to her. I said I enjoyed talking with her and simply tried to be helpful. Cohn insisted that I come over to meet him at his office in an East Side townhouse.

He and his partner offered me drinks and *h'orderves*. Cohn was warm and friendly and told me repeatedly how much his aunt had praised me. Over drinks, he paused, and with his part-

---

35 Insulting racism disguised as flattery, something I saw all the time. "You're one of the good ones," is something every Black person hears—or overhears—at some point. I'd think of this guy when I saw Joe Biden, chasing the 2008 Democratic presidential nomination, describing then-opponent Barack Obama as a "clean" African American.

36 We would often bring the catch to the Inn's kitchen, and they would serve our blue fish as part of that evening's menu.

ner looking on, said if there ever comes a time when I need any assistance with the New York City authorities, please call him and he would take care of it. "And, in the unlikely event you ever have a problem with the police," he said with a smile, "you should call me before anyone else, you hear?"

Loud and clear. I told him the only problem that was consuming my time and attention, which I thought I had resolved, was delivery of the *Amsterdam News* by the union, notwithstanding my new friendship with its president.

Cohn asked me to describe the problems I was having. He then said, before the end of that week, I would no longer have a problem. And, indeed, the problem with the Newspaper Deliverers Union disappeared.

Ironically, I would later come to learn that the union president also had a major interest in a beach-front hotel on Long Island. The Sea Spray Inn.

In the mid-1980s, I was involved in a matrimonial case in which I represented the soon to be ex-wife. One afternoon the husband, who apparently had Mob connections, showed up in a rage at my office. After shouting at me for several minutes, he pulled out a pistol and placed it on the desk between us.

He said, "If you don't call my wife and quit her case, I'm going to kill you."

I was shaking and tried to reason with him. I didn't actually feel like my life was in danger at that moment. He wasn't stupid enough to kill a lawyer in his own office, but he was trying to rattle me. It worked.

He snatched the gun back up and stormed out of my office.

Now, I had recently made friends with several DEA agents who worked undercover, which is an incredibly intense way to make a living. I'd met—let's call them Bill and Bob—at the Showman's Jazz Club, where I sometimes grabbed a drink after work. Like me, they were there blowing off steam. We got to talking about what we did and, perhaps because I was a lawyer and an officer of the court, they felt like it was safe to divulge their profession. We didn't know each other terribly well, but we ran into each other from time to time at Showman's or the Oak Room.

The night that the opposing party pulled his weapon on me, I saw the DEA boys at the bar. One of them noticed I seemed upset, so I told them what had happened.

They looked at each other. Some communication passed between them that I couldn't identify.

"Can you describe this guy to us?" Bill asked.

"Or better yet, do you have a photograph of him?"

"No," I said, "but I know his name and I have his address in my office."

That suited them just fine. "Let's go, then." They convinced me to head back downtown and get them that information on the husband.

"What are you going to do?" I asked.

The reply: Don't worry about it, Clarence.

About three days later, the husband called to make an appointment to see me. When he stepped into my office I offered him a seat, but instead he knelt in front of my desk like he was at church. He placed his hands right where the gun had been and clenched them together, fingers laced so tight the blood was getting pinched off. And the man begged me:

"Please, please, Mr. Jones. I'm so sorry. I was out of line when I came in before. I'm so sorry if I upset you." He began sobbing. "I was out of my head; I didn't know what I was thinking. Can you forgive me? You *have* to forgive me."

I told him not to worry about it. I said it was forgotten and that I'd see him in court for the divorce matter. Of course, I wondered what had caused the change of heart. I thought I knew the who, but not the how.

The next time I ran into the undercover cops at The Showman, they asked me how things went with the husband.

"He came to me, begging for forgiveness," I said.

"Did you forgive him?"

I nodded. "What did you do?"

"We motivated him." Bob smiled. "What we did was, we went by his place, grabbed him up, threw him in the back of our van, and took him down to the stanchion of the George Washington Bridge right by the water. We put him on his knees, dropped a bag of heroin in front of him, and then Bill stuck a .45 in his mouth."

Bill jumped in. "I said we know who you are, we know where you live, and we know what you did to our friend Clarence Jones. We're going to give you one chance; we'll let you go so you can go apologize to him."

They told the man that if I could forgive him, they could too. Otherwise, he'd find himself back in the same spot, only this time the trigger would get pulled.

As with the guy in the Copa's coat check line, I found it difficult to have a lot of sympathy. And yet, I wouldn't wish an experience like that on my worst enemy.

But mine are small-time gangland stories compared to the tales someone like Jimmy Hoffa could likely tell. Which brings us back to the Teamsters and the SCLC's challenge in working with them.

Despite mutual interests, both sides had been keeping their distance from one another through the early Sixties. Then came March 1965 and the Klan's assassination of Viola Liuzzo, who happened to be the wife of the president of the Teamsters local in Detroit. Her husband, James Liuzzo, was one of Hoffa's close friends and supporters. Her death not only shocked the conscience of the nation, it provoked Hoffa into finally reaching out to meet with Dr. King. Hoffa had Teamster official Harold Gibbons call Martin who, in turn, referred the matter to Stanley and me.

My first reaction in discussing Gibbons' call was somewhat cynical: Somehow this incident was going to provide Hoffa with another opportunity to take a shot at Bobby Kennedy in their war of words over the Attorney General's investigation of the union. Stanley, on the other hand, counseled that the

DOJ's inquiry into the Teamsters was not going away and that we simply had to avoid being caught in their crossfire of name-calling. This proposed meeting with Hoffa might provide SCLC with a real opportunity to develop Teamster support for Martin's work.

Some of Martin's friends opposed meeting with Hoffa. They worried it would anger Kennedy and be perceived by some as "the Movement courting the Mob." I advised Martin that the killing of Mrs. Liuzzo provided us with a unique opportunity to engage Hoffa and the Teamsters to support our work and that we had to be neutral in their battle against the DOJ. We'd always sought support from union leadership on both the left and right. I reminded everyone of Randolph's famous teaching: *Negroes have no permanent friends, no permanent enemies; only permanent interests.*

Martin agreed and decided to meet with Hoffa at the Teamsters' offices in Washington. Along with me, Andrew Young, Walter Fauntroy, and a union lawyer also attended. Hoffa was a stocky man with muscular upper arms. His black hair was swept straight back from his blocky, authoritarian face. After some pleasantries, Martin opened by saying we were glad to have the opportunity to talk to him about our Movement and particularly what we are doing in Alabama, where Mrs. Liuzzo had been killed. Hoffa sat passively and listened, then indicated how well he knew Mrs. Liuzzo and her husband.

Martin continued on about the awful nature of assassination. Hoffa interrupted him and said, with all due respect to Dr. King's non-violence, that he and the Teamsters were "decidedly *not* non-violent when it came to protecting union members and their families." He asked, rhetorically, what we thought that "cocksucker" Bobby Kennedy was going to do to protect him and the SCLC.

We didn't have a great answer.

"Well," Hoffa said, as he got up from his chair and walked over to the corner of the room and picked up a baseball bat,

"Let me tell you: The only thing the Klan understands is this." He smacked the bat across the palm of his hand.

Martin said he understood Hoffa's anger, but he had built a movement on non-violence and remained committed to that, despite the various incidents of brutality committed against us.

Hoffa said he understood and that Dr. King should do what he thought he had to do, but the Teamsters were going to do what they had to do. Hoffa then asked three men from an adjoining room to come into his office. In walked three presumably Teamster members who looked like the defensive linemen of a professional football team. They had thick necks and arms as large as the thighs of most men. Hoffa said, "Dr. King, these men are going to go down to Birmingham when you return to be available in case you need security. You don't still think those pricks Kennedy and Hoover are going to protect you, do you?"

Looking a little uncomfortable, Martin said he appreciated Hoffa's concern, but that he did not need security, he had lots of people around him most of the time. Hoffa added something to the effect that he wanted to send his men down anyway to talk to the Klan so that they would understand that he wasn't looking for trouble, but that he was prepared to protect his members and their families. He wanted to be sure the Klan got that message. If some Teamsters in Alabama were members of the Klan, he wanted to make sure that they stayed home and left the Civil Rights people alone.

Then Hoffa gave Martin a $25,000 check made out to the Southern Christian Leadership Conference.

Jimmy Hoffa may well have been involved in organized crime, but my experience was of a man with a baseball bat, a checkbook, and a broken heart.

The earliest details of my meeting Malcolm X are slightly hazy, which is surprising since history shows that the man certainly tended to make an impact on those he encountered. Nevertheless, in the middle of 1963, I had a lot of plates I had to keep spinning. I believe my first sight of Malcolm in person was in Harlem, on 125th Street across from the Theresa Hotel, in the fall of that year. He was standing on a step ladder podium addressing a crowd of supporters who had assembled around him.

He would be dead two-and-a-half years later.

As I've noted, my barbershop in those days was Golden Gloves. It, and nearly the entire Harlem block it was on, was owned by then-heavyweight boxing champ Sugar Ray Robinson. One day after getting a trim, I was walking west on 125th Street. As I approached the intersection at Seventh Avenue, I was stopped in my tracks by Malcolm, on that ladder with a hand-held microphone and a battery-powered amplifier. It was clear he drew strangers to him with his rhetorical power. Whoever passed by would stop, pulled in by his cool but somehow seething voice.

Malcolm was charismatic, humorous, and scathingly sarcastic about the history of Black people in the United States. Most of the assembled crowd was African Americans. A few, like me, were dressed in business suits and ties. Eventually he noticed me and a few others of my ilk; *the briefcase crowd.* Malcolm said some of us listening might think he was exaggerating or being outright untruthful when he described how the white man treats Black people.

Looking at and speaking directly to me, but of course addressing the entire crowd, he said: "Some of you, I can tell, don't believe what I'm explaining to you today. There may be some so-called professionals among you who think that because you have some education, a crisp shirt and tie and a briefcase, you're all right with the white man. But you haven't really tested my hypothesis against yours.

"If you think I'm exaggerating, I suggest you take your briefcased selves downtown and walk along Park Avenue in the Upper East Side around nine or ten at night, see how soon it is before you're stopped by a patrol car or a cop on the beat. With no what they refer to as probable cause, that white cop is going to make you explain—to *his satisfaction*—what you're doing and where you're going.

"Don't be surprised, don't say I didn't warn you. I'll tell you, it will be: 'Nigger, what are you doing here?' It won't matter how well you speak the white folks' English grammar. To the Man, you're just another nigger not in the neighborhood where we belong.

"Now if you say, 'Yes, Sir' or 'No, Sir' politely enough you *might* be *allowed* to go along your way. But keep your hands out of your pockets, brothers, because you run the risk—with all your education and your high price suits and ties and watches—of getting your head blown off. You were a proud Black man with your education and your job? Now you're a dead nigger who probably has a gun in that pocket. And if they need to find a gun to put in that pocket later, well... that can be arranged."

While Malcolm was speaking there were shouts back from the crowd, "Tell it like it is, Malcolm!" and "Preach, Brother Malcolm, preach!"

Malcolm went on, "Your title, your degree, doesn't mean a damn to that white policeman when all he sees is just another nigger. Another nigger that does not know his place, one who's crazy or arrogant enough to think he can walk through a white neighborhood at night without being held 'accountable.' Your briefcase doesn't exempt you from the racism of the NYPD, friends."

This was Malcolm X's *modus operandi*; direct, intense, and inflammatory. He made quite the first impression on me. After reading "The Bullet or The Ballot," the speech Malcolm gave in Cleveland on April 3rd, 1964, I concluded the man was a serious political thinker. Given my work for Dr. King, I had the responsibility to better understand him and make a concerted effort to connect with him. My goal was to exchange ideas and hear his thinking on the issues of the time. My friend Percy Sutton, a powerful man in New York City politics, was Malcolm's lawyer and was happy to make the introductions.

So, not long after this chance encounter uptown, I was able to develop a relationship with Malcolm X. Friendship with Malcolm was always on his terms, of course. He used to ask me questions warmly, but with an edge of sarcasm, about my relationship with Martin. I would always insist that, though their methods differed drastically, their goals and determination gave them much in common.

Not long into our friendship Malcolm asked me if I would take a message from him to Dr. King.

I told him I'd be pleased to do so. "What would you like me to tell him?" I asked.

"I'd like you to write it down."

I assured him my memory was strong and it would be unnecessary to write down his message unless it was a very long one.

Malcolm replied, no it wasn't that long, but he still wanted me to write it down. So, I did. The message was: Tell Dr. King, when he is speaking to a mostly white audience, I want him to say at the end of his speech, "If you don't respond to what I am asking, you'll have to deal with Malcolm X."

I delivered the message to Martin as Malcolm had requested. Martin gave me a wry smile. He responded that he often suggested just that, though not in the exact words that Malcolm X had proposed.

I had to think about that; subtext is a tricky thing when speaking to a crowd. Malcolm had suggested a not so veiled threat, and Martin seemed to say he'd done so. It occurred to me that the empathetic Martin did not issue threats; a better interpretation would be a warning. And he would make such warnings to his white audiences as an appeal to their own conscience, an attempt to force the listener out of their complacency—the threat of the enemy within, not an external force.

Then again, Martin's SCLC was offering one path: A non-violent end to racism. The idea of an alternate path, one perhaps marked by bloodshed, couldn't be ruled out.

After Malcolm broke with leader Elijah Muhammad and his Nation of Islam, he formed an independent group, the Organization of Afro American Unity (OAAU), which resulted in our having more frequent contact. Malcolm would occasionally ask me for advice with respect to organizational matters.

Shortly after Malcolm returned from his pilgrimage to Mecca, the leading scholar John Henrik Clarke invited several people to constitute a Research Study Group to advise Malcolm X: Writers John Oliver Killens and William Branch, entertainers Ruby Dee, Ossie Davis, and Harry Belafonte, the scholar John Mitchell, and me. Everyone was eager to attend, but our inaugural meeting with Malcolm X and his advisors came up one short; Harry Belafonte had a booking he couldn't get out of, but he figured there was always next time.

It would turn out that wasn't exactly the case.

Saturday evening, February 20th, 1965, was the kickoff in the Brooklyn home of John Oliver and Grace Killens. It was a rousing evening. We spent considerable time hearing Malcolm talk of the various threats he had been receiving from the Nation of Islam following his public break with Elijah Muhammad. We talked about the best strategy Malcolm could employ to broaden support for his new organization and what resources were needed (other than the always-in-short-supply money). There was some discussion about the status of the Civil Rights Movement and its leadership and the various requests for Malcolm to speak or appear at different venues to discuss and debate with other Civil Rights leaders.

The underlying theme was how best to "internationalize" the Civil Rights struggle within the United States, at the United Nations and in other countries. Most of the discussion that evening was political, philosophical, and practical about the OAAU going forward, including Malcolm's plan to hold a rally at the Audubon Ballroom on the Upper West Side the next day.

Our meeting didn't adjourn until nearly midnight. Malcolm wanted to make especially sure that I was going to come to the Audubon Ballroom rally. I said that I would try to make it, but I wasn't sure what my wife's plans for our children and me were that next day. I asked Malcolm why he felt it was so important for me to be there, and he responded by saying he needed other members of the OAAU to meet me in person.

He said that he had talked about me often and described me to many of his people. "They simply do not believe that there is a Negro 'professional' who has not already lost his mind and been brainwashed by the white man out of identifying with and supporting our struggle," Malcolm told me. "They need to see you for themselves. You're like Santa Claus."

Everyone went outside to get in their respective cars, but I hadn't driven to Brooklyn. I suggested to Malcolm I could ride with him and continue our conversation. Malcolm turned to me and said, "No, Brother Jones, I have some things to attend to." But he offered that three of his associates could take me home. Then, Malcolm opened the trunk of the car, reached in, and came up with several shotguns and handguns, which he passed out to the men who were to get me home. Malcolm's next words to me were simultaneously soothing and terrifying: "Brother Jones, you are too important. We don't want anything to happen to you because you are associated with us. We have the same duty to protect you as we do to protect ourselves. The Honorable Elijah Muhammad has ordered my assassination."

And so it was that I, confidant to the world's teacher of peaceful protest, was driven home safely late that night with an armed detail. Meanwhile, the last word Malcolm X ever said to me in this world was *assassination*.

Let that sink in.

. . .

The next day was a beautiful, mild, and sunny Sunday. I drove down from The Bronx along the Westside Highway overlooking the Hudson River. I exited at 168th Street and headed toward the Audubon Ballroom, which was on Broadway at West 165th Street. As I pulled up near the entrance, I registered a lot of commotion. I could see people were running out of the ballroom and I could hear screaming. I felt a tightening in my chest; I didn't like the atmosphere I'd just driven into, and I didn't know what to expect. I've since learned to expect the worst in those kinds of situations. Rarely do you find you're overestimating.

I was listening to the car radio as I scoured the area for a parking spot. A news flash came on: Malcolm X had been shot in the Audubon. There was no indication in that first announcement whether he was alive or dead.

Finding a parking space, I ran from my car toward the entrance. Police were there, not letting anyone in. Trying to persuade the policeman to let me by, I told him that I was a guest speaker on the day's agenda.

The policeman responded that the event had abruptly been canceled.

"They said on the radio Malcolm X may have been assassinated," I told him. The policeman said he couldn't confirm that, but from behind us we both heard a group of other police officers say Malcolm was dead from gunshot wounds to the chest.

Manning Marable, in his definitive biography of Malcolm X, *A Life of Reinvention*, described the assassination like this:

> *An incendiary smoke bomb ignited at the extreme rear of the ballroom, instantly creating panic, screams, and confusion. It was only then that Willie Bradley, sitting in the front row, got to his feet and walked briskly toward the rostrum. When he was fifteen feet away, he elevated his sawed-off shotgun from under this coat, took careful aim, and fired. The shotgun pellets ripped squarely into Malcolm's left side, cutting a seven-inch*

wide circle around his heart and chest. This was the kill shot, the blow that executed Malcolm X. The other bullets caused terrible damage but were not decisive.

The single shot gun blast oddly failed to topple Malcolm. As Herman Ferguson recalled, "There was a loud blast, a boom that filled the auditorium with the sound of a weapon going off." On cue, two men—Hayer in the first row, with a .45 next to his stomach, and Leon X Davis sitting next to him, also holding a handgun—stood up, ran to the stage, and emptied their guns into Malcolm."

Upon returning home later that day, I mixed a martini and took a moment to simply reflect. I remembered what Malcolm had said to me early on in our friendship: "Brother Jones, always remember how the Man treats a person he regards as a threat. Friendly at first, he tries to dissuade you from your views, encouraging you to rethink your outlook. To help smooth the way, he often provides some breadcrumbs of potential benefit to you in your business and personal life. He might arrange for you to serve on the Board of an important company or community organization to enhance your professional or personal status, with potential financial benefits. Offer you little goodies from the government till.

"If that doesn't succeed in dissuading you from your 'foolish' revolutionary ideas, the next step is that he'll seek to undermine your professional or personal integrity. Spreading rumors—like you're having an affair with one of your neighbor's wives. Circulating doubts—this church or that organization where you serve as treasurer seems to be missing money, and that you seem to be living more lavishly than usual. He'll try to ostracize you from your base of support, cut off your power in that way."

And then Malcolm leaned in close to me and said quietly, matter-of-fact, "If Step One and Step Two don't work, Step Three is they kill you. They simply kill you."

If I hadn't believed that before, I certainly did from that Sunday onward.

• • •

To the everlasting disgrace of many of the pastors in Harlem and lay leaders of organizations that had the space to accommodate a large number of people for a funeral, all of them refused to host Malcolm's service. Eventually, those of us who respected Malcolm used our collective clout and various relationships to find a venue for a public funeral. It finally took place at the Faith Temple, Church of God in Christ, in Harlem. More than a thousand from Harlem and elsewhere came to pay their respects on February 27th. Loudspeakers were set up outside the Temple so the overflowing crowd could listen, and a local television station broadcast the funeral live. The powerful and poignant eulogy delivered by Ossie Davis, the celebrated African American actor and friend of Malcolm, left the crowd thunderstruck.

> *"Here—at this final hour, in this quiet place—Harlem has come to bid farewell to one of its brightest hopes—extinguished now and gone from us forever. For Harlem is where he worked and where he struggled and fought—his home of homes, where his heart was, and where his people are—and it is, therefore, most fitting that we meet once again—in Harlem—to share these last moments with him. For Harlem has ever been gracious to those who have loved her, have fought her, and have defended her honor even to the death.*

> *"It is not in the memory of man that this beleaguered, unfortunate, but nonetheless proud community has found a braver, more gallant young champion than this Afro-American who lies before us—unconquered still. I say the word again, as he would want me to: Afro-American—Afro-American Malcolm, who was a master, was most meticulous in his use of words.*

> *"Nobody knew better than he the power words have over minds of men. Malcolm had stopped being a 'Negro' years ago. It had become too small, too puny, too weak a word for him. Malcolm was bigger than that. Malcolm had become an Afro-American and he wanted—so*

desperately—that we, that all his people, would become Afro-Americans too.

"There are those who will consider it their duty, as friends of the Negro people, to tell us to revile him, to flee, even from the presence of his memory, to save ourselves by writing him out of the history of our turbulent times. Many will ask what Harlem finds to honor in this stormy, controversial, and bold young captain—and we will smile. Many will say turn away—away from this man, for he is not a man but a demon, a monster, a subverter, and an enemy of the Black man—and we will smile.

"They will say that he is of hate—a fanatic, a racist—who can only bring evil to the cause for which you struggle! And we will answer and say to them: Did you ever talk to Brother Malcolm? Did you ever touch him, or have him smile at you? Did you ever really listen to him? Did he ever do a mean thing? Was he ever himself associated with violence or any public disturbance? For if you did you would know him. And if you knew him you would know why we must honor him.

"Malcolm was our manhood, our living, Black manhood! This was his meaning to his people. And, in honoring him, we honor the best in ourselves.

"Last year, from Africa, he wrote these words to a friend: 'My journey', he says, 'is almost ended, and I have a much broader scope than when I started out, which I believe will add new life and dimension to our struggle for freedom and honor and dignity in the States. I am writing these things so that you will know for a fact the tremendous sympathy and support we have among the African States for our Human Rights struggle. The main thing is that we keep a United Front wherein our most valuable time and energy will not be wasted fighting each other.'

"However, we may have differed with him—or with each other about him and his value as a man—let his going from us serve only to bring us together, now.

"Consigning these mortal remains to earth, the common mother of all, secure in the knowledge that what we place in the ground is no more now a man—but a seed—which, after the winter of our discontent, will come forth again to meet us. And we will know him then for what he was and is—a Prince—our own black shining Prince!—who didn't hesitate to die, because he loved us so."

While Malcolm X was alive—and for years after his death, up to this very day—I would continue to be asked how I compared Martin to Malcolm. How could I be friends to both men and offer advice, from time to time, to each?

I remind everyone who asks that although I was honored and devoted to assisting Dr. King as a political advisor and lawyer from 1961 until his death in 1968, I was equally honored to have earned Malcolm X's respect and trust. Both Malcolm and Martin were revolutionary patriots, irrevocably and unswervingly devoted to fighting for the full unencumbered freedom of African Americans. Martin was a devout Christian steeped in the religious doctrine and legacy of Jesus Christ and committed to Mahatma Gandhi's form of non-violent protest. Malcolm was committed to the defensive use of violence if he or other Black people were attacked by anyone with racist intentions.

He didn't champion a first-strike outlook. I never heard Malcolm advocate offensive violence—that is, *initiating an act of violence against the white man* in the absence of a white person initiating violence against him or his followers first. This is a distinction with a major difference, which those who opposed Malcolm had a tendency to overlook.

As Ossie Davis said in his eulogy, Malcolm was to many Black people their "Black shinning Prince," so, interestingly, I was privileged to know and work with both a "King" and this "Prince."

I encourage readers to put the man in proper context. Do not to think of Malcolm X as disconnected from so many of our earlier Black patriots. Men whose strategies and tactics were different before Malcolm and Martin, but whose goal remained the one we all shared and share to this day: To build a distinct link in the historical chain of their quest for achieving freedom and human dignity of our people. Whatever successes Martin or Malcolm may have had, they would not have been possible (nor would any "success" I may have achieved during my journey) had it not been for people like Alain Locke, Dr. W.E.B. Du Bois, Ralph Bunche, John Lewis, Paul Robeson, A. Philip Randolph, Bayard Rustin, and so many others. Yes, there are faces to movements, leaders that become heroes and lightning rods, but never forget that movements only yield fruit when many others before these leaders have sown the seeds.

With much consideration, I find it extremely unlikely that the assassination of Malcolm X occurred without the prior knowledge of the FBI, and paid informants within the Nation of Islam, especially those closest to Elijah Muhammad. John Ali was secretary and chief of staff for the Nation of Islam. He was also a paid FBI informant. Lewis Farrakhan was one of the Elijah Muhammad's most trusted and closest advisors. The 2021 exoneration of two of Malcolm X alleged assassins by the Manhattan District Attorney requires us to consider the assassination of Malcolm X in a new light after all these years.

It's important to understand that Malcolm's trip to Mecca to participate in the annual Haj was ideologically and spiritually transformative for him. It took place after he had severed his ties to the Nation of Islam, following the disclosure that Mohammed had fathered several children by women who worked for him as secretaries in his office. This knowledge shook the very foundations of Malcolm's belief in the Nation of Islam, which required its members to be faithful to their wives, to honor and protect them. To consider family sacred.

During his time with the Nation of Islam and as a follower of Mohammed, Malcolm was taught that all white people are inherently evil and racist and hate Black people. But the revelations about Elijah Muhammad, combined with his experience at Mecca of praying with and sharing a bowl with Muslims with white skin and blue or gray eyes made him reevaluate. Returning to the United States, Malcolm became focused on the creation of a new organization where white people would be welcomed. His organization of African unity planned to refocus on internationalizing the "Negro Question" by bringing to the attention of the United Nations racist conduct by the United States government and various states. Disentangling the issue from the domestic struggle was essential for Malcolm to move forward, but it also made him exponentially more dangerous to the federal government. Just as Martin's receipt of the Nobel Peace Prize and his 1967 speech opposing the war in Vietnam marked him as a target, Malcolm became one of the most menacing people in America in the eyes of the status quo. Malcolm X, in the opinion of the FBI and the United States Government, became the most dangerous Black man in America, particularly in contrast to the leaders of other Civil Rights organizations like CORE, the NAACP, the National Urban League, SNCC, and the SCLC.

As with Martin, the FBI conducted electronic and visual surveillance of Malcolm, around the clock. The FBI was likely aware of any plans to assassinate him, given their electronic surveillance of Elijah Muhammad, John Ali, Louis Farrakhan, and others. The FBI and certain members of the NYPD knew that the men arrested for the assassination of Malcolm X did not shoot him without the prior knowledge of Elijah Muhammad. Accordingly, those agencies knew that the men arrested and incarcerated for the killing of Malcolm X were not ultimately responsible for the murder.

Time and further disclosure by the NYPD and the FBI will ultimately reveal who planned the assassination. But there already is enough information to implicate John Ali, Lewis Farrakhan, and others. And just as James Earl Ray may have purchased the rifle and pulled the trigger to kill Martin, this assassination did not occur without the prior knowledge of the FBI.

I won't be around to witness it, but government files to be declassified in 2050 will undoubtedly confirm what I speculate here.

I thought I hated being so close to an assassination. What I didn't realize was the opposite—being too far away—was even worse...

I wouldn't remember a certain comment the tea-totaling Martin King said to me until almost ten years after his assassination. It would have been useful to remember it within the first ten days of Memphis. It might have saved my family if I'd done so. But it was just another Martin *bon mot*, tucked into the folds of my memory and temporarily exiled.

It was five o'clock on a 1966 afternoon. We were discussing business while sitting in a midtown Manhattan lounge, and Martin, who had never taken an alcoholic drink in his life, looked over at me with one of those wry smiles of his. "Man, I can only imagine how good a martini must taste. Just the way you're holding it, I know the answer is very good indeed."

Minor enough at the time, particularly if you knew me. But then, that's exactly what's so devastating about this comment. Martin probably knew me better than I knew myself. That glass would've looked perfect, sweated perfectly, and I would've—subconsciously mind you—modeled it, along with my Rolex and my Pierre Balmain suit that would've cost $800 back then. I would've looked like a goddamn advertisement for that martini, or the vodka in it, because I had bought into the *vie en haute* without realizing it. It wasn't about the taste or the kick the alcohol gave as much as it was what the drink said about me. I was making statements, and that fell far afield of what Martin believed in. When he made statements, they were on issues of importance to the spirit, not imported spirits.

Regardless of whether or not he felt liquor was dangerous or unholy (check and double check), he was calling me out to tell me a little bit about myself. I didn't hear him, or perhaps I chose not to hear.

"Man, I can only imagine how good a martini must taste."

Yeah, it tasted good. Of course, there came a time when I hardly tasted it at all. I was on autopilot with the drinking, never getting particularly drunk nor ever probably being clearheaded. Just a smear of time passing with cocktails mixed and pouring, freshening up. Wash, rinse, repeat.

I can remember exactly when I got drunk for the first time. It was 1953, during my purgatory as a draftee in the United States Army at Fort Dix, New Jersey. One night, on base for the weekend, my barrack mates invited me to have a can or two of cheap beer. Following that, we all shared some Anna Marie red port wine. This made the cheap beer look like champagne in comparison; the soldiers called it "Sneaky Pete" and it cost thirty-five cents a pint.

We sat around the barracks, shooting the breeze. Mostly about women, professional sports, or life in the Army. The more we drank, the more animated and loud our conversation became. I'm sure you know the drill; it was fun until it wasn't. The Sneaky Pete snuck up on me. At some point, I stood up and felt nauseous, ran outside the barracks, and vomited up the wine-soaked contents of my stomach. Dizziness and a headache ensued. I eventually threw myself down on my bunk and the world went black. It was the first time I passed out from drinking too much. It would not be the last.

I learned my lesson temporarily. I figured that the harder alcohol was not for me. During my time off base, I can't recall drinking anything other than beer until after my undesirable discharge in 1955.

I went to stay with my Uncle Clarence and his wife Charlotte on West 18th in Manhattan. There, I began to drink martinis, initially gin because that was what my aunt and uncle drank. Uncle Clarence considered himself a connoisseur in the making of a gin martini (I believe he used Tanqueray). Quickly, I learned that a martini's dryness depended on the proportion of gin to white vermouth and that a Gibson was a martini with a small cocktail onion instead of an olive. In dire circumstances a twist of lemon could be substituted.

At this time, Uncle Clarence was working as a waiter at the Lexington Avenue and Park Lane Hotels.[37] His schedule changed weekly, but on most days, he'd be home by late afternoon. Around 5:30 he would commence mixing martinis. He taught me that there was artistry to the making of an excellent (as opposed to merely serviceable) cocktail.

"Any ape can stir together ingredients," he would say. "But a talented barman is like a chef."

We would often watch the evening news drinking martinis while awaiting Charlotte to arrive home from Macy's where she worked as a buying executive. I was 24 years old at the time, drinking typically just one martini a day. It became part of a routine ritual of bonding between me and my uncle, whom I admired and adored. As we drank, he would often talk about his sister, my dear departed mother. I couldn't get enough of those stories, and I suppose the drink and the tales about my mother became intertwined in my nervous system somehow.

Years later, I was told Uncle Clarence died of a heart attack in his living room as he got up from his favorite chair to change the TV channel. With a martini in one hand. Maybe not a terrible way to go, depending on what program was on.

While I attended law school, I had neither the time nor the money to drink on a regular basis. Beers with our landlord on the weekends was about the extent of it.

In Los Angeles, I certainly had the money and a bit more social time than at law school, but then, as now, Southern California was an odd mixture of health-consciousness and drug culture. Sure, lots of dinners with expensive wines and the parties in the Hollywood Hills, but only occasionally during these years did I drink excessively. On the road away from Anne, working with Martin or Arthur Kinoy, I barely drank at all.

---

37 It was my uncle's association with the Lexington Avenue Hotel that enabled Anne and me to hold our wedding reception there several years later, right before our move to Boston.

When we finally moved back to New York in 1961, I returned to the habit of drinking martinis on a daily basis. In our law partnership, I was the one who generally appeared on behalf of the firm in state or federal court. Both were located on lower Broadway, and we could walk to those and most of the civil and criminal courts. Besides trial, there were always pretrial motions that needed to be filed, so I developed a ritual: After appearing in court in the morning, I'd stop and have a lunch and a drink either before heading back to my office or returning to court in the afternoon. There was a bar and restaurant where many other lawyers would do the same. I began to develop friendships drinking martinis at the bar with other lawyers or having lunch standing at the high-top tables. For most of those years, I generally would be the only Negro lawyer in the restaurant filled with lawyers, most of whom were Irish or Italian. This was early '60s, and anti-Soviet feelings were simmering. In the restaurant, the bartenders would grumble about how much they hated the communists... but damn, didn't the Russians make fucking good vodka![38]

It was customary in those days for the bartenders to monitor us and asked whether we were just finishing up an earlier court appearance or whether we had to return to court. This information would guide them on when to cut us off before our next court appearance. They kept the justice system in check but well lubricated.

I would often have one vodka martini with lunch and another at the end of the day before heading home, either at a bar in Grand Central station or the bar of a restaurant near my office. This was when I would commute from Grand Central to Riverdale. If I'd had a martini earlier during the day, I'd drink another one as soon as I arrived home. Anne, no fan of Russian politics, was drinking Tanqueray Gin martinis at the time.

---

38 Later, in the early seventies, a thawing in the Cold War was underway. It was symbolically expressed at Carnegie Hall by the first-ever United States performance of David Oistrakh, the celebrated concert violinist from the Soviet Union. By this point, drinking newly imported Stolichnaya vodka was all the rage.

After Anne and I finished our house in Riverdale, we would often have parties with lots of dancing. Ray Charles was at the top of the charts, and we would dance to "I Got a Woman Way Over Town," "Unchain My Heart," "Georgia," and "What I Say Now." My neighbor Doug Pugh would always jump up and dance when the Stevie Wonder sang "Signed, Sealed, Delivered" or Johnnie Taylor wondered "Who's Making Love to Your Old Lady?" Our music also included heavy doses of country and western and sophisticated early rock. We loved Eric Clapton and Joe Cocker.

Alcohol fueled the fun. Whether it was the vodka or gin martinis, bourbon, Dewar's or Cutty Sark scotch, the drinking would keep everybody mellowed out. And flirtatious. At parties several women sought my attention. Doug and I would case out who we referred to as "the foxes" and take inventory of the women who had hit on us.

Of course, everybody talked local, state, and national politics. These gatherings took place took place at the height of the Civil Rights Movement and protests against local housing segregation. Guests would occasionally include Miles Davis, local Bronx political officials, or lawyers in the entertainment and music business. Anthony Browne, Spencer Jourdain, and other prominent successful Negroes would show up regularly. It was as if our home was a beehive filled with seductive honey and everyone was looking for a taste.

In the early years, when my work with Carter, Berlind & Weill overlapped with my assisting Martin, I would go to dinner meetings in the evenings. I started ordering vodka martinis at the restaurant bars again. Sometimes these dinners would also involve expensive bottles of wine as part of our dealmaking process. In virtually all such cases, I was driven home, either by another meeting participant or via car service.

When I returned home to Riverdale, I would often have yet still another martini. Sometimes later in the evening, during a conference call with Martin, Stanley Levison, Andy Young, and Ralph Abernathy, Martin would say, "I hear our lawyer is animated this evening. We can thank our good friend Dr. Martini for this late-night energy."

Interestingly, when I traveled South—which was often during those years—I rarely drank vodka. Most Black bars and homes that I visited did not have Stolichnaya yet. Bourbon was the drink of the South, so I'd drink Jack Daniels or Old Grandad with a splash of club soda and a lemon wedge.

The first signs that my martinis were becoming a form of self-medication were when I started looking at my watch to see whether it was after 12:00 noon. If so, it was then okay in my mind to begin to think about a martini (or perhaps actually *have* one). I had never really considered myself an alcoholic. But perhaps I should have known I was at the threshold of a drinking problem when, like Pavlov's dog, while walking in the street or standing on a subway or commuter train platform, if I saw an ad featuring a bottle of vodka, I would feel the need to have a martini. In 1972, importers put a giant Stolichnaya billboard outside the window of my law office, and it almost seemed personal. Often when talking on the phone I would look out at the billboard, craving a drink.

I didn't like the fact that advertising could work that well. At least on me.

INTERLUDE

THE INFLECTION POINT

FOR THE LEAST OF THESE

The last time Martin phoned me—on the day of his assassination—the call came into my office. I had my secretary do my talking for me.

Important lawyer. Too busy to pick up the damn phone.

I knew Martin so well that I could reasonably anticipate the purpose of his call. He was in Memphis with Andrew Young and Rev. Billy Kyles, going over the details of his schedule. He wanted to make sure he knew exactly when I'd be arriving in town to assist him. Logistics—clerical stuff, really—and I was buried in other work. It's not that I was distracted, it was simply a matter of cutting to the chase. Why get on the phone when I knew the entire point of the conversation? Why indeed. I shouted to my secretary, "Tell him I'll be there on time."

I would later have a bible verse from the Book of Mathew stuck in my head, repeating... haunting me in its way:

> *The King will reply, "Truly I tell you, whatever you did for one of the least of these brothers and sisters of mine, you did for me."*

Everything Martin did, he did for the least of us. He did the most for the least. And I couldn't even be bothered to answer my friend's call.

"You don't want to speak with Dr. King?" my secretary asked.

Not really; I'd had the conversation a hundred times before. And thus, I missed my chance at goodbye. "Just let him know I need someone to pick me up at the airport. I'll be there on time."

I wasn't on time. As with Malcolm, I pulled up late once again.

• • •

February 1968 had been rough for the city of Memphis, Tennessee. The bad news for the mostly Black Local 1733 of the American Federation of State, County, and Municipal Employees started on the first day of the month, when two of their workers were literally crushed to death in the faulty trash compactor of their own garbage truck. Within two weeks, to protest the city's lack of urgency in dealing with outdated equipment and dangerous working conditions, the union members staged a work stoppage. Only a quarter of the trash trucks were on the streets, and almost none of the more than 200 sewer workers showed up. Within days, garbage was piling up in front of houses and businesses, and the mayor, the stubborn former head of the Department of Public Works (in which role he oversaw the sanitation workers), was not interested in negotiation. He brought in white strikebreakers, who just added fuel to the fire.

I'd been opposed to Dr. King going to Memphis in support of Local 1733. My opposition had nothing to do with the merits of the workers' issues; it was based solely on the fact that Martin had repeatedly requested me to set up meetings in New York with possible donors in support of his work for the same time frame. I had already scheduled several meetings in Manhattan with potentially major financiers. The dates conflicted with the schedule for Martin to go to Memphis. Moreover, events on the ground there, between the striking African American garbage workers and the city of Memphis, had become more bitter and antagonistic.

A few weeks later, Roy Wilkins, Bayard Rustin, and Billy Kyles had convinced Martin that his presence in Memphis would be invaluable to the cause. He marched with the sanitation workers on March 18 and was supposed to do so again four days later, but an unseasonable snowstorm forced the union to postpone the demonstration until the 28th. During that march, rioting and looting began, and the clash between protesters and police resulted in the shooting death of Larry Payne, an unarmed sixteen-year-old boy.

In the wake of that horror, the mayor called in the National Guard.

If you can't beat 'em, join 'em, I figured. I needed to prep Martin for the fundraising meetings, and he wasn't leaving Memphis anytime soon. So, if he wasn't going to be in New York to do the prep work, I'd have to bring the prep work to him. I planned a trip to Memphis; my plane was scheduled to land the night of April 4th, 1968.

In that context, I was pretty sure I knew why Martin was calling me earlier in the day. And so I didn't take the call.

That evening I was packing, getting ready to leave for the airport for the Memphis flight, when my home phone rang. My initial instinct was to ignore this call too, since I was running late. But something told me to answer it.

It was Harry Belafonte calling. "I can't talk now," I told him. "I'm jumping in a cab for the airport."

Harry simply said, "Turn on the TV. Martin's been shot." He hung up.

Numb, I turned on my bedroom television. There it was, breaking news—Walter Cronkite repeating Harry's words, telling me, "Martin Luther King has been shot."

I was stunned. I went to the phone to call my contacts in Memphis. Every line was busy. My own phone rang again; it was Harry. "If you don't already have the TV on, they're now saying he's dead."

The feeling of a cold and overwhelming resignation swept through me. *They finally got him.* The day after the assassination of President Kennedy, I had met Martin at LaGuardia. He had said when they want to get me, they will kill me too. It's not a question of whether they can do it; it's only a question of when. We didn't stop worrying, but he'd been right.

"Harry, am I getting on the plane to Memphis?" We talked and agreed that I could do more from my home base in terms of coordinating with our SCLC colleagues, some of whom were in Memphis but most of whom were still in Atlanta.

At first there was a simple numbness that comes to any family with a sudden death. Anyone who's lost someone close knows this almost robotic reaction. There's so much to be done that deep-seated social norms take over the mind and body, and the psychological processing of grief gets put on hold.

I tried to help long distance, making calls and connecting people, responding to press inquiries, assisting with logistics. But it quickly became apparent that I needed to be down South, so Stanley Levison and I traveled to Atlanta to meet up with Harry.

Most of the next few days were a blur.

It would all hit me later, and hit me hard, but for the time being, there wasn't a moment to waste on honest reflection. I held steady assisting in planning for the funeral. The other two men rushing to help were Harry and Stanley. They were two sides of the same coin, one so famous and out front, the other, by necessity, in the shadows. Both men always offered such stalwart support in Martin's life and work; here at the end, they did anything they could to help.

Together, the three of us tried to take as much off Martin's widow Coretta's plate as possible and button down the details of the massive undertaking of the funeral. The Kings' living room doubled as the command post. There seemed a million details.

The racist governor of Georgia refused to let Martin's body lie in state, and even kept the flag flying at full staff... at least until he was ordered to by the White House—it was a federal mandate.

Xerona Clayton, the groundbreaking Black female journalist who had been working for the SCLC, came downstairs and announced that she was heading downtown to pick out some outfits that would be appropriate for Coretta to wear over the next few days and to Martin's funeral. Harry, Stanley, and I all took out our American Express cards and handed them to Xerona, telling her to split the charges up among all three. "And if there's any problem," I told her, "Have the clerks call here for approval."

We didn't hear from any department stores, and when Xerona retuned hours later, she gave us back unused credit cards. All the merchants had refused payment, wanting to support the King family in their time of grief. "They felt it was the least they could do," Xerona said.

The day before the funeral I received a call from William Vanden Heuvel. Bill was a good friend of mine and close to the Kennedy family. In fact, he told me that he was calling on behalf of Jacqueline Kennedy. The former First Lady would be attending the funeral and wanted to visit Coretta beforehand. I worked the logistics out with Bill. I met Mrs. Kennedy at the door and escorted her into the private area off the dining room where Coretta had been spending most of her time.

"Coretta," I said. "I have someone who wants to give her condolences." The world's second most famous widow turned to face the first. It was certainly no pleasure, but it was a surreal kind of honor to introduce the two of America's most prominent living victims of political violence to one another.

The funeral procession—three miles with the casket on the back of a farm wagon pulled by mules. A symbol if there ever was one.

The eulogy—Martin's own recorded voice delivering a sermon on how he should be remembered. Asking no one mention awards and honors, but only the simple good he tried to do.

Mahalia Jackson—always his favorite. Singing "We Shall Overcome."

I didn't think we would. Not this time.

In the days after the funeral, I returned to New York and tried to get back to some form of normalcy. In the back of my head, I kept hearing a voice asking again and again, *Do you really think you can continue to live in a country that lets something like this happen?*

I tried to process the bitter heartbreak of Martin's assassination, and I didn't do a very good job with it.

Soon there were calls from the SCLC that I didn't take. On other occasions, I made calls to people there and mine went unreturned. I hadn't exactly made a decision consciously, but as the days slipped into weeks and there was radio silence between me and Atlanta, I began to form a picture of my relationship with the Movement that I hadn't fully grasped previously: While I knew I was inspired by and worked for Dr. King, I did not really understand until circumstances forced me to that I was really working *only* for the man. Not his organization. That is not to say that I didn't continue to believe in mission of the SCLC—that was a mission that Dr. King had sculpted.

But the fact of the matter struck me clearly: The SCLC was an organization, not much better than most organizations. That meant ego, posturing, sabotage, blaming, angst over employment and salary and status. In short, it was a group of people, well intentioned as they might have been in the abstract, who acted like people at work act. There was no magic without Martin Luther King, Jr. And in the grander sweep of the Civil Rights Movement, Martin had his enemies: Those who were jealous of the impact he made on the national stage. And I was his man. Now *persona non grata.* Fine with me. I was so angry I lost all interest in the SCLC version of theCivil Rights Movement. Some organizations work at the nuts-and-bolts level, and others are meant to rise or fall with a "key man." As far as I was concerned, I lost my faith in the SCLC as an ongoing concern when they lost their leader.

There was nothing anybody could do about it. I was tired of giving and getting nowhere with it. I pulled away, I retreated north, where I felt I really belonged. To a life that I planned on being more self-centered.

A return to form, I suppose.

During the period where James Earl Ray was arrested, indicted, tried, convicted, and sentenced for terminating Martin's life on the balcony of the Lorraine Motel, I accepted the finding that Ray was the one who pulled the trigger.

What I have not accepted to this day is the widely circulated U.S. Justice Department conclusion that James Earl Ray acted alone. I believe Martin's death was the result of a premeditated, calculated conspiracy to assassinate him. James

Earl Ray simply was the person who carried out the execution. He was undoubtedly the trigger man, but that doesn't make him the brains of the operation. My continuing belief is that Martin's assassination was planned and financed by the Dallas oil millionaire Hunt brothers, who were as rabidly afraid of communism as Joseph McCarthy had been.

I also believe the government let it happen. Martin Luther King Jr.'s change of focus—moving from demands of desegregation to demands of economic parity and an end to the unjust slaughter overseas—led to his assassination. If he was the most dangerous Negro leader in 1963 just worrying about Black folks, the least of these... just imagine what they thought of him by the time he was at Riverside Church, attacking the President of the United States about the war.

I met with then-FBI Director James Comey for an hour in his office in Washington, D.C. in 2015. We spoke of many things, including the assassination. I shared with him my view as to who was behind and funded James Earl Ray's activity. I told him, "It may not happen in your lifetime or mine, but I'm convinced that, as the old folks say, 'The truth will out.'"

Comey didn't take a stand on the issue one way or the other, but he showed me what was beneath the glass on his desktop: A photocopy of the memorandum from former FBI Director J. Edgar Hoover requesting authorization from Attorney General Robert Kennedy to wiretap Dr. King and Kennedy's authorization to do so. Comey said he kept a copy in plain sight so when his agents visited him in the office, they could be reminded of what the FBI should *not* do.

Throughout the summer of 1968, I honestly considered becoming a militant. I could actually imagine taking up arms against the government. For real. That was how angry the assassination had made me. If you can do this to Martin King, who stood for nothing but peace and dignity, if you can bring your copper-jacketed tools of destruction and oppression to such a man, maybe I'll do the same thing to you. Why not join the Black Panthers? Learn bomb-making? Get armed to the teeth and burn the whole motherfucker down?

PART V

AFTERBURN

I had been drinking heavily (socially, but heavily) for nearly a decade, but in 1968 my drinking escalated. If I had been asked directly to think of the reasons why I drank so much at that point, I probably would've said to blunt my pain, the pain over the assassination of Martin. Yet in 1952, I had suffered and grieved over the loss of my mother, and I'd pulled myself out of a self-destructive nosedive without the aid of mood-altering substances. As much as I loved Martin, if I didn't need to find the bottom of a bottle to get through the anger and resentment of losing my mother, I didn't need to do that for anyone.

What I hadn't realized was that Martin's death, because of what he represented and what he was trying to accomplish in America, meant something different to me as a Black man. That, of course, is what the ideology behind assassination is all about—taking down the *figure*, the *representation*, the *iconography*. Losing Martin felt different than losing Mary Jones; not worse, but more *philosophically* painful. With Mary, I was one man losing his mother. With Martin, I was one Black man losing all hope for his kind.

Big fucking difference. Personal or profound—how do you take your heartbreak?

The rage I felt at the system—at the world—didn't burn clean in me, but it sure as hell burned bright. After Dr. King's death, the drinking would mean less, but do more.

For me, I thought.

To me, as it turned out. It stopped mattering how I looked holding the martini and started mattering how the little chemistry-set-in-a-glass made me feel. I used the alcohol to keep the pain from surfacing as surely as a tourniquet cuts off the flow of blood out of the body. There was plenty of pain to try to press the mute button on. My friend and mentor had been gunned down and our government not only did nothing to prevent the murder but, I suspect, secretly *celebrated* it.

Pour me another.

After the assassination and funeral of Martin, I turned my attention away from the SCLC and the general Civil Rights Movement to focus on my work at Carter, Berlind & Weill. However, I increased my active participation in the growing anti-war movement, and I decided to get involved in politics.

My first step was joining a new organization called the Coalition for a Democratic Alternative, where I shortly became one of their three statewide co-chairmen. But I soon realized that outside interest groups could only influence policy so far. Being meaningfully involved in the political landscape meant being involved in actual government.

In 1968, just days before Martin's final sermon and assassination, Lyndon Johnson announced to the nation that he had decided not to seek reelection. He wouldn't even accept the nomination. This was unprecedented in modern American politics, and the Democratic Party—which at that point held the Oval Office and both houses of Congress, was thrown into a tailspin.

President Johnson's decision resulted in Minnesota Senator Eugene McCarthy running as an insurgent anti-Vietnam candidate in the Democratic primary in New Hampshire. He came in a strong second, and his showing shocked the Democratic establishment.[39]

Robert Kennedy won the California primary a month later, but he was killed the night of his victory. Over the next month, it became clear that for the first time in memory, there was no one candidate for president the party could rally behind. It was looking like a three-way fight between then-Vice Pres-

---

39   Our nation was deeply divided over the issue of the U.S. government's role in Vietnam. The candidacy of Vice President Hubert Humphrey rattled many because of Humphrey's association with the hawkish President Johnson.

ident Hubert Humphrey and Senators McCarthy and George McGovern (South Dakota).

I saw this situation as my opportunity and knew I had to act fast. So, I established residency in Manhattan at the Cambridge House Hotel apartments on West 86th Street, a strategic address that just happened to be in a particular Democratic Party precinct. At that time, the New York Democratic Party appointed its slate of electors in each precinct, people almost always chosen from the loyal ranks of the Party's machinery. In order to become an elector from outside of the organization, a person like me had to challenge a current office holder, contest the seat, and force a caucus-style election with the Party leaders. I'd chosen my apartment based upon my reading of the political weakness of the elector in that particular district. I suppose, like Boston's favorite son Robert Kennedy, I became a New York carpetbagger... but I was only coming in from five miles upriver.

In any event, I got the gig. As an elector, I then ran as a McCarthy delegate in the statewide elections to determine which electors would attend the National Democratic Convention in Chicago and wound up as co-chairman of the New York State delegation. Meanwhile, a group of McCarthy supporters in Connecticut, disgruntled at being under-represented in their state's delegation, met to create a "Commission on the Selection of Presidential Nominees." They planned on submitting complaints to the convention's Rules Committee calling for an end to the practice of winner-take-all in state delegations.[40]

Complicating matters further, about two months before the convention, more than a thousand frustrated Democrats met in Chicago as the "Coalition for an Open Convention," an effort largely organized by Allard Lowenstein, a New Yorker whose "Dump Johnson" campaign is considered to have influ-

---

40 The 1968 Convention agreed to study the issue. The resulting committee, the Commission on Party Structure and Delegate Selection, chaired by Senator George McGovern, made recommendations that were adopted by the Democratic National Committee in 1971. These were designed to take control of the Democratic presidential nomination process out of the hands of the Party bosses. McGovern, coincidentally or not, wound up the Party's nominee for President in 1972.

enced the President's decision to abdicate the '68 nomination. The Coalition couldn't quite organize a way to mount a bid for their own candidate for the presidency. They settled instead for passing a resolution opposing Humphrey, who should have been the favorite but was saddled with anti-Vietnam War blowback due to his time as Vice President.

In Chicago, as the date of the convention approached, various groups were applying for permits for their planned protests. Almost all were denied. Around the same time, the ever-vigilant J. Edgar Hoover sent a memo to all the FBI field offices initiating a vast counter-intelligence program to disrupt new leftist groups.

In retrospect, it should've seemed like a powder keg to me.

It seemed precisely like that to Chicago's Mayor Richard J. Daley, who had always been a law-and-order man, nearly to the point of fascism. With the shadow of mobs of protesters looming over the city, he'd put his 12,000-man police force on 12-hour shifts in late August. He also brought in an equivalent number of National Guard and federal troops, doubling down on his show of force. Daley was going to keep an iron grip on the dissent. With the spotlight on his city, he would make sure nothing got out of hand.

But the best laid plans...

Four months after Martin's assassination, I was in Chicago as an elected McCarthy delegate, and the city felt as charged as I'd seen in Birmingham. The protests during the convention covered a lot of political territory. It was an amalgam of simmering resentments—racial tensions, anti-war sentiments, suspicion of the so-called democratic process itself. The emotion was too much to contain, and with the protesters baiting law enforcement with thrown bottles and vicious insults, the small one-on-one skirmishes (billy clubs against skulls, mostly) eventually blossomed into a pure widespread riot.

Daley did his best to keep the convention insulated from the chaos on the streets, but once a television was turned on

Wednesday afternoon, August 28th, the cat was out of the bag. The proceedings on the convention floor were halted as we all started to understand what was taking place outside.

The New York delegation was one of the largest, second only to California, and many of the electors I was responsible for rallying turned to me for guidance on the protests. And, like many other delegate leaders from nearly every other state, I voted with my feet and led a large group of my fellow New Yorkers into the breach.

We marched past the Conrad Hilton on Michigan Avenue, which was the hotel of choice for the convention. It was hot, ugly, loud, violent, insane.

Looking to the hotel on the right, I could see at the huge windows of the lobby's mezzanine that many of the party leaders were staring at our protest like it was a spectator sport. There was Hubert Humphrey, watching it all unfold. I'd say watching it all slip away if I believed the man was at all self-aware.

Looking to the left, I could see the cameras of ABC, CBS, and NBC.

We, the mob, were right between the two.

I knew then that the Humphrey campaign was finished. So was McCarthy's and McGovern's. The Democrats had lost a sitting president and another martyred president's brother to head our ticket, and now with the news trucks shaping public opinion and passing judgment on us, we'd lost the moral high ground.

Richard Nixon, triumphant out of Miami's Republican Convention two weeks earlier (despite Ronald Reagan and my old friend Nelson Rockefeller attempting to block his nomination) was going to get elected president.

Two days later, as my flight to New York took off from O'Hare, I glared down at the glistening and still simmering Chicago streets and felt sick. I was in first class and already had a drink in my hand. I turned away from the window and looked at the glass—real glass back then.

264 LAST OF THE LIONS

The splintering of the Democratic Party was not the only casualty of the 1968 Democratic Party National Convention in Chicago. The Clarence Jones who'd landed in the Windy City wasn't the same man who was leaving. I suspect many other delegates were suffering a similar post-convention traumatic stress disorder.

I had called home from payphones throughout the convention, to tell Anne what was going on and, near the end, to reassure her and our children that I was safe. Most of these calls were placed in the late afternoon or early evening. Yet even accounting for New York's time difference, Anne sounded mealy-mouthed and slow during these calls, repeating herself and making little sense.

With a bit of distance, I could see the problem. Or rather, hear it. "Anne, you've had too much to drink," I would tell her.

"That's your opinion and you're entitled to it, Clarence," she would fire back with slurred contempt, "but you're wrong."

On the plane, I made the decision staring at the cut glass vodka tonic. The man who'd left Anne to come to Chicago wasn't the man who was returning. *That* man was never returning.

What occurred in Chicago during and on the floor of the Convention and—equally important—outside in the streets of Chicago, was an extraordinary, once in a lifetime experience. That was the only time I ever seriously considered whether or not I could continue to live in America. What I saw and heard as a Co-chair of the New York State McCarthy delegates on the floor, and, more importantly, what I saw the government do to the peaceful protesters outside made me ask myself, *Is this really happening in the United States? Is this really my country?*[41]

• • •

---

41 I recall being in France, Tunisia, Egypt, Iraq, Saudi Arabia, and Switzerland and occasionally having conversations that included criticisms of United States foreign policy or the perceived treatment of me and other Negroes. I'd be asked why I would continue to live in the U.S. when I had options to live abroad. Fundamentally, it was my kids. I could not separate myself from my children like that—they provided an anchor of sanity against any momentary angry impetuousness.

When I reunited with Anne at the Riverdale house, I told her I couldn't continue in the marriage because she was drunk too much of the time.

When I announced this, Anne laughed. She was drunk, naturally.

I told my wife that if I continued to be married to and live with her, I would be dead within five years. Her growing dependence on alcohol and the consequence of that on our relationship had developed in a way that appeared beyond my capacity to constructively manage. Most of the arguments we had—about the children, about my traveling when Martin was alive and thereafter on business, and especially after the formation of Intramerica—occurred after both of us had been drinking a lot.

"I may be vain, and I may like martinis," she said, "but I'm not stupid." She wondered why I would have to leave to protect myself from becoming an alcoholic since, if I really wanted to stop drinking, I could just stop. Then all that would be necessary for us to get along would be for me to avoid lecturing her on her consumption, since she had no plans to stop drinking. "What did you always say about white people whose skin color gave them privilege?"

"Free, white and twenty-one," I muttered.

Anne said, "Clarence, honey? I am free, white, and it's been a while since I turned twenty-one. I will drink as much as I goddamn want, and it's none of your goddamn business."

She was going down and practically daring me to go with her.

This was the exact attitude that had persuaded me that my survival was at stake; I could not be a good father to my children if I was seriously ill, medically impaired, or dead.

Anne thought I was a coward. I thought I was just seeing the writing on the wall. If we both drank ourselves to death, who would be left to take care of our four kids?

That, of course, felt like hyperbole at the time; a lawyerly argument *ad absurdum*. Nobody was really going to go down by drinking, right?

. . .

It probably comes as no surprise that, despite my sweeping declaration, I didn't sober up. My drinking persisted through the years of our separation and my eventual divorce from Anne. But it didn't accelerate like her drinking did. According to the kids, Anne's drinking just kept getting worse and worse.

I moved to Manhattan, at first staying at a short-term weekly rental at the Hudson Hotel on West 57th Street. After several months, I settled into an elegant apartment on West 72nd. It was just off Central Park, next to the Dakota and my songwriting friend Bob Crewe. I lived on the 37th floor with a terrace and view of the Manhattan skyline, looking west toward the Hudson River and New Jersey beyond.

The '60s bled into the '70s. Single and rich in Manhattan in the early '70s was the way to do it. For a period, the place on West 72nd was a "playa's" playpen. The women came and went. I met them at discos and bars and concerts and restaurants. Some were well known, some were married, some were friends' wives. I never smoked cigarettes or much pot. I never snorted cocaine. And I tried, with limited success, to keep my drinking level.

Counter-intuitively, during this period I began to jog six days a week, between four and six miles a day. I often thought the rigorous daily exercise in the early morning must have arrested or delayed the debilitating consequences of heavy alcohol consumption.

I also spent time back at the hotel on West 57th, where I kept my access to the health club. The gym at that time was managed and operated by fitness guru Jack LaLanne. He would wear a one-piece jumpsuit in orange, blue, or tan as he instructed members through their exercise routine.

Occasionally an announcement over the loudspeaker would summon a member to respond to an important phone call. The member would leave the workout area and go to the nearest house phone. As a rule, that was a rare occurrence; members were discouraged from allowing people to call them while they were working out. Jack felt the phone should be for emergencies.

One day when I was a partner at Carter, Berlin & Weill, I'd been working on a transaction that was time-sensitive. I took a break to get a workout in, but during the time I was at the gym received two or three announcements over the loudspeaker to return phone calls.

Jack came up to me and asked what line of work I was in that prompted so many interruptions to my workout. I explained apologetically that I was a lawyer and investment banker and told him I'd *tried* to discourage people from calling me at the gym.

Jack came up close to me, pressing his finger against my chest. "Do you know what this is? Your body is a Rolls Royce," he proclaimed. "It needs daily attention and care. If you don't allocate the necessary time and attention it deserves, it will begin to malfunction. And you only get the one, so it doesn't matter how important the deal you're working on is. Tell your business associates that your time here is needed to fine tune your Rolls Royce!"

I wish I'd thought to pass LaLanne's advice on to Anne.

Hanging on the wall of my divorce lawyer's office was a framed sign that read:

In every matrimonial case there are always three sides:
the wife's, the husband's, and the truth

In keeping with the wisdom contained therein, my discussion of those years following the breakup of my marriage is constrained by the fact that Anne is now deceased. It is difficult for me to write about the events associated with my leaving our marital household and children, because my ex-wife isn't here to provide a counter-narrative to anything I now explain.

However, one point is indisputable: Anne's dependency on alcohol killed the marriage. What role I played, in terms of my conduct or character flaws, that contributed to Anne's growing dependency remains an open question. Clearly, it was a

factor, but I can't estimate the impact of that behavior.

Leaving the children was painful. Doug Pugh, one of my closest friends at the time, told me it would be better for me and my children if I simply endured and remained in our home. The advice was lovingly given and difficult to ignore, but in the end, I did what I believed at the time was in my and the children's long-term interests.

One of the most difficult things for me to handle was the awkwardness of visitation time. If the weather was warm while they were still in school, I'd pick up my oldest son Ben and drive to nearby Van Cortlandt Park and play baseball with him or ride bikes. The physical activity made it easier for us to ignore our pain.

I stayed on West 72nd Street throughout the seventies. It was the place where, as a young teenager, my oldest daughter Christine sought refuge from those instances of Anne's worst episodes of drinking and verbal violence. Tina was still attending Fieldstone in Riverdale. During the week, when she decided she couldn't be in the same house with her mother, she would come and stay with me and commute to Riverdale for school.

Those were also the years when my investment banking work would take me to the Bahamas or Jamaica. I often stayed over the weekend and returned to New York Sunday evening, but one trip Ben's birthday fell on a Saturday. The other partners pressured me to remain because a special dinner party was taking place at the Nassau Beach Hotel to celebrate our client. I was told that my son would understand.

"Tell him you'll celebrate his birthday on Monday or Tuesday."

I told my partners I couldn't, because it would make a big difference to my son if I was there to celebrate his birthday on the date it *actually occurred*.

Look at me, showing up. Making the hard calls. Of course, it's easier to remember the moments of being the good father than it is to remember the other ones.

• • •

Then, in March of 1977, Anne Aston Warder Norton Jones, my ex-wife, the mother of my children, was found dead in the front seat of her car in the driveway at her mother's home in Wilton, Connecticut. Empty bottles littered the cabin of the vehicle. She'd drank herself to death.

Nobody was really going to go down by drinking, right?

If we both drank ourselves to death, who would be left to take care of our four kids?

I suddenly found myself a sole parent. The youngest of our four, Dana, was twelve years old at the time. His sister, Christine, was a senior at Brown University.

How the hell was I going to do this?

Losing my mother, Malcolm, Martin, the Kennedy brothers—that had all been bad. But Anne... this threatened to destroy the kids' lives. That internal gyroscope that had stood me in good stead over all the years and all through the heartbreak seemed to be out of order, malfunctioning. I felt rudderless.

Nobody told me the road would be easy. But, Lord, I don't believe you brought me this far just to leave me. James Cleveland may have said it, and once I may've believed it. In March of '77, I wasn't so sure.

New York City was good for someone like me in the 1970s. The pace and the hunger that vibrated through the city blunted the everyday racist aspects of life there. Everyone was on the hustle, and pushing the limits was job one for anyone who wanted to get ahead. My skin may have been black, but my cash was green, and that's really what mattered in Manhattan.

Of course, the average white New Yorker was still *terrified* to wander up to Harlem. The national—and certainly the borough-wide—perception of the crime-ridden, graffiti-wasted, and drug-scarred streets of urban America made it feel as if Harlem would terminally play its role as what Bobby Womack referred to as "the capital of every ghetto town." Those people didn't know what they were missing: Sure, there was public housing, sure there were street gangs, sure Frank Lucas was a heroin kingpin, but in general, the vibrancy, culture, music, and food were all among the best in the world at that time. Some thirty years before former president Bill Clinton raised some eyebrows by choosing New York City's 125th Street for his foundation's world headquarters, I had held onto a vision of a reinvigorated Harlem. This was the early '70s though, and it would take some time to get to the point where tourists would wait in line for a table at Sylvia's or the Red Rooster.

I wasn't alone in having notions of grandeur for Harlem. Percy Ellis Sutton saw it from the beginning.

Percy is an unsung hero. He had been a barnstorming circus pilot, an intelligence officer in the Tuskegee Airman unit in World War II, a Freedom Rider, and a well-regarded Civil Rights attorney (one of his clients was Malcolm X). He was even an Eagle Scout.

I first met Percy when I began to get involved with New York politics. He was part of the regular Democratic Party establishment and attended the 1968 convention in his capacity as President of the borough of Manhattan. At the time, the delegates to the national convention in Chicago had to be committed to a specific candidate, and they conducted their affairs separately from the other New York delegates committed to a different candidate. In my capacity as Co-chair of the McCarthy delegates from New York State, part of my job was to exclude people like Percy Sutton from our caucus meetings. He didn't take it personally.

A few years after the convention, I had made a bid to purchase the *New York Amsterdam News*, at the time the largest African American weekly newspaper in the United States. It was a kindred spirit to the *Village Voice,* but the voice it echoed was that of the men and women of Black New York. Historically, Black newspapers have played a major role in providing the white community with a window into the African American experience. In 1827, John Russwurm and Samuel Cornish started *Freedom's Journal* in New York. By the start of the Civil War, nearly four dozen Black newspapers were being published. So, I was standing on the shoulders of those trailblazing giants of publishing when, at the age of forty, I attempted to take the helm of one of the most venerated papers of the genre.

I didn't realize until well into the negotiations with my banking partners and the newspaper's owner that Percy Sutton was also one of the parties bidding against me. It made sense to me was that we team up; I figured the two of us coordinating could likely snuff out any other competition.

I called Percy and we sat down to discuss it. Together we decided that we would jointly bid for the *New York Amsterdam News*—his group and I would each acquire 48% of the paper with the remaining 4% ownership held by a small group of independent investors. Ours was the winning bid. Just like that, we were in the publishing business.

The small investors had no real interest in running the paper, and as it turned out, neither did Percy—or perhaps with all his other projects he simply didn't have the time. As a result, I took on the roles of editor and publisher. Percy and his team were most interested in the political value of the paper— or to put it more bluntly, interested in using the newspaper as a media platform to advance his agenda in local New York City politics.

I was more concerned with reporting the news as it happened, to give the community of readers real insight into their day-to-day conditions. Percy and I agreed that we would periodically switch writing editorials or supervising the writing of editorials so we could focus fairly on the issues of importance to each of us.

However, one of the first changes I initiated was re-formatting the op-ed page. Shortly after taking the helm, I learned that our paper was one of the few permitted for distribution and purchase in the various prisons throughout the State of New York. Like most media outlets, our paper was constantly inundated with letters from prisoners complaining about the inhumane conditions they endured (sadly, inmates had and have both horrible conditions and a lot of free time to complain about them to anyone, whether they'll listen or not).

And the number of letters had been on the rise. In 1970 and '71, there were several news reports about disquiet and disturbances in prisons throughout the state, most notably on Rikers Island. Growing discontent within the New York State prisons became an issue of widening concern for *Amsterdam News* readers. Given incarceration demographics, I decided the subject might be of more interest to my readership than, say, that of the *New Yorker*. We began to run a new column, "From Behind Prison Walls." Our weekly receipt of letters soon began to exceed our capacity to reprint excerpts. I created "From Behind Prison Walls" to provide inmates a voice, the opportunity to have their letters read by the public at large. It turned out I was perhaps the only editor in the country who actually published letters like this.

Though this wasn't my first brush with letters from prison —that came in Birmingham—it would certainly not be my last experience with the pains of New York's prisoner population.

• • •

Percy and I continued our joint business venture in 1972 by purchasing New York City's largest Black-owned AM radio station, WLIB, and acquiring right of first refusal on its sister FM station, WBLS. We took on some other investors, including David Dinkins, who would become the first African American Mayor of New York, and Hal Jackson, a legend in radio and one of the first Black disc jockeys to reach a large white audience. Together we founded Inner City Broadcasting. We exercised the option on WBLS two years later and branded the twin stations "The Total Black Experience in Sound." Before long we expanded to the San Francisco, Los Angeles, and Detroit markets.

During this period in the radio industry, some station owners and disc jockeys got caught up in the "payola" scandal. This occurred when a PR person or agent of the label or artist seeking airplay on a top radio station would slip a wad of hundred dollar bills or bags of cocaine to a disc jockey to get him to play the artist's record. The FCC would threaten the licenses of station owners and impose hefty fines if payola was discovered. In some limited cases, the offending DJ would be fired and banned from working at other stations.[42]

To protect Inner City against such exposure, we sat down with our disc jockeys to decide which songs were going to be played during their broadcast segment. These playlists were then kept under lock and key by the station manager, who could compare the actual broadcast to the plan.

During my early years in media, I became friendly with Bobby Schiffman. Bobby's family had owned and operated the Apollo Theatre for decades. It was located on 125th Street between 7th and 8th Avenue, just a few blocks from my office at the news-

---

42   It is not by coincidence that payola became an issue of governmental attention only after Black artists began buying their way on-air with stations that otherwise had a policy of playing only white artists. In truth, the radio industry had pay-for-play activities since its invention, Alan Freed's case being an early example. This is another example of the racism baked into the very soul of American culture.

paper. Built in 1913, it was a grand and classic uptown music hall. At that time, the Apollo was beginning to confront the competitive pressures of larger entertainment venues outside of Harlem.

It was a simple lesson in economics. For years, Black artists could not get bookings at the city's white-owned venues. By default, the Apollo Theatre became their cultural performance home. However, when those larger venues began to open up in the late '60s, they presented the Apollo artists opportunities to make more money per performance. The Apollo, with its intimate capacity of 1,500 seats, could not competitively pay artists who had played there for years.

Bobby Schiffman and his family fought back by offering artists two sets per night, which meant the opportunity to sell twice as many tickets. They also started showing movies, but none of this really staunched the bleeding. It was sad to see the decline, and I kept thinking there should be a way to save the beautiful Apollo.

My role as publisher of the *Amsterdam News* gave me a public profile I hadn't previously had. I was invited to serve on the Board of Directors of the New York Plaza Hotel, the crown jewel in the Sonesta chain. In addition to the Plaza, Sonesta operated hotels in Boston, Bermuda, Los Angeles, and New Orleans. While working with Sonesta, which was actively looking to develop another Manhattan property, I began forming a plan that might be able to help the Apollo Theatre.

During my last years at Carter, Berlind & Weill, I met Frank J. Biondi, Jr. A newly minted Harvard Business School MBA, he was the firm's young hotshot hire of that year. Prior to Harvard, he'd attended Princeton University, an institution where the white South sent its sons to be educated "up north." But Frank was from New Jersey, and Frank didn't change to suit anybody but Frank. He didn't turn into a Southern white boy while at Princeton, and he didn't turn into an insufferable know-it-all when he attended Harvard. Early on, I needled him, saying the only other nice white person I ever met who went to Princeton was my partner, Roger Berlind. "You seem like another one."

Frank responded, "Well, you'll just have to wait and see."

He was one the few white men I ever met that was entirely bereft of the trappings of white male racism. It was an amazing phenomenon to experience.

The two of us became socially friendly, our interests aligning around baseball and music—particularly blues and Southern rock. At his apartment, we would listen to his record collection. Once we were discussing the uniqueness of the Black singer—how you could just listen to their voice and instantly know it was a Black performing artist. Frank put on a record of a performer I had never heard of named Joe Cocker. I thought the guy was fantastic.

Months passed, and one day Frank let me know that he bought two tickets to go see this performer Joe Cocker that I had liked so much. Cocker was performing at the Bottom Line, a jazz music venue in Greenwich Village. When we arrived, we got in line out front and wound up standing right next to the poster the venue always put up for that night's act. I looked at the large pen and ink poster of a white guy—Joe Cocker.

After all these years I can still remember the grin Frank had on his face. I had never heard nor seen a white person whose voice sounded so much like a Black soul singer when you closed your eyes.

Thinking back on that evening out, I realized that Frank was the perfect person to help bring my big idea to fruition: A business complex on 125th Street that would include the Apollo Theatre, offices for the *Amsterdam News*, and a Sonesta Hotel. The idea was to build the hotel rooms and offices above a newly renovated Apollo, which would act as the crown jewel of the project.

I called Frank, who at this point was no longer at the firm. He had gone on to help found and finance the Children's Television Workshop, producer of *Sesame Street* and *The Electric*

Company. He had also joined Teleprompter, which was eventually bought by Warner Bros.[43]

Frank loved the idea and began coming to my office to work at a desk I provided. He would often bring his lunch and eat as we outlined the parameters of this endeavor and how it might be financed. I was the beneficiary of one of the most brilliant financial minds I have ever encountered. Frank and I created a private placement of eager investment and borrowed bank financing.

Subject to us obtaining financing, the Sonesta agreed to locating a hotel on 125th Street. I had negotiated a purchase price for the Apollo with Bobby Schiffman. Architectural drawings and renderings were in the works. The complex was to be owned and operated by a newly created holding company we called Center City Communications.

Sonesta's willingness to locate a hotel on 125th Street during those years was historic. Harlem had a terrible reputation for drugs and crime at the time, and being the first mover in that market took real courage and trust. It was, of course, subject to structuring an innovative institutional investment package that could attract commercial banking paper on top of more private equity.

We lined up the debt/bank financing easily enough, but we had only a tight window of time to make up the balance in equity investment. Frank and I knew we needed to swing for the fences in our proposal. We made presentations to Prudential Life Insurance and ITT, and each company agreed to invest a half million dollars. None of this would have been possible without Frank, his pedigree, and his brilliance.

We were on a roll, but we were unable to parlay the early affirmatives into full equity. We needed a miracle, another deep-pocketed yes, but it didn't happen. The debt period elapsed, and the bank withdrew. In short order, the Sonesta Group decided a hotel in Harlem might be too risky, and the project fell apart.

---

43 At Warner Bros, he created and wrote the five-year business plan for Home Box Office, what is now known as HBO, and became its President and CEO.

Center City Communications was too early for its time.

Frank died in 2020. Often in life we can measure a person not solely by their successes or failures, but the quality and magnitude of the effort they undertook. Frank was, by any measure, an extraordinary human being who provided exemplary corporate leadership and left an enduring impact in the entertainment, television, and motion picture businesses.

Frank has never been in given sufficient credit for his imaginative business and creative genius. After years as an experienced wordsmith, I remain challenged to choose the correct words to describe the love and admiration I still have for Frank. So, I'll simply repeat what I posted on social media shortly after his death: They don't make white boys like Frank J. Biondi, Jr., anymore.

Despite my disappointment in Sonesta, I understood the pragmatic business decision regarding Harlem. I continued as a director of the Plaza Hotel. I left the newspaper in the late '70s and had an office at Inner City Broadcasting with Percy Sutton at 2nd and East 42nd Street and worked primarily in the radio business.

Then I got another bite at the apple that was the Apollo Theatre.

It had shut down briefly in 1976, then was sold and reopened quickly. The theater struggled for several years, and by the turn of the decade it was up for sale again.

Percy Sutton was interested. Remembering my Sonesta plan, he came into my office and we talked about what could be done with the Apollo now. We decided the office complex was too much to undertake. The goal was: Buy, renovate, promote, and find a way to create revenue beyond renting seats to patrons. We drew up a rough budget and plan and Percy, a former Manhattan borough president who had everyone's phone number, started through his Rolodex.

Percy delegated the negotiation of the bank loan and other financing to me. There was no ITT or Prudential this time.

With the assistance of the New York State Economic Development Corporation, Inner City purchased the Apollo Theatre. Financing for the project included $4 million in state and federal loans and a $1.5 million infusion from private investors.

Working with Percy Sutton and the group he assembled to renovate the Apollo Theatre was one of the most remarkable experiences of my life. In addition to members of the Sutton family who undertook various duties during the renovation, one of the most memorable people was Jerry Kupfer, Inner City's resident radio station broadcast engineer. Percy Sutton had great confidence in Jerry, who was given on-site responsibility for working with the construction company that was performing the renovations.

Percy saw the renovation of the Apollo as a statement about the pride he and others in his generation (including me) took in that theater. Percy's mantra was "excellence and majesty." He wanted the renovation to have a certain contemporary elegance that the Harlem and broader Black communities would be proud of. His vision was to have the Apollo serve as the broadcast venue for music videos and television shows as well as a theatre for live entertainment.

New carpet was installed in the lobby and in the theater. The seats were refurbished. Most important to Percy, the men's and women's restrooms had to be first class. Around midnight before the official opening, Percy and I were on our knees in the men's restrooms, checking that the newly laid tile floor was completed and that all of the toilets and sinks, soap, paper towel dispensers, and toilet paper holders were in working order.

I joked with Percy, asking how men of our stature—former President of the Borough of Manhattan, Ivy League lawyer— found ourselves on our knees at midnight in a men's room?

Percy calmly responded, "No matter how much glitter and glitz the Apollo has now, patrons will remember their experience by the condition of the restrooms. Favorably or unfavorably. I want to make sure it's favorably."

Percy's vision for the Apollo was soon validated. *Motown Returns to the Apollo*, a three-hour television special featuring 60 entertainers representing a wide spectrum of pop, soul and jazz talent over the previous 50 years was taped by NBC. It provided the backdrop for the grand reopening.

Prior to the taping, Coca-Cola sponsored a reception in the mezzanine of the subway station at 57th Street and the Avenue of the Americas. A sextet featuring members of the original Duke Ellington orchestra performed alongside the Apollo's 12-member dance ensemble. After the show, the surprise: We had worked with the Transit Authority and arranged for a vintage 1948 subway train to take them to Harlem for the opening.

Of the theater itself, the *New York Times* reported:

> *The newly refurbished theater has all the glamorous trappings of a Broadway house—plush purple carpet, crystal chandeliers and red-and-gold trimmed box seats. It was a splendid setting.*

Not long after The Apollo opened, Percy began to think about taping and rebroadcasting the centerpiece of the theater's long history, *Amateur Hour at The Apollo*. It consisted of having performers from all over the country on the Apollo stage every Wednesday evening before a live audience. It was widely acknowledged in the entertainment business if you performed at The Apollo's amateur night and survived, you had arrived as an artist in show business.

The Amateur Hour audience was regarded as one of toughest anywhere in the world. If an audience didn't like a performer, they would shout boos and scream for the performer or group to be pulled off the stage by comedic tap dancer Sandman, who would grab the performers with a curve handled wooden cane to the booing audience's delight.

On the other hand, if the audience liked the act, they would shout and scream their approval, sometimes throwing flowers on the stage at the feet of the performers. Apollo audiences have shouted and screamed approval toward Amateur Hour performers who went on to become huge stars.

From this concept emerged the idea of a possible late-night show or variety show that would be taped and syndicated on broadcast television.

This was the heyday of syndicated TV shows. Percy designated me as Executive Vice President of Apollo Entertainment Company. I was to go out and solicit TV producers and TV networks that might be interested in airing our shows on late night television.

During this time, I became friends with Mersh Greenberg and his oldest daughter, Bonnie. She was a lawyer involved in clearing the rights to use various songs and music in the soundtrack of motion pictures. Mersh was a cofounder and manager of a newly created television and motion picture facility in Queens, converting a former bread factory into Silvercup, the center of New York production.

I introduced Percy to Mersh. The two of us toured Silvercup Studios, and Mersh came and visited the Apollo Theatre. To give us some production expertise, I arranged to have Percy's daughter, Cheryl, work at Silvercup with Mersh as an apprentice.

To sell this idea of an entertainment variety show for late night television, Percy, Jerry Kupfer, and I (along with others from the Inner City Broadcast Corporation family) created a five minute sizzle reel of *It's Showtime At The Apollo*.

Every year, the television production business holds a national conference or convention of TV producers (NATPE). In 1982, the convention was held in March in Las Vegas. We decided to have a booth at the Convention showcasing *It's Showtime at the Apollo*. This required us to rent space and construct a space to exhibit our reel. Jerry was placed in charge arranging for space of our booth on the convention floor and supervising its construction.

Our exhibit booth consisted of an enclosed space with TV monitors overhead playing the pilot on a loop. Percy and I had developed a friendship with the then station manager of WNBC in New York. He then introduced us to the station managers of all the NBC-owned and operated TV stations in the U.S.

A new syndicated show that could amass commitments from TV stations collectively covering 80% was the gold standard. This is critical, because the amount of nationwide coverage your show had determined the rate you could charge advertisers seeking spots during your show's time period. We returned from Vegas beating the 80% threshold.

I had developed a friendship with Bob Banner. His company, BB Associates, was the producer of TV programs such as *The Dinah Shore Show* and *Star Search*. I introduced Percy to Bob and his company. Thereafter, the Apollo and Inner City Broadcasting entered into a joint venture to produce *It's Showtime At The Apollo* for nationwide syndicated broadcast. The show ran for five years and featured preforming artists such as Destiny's Child, Eartha Kitt, A Tribe Called Quest, Boys II Men, Mariah Carey, M.C. Hammer, and many others.

Working with my beloved brother Percy Sutton at Inner City Broadcasting Corp and the Apollo gave me some of the most enriching and exciting years of my life. Seeing Harlem blossom again over the decades has been one of the small victories in my lifelong struggle for equality and dignity.

The last time I'd spoken to Nelson Rockefeller, we were standing in the vault of one of his banks and I was getting a briefcase containing $100,000 in cash handcuffed to my wrist. You could learn a lot about a person that way, or at least I thought you could. But people can fool you. Or people can change.

Or both.

Nearly ten years after that briefcase, Rockefeller was New York's governor, and I was talking to him from a graffiti-smeared phone booth off of Broadway. Grim news: It seemed a huge number of angry inmates had wrestled control over Attica Penitentiary upstate, hostages were taken, and some killed. It was a lock-down, a major standoff.

What did this have to do with me? Nothing. Except for some reason, the leaders of the uprising were demanding that I show up there and act as one of their representatives in negotiating their release. I'd been in the car on the way to publish my newspaper, and I'd just been flung head-first onto my own front page.

The Rockefeller family's history of concern over minorities' rights was well known. Spelman College was funded by the family and christened with Nelson's mother's maiden name. Despite this kind of "advertising," they were quiet about their participation in the Movement. Gov. Rockefeller practically swore me to secrecy in the spring of 1963 when he gave me that briefcase full of cash to bail out Martin King and the hundreds of others imprisoned in Birmingham's city jail by the psychopathic so-called Public Safety Commissioner "Bull" Connor.

But this was after all that. Martin was gone, "Bull" Connor was gone, and I was living along Central Park and running a newspaper in Harlem. Things were going well, and I'd taken on a luxury or two that very quickly turned into something close to feeling like a necessity. One of those was having a driver take me to work in a town car while I sat in the back and planned out an attack for my day. Even back then, the snarl of Manhattan traffic was nothing a sane man would be interested in dealing with if, with just a signing of a check, it could become someone else's problem. Needless to say, this was long before cell phones. Some high-end doctors had "beepers" that could track them down and hum, forcing them to call into their offices for an urgent message. But the rest of us were on our own. If you weren't by your phone, you could've been anywhere. In the wind and out of reach. So, imagine my surprise when my driver caught my eye in the rearview mirror and said, "They're calling your name, Mr. Jones."

"Who?"

"On the radio."

"Are you sure?" I replied. I had been reading the *New York Times*; I was aware that the car radio was on, but I hadn't been listening to it.

"Is there another Clarence Jones who's the publisher of the *Amsterdam News*? Listen!" My driver George had the habit of quietly tuning in WINS AM each morning to check the scores of the previous night's games. We were somewhere on the West Side Highway in New York, below 125th Street, headed to the newspaper offices.

As George cranked the volume dial, something I had never heard came out of that one tinny speaker that passed for fidelity in 1971. The sound akin to a news bulletin filled the air, but it wasn't exactly the news. It was the authoritative voice of an announcer saying: "– can hear this message, it is urgent you contact the Governor's office in Albany immediately." A phone number was rattled off, and then the message started again. "This is an urgent request by the State of New York to contact Clarence B. Jones. Governor Rockefeller requests if Clarence B. Jones, publisher of the *New York Amsterdam News*, can hear my voice right now, please go to the nearest phone and call his office immediately. Again, if Clarence Jones can hear this message..."

No telling how long it had been repeating. George and I looked at each other. Neither one of us had ever experienced anything like this before. It was a little bit like encountering a personalized version of the emergency broadcast system alert test. Quite unsettling. I had no idea what it was about. I'd received some bad phone calls before, but nothing like this.

"What do you want to do, Boss?" George asked.

I told him to get off the West Side Highway the first opportunity he saw. We exited at 96th Street and drove east toward Broadway. Ten minutes later I found myself leaning in a barely maintained phone booth making the call. Eventually, I was talking to Nelson Rockefeller once again.

"I'm glad we got through to you, Mr. Jones." Grateful for the call, he quickly explained the nature of the emergency. Upstate, near Buffalo, a riot had broken out in the Attica Correctional Facility, and the prison had literally been taken over by inmates. Rockefeller said, "If you were near a television, if you could see it, Mr. Jones, you'd know how serious it is. Extremely serious."

There was no movie-set appliance store filled with TVs nearby. I had only my imagination to fill me in. As the Governor searched for clarifying words, I rubbed my face, full of dread and feeling the weight of the world on my shoulders. "I take you at your word: You're talking about a full-scale riot."

"The riot's over. The inmates are in control. These people have killed at least one guard and taken nine hostages."

By now, there was no dancing around the big question. "But what does it have to do with me, Governor?" It had *something* to do with me, clearly. I knew that from the radio station all points bulletin. But I still had no idea what.

"The inmates are making a number of demands. One is that I send a group of 'observers' to hear their complaints and grievances. Your name was one of the first mentioned. They're demanding you show up at the prison, Mr. Jones."

Me? How did they know me? I wasn't famous. Yes, I'd been a part of some history, but from entirely within the shadows. Then it hit me. The newspaper. *Their* newspaper. The ones with their letters of complaint.

It turned out I was one of the very few—perhaps the *only*— editor in the country who actually published letters like this.

So, when the convicts of Attica's Cellblock "D" had their hostages and the government waiting for them to make their first move, they wanted some righteous representation. They wanted me to do their talking for them. To speak truth to power. From the rioting inmates' perspective, it was a perfect fit.

Without my realizing it, printing these letters had made my name intertwined with prison reform. I had become a beacon for inmates' rights. And now it was time to see what I could do with the power.

Almost three hundred miles away from Manhattan, the deadliest prison rebellion in U.S. history had very inauspicious beginnings.

A few hours before my call with Governor Rockefeller, on the morning of September 9th, 1971, an incident occurred at the Attica Correctional Facility when several inmates were on their way to breakfast. A minor conflict had developed between the prisoners and the guards the previous morning, which ended with the disciplining of two prisoners. A rumor spread that the two prisoners had been beaten as punishment. The inmates had no direct proof of this, but the rumor was nevertheless a tipping point.

By the fall of 1971, the prisoners of Attica were likely just waiting for an excuse to riot. The inmates, who had long been upset with the harsh conditions and (since the vast majority were African American) the overt racism of the guards, saw the rumored and unwarranted beatings as the last straw, and began to react. At lineup that morning, several inmates refused to come out of their cells, in solidarity with their supposed-tortured comrades.

. . .

There was no question that on some level, the violence had been foreshadowed. That entire summer, the facility had been an epicenter of complaint from inmates and their families. High prisoner density was the overarching issue (the prison was packed to nearly double its designed and approved capacity), but overcrowding was the fountainhead from which spilled out tributary complaints of deteriorated living conditions like cold water showers, scarcity of toilet paper, and the utter disregard for the beliefs of Islam, a major and growing religion among Black inmates. The inmates voiced their frustrations, which for the most part fell on deaf ears. New York State Commissioner of Corrections Russell Oswald had made several appointments to meet with the leadership but had canceled them all with feeble excuses.

Adding to the tension, a little more than two weeks before the riot, a prisoner was shot by a guard at San Quentin State. Many of the convicts had developed a new mindset. Rather than embracing their identities as run-of-the-mill criminals, some were possessed of the radical spirit that was sweeping the country at that time and began to look at their situation more as if they were prisoners of war or political prisoners. As a result of the indifference by those in charge and the agit-prop thinking of those incarcerated, the situation in Attica was, in retrospect, turning into something of a powder keg. All that was needed was a flame to touch off the fuse.

In an effort to straighten out the situation with the no-shows, several guards headed back to Cellblock "D," where the protesting inmates overpowered them and escaped. One guard attempted to use a phone to call for help but was beaten with the phone's handset. The inmates broke into a spontaneous riot. They made their way to the prison's central intersection—an area dubbed "Times Square"—and accessed the rest of the cellblocks from there, releasing dozens of inmates.

The steam whistle at the powerhouse was blown as a signal to everyone that anarchy had replaced order. The riot was on, without any planning or strategy. Not the best situation, but they all knew it was the one chance they'd ever get to make a stand, so they took it. Many of the inmates joined in the riot, making weapons and starting fires, taking guards hostage. One guard was severely beaten and thrown out of a second-floor window.

A group of inmates broke through a gate and took over an exercise area—"D" Yard.

Once in control of the prison, the inmates placed a series of demands at the feet of then Commissioner Oswald, for future delivery to Governor Rockefeller and then on to President Richard Nixon.

They demanded the removal of the warden (Vincent Mancusi, who they blamed for many of their woes), improvements in their living conditions ("more recreation with better equipment"), an end to censorship (the prison redacted newspapers and magazines as well as personal letters), and more.

There were fifteen demands in all, in a letter with the opening line: "From all inmates of Attica Correctional Facility to Sirs."

This missive also contained several "immediate" demands, including amnesty for revolt participants ("from all physical, mental and legal reprisals") and—here's where I come in— they demanded "urgent, immediate negotiation" through a list of heavy hitters both in the public eye and, if not actually vocal on the Civil Rights Movement, then at least left-leaning and humanistic in their social and political views. The requested group of eleven, many of whom would in fact make the trip to Attica included: Civil Rights attorney William Kunstler, famous from the Chicago Seven trial; New York State Assemblyman Arthur Eve; David Anderson of the Urban League of Rochester; Nation of Islam leader Louis Farrakhan; *Michigan Democrat and Chronicle* journalist Jim Ingram; Black Panther Party leader Bobby Seale; *New York Times* assistant editor Tom Wicker; Richard Roth of the *Buffalo Courier Express*; Juan Oritz of the Young Lords, a Puerto Rican nationalist group; Eva Bond, a literacy activist; and me, the man who printed their letters of outrage and injustice.

• • •

288 LAST OF THE LIONS

"We don't know where all this is going to go, as we try to sort things out," Governor Rockefeller told me. He thought it was a good idea to give the prisoners at least this much: To deliver to them as many of their requested "observers" as it was possible to reach—if for no other reason than to try to forestall the chances of any more violence erupting. The governor told me Tom Wicker, the associate editor of the *New York Times*, had also been requested by the inmates to act as an observer. He had agreed to fly to the prison, as had Herman Badillo, a congressman from a district in the Bronx who wanted to help. Also, although not requested as an observer, my old friend Wyatt Tee Walker, the former Chief of Staff of Dr. King's SCLC and then-Special Assistant on Urban Affairs for Rockefeller, would be coming along to lend his support. And if I would go along with it, the governor wanted me there.

"You would be doing a great service to me personally and to the people of the State of New York if you could come to Attica. If you can get over to the airport in New Jersey, we have a plane that can take you."

"Maybe," I told him.

He gave me the full court press. "If you don't have transportation, tell us where we can send a car to pick you up and drive you there as quickly as possible." He told me Bobby Douglass, his official secretary and chief of staff, would make all the arrangements.

"No, it's not a question of transportation." I considered the request for a moment. Negotiate a prison riot. Walk into a war zone. It was new territory, but new territory was always a challenge I found intriguing. I said to the Governor, "I'll have to call Mr. Douglass back after I determine if and when I can go there for you."

At the time of Rockefeller's request that I show up to the Attica rebellion, I had been living in Manhattan, and was in the process of divorce from Anne. To be geographically closer to the residence of my children with their mother, I relinquished my Manhattan apartment to move back to Riverdale a few blocks from where they lived. This would enable them to see me more frequently, especially on their way to or from school.

The timing was less than stellar; on the day of the radio announcement, a moving company had arrived at my West 72nd Street apartment to move me to the home I had rented in Riverdale.

My "significant other" at the time (she would later become my wife) was Charlotte Grad Schiff. She was the point person that day in arranging our move, and she was packing when I called over there. When I told her about the series of events and the conversation with Rockefeller, her first reaction was that she would've thought I'd come up with a much more believable excuse to get out of being around to oversee and participate in the move: "A prison riot? And Nelson Rockefeller called you to assist in resolving it? Give me a break."

But truth can be stranger than fiction.

I called back the Governor's office after I finished explaining the situation to Charlotte. "All right, Governor, I'll do what I can to help," I said. "I'll see you upstate."

Then Rockefeller said, "I hope not." It would have been telling had I paid closer attention. "If you guys handle this right, there might not be a need for me to go."

As I climbed into the back seat, I passed along the new game plan to George. The Governor had told me to head to Teterboro airport, a private airstrip in the northern New Jersey Meadowlands. There, the Rockefeller Family's personal plane would be waiting to take me to the prison.

"Do you want to stop back home first?" my driver asked.

But I traveled light. "The plane's waiting," I told him, not wanting to go to the apartment and get into it again with Charlotte in person. And certainly not imagining that the clothes I had on my back right then would be the same ones I'd still be wearing four days later. I picked up a new toothbrush at a drug store on Broadway and had George take the Lincoln Tunnel out of the city.

• • •

The plane took off with me, Tom Wicker, Herman Badillo, and another politician who would end up in an observer role, New York Senator John Dunne. As we soared over the Manhattan skyline and banked north along the Hudson, I felt lost in a receding sensation, a feeling of turning back the clock. Since Martin's death, I'd channeled my energies into business, and the little time I managed to set aside for social justice leaned more toward the political end of the spectrum. Of course, I still wanted change, the change Martin demanded, paid for with his life, and still hadn't gotten. But I'd fought back the pain of losing my friend by skewing my efforts into an approach that much more closely resembled the viewpoint of Roy Wilkins' NAACP and Whitney Young's National Urban League—that of "changing the system from within." In this area I'd made only minor inroads, so coming in like the cavalry to confront the prison system and its inherent inequities felt like an invigorating throwback. It revived in me some long-buried sense of street-level fighting I hadn't really noticed missing. But miss it I did. I was glad to be alive, glad to be one of the people to whom the downtrodden reached out. Did I condone prison riots? No. But I saw much of the same gray area those prisoners saw, and maybe together we could shed a little light on some of the problems. History would have a say in the matter, though. I had no way of knowing at that moment, but it wasn't going to be light that was shed there in Attica.

It would be blood.

The first afternoon at the penitentiary, the sky was upstate gray, the air was thick and humid. The four of us stepped out of the car that had brought us from the airstrip and approached a phalanx of state administrators who could barely hide their panic. You would've thought *they* were the hostages. These functionaries were waist-deep in a public relations nightmare and their boss, the Governor, had designs on the White House. You could see it in their eyes: Control had to be re-established as fast as humanly possible.

Shortly after our arrival we were escorted into the Cellblock "D" Steward's Room, which had been set up as a sort of base camp for the observers. There were some VIPs from the Buffalo area who'd been waiting for us. Along with the men with whom I'd flown from New Jersey, two others were on-site so far: The first man on the prisoners' requested observer list, William Kunstler, and William Gaiter, the director of a Buffalo-area anti-poverty group called BUILD (who, like Sen. Dunne, would end up as an observer though he wasn't part of the initial request). I knew Kunstler fairly well; I'd advised Stanley Levison to engage Kunstler to represent him before the Senate, and I'd been at the '68 convention where Kunstler caught the case that skyrocketed him to national prominence. Abby Hoffman and the rest of the so-called "Chicago Seven" were charged with conspiracy to incite a riot. Bill Kunstler had represented the group in the subsequent media circus trial (that included, among other chaotic displays of contempt for the process of justice, defendants taking the stand dressed up in Chicago Police uniforms and recommending to the judge that he take LSD).

Well, here was another media circus. There was already lots of press, local and national, assembled outside the prison.

We were immediately "briefed" by Commissioner Oswald. As far as the information went, it was limited. We were told about what had transpired prior to our arrival and the current situation in Cellblock "D." Oswald's posture and attitude made it clear that he didn't think any "observers" would make one bit of difference in the crisis, and he wasn't interested in playing babysitter.

Fine with me. I wasn't interested in having one.

As he spoke, Commissioner Oswald passed around a mimeographed sheet of the inmates' demands. We were told that they believed one guard had been killed in the uprising, but they did not know which inmates were responsible for his death. Oswald then told us something that didn't really require clarifying: If a guard had been killed, that took the prospect of "amnesty" right off the table. I had already come to that conclusion, as would any first-year law student.

However, this issue of addressing the demands was at the forefront of the operation. Oswald and Rockefeller were anxious for all the observers to be admitted into Cellblock "D" simultaneously, as evidence on their part to the inmates that they were negotiating "in good faith." As if to say, "You asked us to bring certain 'observers' to meet with you, and see, we have complied with your request." So, although several of us were inside the Attica prison facility, we had not yet been allowed into Cellblock "D." I wouldn't be going into the belly of the beast that day. And in fact, before we'd be allowed in at all, there was a small business matter that needed our attention.

One of the prison administrators came over and introduced himself, but instead of a handshake, he thrust a sheet of paper into my hand. "This is a document we need you to sign." And then he moved on to the other observers.

I eyed the piece of paper. Lawyers, I thought, and it was hard to imagine I was actually one of them. Part of the problem, as it were, not the solution. I did the state the courtesy of reading through the form which said, in substance, if anything happened to us as a result of being in "D" Yard or at the prison, the State of New York was absolved from any legal liability for any injuries or death we might sustain.

I turned to Commissioner Oswald and said, "You request me to come here to assist you and the Governor in resolving a prison rebellion, but you take or assume no responsibility or liability if I sustain any injury or am killed during the course of this visit? Thanks, but no thanks."

"Well, it's just in the event of something unforeseen..."

I couldn't help smiling at that. The document made it clear the worse potential outcome—the observers' death—was in fact well foreseen. It was possibly even the more likely scenario, despite the written proclamation from the inmates that, "We guarantee the safe passage of all people to and from this institution." I wasn't necessarily opposed to the idea of dying in the attempt to help if it came to that, but by the same token I didn't want the system that would be responsible for my death getting away scot-free.

The man who'd handed the form to me looked around. "Everyone else signed it," he said in a hushed voice, as if that would matter to me. As if we were all members of the same fraternity.

"If you bring in people to clean up your messes," I suggested, "you have to be prepared to take care of them."

"We'd need to talk to the Governor to get around this, Mr. Jones."

I returned the form and the fountain pen and grabbed a seat in a nearby folding chair, ready to wait as long as it took. "Someone can take me to the airport for the first available flight back down to New York City." I settled back, waiting for their move.

After discussion and consultation with someone over the phone and at the prison, the requirement for my signature on the form was waived, and I resumed being processed for admittance into Cellblock "D." If we all came back out in body bags, my family, alone among all the observers' next-of-kin, would maintain their right to sue. Cold comfort, indeed.

Most of the observers were still to arrive, so not much could be done that afternoon. This first wave of us discussed how we might be able to help for a number of hours, and then I found a ride to a nearby motel.

That night in the motel room was a blur. I stumbled in, pulled off my tie, kicked off my shoes, and collapsed on the bed. I was exhausted from just those few hours at the locked-down site... without actually working with the Attica prisoners. I knew the next day would be three times as long.

I didn't turn on the TV. I'd just get sucked into the Attica coverage. It was a national story by now; I'd seen the cameras and anchor people descend, vultures smelling fresh kill. I simply tried to relax and come up with some way of explaining to the inmates, whose situation was similar to that of cornered rats. They really weren't in a position of power. My mind racing at 1,000 RPM, I finally realized I needed to strip out of my suit and shirt and get them hung up. This was the only clothing I had with me, and I'd be wearing it until things were resolved. Maybe I could've dug up a ride from one of the state troopers to some suburban Buffalo mall to get some fresh clothes (or at least a razor and some shaving cream), but I was bone tired. So, I let the small, hopeful voice inside me drown out the harsh reality and tell me it wouldn't be too long before I was back home.

The next day, Friday, was a waste of anxious energy. We were still waiting for the rest of the observers to arrive. That didn't happen until the afternoon.

In the meantime, I had gotten a clear sense that from the Department of Corrections' standpoint, the only way to put a bow around this was to take back the prison by force. Wicker wrote in his excellent book about the riot, *A Time to Die*, that, "In Oswald's mind it was up to (the inmates) to arrange a settlement and avoid bloodshed."

As the observers arrived, each picked up on this entrenched point of view of the prison officials, and I could only imagine how much more of a bunker mentality was prevailing inside the prison. If both sides were so dug in, we all felt the responsibility to bridge the gap and find some compromise. In the end, Julian Tepper, a DC-area lawyer, and Jaybar Kenyetta, head of the Los Angeles Muslim Mosque, joined the observer team, taking the places of David Anderson and Eva Bond. Meeting in the Steward's Room, we tried to anticipate how we could work as negotiators to bring the sides together.

The prison officials escorted us to the entrance to the yard, which looked like something out of a movie. Then, with a *you're-on-your-own* sort of shrug, they backed away, leaving us literally to enter on our own.

The group of us made our way through the entrance of Attica to Cellblock "D," then down a corridor lined on either side with "sprung" prisoners toward "D" Yard. I still remember the expressions on their faces. Some of these men I would be seeing ten years later, some of the luckier ones, when they'd come by my office looking for handouts—what they referred to as "loans"—to help them survive on the outside. The look in their eyes at that time would be the same as they were at that moment: Lost.

The yard gate opened onto a dusk-lit throng of nearly a thousand agitated and fearful inmates. We were escorted to the makeshift bargaining table in the middle of the prison yard.

There were two long benches inside the cellblock, where all the observers sat. Immediately after we entered, our names and descriptions were shouted out to the inmates. As each observer's name was shouted, there was a roar from the crowd. One of the riot's leaders, a Black Muslim, told the inmates in "D" Yard that each of us would be called up to the microphone and makeshift podium to say a few words to them.

All through the night, the inmates made speeches and so did the observers. As important as it was for us to be there for them, they spent more time making proclamations to each other than they did listening to us. They were merely, in street parlance, "sellin' wolf tickets" to one another. When the observers did have a chance to speak, there was a thematic consistency threading through our comments. The idea behind nearly every one of the observers' remarks was that we were individually committed to facilitate a peaceful resolution of the uprising and to try to get the prison authorities to respond to and redress the inmates' demands.

It was extremely late when the prisoners began reworking their list of demands. Instead of narrowing it down, it grew. The prisoners' list of fifteen so-called practical demands had more than doubled. They were now asking for 33 concessions, including a plane to fly them out of the country. Cuba was mentioned several times. Things were moving in the wrong direction. The issue of amnesty was still paramount; it was listed third after getting food and water and replacing the warden. One of us suggested that before we could advise or comment on the issue of amnesty, we would have to arrange for a meeting with the local prosecutor.

We exited "D" Yard in the early hours of Saturday morning and immediately requested to meet with the district attorney as soon as he was available. We all felt it was crucially important that we follow through with the representation we had made to the inmates. It was an issue of trust.

Wicker, Tepper and I became the "amnesty delegation" and met Wyoming County District Attorney Louis R. James at his home. He was very gracious. We discussed the situation then prevailing inside "D" Yard in considerable detail. We indicated to the district attorney that we wanted to be able to report to the inmates that we had met with him and that the result of our meeting would somehow help to stabilize the situation. Their biggest concern was when the standoff was over (and I think most knew deep down that it wasn't going to end in victory) there would be a widespread, vendetta-driven, malicious prosecution for the murdered guard—a witch hunt.

That said, we were all realists. We knew that it was unlikely for the DA to grant amnesty to the inmates for a homicide that has occurred during a riot. We did what we could and negotiated a statement approved by the DA, Commissioner Oswald, and the Governor. Based on our meeting with James, this letter was issued:

> *I have been asked by Messrs. Clarence Jones, Tom Wicker and Julian Tepper, representing the Committee of Observers at Attica Correctional Facility, to express my views as to the possible prosecutions that might arise from the recent events at the Facility.*
>
> *First, I deem it to be my duty as a prosecuting attorney to prosecute without fear or favor ALL substantial crimes committed within this county, if sufficient evidence exists to warrant prosecution.*
>
> *Second, in prosecuting any crime, I do and would endeavor to prosecute fully and impartially and for the sole purpose of attempting to see that justice is done.*
>
> *Third, under the circumstances of the present situation at Attica, I deem it to be my obligation to prosecute only when in my judgment there is sufficient evidence to link a specific individual with the commission of a specific crime.*
>
> *Fourth, in this particular instance at Attica, I am unalterably opposed to the commencement of indis-*

criminate mass prosecutions of any and all persons who may have been present, and to prosecutions brought solely for the sake of vindictive reprisals.

Fifth, in the prosecution of any crime, in this as in every other situation, I would endeavor to prosecute honorably, fairly and impartially, with full regard for the rights of the defendants.

Finally, as prosecuting attorney, I regard it as my paramount duty to attempt to assure justice, both in the trial itself, the outcome of the trial, and in the possible sentence.

> *Louis R. James*
> *Wyoming County District Attorney*

While on its face that was certainly no grant or offer of amnesty to the rioters, a careful look given the context of the moment reveals a savvy political mind. There was no way in general, and with his Governor seeking the White House in particular, that this district attorney would cave in, but he had tried to give us something. As we were leaving James' house I remember saying, "I wish all district attorneys were like that."

The following, from my testimony in the aftermath of Attica before the McKay Commission, illustrates my state of mind about the letter:

I would say the best that we got from that was a quasi-amnesty. What do I mean by quasi-amnesty? Did the letter in fact say that all acts of criminal conduct would in fact be excused? No. It didn't say that, but we tried to get something... we tried to get something which would indicate that the state would not go in with vindictive and... you know, vindictive reprisals, would not seek to get blanket indictments, and would not seek to use their prosecutor, their prosecution powers in a way which essentially would be in a vindictive manner. That's what we tried to get. We tried to get something—well, we tried to get absolute amnesty but what we in fact

got in my judgment was something less than that but
something much better than nothing at all.

The letter walked a political high wire, helping both sides save face with just enough wiggle room without it ever looking like the DA was soft on crime or giving in. Now it was the observers' job to make the inmates see it the way we did. As a form of victory, as an indicator that the standoff could end without bloodshed. As, honestly, the best they had any right to hope for under the prevailing circumstances.

When we arrived back at the prison that afternoon with our letter in hand, we were met with another document. While we'd been out on the wild goose chase of amnesty from the county, the prison officials had been reacting to the list of 33 demands. Unbelievably, we were handed a counteroffer to that list. It was a list of 28 "concessions" Oswald was willing to make in exchange for an end to the siege. It was not a simple return checklist of the inmates' demands, of course, because the lawyers had to have a go at it, but it was remarkable in its wording. It sought to give the appearance that Commissioner Oswald had agreed to most of the 33 demands for change the prisoners were asking for. It appeared he'd given in on everything, essentially, except the spectacularly unrealistic expatriation and the real sticking point—the legal amnesty. He went as far as agreeing to half their demand, that of administrative amnesty, but in purposely singling out and parsing the specifics of the legal amnesty (property damage and civil suits), it spoke volumes about the potential of criminal prosecution. Whatever enthusiasm I'd managed to wring out of the letter from DA James had been trumped. Here was the state saying flat out, *No amnesty.*

I knew that would be the way the dice rolled on that issue. Not only had one guard died in the initial riot, but I was informed that William Quinn, the guard who'd been beaten and pushed through the window on Thursday morning had just died in the hospital. Another body. I could see an uphill battle was in the cards for the inmates.

In Bert Useem and Peter Kimbal's book *States of Siege: U.S. Prison Riots, 1971-1986*, the authors wrote, "In fact, as the inmate-state dialog collapsed, the observers more and more took on the (proactive) role, trying to come up with an idea to fend off catastrophe." It's an accurate description of our mindset at the time.

Telling people what they want to hear is a great way to get a crowd on your side, but I'm from the school of sales that says under-promise and over-deliver. I could read the crowd, and despite the haunted eyes, their attitude told me they'd been over-promised at least a thing or two. Probably by their own leadership, or perhaps by some of the observers we'd left behind. It was easy enough for any one of us to rally around their mindset and begin to think the chances were better than reality would dictate.

I was chosen as spokesman for the delegation that had gone to see the district attorney. I was brought into the yard and the crowd gathered around me. I read Oswald's 28-point letter verbatim. Point number three included a reference to the letter from the district attorney, so I read the letter as well.

When I finished reading aloud, I told the crowd, "You have earned our respect for your ongoing commitment to the journey down 'Freedom's Road.'" I took a breath, and then started in hard and deep. Just like with a cold ocean, wading in doesn't make it any easier. That's an illusion. I knew then and there I had to pull the trigger. An apt metaphor for the situation.

"In the Civil Rights Movement, several organizations sought the same objective: The end to racial segregation and the fostering of equal political and economic opportunities, regardless of race, color, or creed. But these groups considered and chose different political methods to achieve their similar objective. That is close, if not identical, to the situation we are facing here today.

"Sometimes during the course of a particular battle for what we're all seeking, some of the best-intentioned and committed brothers or sisters can let the intensity and passion of their devotion to a just cause emotionally cloud their otherwise sound political analysis and judgments."

The crowd quieted down.

I kept going. "One of the things I learned during those years I served and worked with Martin Luther King, Jr. as his lawyer, advisor, and speechwriter, was to always provide him with what I believed to be the best dispassionate political analysis of the power relationship of our committed foot soldiers to those of the segregationist opposition. Too much was at stake; too many people followed and depended on our leadership for us to avoid a daily assessment of the reality of *our* power in relationship to the opposition we faced, at any given time and place.

"We were passionate in our commitment to achieve racial justice and an end to segregation," I continued. "However, we were also clinical and dispassionate in our analysis of the reality of the possible options of actions we should choose to maximize the possibility for our victorious success; and minimize the possibility of our loss. Or defeat.

"So allow me to be the bearer of some sobering news."

There was dead silence. One of the riot's leaders leaned across the table. He glared down at me. His voice was laced with practiced menace. "We're not lookin' for *news*. This is a revolution, brother. This is no time for endless talk or analysis, only time for action. There's only victory."

Politics has a phrase for what was happening then: The man was "playing to his base." The Attica inmates ate it up. They were invested in this never-turn-back mentality, but there was a whole different audience outside the walls. They were not likely to greet the revolutionary rhetoric with nearly as much enthusiasm.

"If you want me go out there and tell the Governor everything you tell me, we can work it that way. Or... or we can deal with reality and try to figure out what's possible given this grim situation," I said, trying to inject a little reason into this kabuki performance to which I was suddenly a party.

The leader looked at me like I was crazy. The sea of faces surrounding him followed suit. Kunstler had been saying the issue of human dignity underpinned this whole mess. I could see that was true in all their eyes. But two innocent men were still dead, and that doesn't get erased from the debit column in these kind of situations.

I said, "No one's denying the mistreatment, the dehumanizing conditions, the crowding... but you've got to be realistic. I have experience in negotiating with institutional power. I know you can get something positive and *meaningful* out of this. Real change. Yeah, sure, we'll take care of these crowded conditions, you'll get your toilet paper, life will be better here. But this talk of a jet, this Havana freedom...? Listen to me, it's a fantasy. Blanket amnesty for that dead guard will not happen. Under the circumstances of this place, and this time, it's a fairy tale, brother. And in a situation like this, you can't afford to be telling yourself—or each other—bedtime stories."

"William Kunstler says—"

I cut him off. "Bill Kunstler and Bobby Seale are making a different assessment of the political strengths and weaknesses of Governor Rockefeller. I doubt they know the man like I do." Kunstler, a superb trial lawyer with a theatrical flair, had done a job whipping them into believing they had some leverage, and it was something I had to undo. "Nelson Rockefeller's got his sights set on the Oval Office. You think he's going to let the voters see a bunch of angry niggers push him around from inside a prison? He's not firing the warden just because you hard cases say the warden's a prick. He's not letting you fly off to Cuba. Now we all have to think straight about what you can hope to gain here, because these 28 points of Oswald's, I guarantee you, are the best offer you're going to get."

The leaders all looked stricken. Nobody wanted to tell any of us much about how decisions were made by the group. I was trying my hardest to get through. These weren't kids in a lecture hall struggling to understand history and what's going to be on the test you throw down in front of them next week. These were people with their lives on the line. Their struggle was not the opening gambit of a negotiation; it was a full-bore commitment. And they'd committed without thinking things through. It was rapidly approaching the immovable object-irresistible force dichotomy, and history showed that never ended well.

"You have to separate out the opportunities here," I said. The prisoners needed some straight talk. The Governor that *I* knew was never going to fold. "You don't have the power to force your demands down Governor Rockefeller's throat."

One leader looked as angry as I'd seen any of the prisoners look yet. "Political power comes from the barrel of a gun." Throwing a little Chairman Mao my way.

I nodded, letting him understand I knew where he was coming from. Mao Zedong had led one of history's most successful revolutions. He'd created the People's Republic of China. The man was probably spitting back what he'd heard Bobby Seale say a day earlier, when the Black Panther was busy convincing these guys *they* had the upper hand in all this. They should've been quoting Rev. Walker, who'd also told them the 28-point plan was a great concession by "the man." But no, they were going all in with the revolutionary mindset. Well, I knew a bit about Chairman Mao myself.

"Right, brother," I told him, "I too am quite familiar with that quotation from Chairman Mao. It goes, 'Real political power comes from the barrel of a gun, not from revolutionary-sounding speeches.'" I reminded the inmates that those words were spoken when Zhou Enlai, Mao and others were leading several thousand armed followers in their 6000-mile "Long March" across China to defeat General Chiang Kai-shek. "Mao could only say that because he had *guns*."

The inmate got right up in my face. "We've got guns!"

"You've got a couple of noisemakers," I pointed out. I glanced up to the towers surrounding us. "You want to see guns? Look up there. Those are the ones with the power here." The snipers from the New York State troopers and the armed Attica prison guards were leaning on the walls with their assault rifles aimed at all of us assembled in the prison yard. "Having a few dozen hostages gives you the *illusion* of control. They'll only let you hang onto that illusion so long. Those men are simply waiting for the order from Rockefeller to retake this yard by force. Like it or not, the barrels of your guns don't bestow any political power right now."

I let them think about that for a moment, then drove the point home: "You have to make your choices based on the reality of your limited power against state police and armed prison guards waiting to commence an assault to retake the prison. We're running out of time."

The leader leaned back. "Amnesty. A plane to a non-imperialist country. Those are our demands. Beyond that, we ain't got nothin' to discuss."

"I wouldn't count on that," I told him, "The Governor's sick and tired of waiting for this thing to evolve. Patience isn't running thin, brother, it's running out. I'll tell you my concern. Honestly. When I go, there's a good chance the next thing they'll be sending in from out there is bullets."

The crowd responded to the tension, the mob mentality taking hold once more. It began as a murmured chant, and then built to a crescendo of unmistakable clarity: "...kill him! Kill him! KILL HIM!"

There was movement in the crowd now. A real threat of violence. I looked around. To say I felt surrounded would be the understatement of my long life. I felt like a Christian thrown to the lions.

My heart was racing, but I was smart enough to know you can't let them see you sweat. I brought the focus back on the chain of events. After all, I didn't just drop out of the sky. I was there for a reason. I held up my hand. "Hold up one minute, now. Just hold up. Remember, you invited me here! I came at your request. I'm your *guest*. Does that ring a bell? Forty-eight hours ago, I was riding along the West Side Highway, minding my own business." I tried to catch as many of the prisoners' eyes as I could, making the point. Making the sale. "Now if you don't want me here anymore, I will leave. It's as simple as that. But you do not threaten an invited guest. You do *not* treat a guest like this. I know you all know better."

The cries for my head on a platter continued, though.

I swallowed, choking back the sawdust sensation in my throat. I tried another angle. "You know, Dr. King would often say to me, 'Clarence, don't tell me what you think I want to hear, tell me what I need to hear. Tell it to me like it is.' So, my brothers, in keeping with that ideal, I'm telling you about the reality of the limitations of your negotiating leverage on this day, in this place, under these circumstances."

Another man, a Muslim, raised his hands. And the crowd hushed immediately. This was a man who commanded respect. He cleared his throat. "Brother Jones speaks the truth. He's telling it to us like it is; he's helping us the best he can. We don't have any beef with him. I'm telling you all, if anyone makes a move on him, I will kill you personally before you can touch one hair on his head."

And just like that, I was safe again.

The sun had almost set, forcing the shadow of the prison wall completely across the courtyard. The light had a heavy quality to it. I got up from the table. "We'll see what we see." I wanted it to sound hopeful, but everyone saw right through that. I'm not much of a liar. It may be a character flaw. As I made my way out of the yard, the prisoners parted to make a path for me, and I could feel the tension in the air shift. It was a deflated sensation, all that pent-up hostility turning in an instant to despair. On either side, I could hear the sobbing.

Convicts' emotions poured forth—a litany of swearing, praying, moaning, and crying. A jumble of lost voices sifting through to my ears, drumming into my head:

Tell my boy daddy loves him...

Oh god, save us...

It's not our fault...

Don't go, brother...

Because they knew, just *knew*, they were watching their last hope walk out that door. Black and brown hands reached

out, forcing into my grip notes written on the inside of cigarette packs and torn-out edges of Bible pages.

Outside of the yard, I sifted through the dozens of hand-
scrawled notes. They were all written to loved ones or family
members, many with phone numbers or addresses for me to
reach out to on their behalf. They thought they would never
get the chance themselves. These inmates were being realistic now. They didn't expect to survive in "D" Yard once the
order was given by Rockefeller to take the prison back. And
that order was coming sooner or later.

I began to reflect on the looks on the faces and the sound of
the voices of those inmates who had pleaded with me to take
their message out with me. I thought about my parallel experience with jail cells: How in 1963 when Martin Luther King,
Jr. was imprisoned in Alabama, I was the man who was given
those tiny scraps of paper upon which he'd written his "Letter
from a Birmingham Jail" to deliver to the world outside.

This was some kind of crazy mirror image of Martin's
by-then famously scrawled letter. Again, I was leaving a
prison, and again I was the one charged with carrying to the
outside world the written aspirations of those held inside.

Everything swirled in motion around me. I closed my
hands around the inmates' scrawled notes and then stuffed
them into my pockets for safe keeping. Shortly after I exited
the prison, the telephone line the officials had been using to
communicate with the inmates was shut down.

When I left "D" Yard, things seemed hopeless to me. I was
running on fumes and home was feeling very far away. Even
that disgusting phone booth, pretty much the last thing I
could remember from New York, felt comforting in retrospect.
Many of the observers had been sleeping in the makeshift
headquarters of the Steward's Room the state had made available to us and would that Saturday, but I was too depleted.
I went to the motel and tried my best to summon the blissful
nothingness of sleep.

• • •

Three days and my beard was really starting to take hold. Other than that, everything was the same. I was still in that same suit; the demands were still the same. Nothing had budged. The only difference regarding this day was invisible to everyone: The Governor had decided it would be the last.

When the day had started it was apparent that the prison officials had decided that our role as observers wasn't helping to achieve their goals. Oswald's people eventually came straight out and told us that we weren't going to be allowed back in the yard anymore. When we heard this, I experienced an immediate icy feeling, a brutal cocktail of foreboding, fear, and anger.

Clearly, the tide was shifting. It seemed like there was a Kent State kind of tension in the air, as if everyone was so wasted from lack of sleep that anything could happen—and happen in the blink of an eye. At Kent State in Ohio, National Guardsmen, untrained and unprepared for the peaceful confrontation of students opposed to the Vietnam War, fired live bullets at the demonstrators, killing four students for merely exercising their First Amendment rights to peaceably assemble and express their opinion. Attica was qualitatively different from a rights standpoint, but inmates were still human beings petitioning for improved conditions. I could see a gun going off by mistake starting a domino effect. I could just as easily see its firing as no mistake at all. There was an exchange of ultimatums that tinged the entire crisis with an air of inevitability.

The observers realized this might be our last chance to stave off disaster. We wanted to get through to Governor Rockefeller personally. It was Sunday, and he was at Kykuit, his family's estate in Pocantico Hills, Westchester County. Sen. Dunne, however—a Republican and political ally of the governor's—had Rockefeller's home number.

We got him on the line and tried to convince him to come to the prison in person. We thought it would show he was negotiating in good faith, but he didn't see the upside of that suggestion at all. Sen. Dunne had the sense that a decision to use force had been made.

I got on the phone and pleaded for Rockefeller to give us more time. "Governor, you have to let us do what we came here to do."

Rockefeller's voice was even. Stone cold. "Mr. Jones? I understand your feelings, but this situation is out of hand."

"It was out of hand from the beginning. Just how is a bloodbath going to make it better? Tempers need to cool. I propose we—"

The Governor cut me off. "No one's going back in. The people of New York thank you for your service, Mr. Jones."

This took a moment to register. I said the only thing I could think to say, my voice dog-growl low, full of dread, but impotent. "No," I told him. "You haven't looked these men in the eye like I have."

Without tipping his hand, Rockefeller made it clear what he had decided. "Again, on behalf of the people of New York, we thank you for your service in this matter."

The next morning, Monday, September 13th, 1971, turned out to be the last day of the standoff. It wasn't much of a surprise after the terse phone conversations the day before. The writing, as they say, was on the wall.

The observers were ordered to leave the premises. We refused as a group, feeling the most honorable thing we could do at that point is act as witnesses for whatever was about to happen. If we couldn't stop it, at least we could make it as difficult as possible for Rockefeller to whitewash it.

The sound of hammering air suddenly surrounded us. The source was two enormous National Guard helicopters swinging in low over the prison walls. A clearly pre-designated system of attack whirred into motion. I watched as the state troopers up on the garrisons all snapped to attention. The helicopters dropped teargas canisters into "D" Yard and drifted back out. Then, six hundred state police officers that had amassed on the walls surrounding "D" Yard stormed Attica. Then the gunfire started.

There were reports that inside, the inmates threw a number of their hostages into a trench that had been filled with gasoline with the intention of immolating them. Apparently, none of the rebels had the stomach for it. Even at that last desperate moment, as their numbers were getting cut down.

We stood outside, seeing little but hearing everything. Listening to the firing of the rifles and the screams, watching the ambulances scramble outside the prison. I struggled, divided against myself—one moment trying to walk away, turn my back on the prison, the next moving toward it as if drawn.

The whole thing took less than an hour. It was like watching a medical procedure go horribly wrong, then watching the crash carts getting dragged around while the surgical team desperately runs through the entire playbook. It was organized chaos. It was a massacre. And it was exactly what our presence had been intended to avert.

When it was all over, I watched as the prison disgorged stretcher after stretcher. The body count rose. Thirty, thirty-five, then forty. The final body count came in at forty-two. The dead were a mix of prisoners and guards. Ten of the hostages had been shot, all accidentally, by the men Rockefeller sent in.

One of the news producers approached me. He worked for David Frost's late night television interview show. He'd been at the prison for the last two days of the standoff. He seemed very sympathetic and could tell I was in no mood to be interviewed. I told him I just wanted to get home. I was unshaven and still wearing the custom-tailored Pierre Balmain suit I had on when my ride on the West Side Highway was diverted to Teterboro Airport. I was on the verge of exhaustion and tightly wound from the stress of my last hours in "D" Yard. What I had been through was nothing compared to what had happened inside those concrete walls, but still... I felt dead on my feet.

"How are you getting back to New York, Mr. Jones?"

"I don't exactly know. I got here in Rockefeller's plane. He didn't offer me a lift back."

"CBS would be honored to take you home," the producer said.

"Mmm-hmmm." I stood there, waiting for the catch.

"Not a problem. Now there is one stop I'd love for us to make on the way."

Of course. No such thing as a free lunch. So, I was able to pay for my passage from the Attica Correctional Facility to New York City by agreeing to appear on the David Frost Show live that evening.

I can speak for all the observers: We were tormented by the Governor's decision. Arthur Eve would even go so far as to testify in front of Congress the following year and accuse Nelson Rockefeller of engineering a massacre and then lying to cover it up. For my own part, I too would have a reactionary opinion about the Governor with the spotlight on me. And a lot sooner than Rep. Eve.

On the ride back to New York City, I tried to decompress a little bit. But the tension, fear, sadness and anger I experienced during the ride back in the car remained very strong. Repeatedly, I was asked how I felt by one or more of the other passengers, including print and electronic media people also in the car. I remember saying over and over: "I can't believe this, can't believe this."

The car radio simply said an unknown number of inmates had been shot, several killed, no definitive number indicated, as news reports described the retaking of the prison by New York State troopers and prison guards. I felt the reporting underestimated the profound violence of the event.

After sleeping a little bit in the car, I awoke and was taken to Frost's studio. All late-night news was pre-occupied with the events that had transpired at Attica only a few hours earlier that day. I was likely in some kind of shock. I don't remember any green room or makeup artist dealing with me before being ushered on stage to sit in a chair across from David Frost.

Still in that suit, knowing I looked as ragged and edgy as I felt, I sat in a swivel chair facing David Frost. At the time, the British journalist had a live, late night program broadcast from ABC Television's headquarters on the Upper West Side. It was a fairly hard-hitting counterpoint to Johnny Carson's *Tonight Show,* necessary in the days before 24-hour cable news. The red light on one of the cameras winked on, and

Frost went into action. They rolled some news clips and discussed the initial outbreak at Attica and the events that had transpired only a few hours earlier. I don't remember the exact wording of the question Frost posed to me. But after introducing me and describing my role in unsuccessfully negotiating a peaceful resolution of the incident at Attica, he asked me to tell the audience what it felt like for me there at the prison as everything I'd been working toward started to unravel.

I thought for a moment and came to the conclusion that this was possibly the only time I'd get a voice in this. I had the eyes of the world, and an obligation to tell the truth as I saw it: "The hands of the Governor of the State of New York are dripping with the blood of the inmates killed at Attica during the retaking of the prison."

I turned on the man who had once been so helpful to my cause, the cause of Martin Luther King, Jr. But he was no longer that man, was he?

Frost, not one who was easily thrown off, turned pale. My statement had taken him utterly by surprise. He then invited me to clarify what I had said. In response I repeated: "The hands of the Governor of the State of New York are dripping with the blood of the inmates killed at Attica during the retaking of the prison."

Frost said something along the lines of, "Mr. Jones, you appear very upset by events that you observed earlier. Those are strong words you've used describing Governor Rockefeller's exercise of his executive authority to restore law and order at the prison."

He was giving me the chance to soften my response, give me some political cover.

I responded something to the effect that I had been minding my own business and the Governor asked me to come to Attica immediately. I did. And when we asked for more time to negotiate, he refused. Instead, he ordered the prison be retaken by armed force, undoubtedly killing many innocent inmates whose only crime was to "protest" for better prison living conditions.

When I left the sound stage, I was told that the CBS telephone switchboard lit up like a Christmas tree during my time on the air.

Following my appearance on the show, I headed home. My old apartment was mere blocks away from the studio, but it was empty, not mine anymore. I caught a cab and made it to Riverdale by about 1:30 in the morning. As I was getting ready for bed, the telephone rang.

It was Governor Rockefeller on the line. He said something like, "I caught you on the Frost show tonight. I guess you were really angry, Mr. Jones."

That was an understatement. I said nothing.

"I'm calling to say I know you did what you believed you could do as best as you could. For that, I and the people of the State of New York are grateful to you. You did what you had to do on David Frost. I did what I thought I had to do at Attica as Governor of the State of New York."

I was too exhausted to be argumentative. I just listened and may have said something like, "I guess so." However, what he said and his reason for exercising his gubernatorial "Executive Authority" was not merely to restore order at the prison. He was running for president and wanted to make sure he demonstrated his "law and order" credentials. What he had done he'd done for himself. How could it have materially worsened the outcome at the prison if he had given us a couple more days to negotiate with the inmates as Tom Wicker has requested on our behalf? As Wicker's book poignantly reminded us and Gov. Rockefeller, "There is always time to die." No, the only outcome it could have conceivably worsened was Rockefeller's future election results.

Years later, writer Bruce Jackson would share the following story:

Sander Vanocur, for decades the senior Washington correspondent for CBS and ABC, asked me, "Who do you think is the most cynical politician I ever met?" I went through a string of names and he kept shaking his head, and finally he said, "Rockefeller, Nelson Rocke-

feller. No one else came close." Vanocur and I had been talking about Attica just before that so I asked him if he thought Rockefeller would have permitted the slaughter just because of political ambition. He said, "I just told you: Nelson Rockefeller was the most cynical politician I ever met."

"Those were people under your care," I told the Governor over the phone that early morning. It was an accusation.

"You can't save everyone, Mr. Jones," Rockefeller told me calmly.

This was something I'd long ago figured out. The trouble was, I couldn't seem to save *anyone*.

I hung up on the future Vice-President of the United States.

In the weeks following the Attica riot and its retaking, following the death toll tabulation and the finger-pointing, the crisis was the subject of nearly endless newspaper column inches and hours upon hours of radio and television time. For my own part, I dug out those scraps of paper I'd been handed and made all those painful phone calls. I thought that was the last of it, that I'd be free of Attica.

Dean Robert McKay of the New York University Law School established his New York State Special Commission on Attica to investigate and review the events and circumstances of the rebellion and the death of those killed in the retaking of the prison. In short order, it would be known as the McKay Commission. Those in charge made it clear to me that the Commission urgently wanted my participation.

Personally, I wanted nothing more to do with the memories of failure at Attica, but I had developed a personal friendship and professional relationship with Arthur Liman, who had been appointed Chief Counsel to the McKay Commission. Arthur was the senior litigation partner at Paul, Weiss, Refkind and Garrison, and former Assistant United States Attorney for the Southern District of New York under President Kennedy. He was smart, thoughtful, honest, and reasonable. So, when he specifically asked me to assist him in his *post facto* investigation of the events at Attica, I agreed to do so.

Everyone knew the Commission's so-called findings would carry the personal imprimatur for professional and personal integrity of both McKay and Liman. These men had reputations to uphold and conducted the proceedings to reflect what they referred to as "the conscience of New York."

The process of gathering testimony was laborious and serious. Hearings took place starting in Rochester (fairly close to the riot site for access to people in the community around Attica) on April 12th, 1972, for three days. Then the Commission moved to New York City. I testified during the afternoon session on April 19th.

After two weeks of testimony from approximately thirty witnesses, the hearings were adjourned. The principal findings of the New York State Special Commission on Attica were that the government had acted in a vindictive and deadly way. It said in the report that, "The strike virtually assured the death or injuries of innocent persons," and noted, "With the exception of Indian massacres in the late 19th century, the state police assault which ended the four-day prison uprising was the bloodiest one-day encounter between Americans since the Civil War."

With the benefit of fifty years' worth of perspective, I believe there were two areas of inquiry that both the Commission and those of us who were observers should have considered more carefully. First was the internal decision-making process for retaking the prison by force. The on-the-spot operational role of Vincent Herd, Director of State Operations, Commissioner Oswald, Warden Mancusi, and particularly the leader of the special sniper unit of the New York State troopers should have been more closely examined. This group was feeding Bobby Douglass (Rockefeller's chief of staff) misleading information based on rumors of inmates committing brutalities and mutilations against the captured prison guards. Thus, they presented boots-on-the-ground "facts" from "D" Yard that were inflammatory and false to a Governor trying to weigh the pros and cons of a major life-and-death decision.

The questions are clear: Should Douglass have delegated the basis for the Governor's decision to retake the prison by armed force to Herd, Oswald, Mancusi, et al, without further due diligence in cross-checking of the information presented to him? And if he had, would Rockefeller's decision have been different?

The other area of inquiry that should have been more fully scrutinized was that a substantial number of Attica prison guards were also members of the local chapter of the Ku Klux Klan or its equivalent. Attica was a bastion and conclave of racism. The impact of this philosophy on the guards' behavior toward Attica inmates before the uprising and during the efforts to retake the prison should have been the subject of more careful review.

In the end, however, I feel the McKay Commission report fell on deaf ears. Dozens of inmates were charged with felonies, and not a single one of the officials was brought up on any charges. This, despite illegal activities in the aftermath of the assault such as abusing injured prisoners and trying to pin inmate deaths at the hands of prison officers on the inmates themselves. (Observer Jim Ingram would go on to claim, in his *Ebony* piece "Bill of Wrongs at Attica Prison," that his life was threatened by a prison guard and that at one point he was told he was a prisoner of the state.)

The jury is still out as to what constructive lessons were learned from the McKay Commission's findings on the Attica Prison rebellion. Regardless of whether one believes that prison incarceration is principally for punishment or principally for rehabilitation, the unavoidable question, fifty years later is: In retrospect, was retaking control of the prison, during which 42 inmates and prison guards were killed, a reasonable and prudent response to the list of demands for the changes in prison conditions that the inmates presented to Warden Vincent Mancusi, Commissioner of Corrections Russell Oswald, and New York State Governor Nelson Rockefeller?

Not if we're a society that lives by its own rules of conduct. An eye for an eye is Old Testament bullshit, inconsistent with the moral values of a humane society, particularly for a nation allegedly built upon Christian love.

But the rock we claim we're built upon and the rock we actually are built upon may not be the same. Historical, empirical evidence suggests that the wise truth Fyodor Dostoyevsky offered us in *Crime and Punishment* remains a solid thesis: The degree of civilization in a society can be judged by entering its prisons. I would ask a follow-up question: How much more so can we judge the degree of civilization by the way it gasses and opens fire upon its prisoners?

It's axiomatic that a single spark can start a prairie fire. We will probably never really know what specific event caused the angry flare-up of individuals in a few cells to erupt into a full-scale rebellion. Was it the death in San Quentin? Was it the censorship, the absence of one single Black face among the corrections officers and administration? The institutional racism? Or simply the heat and pressure of the overcrowding? No one can say. However, there is one thing we do know: You can push, degrade, or humiliate another human being only so far before, at some time, some place, he or she will, motivated by anger and the instinct to survive or to end their persecution, strike back. This is especially true when all alternative, non-violent avenues to redress their injustice are closed. It was President Kennedy who reminded us that those who make peaceful revolutionary change impossible make violent revolution inevitable.

"I am proud to have been involved in it," Akil Al-Jundi, one of the inmates who participated in the uprising, is reported to have said, "Because I think it was a momentous historical happening and I daresay one of the most important events that happened in the 20th century.

"Because one thing I know for sure is that, although the rebellion and the massacre technically speaking ended in 1971, it didn't. It's a continual process."

From the point that I hung up on Nelson Rockefeller early in the morning of Tuesday, September 14ᵗʰ, 1971—the first day in my new house—hardly three months would go by for the rest of that decade without a call from the Governor's office with an offer of some board appointment or another for me: Sitting on the Board of Regents, the New York Power Authority, the State Museum Board, New York City Public Works, the Board of Elections. For nearly two years I turned every one of the offers down.

Still, I liked getting the calls. It made me think about guilt, about responsibility. As long as I was getting those calls, I thought I could sense something of the Nelson Rockefeller who once cared enough to open his heart and wallet to my friend Martin King. I could see something pink and raw and real poking through the gray political crust that wound up passing for skin in those hard, hard days following the sorrowful events at Attica.

I finally did accept an invitation to help Gov. Rockefeller with something. In the summer of 1973, there were 49 vacant Court of Claim judgeships in New York State. Rockefeller was a master politician and he'd led a successful legislative effort to have those judgeships converted into New York State Supreme Courts judgeships, complete with full plenary jurisdictional power. He then created a five-person Judicial Review Committee to interview and recommend candidates to fill those judgeships, which were all political appointments and completely at Rockefeller's discretion. Judge Miles Lane was appointed as chairman of the committee, and Rockefeller asked me to fill one of the remaining four seats.

Rockefeller said, "Clarence, I don't care if a candidate was first in their class at Harvard or last in their community college law school," he said. "The only thing I want to know from them is: If appointed, will they apply the law as written? You find out the answer to that question and recommend them to me on the basis of that answer only."

You see, one of the Governor's crowning achievements had been New York's enactment of the toughest drug laws in the country. Long sentences were mandated by statute. No matter how small the amount involved in a drug transaction, mitigating circumstances, or an otherwise spotless criminal record the law did not mitigate or allow for possibility of a reduced sentence for a drug felony conviction.

What few people know about these infamous drug laws are that they came about, not as a result of the political or economic ramifications of the situation, but directly as a result of how Nelson Rockefeller perceived his own authority. At the time, the heroin epidemic was sweeping though the Black neighborhoods of Harlem and Bed-Stuy. This widespread addiction problem led to a lot of low-level crime; stolen 8-track tape decks from parked cars, purse-snatches, first-floor burglaries and the like. When promoting the drug legislation, Rockefeller had often repeated a story about delegations of Black church leaders complaining to him about the drug dealers in their communities. He said that Black pastors would tell him their senior congregation members were afraid to leave their homes to go to church out of fear that they or their homes would be robbed by drug dealers. Rockefeller, who immediately saw this as a direct affront to his power. It wasn't that the junkies had taken the streets from the law-abiding residents of Stuyvesant Avenue and 123rd Street, they'd taken them from him personally. His "taking back" of these crime-ridden streets was an issue of personal pride, of ego. He assured Black church members, especially in Brooklyn and the Bronx, that with him on the job they attend churches safely.

And he needed the right judges to do it.

So, by "will they apply the law as written?" he was referencing his new drug laws. In other words, if they weren't going to back up his ideology, they weren't in. No bleeding-heart judges was the order, but it went unspoken.

The committee did exactly that.[44] After that successful process, and as some of the raw wounds of Attica had begun to turn to scar tissue for me, I found myself a bit more open to working with Rockefeller on other matters. But looking back, I see the impact those laws and those fundamentalist judges have had on our prisons. It wasn't in keeping with my political ideology.

---

44 As a result, I must accept some small responsibility in the systemic problems of our prison system, at least in New York State.

The controversy of Attica did not go away, however. There was that unusual moment years later when we were both attending an event. At an evening dinner banquet, people with picket signs had gathered outside the building. The signs were directed at Rockefeller for his use of deadly force at Attica and featured graphic images of the carnage his executive order created.

Nonplussed, the Governor came over to me in the line that had formed among guests to the banquet and said, "Clarence, I guess we are going to have to show these people that healing has begun among adversaries at Attica." Then he grabbed my arm and we walked, linked together, past the picket line and into the building. He smiled the entire way. Sander Vanocur may have called him the most cynical politician in history, but I consider him simply one of the most effective.

By the early '80s, several of the Attica Cellblock "D" inmates who had survived, served their time, and left the prison life behind them would come around to my office at Inner City Broadcasting. They were looking for a little extra money because they were having a hard time finding work that would pay them much. This was the time before ATMs, so on Fridays I would sometimes go to the bank and make a sizeable cash withdrawal, often hundreds of dollars, and proceed to pass the money out. Such was my feeling of responsibility toward these men for what they had gone through.

Several of the ex-cons would say to me in hushed tones things like, "If you ever have any trouble, Mr. Jones, with *anybody*, you let us handle it. Understand? Don't go to the police... you tell us, and it'll be taken care of."

It was harrowing, of course. Between the lines, they were talking about threats, intimidation, possibly even murder. But I was helping them, had tried to help them in the past, and that was about the only thing they could offer to do for me in return.

Their hearts were in the right place; thanks to the prison system, it was practically all they knew.

CHAPTER 24 | GEOPOLITICS

Concurrent with my continuing activity in investment banking and deal work, I began to pay more attention to several major political and business developments that were occurring within the national African American community. These were happening in the media, motion picture, broadcast television businesses, and with cable television franchises being awarded in several major cities with substantial African American populations.

These developments were accompanied by a growing political cynicism and greater awareness manifested by a disenchantment, among substantial segments of the Black political leadership and the Black community in general, with the leadership of both major national political parties. This disenchantment spread like a wild fire among the citizens and political leadership within African American communities nationwide.[45]

This disenchantment with the effectiveness of African American political power was reflected in 1972's Call for a National Political Convention of African Americans to assemble in Indiana.

In early March of 1972, several thousand of us gathered in the city of Gary for a "new kind" of twentieth century national Black political convention. It pulled together a cross-section of people representing a wide range of political philosophies. Held at Westside High, the event brought together Republicans, Democrats, nationalists, Socialists, and Independents.

The steering committee consisted of Gary's mayor, Richard G. Hatcher, U.S. Representative Charles C. Diggs, and Amiri

---

45 A hundred years earlier—in 1868, '69 and '70—African American mayors had been elected in Louisiana, South Carolina, Tennessee, and even Mississippi. Then came a drought. Not until 1964 through 1970 would there be a resurgence in the election of Black mayors in such places as Richmond, California, Cleveland, Ohio, Flint, Michigan, Washington, D.C., Chapel Hill, North Carolina, Newark, New Jersey, Wichita, Kansas, and more.

Baraka (also known as poet LeRoi Jones). The convention was a culmination of a series of earlier meetings, mostly held in 1971, with an eye toward developing a unified political strategy for African Americans. Convened by Diggs, the first planning session for the 1972 convention was held in Washington, D.C. A convener was identified for every participating state. Delegates were selected from statewide political caucuses (any Black holding elective office in a state was automatically qualified as a state delegate). In addition to the steering committee, participants listed on the program for the three-day conference included Carl Stokes, Louis Stokes, Yvonne Braithwaite, Jesse Jackson, Walter E. Fauntroy, Ronald V. Dellums, Richard Roundtree, Bobby Seale, Louis Farrakhan, Vincent Harding, Patricia Patterson, Kim Weston, Barbara Jordan, and Julian Bond.

The call to the National Political Convention was powerful and worth printing here in full:

Black Politics at the Crossroads

Introduction

The Black Agenda is addressed primarily to Black people in America. It rises naturally out of the bloody decades and centuries of our people's struggle on these shores. It flows from the most recent surging of our own cultural and political consciousness. It is our attempt to define some of the essential changes which must take place in this land as we and our children move to self-determination and true independence.

The Black Agenda assumes that no truly basic change for our benefit takes place in Black or white America unless we Black people organize to initiate that change. It assumes that we must have some essential agreement on overall goals, even though we may differ on many specific strategies.

What Time Is It?

We come to Gary in an hour of great crisis and tremendous promise for Black America. While the white nation hovers on the brink of chaos, while its politicians offer no hope of real change, we stand on the edge of history and are faced with an amazing and frightening choice: We may choose in 1972 to slip back into the decadent white politics of American life, or we may press forward, moving relentlessly from Gary to the creation of our own Black life. The choice is large, but the time is very short.

Let there be no mistake. We come to Gary in a time of unrelieved crisis for our people. From every rural community in Alabama to the high-rise compounds of Chicago, we bring to this Convention the agonies of the masses of our people. From the sprawling Black cities of Watts and Nairobi in the West to the decay of Harlem and Roxbury in the East, the testimony we bear is the same. We are the witnesses to social disaster.

Our cities are crime-haunted dying grounds. Huge sectors of our youth—and countless others—face permanent unemployment. Those of us who work find our paychecks able to purchase less and less. Neither the courts nor the prisons contribute to anything resembling justice or reformation. The schools are unable—or unwilling—to educate our children for the real world of our struggles. Meanwhile, the officially approved epidemic of drugs threatens to wipe out the minds and strength of our best young warriors.

Economic, cultural, and spiritual depression stalk Black America, and the price for survival often appears to be more than we are able to pay. On every side, in every area of our lives, the American institutions in which we have placed our trust are unable to cope with the crises they have created by their single-minded dedication to profits for some and white supremacy above all.

White Realities, Black Choice

A Black political convention, indeed all truly Black politics must begin from this truth: The American sys-

tem does not work for the masses of our people, and it cannot be made to work without radical fundamental change. (Indeed, this system does not really work in favor of the humanity of anyone in America.)

In light of such realities, we come to Gary and are confronted with a choice. Will we believe the truth that history presses into our face—or will we, too, try to hide? Will the small favors some of us have received blind us to the larger sufferings of our people or open our eyes to the testimony of our history in America?

"For more than a century we have followed the path of political dependence on white men and their systems. From the Liberty Party in the decades before the Civil War to the Republican Party of Abraham Lincoln, we trusted in white men and white politics as our deliverers. Sixty years ago, W.E.B. Du Bois said he would give the Democrats their "last chance" to prove their sincere commitment to equality for Black people—and he was given white riots and official segregation in peace and in war.

Nevertheless, some twenty years later we became Democrats in the name of Franklin Roosevelt, then supported his successor Harry Truman, and even tried a "non-partisan" Republican General of the Army named Eisenhower. We were wooed like many others by the superficial liberalism of John F. Kennedy and the make-believe populism of Lyndon Johnson. Let there be no more of that.

Both Parties Have Betrayed Us

Here at Gary, let us never forget that while the times and the names and the parties have continually changed, one truth has faced us insistently, never changing: Both parties have betrayed us whenever their interests conflicted with ours (which was most of the time), and whenever our forces were unorganized and dependent, quiescent and compliant. Nor should this be surprising, for by now we must know that the Amer-

ican political system, like all other white institutions in America, was designed to operate for the benefit of the white race: It was never meant to do anything else.

That is the truth that we must face at Gary. If white "liberalism" could have solved our problems, then Lincoln and Roosevelt and Kennedy would have done so. But they did not solve ours nor the rest of the nation's. If America's problems could have been solved by forceful, politically skilled and aggressive individuals, then Lyndon Johnson would have retained the presidency. If the true "American Way" of unbridled monopoly capitalism, combined with a ruthless, military imperialism could do it, then Nixon would not be running around the world, or making speeches comparing his nation's decadence to that of Greece and Rome.

If we have never faced it before, let us face it at Gary. The profound crisis of Black people and the disaster of America are not simply caused by men nor will they be solved by men alone. These crises are the crises of basically flawed economics and politics, and/or cultural degradation. None of the Democratic candidates and none of the Republican candidates—regardless of their vague promises to us or to their white constituencies— can solve our problems or the problems of this country without radically changing the systems by which it operates.

The Politics of Social Transformation

So we come to Gary confronted with a choice. But it is not the old convention question of which candidate shall we support, the pointless question of who is to preside over a decaying and unsalvageable system. No, if we come to Gary out of the realities of the Black communities of this land, then the only real choice for us is whether or not we will live by the truth we know, whether we will move to organize independently, move to struggle for fundamental transformation, for the creation of new directions, towards a concern for the life and the meaning of Man. Social transformation or social destruction, those are our only real choices."

"*If we have come to Gary on behalf of our people in America, in the rest of this hemisphere, and in the Homeland—if we have come for our own best ambitions—then a new Black Politics must come to birth. If we are serious, the Black Politics of Gary must accept major responsibility for creating both the atmosphere and the program for fundamental, far-ranging change in America. Such responsibility is ours because it is our people who are most deeply hurt and ravaged by the present systems of society. That responsibility for leading the change is ours because we live in a society where few other men really believe in the responsibility of a truly human society for anyone anywhere.*

We Are The Vanguard

The challenge is thrown to us here in Gary. It is the challenge to consolidate and organize our own Black role as the vanguard in the struggle for a new society. To accept that challenge is to move independent Black politics. There can be no equivocation on that issue. History leaves us no other choice. White politics has not and cannot bring the changes we need.

We come to Gary and are faced with a challenge. The challenge is to transform ourselves from favor-seeking vassals and loud-talking, "militant" pawns, and to take up the role that the organized masses of our people have attempted to play ever since we came to these shores. That of harbingers of true justice and humanity, leaders in the struggle for liberation.

A major part of the challenge we must accept is that of redefining the functions and operations of all levels of American government, for the existing governing structures—from Washington to the smallest county— are obsolescent. That is part of the reason why nothing works and why corruption rages throughout public life.

For white politics seeks not to serve but to dominate and manipulate.

We will have joined the true movement of history if at Gary we grasp the opportunity to press Man forward as the first consideration of politics. Here at Gary we are faithful to the best hopes of our fathers and our people if we move for nothing less than a politics which places community before individualism, love before sexual exploitation, a living environment before profits, peace before war, justice before unjust "order," and morality before expediency.

This is the society we need, but we delude ourselves here at Gary if we think that change can be achieved without organizing the power, the determined national Black power, which is necessary to insist upon such change, to create such change, to seize change.

When I read that, I thought, Oh, shit! A seismic political change might just be occurring right before my eyes.

The convention's political call reflected the pain, anger, and unequivocal determination of so many African American leaders of prior generations. Its words echoed David Walker's 1830 "Appeal," as well as earlier voices like Richard Harvey Cain, Claude McKay, Alain Locke, Zora Neal Hurston, John Russwurm, Frederick Douglas, Dr. W.E.B. Du Bois, Langston Hughes, Fannie Lou Hamer, James Baldwin, Martin Luther King, Jr., Malcolm X, Lorraine Hansberry, and Eldridge Cleaver, just to name a few.

After the Chicago Democratic Convention in 1968, the election of Richard Nixon, the increasing domestic protests to the War in Vietnam, and President Johnson's earlier failure to deliver a "Great Society," the call to the Gary Convention reflected anger and frustration among wide segments of the African Americans nationwide.[46]

---

46 I believe the *weltanschauung* reflected in the Call to the Black Political Convention also fanned a creative spark in the film industry during the seventies. Films such as *Trouble Man, Cotton Comes to Harlem, Uptown Saturday Night, Sweet Sweetback's Baadasss Song, Across 110ᵗʰ Street, Shaft, Foxy Brown* and *Superfly* might not exist if it wasn't for our time in Gary.

The Convention also coincided with my growing romantic relationship with Charlotte Schiff, whom I would later marry. At the time, she was the Executive Vice President of Time Warner Cable in Manhattan. The cable company decided it wanted to provide its subscribers access to the Convention proceedings in Gary. They asked me to provide the live on-air description and commentary about the events.

My daily interviewing of Convention participants and national Black political leaders was an unforgettable experience. Selfishly, it also gave me access to those politicians down the road, a situation that would inure to my benefit as an investment banker. Throughout the seventies, the political leaders I had met in Gary facilitated access to people and companies for me.

In 1973, I was asked to join Rockefeller's Commission on Critical Choices for Americans. The four-term New York Governor had created the Commission a year earlier at the request of the Nixon Administration in advance of the country's bicentennial[47], though the gusto with which Rockefeller embraced the project made many—including me—believe it was an effort to project himself on the national political stage as a potential Republican Presidential candidate. Nevertheless, he took the Commission seriously—so seriously that he resigned the governorship to devote his full-time energy to it.

I was invited to be a member of the Commission which consisted of 42 national political, educational, business, and civic leaders; a virtual who's who of American thought leadership (including the majority and minority leaders of both houses of Congress at the time.

The charter of the Commission on Critical Choices for Americans read:

As we approach the 200th Anniversary of the founding of our Nation, it has become clear that institutions and values which have accounted for our astounding

47   In fact, the program had originally been called "America in the Third Century."

progress during the past two centuries are straining to cope with the massive problems of the current era, The increase in the tempo of change, and the vastness and complexity of the wholly new situations which are evolving with accelerated change, create a widespread sense that our political and social system has serious inadequacies.

We can no longer continue to operate on the basis of reacting to crises, counting on crash programs and the expenditure of huge sums of money to solve our problems. We have got to understand and project present trends, to take command of the forces that are emerging, to extend our freedom and well-being as citizens and the future of other nations and peoples in the world.

Among five other areas of study, the Commission focused on "Quality of Life." To an early '70s, die-hard Republican like Rockefeller, that concept had a lot to do with perhaps a general kind of segregation between the well-to-do and those struggling.

While I was a member of the Commission, I continued my work at the *New York Amsterdam News* and my business ventures with Percy E. Sutton. One such venture involved our efforts to acquire additional FM and AM radio stations. Percy had asked me to find the financing needed to exercise one of our purchased options for a radio station in one of the key markets in which we were trying to establish a presence.

The exercise of the option required a down payment of $250,000. The date for the necessary payment occurred during the time I was a member of the Commission for Critical Choices and when we were holding meetings.

If a member of the Commission needed to be reached, the person calling would telephone a number at the Rockefeller Townhouse on East 55th Street where the Critical Choices Commission meetings were held. They would then give a message to the Commission member they were trying to reach.

I received several calls during one particular Commission meeting, as the date for exercising the purchase loomed closer and the urgency increased to find financing. After a few of

33

these calls required me to step out of the meeting, Rockefeller took notice. He pulled me aside and asked me what all the fuss was about. I explained the situation.

At the end of the day's Commission meeting, Rockefeller advised me that the chairman and CEO of Banker's Trust, a prominent business bank headquartered on Park Avenue, wanted to lunch with me the following day.

Per Rockefeller's request, the next day I dined with the stranger in the penthouse of Bankers Trust. The chairman of the bank asked me how I liked serving as a member of Rockefeller's Commission on Critical Choices, about my experiences working with Dr. King and at the newspaper, and generally got to know me in that cocktail-party way.

I began to wonder why Rockefeller wanted me to take valuable time to have lunch with this guy, especially knowing the time pressures I was under to raise money.

At the end of the meeting, over coffee and dessert, the chairman mentioned in a matter-of-fact manner that Rockefeller had spoken to him about my need to exercise the radio station option. "Go down two floors and introduce yourself. They're expecting you."

When I found the right office, the banker there advised me that an account had been opened in my name with a deposit of $275,000, indicating that the chairman of the bank had directed they add an additional ten percent over and above the amount needed as a safety net. I signed some papers and was directed to a teller who drew up a cashier's check for a quarter of a million dollars. I was, to say the least, dumbfounded.

I returned to the Rockefeller townhouse for the balance of an afternoon meeting of the Commission. Rockefeller pulled me aside and asked how the luncheon went with the chairman of Banker's Trust.

I told him I had enjoyed it.

He replied, "Good. I hope now that there will be no further interruptions unless they're family emergencies."

• • •

I had a modest net worth, certainly not one that would comfortably support my borrowing $275,000. It took me more than four years beyond what would normally be permitted to repay the $275,000 I had been advanced. What was most extraordinary was that, about once a quarter, I would have a discussion with Bankers Trust about what a comfortable repayment schedule would look like for me. No rate hikes, no late fees, no demand notes. It was as if I'd borrowed the money from an uncle.

But there at the intersection of political power and banking, anything was possible. After all, this was a *former New York Governor* who called the *Bankers Trust chairman*. I never had to fill out any loan agreement, nor was there any itemizing of collateral assets. I'd just simply signed a(nother) promissory note acknowledging the indebtedness and a discretionary amount of repayment that would be made against the loan. Clearly, this loan arranged by a power broker calling in a favor, not by a bank coldly calculating upside vs. risk.

I raise the point because it's important to see that banking, despite being a nuts and bolts financial numbers business, is also part of the vast old boys network. There are worlds of finance where handshakes and backslaps seal deals, while at the same time there's an entire strata of society forced into being victimized by predatory loans, crippled by insane credit interest rate debt, forced into usury payday advances. There is deep amorality—if not immorality—in the finance industry, and like so many things, it negatively affects minorities disproportionately.

Recently, I watched a news story commemorating the anniversary of Civil Rights icon and Congressman John Lewis, Hosea Williams, and others seeking to cross the Edmund Pettis Bridge in Selma, Alabama to register Blacks to vote. In recreating the crossing, the footage was especially poignant because it showed President Biden alongside Reverend Jesse Jackson in a wheelchair, pushed by his son Congressman Jonathan Jackson. This sparked memories of the earlier role Rev. Jackson and another President played. Jackson and Bill Clinton, along with Sandy Weill of Citigroup and Clinton's

Secretary of the Treasury, Robert Rubin, coordinated the repeal of the Glass-Stegall Act.

The act, signed into law during the Presidency of Franklin D. Roosevelt, was designed to regulate the banking industry by separating commercial banking activities from those of investment banking. The aim was to protect the public from the high risk of bank credit speculation and avoid a future Great Depression.

The Gramm-Leach-Bliley Act reconnected the affiliations between security firms and banking institutions. For his part, Jesse Jackson had been using his organizations—PUSH and the Rainbow Coalition—to open Wall Street jobs to more minorities and encourage inner-city investment. He believed, perhaps rightly, that Glass-Stegall had been stifling those opportunities.

But by loosening the government reins on the banking industry, Gramm-Leach-Bliley opened the door for the subprime mortgage crisis in the early 2000s and the 2023 Silicon Valley Bank collapse.

The machinery of pure capitalism has no conscience; it's up to the citizens to empower their government to provide boundaries against unbridled greed. We can't all be Nelson Rockefeller... or those lucky enough to have his ear when complaining about a radio station purchase.

American finance, however, was only a part of my story back then.

During 1975-76, I became friendly with an Iraqi oil businessman as a consequence of my relationship with Gus Solanika, a successful broker at Cogan, Berlin, Weill and Levitt. The firm had moved from its downtown offices to new digs at the General Motors building on East 58th Street and Fifth Avenue. The Sherry Netherlands Hotel was across the street and at least once or twice a week after work, Gus and I would have drinks at the bar on its ground floor. We called it our after-hours "conference room." Gus was a handsome, 6'2" Greek American, and we referred to ourselves as "brothers from another mother." Our usual after-work drinks were vodka martinis or champagne, depending on the attractiveness of the women we would meet and chat with at the bar. After a couple hours, we would usually go our separate ways, though occasionally we would continue our conference at the Oak Room of the Plaza Hotel across the street. The Plaza bartender knew my drink and would start mixing a Stoli martini as soon as he saw me enter.

At some point, Gus had left the firm and shared offices with Rashad Alhasseni, an Iraqi oil trader. I would often visit Gus there and soon became friendly with Rashad as well. Occasionally, at the end of the business day, I would join the two for drinks.

On one such occasion, I met one of their friends, the Iraqi ambassador to the United Nations. From that point on, when there would be a diplomatic party or reception at the Iraqi Embassy on East 77th Street, I was invited and often attended. I met the Iraqi information minister during one of his visits to the United States at one of those diplomatic parties.

The next time I saw him he was with the U.N. Ambassador, and the two of them invited me to be part of a delegation of businesspeople and politicians to go to Iraq for a week, paid for by the Ministry of Information. So, in '76 I traveled to Iraq for a visit. One of the highlights of the trip was to Bashara, where date trees grow and their fruit is shipped all over the globe.

When walking along one of the main streets in Baghdad, shop owners would come out to the sidewalk to introduce themselves to me. They had not seen many Black people, and certainly not dressed in a business suit. I spoke no Arabic, but the shopkeepers would shout out names to me like Muhammad Ali! James Brown! Ray Charles! A language we *all* understood. I was such a novel presence they offered me coffee and snacks to come into their stores.

Though we were told a meeting with Saddam Hussein might be possible, in the end we did not meet with him. It turned out that during our visit he'd been meeting Donald Rumsfeld, who was President Ford's Secretary of Defense at the time. Famously, relations between the two did not remain so cordial a few decades later.

Instead of immediately returning home, I was invited to travel to Egypt. I stayed in Alexandria and day-tripped to

Cairo, visiting the pyramids and watching them glisten as the sun set and the lights came on. I stood in the shadow of the pharaohs and thought of myself in the third person—as the son of domestic servants, seeing the wonders of the world.

I moved on to Tunisia and stayed on the beach overlooking the beautiful, otherworldly turquoise water of the southern Mediterranean. While there I accompanied some friends I'd made in Iraq to a plenary meeting of the Palestinian Liberation Organization. Under the leadership of Yasser Arafat, the PLO had been fighting Egypt for over a decade. In the news, the PLO had always seemed quite organized. But I was bemused to see that, like the March on Washington, different factions with the same goals spent time infighting. I listened in on vigorous and heated debate between Arafat and the leader of a more radical wing of the PLO. The proceedings were translated in both French and English. I held my headset tight to my ears, thinking only that revolution was somehow a universal language.

Traveling the Middle East was educational and exciting, but it was also an escape. I had responsibilities back home. I was thinking maybe some of what I learned on this trip could be useful on Wall Street. Perhaps I should've been thinking more about my family.

CHAPTER 25 | THE CRADLE AND THE GRAVE

I was on a British Airways flight to London from Nairobi in 1976, seated next to a white woman—a flight attendant from South African Airways. She had red hair, was extremely attractive in that spangling, eye-shadowed, polyester way that defined beauty in the disco years. I'd spent nights with women just like this. Many nights, many women. It was something, fueled by depression and alcohol, I'd become virtually programmed to do. If anyone had asked me if I would turn this woman down if she offered to spend the night with me, I would've laughed in their face. Not likely. Yet, less than twenty-four hours later, there she was, sitting on the edge of my bed at the London Hilton, asking if I'd like her to spend the night. And as unbelievable as it may now sound, I sent her away without so much as a kiss.

During the course of our flight from Nairobi, woven within flirtatious banter, she had explained she was a supporter of apartheid and the racist South African government that had continued to imprison Nelson Mandela. Yet she seemed oddly drawn to me, a man who, if he lived in her country, would be a member of an "underclass" she freely described as inferior to her own. Now I've often thought, if this had been a crusty old man, would I have engaged in such a racist discussion so calmly? I'd like to think so. It was, after all, not heated. It was philosophical, a discourse on how our heritage affects our understanding of the world. But she *was* stunning, and it *was* a ten-hour flight.

After a few martinis the redhead remarked that if there were more "keffers" (South Africa version of our word nigger) like me in her country—educated, sharply dressed, well-spoken—South Africa could make more "racial progress."

Ah, I thought, another of the endless ways the human mind warps, justifying irrational thinking without breaking a sweat. Psychology on parade. As it was, she didn't think much of her Black countrymen. But she was certainly curious about me. I think I struck her as some kind of freak of nature. Those of a certain age, perhaps thirty and younger, don't remember a time before the phrase "African American" first came to prominence, but it was a concept that this woman never would've encountered in 1976. Still, there was something about the way this Afrikaner interacted with me that made it seem like she was enthralled by someone who was simultaneously representing the people she looked down upon and the strong Westerners she idolized.

I was African to her, *and* I was American. I was safe *and* dangerous. I was taboo. In the way that we can hold two ideas in mind that are diametrically opposed, she found the tension exciting. She felt about me the same way that I felt about the entire continent of Africa. Within it, there were contradictions and possibilities.

Two years earlier, in 1974, the big news coming out of Africa was that Emperor Haile Selassie had been overthrown in Ethiopia. On the international beat, it barely made the headlines, overshadowed by India's first nuclear test. And every American eye was on the White House. While President Nixon was tangled in the final throes of the Watergate scandal, most of my attention was consumed by something further away from home than Washington. For me, 1974 was the summer of Zaire.

I was still working through my divorce and had agreed to spend August vacationing with my children. I'd rented a beach house on Long Island for the period, a block away from the beach. I thought it was going to be a quiet month. On August 8th, 1974, Nixon became the first President to resign office. On the drives between Riverdale and the beach, radio coverage was exhausting. I often listened to music instead. Barbara Streisand on the car stereo singing "The Way We Were" and Gloria Gaynor, who "Never Can Say Goodbye." Like many going through a breakup, love songs during summer vacations could make me melancholy. Frequent thoughts echoed and repeated; what ifs, or if I would've, I could've, and maybe things would have been different.

I suppose, like Nixon's presidency, my marriage to Anne had imploded, not exploded. My August vacation with my kids was intended to put all of that out of my mind. For at least a month, I would enjoy the beach with them and friends in East Hampton or Sag Harbor.

I was wrong.

Earlier in the year I'd developed a business relationship and friendship with Nicholas Simunek. Nicholas had been a London West End and Broadway producer; a consummate British aristocrat, straight out of central casting for a sun-setting-on-the-Empire melodrama. I could easily picture him impeccably dressed, sipping Tanqueray gin on a veranda overlooking a colonial African plantation. Nicholas was a close business associate and friend of the late John Daly, a film producer and entertainment impresario from London's Hemdale Film Corporation, a British company founded by John and actor David Hemmings. Nicholas introduced me to John in New York in 1974.

As I was making plans for my Amagansett vacation, Nicholas told me that Don King was negotiating with Muhammad Ali's manager and George Foreman (then-heavyweight champion) about a match between the two in Africa.

In an Africa in the early stages of throwing off its colonial chains, it seemed like *anything* could happen. But even in that context, what was being proposed was unimaginable. As a result, King was having difficulty raising the required money. Consequently, he was trying to package and promote the Ali-Foreman fight abroad and make it the centerpiece of an African Music Festival. This hypothetical festival would be an unprecedented meeting and sharing of American soul and indigenous African music. Which didn't make much sense until I learned the details: King had managed to get both Ali and Foreman to sign five million dollars contracts, payment for a fight win or lose. This was one of King's early stabs at boxing promotion, but he instinctively knew how to swing for the fences. He didn't have the money, of course, so he spent his time working out a way to have a major entity sponsor the event.

He found it in Zaire, one of those many troubled post-revolutionary 1970s African hotspots. Zaire's flamboyant president, Mobutu Sese Seko Kuku Ngbendu wa za Banga, had the kind of image problems dictators do, and he seemed to believe a high-profile event like King's idea would provide him a kind of PR makeover. Formerly Joseph Desiré Mobutu, the president had changed his name. According to most translations, his new name meant "the all-powerful." This boxing event was intended to show the world that power.

And Mobutu had found the perfect partner in Don King, who brought together a team that included an American television production company, Video Techniques, Inc. and Hemdale. John Daly, who had bought Hemmings' share of the Hemdale business, was and would be the executive producer of many acclaimed motion pictures: Robert Altman's *Images* (1972), Ken Russell's *Tommy* (1975), Michael Schultz's *Carbon Copy* (1981) (an interracial comedy in which Denzel Washington made his big-screen debut), John Schlesinger's *The Falcon and the Snowman* (1985), and James Foley's *At Close Range* (1986). The company also acquired the worldwide stage rights of Lionel Bart's hit musical *Oliver!* And it produced a new stage version of *Grease* starring Richard Gere.

But it was James Cameron's *The Terminator* (1984), starring Arnold Schwarzenegger as an android assassin, made for about $6.5 million, and grossing more than $78 million worldwide, that made Hemdale one of the most successful independent film companies of the 1980s. John and Hemdale also produced Oliver Stone's *Platoon* (1986), a script written ten years previously that no one in Hollywood would touch. The film, which portrayed the mindless jingoism and brutality instilled into the psyche of the ordinary American soldier, went on to win Oscars for Best Picture, Best Director, Best Sound and Best Editing. Made on an incredibly low budget, it grossed more than $125 million.

My friend Nicholas also served as president of Remarkable Partners LLP and was co-owner of the Aldwych and Adelphi

theatres in London and the Marquis in New York. He'd been
a producer of the revival of *Who's Afraid of Virginia Woolf?*
which recently had been staged in London. According to him,
Don King's music festival would be headlined by James Brown
and include B.B. King, Celia Cruz and the Fania All-Stars,
the Spinners, and Bill Withers, as well as African musicians
unknown in the west. It would be filmed by the same video
production crew that was going to broadcast the fight through
"pay-per-view" television, a business still in its infancy. He
said the event would need a lawyer who knew finance and
business. For reasons unclear to me, Zaire purportedly preferred a Black lawyer to help them with the business arrangements. Nicholas had recommended me to John Daly for the
gig.

A few weeks later, he invited me for drinks with John at
the Four Seasons Restaurant in the Seagram's Building on
Park Avenue. John's interest in boxing ran deep. His father
Tom was a veteran boxer in England with more than three
hundred fights to his record and he ran a boxing school in
London. The Daly men believed co-promoting and co-produc-
ing this heavyweight match was great commercial exposure
for the school. He seemed comfortable doing business in Zaire
(formerly—and now once again—the Democratic Republic of
the Congo) and said he had pretty much decided to join Don
King in the proposed "Rumble in the Jungle." The event had
by this time been scheduled: September 24th in Kinshasa, the
capital, in the Mai 20 Stadium, with the festival unfolding the
22nd through the 24th. John said it would be a historic boxing
match, pitting then World Heavyweight Champion George
Foreman against former world champion and challenger
Muhammad Ali.

I was familiar with the Belgian Congo's history of struggle for independence. The leader of its successful "liberation movement" and first Prime Minister of the then-new-
ly-independent country, was the Congolese patriot Patrice
Lumumba. In an effort to overturn Lumumba, the man President Eisenhower regarded as the "Castro of Africa," Belgium
and our CIA engineered a counter-*coup* against Lumumba

and installed then-Congolese Army Sergeant Joseph Desiré Mobutu as the new Prime Minister. After assuming power, Mobutu renamed the country "Zaire."

In *Legacy of Ashes: The History of the CIA*, Tim Weiner wrote:

> *Lumumba had been freely elected, and he appealed to the United States for assistance as his nation shook off Belgium's brutal colonial rule and declared its independence in the summer of 1960. American help never came, for the CIA regarded Lumumba as a communist dupe.*

> *The agency had already selected the Congo's next leader: Joseph Mobutu, "the only man in the Congo able to act with firmness..." The CIA delivered $250,000 to him in early October, followed by a shipment of arms and ammunition in November. Mobutu captured Lumumba and... delivered him to the hands of a "sworn enemy." The CIA base in Elizabethville reported that 'a Belgian officer of Flemish origin executed Lumumba with a burst of submachine gunfire' two nights before the next president of the United States (Kennedy) took office. Mobutu finally gained control of the Congo after a five-year power struggle. He was the agency's favorite ally in Africa and the clearinghouse for American covert action throughout the Continent during the cold war.*

Back then, I didn't have the benefit of this information. However, I'd read enough about the Congo to have developed a cynical opinion of Mobutu and his government. Nevertheless, I took the wait-and-see approach.

I didn't have to wait long.

Nicholas and John had given my name to Bula Mandungu Nyati, Chairman of the "Boxing Commission" of the Government of Zaire, and in late July, John called to say Bula was in town. He wanted to meet at the Essex House on Central Park South. On the phone with Bula, I described myself so he could identify me at the bar. Bula's only description was that he would be carrying a leopard-skin briefcase.

I met him along with two other African men who spoke French to each other. We chatted about nothing important—How far is Harlem from the hotel? Had I ever been to Africa?—but after a second round of drinks, Bula suggested I accompany him and his colleagues to his suite. I sat down on the couch in the living room before a coffee table. Bula sat down in one of the chairs near the sofa, facing me. He told me that Risnelia Trust would post a $10,000,000 Letter of Credit "payment guarantee." First payment was to be made by Hemdale, Don King, and Video Techniques from the pay-per-view revenues. Under this financing plan, if the television revenues were insufficient to cover the five-million-dollar payment to each of the fighters, Risnelia would pay the shortfall. When I inquired about Risnelia and why it was serving as a payment guarantor for the fighters' purse, I was told that the money was President Mobutu's personal guarantee, from his Swiss account, "As a gift to the people of Zaire." (Literally; in Zaire there would eventually be posters plastered everywhere advertising the fight as *Un cadeau de President Mobutu au people Zairois*. The posters also read, *et un honneur pour l'homme noir*—"plus an honor for the Black man.") Some gift, and some honor: At the time Mobutu was reported to be the seventh wealthiest person in the world, yet he presided over a country with a per capita income of $70 a year.

Bula underscored that I had been highly recommended by John Daly and asked whether or not I was interested in helping them. I said I needed to better understand what he wanted or expected me to do, and where I would perform such services? He interrupted me, saying whoever worked with them had to travel to Zaire and be there for several days, if not weeks. He asked how soon I could get on a plane. Taken aback, I replied that whatever might be the professional services I would perform for his Boxing Commission, beginning the next week, the month had been earmarked for vacation. I told him if he was talking about my coming to Zaire during August, it wasn't possible. He then asked what fee I required for my services to be retained. I repeated that if it required me traveling to Zaire in August, I couldn't undertake the matter.

Bula put the leopard-skin briefcase on the coffee table and opened it. Inside were stacks of $100 bills in currency wrappers. Bula removed a stack of bills: $15,000. "We have the money to retain you."

The fight was scheduled for September 24th. If I were to be of any value to him right away, it would have to be from Amagansett. I said I could work by telephone while on vacation, but I wanted to think about it first. Bula conferred with his associates in French, then announced that he wanted my answer before the weekend. At this point, he went to his briefcase again and placed another bundle of $100 bills on the table. An additional $5,000.

They really wanted my help. It suddenly occurred to me that the boxing match between Muhammad Ali and George Foreman was very real.

In 1967, Ali had refused to be drafted into the military based on his religious beliefs and moral opposition to the war in Vietnam. He was arrested on draft evasion charges, found guilty, stripped of his boxing title and boxing license. In '72, Joe Frazier had beaten him. Ken Norton had broken his jaw in a 1973 bout. By 1974, at 32, Ali was past his prime.

In contrast, George Foreman was at the top of his game, younger, and coming off two-round knockouts of both Frazier and Norton. He was undoubtedly the favorite in Don King's matchup.

I agreed to work on the production and immediately installed a second phone line in the rented beach house to conduct business with London and Zaire. I made it through August without having to leave the country.

In September I traveled to Kinshasa. A room had been reserved for my stay at the Inter-Continental Hotel. The boxers had already been on-site for several weeks by that point, constantly working out. George Foreman cut his forehead during a training mishap, then injured his hand. As a consequence, the match was postponed, then re-scheduled to October 30th, the latest day around which they could safely plan the event before the rainy season hit.

Norman Mailer, in his book *The Fight* (Random House, 1975), described the atmosphere in Kinshasa after the postponement:

> *There had been rumors that neither Ali nor Foreman was being allowed to leave Zaire. It was certain at any rate that soldiers surrounded Foreman's villa. In the hour after the Champion was cut, Mobutu's man in Nele, Bula Mandungu, tried to keep the story quiet, only to discover that word had already gone out to America from one Telex machine his assistants had neglected to put out of order. "You must not publicize this," Bula said, "It will be improperly understood in your country. I suggest you forget about such a story. The cut is nothing. Go for a swim."*

When the postponement was officially announced, President Mobutu sent a small squad of soldiers to the rooms of King, Foreman, and key people associated with them from the United States, to collect their passports... for "safekeeping." I sweated the situation, but it turned out I was able to hold on to mine.

The music festival, *Zaire '74*, proceeded on schedule... but was now out of sync with the promotion of the "Rumble in the Jungle."

And there was more drama, what I considered Foreman's attempt at extortion. Norman Mailer discussed it with me, and the conversation made its way into *The Fight*:

> *Clarence Jones, a bright well-equipped Black lawyer from New York, is full of horrendous news that Leroy Jackson, Foreman's lawyer, is now in London attempting to get an extra $500,000 for the fight, and claims Foreman will not appear in the ring until he is given the bonus. It seems much of his $5,000,000 is already attached—and he feels there is nothing left for himself. If Foreman fails to appear in the ring, boxing is not going to recover in a hurry.*
>
> *"Do you think he'll get it?"*

"I'll never speak to John Daly again if he gives another dollar to him," Clarence Jones says in pain. "Foreman is the champ. He shouldn't act that way."

In the end, I could keep on speaking to John; Foreman did his job for the agreed-upon price. Who knows how much of it he got to keep.

Of all the memorable experiences in Zaire, my foolish acceptance of his invitation to jog with Ali early in the morning as part of his training routine takes the cake. I was in great shape, but after three miles, I could barely keep going in the African heat. And I was in the proper attire—Ali would wear combat boots and long sleeves and sweatpants with weights around his ankles. After about three miles, at a moderate pace with sneakers and wearing jogging shorts, I would tire. But Ali would just keep jogging like the implacable Energizer bunny. How did he do it?

When we returned to the building housing Ali's training, I was out of breath and gasping for air. Ali was perspiring profusely. With the assistance of one of his trainers, Ali removed his jacket with the hood. In sweatpants and the same combat boots he had jogged with me, he got up on a narrow slightly raised table and commenced doing 500 sit-ups. I watched in amazement. Afterwards, he suggested I do the same thing.

I said, "Not today, Champ. I'm so exhausted I can hardly stand and walk."

His reaction? "You should stop drinking all those martinis and keep away from all those beautiful women staying in this hotel."

As the day of the fight drew nearer, the more life and activity at and in the lobby of the Inter-Continental became a combination of street theater and the set of a Fellini movie. There were Americans, the Caribbeans, and Europeans, all "players" at such events. Men with their white straw hats, capes, and stylish suits. Women with colorful African-themed outfits and gaudy jewelry.

The betting odds favored Foreman 7-to-1, but Ali was clearly the favorite among Zaire's boxing enthusiasts. In the days leading up to the fight, graffiti turned up on several buildings around our hotel proclaiming, *"Ali Boma Ye!"* i.e., "Ali, kill him!"

The rainy season was fast approaching, and the weather on the eve of the "Rumble" was oppressive. The ring's ropes had stretched in the heat, and the sponge mat had softened. Angelo Dundee, Ali's trainer, worried that this would make it harder for Ali to move around the ring in his unique way. The mood in Ali's camp began to darken. There was genuine concern over whether Foreman could seriously injure, if not outright kill, Ali.

At 2:00 a.m. on fight day, we received word that Ali was leaving for the stadium. I was transported from the hotel by the bus carrying the media people from all over the world. The convoy bringing Ali to his destiny in Kinshasa had made it less than a mile before it stopped. Ali had forgotten his robe, so the vehicles waited while it was retrieved.

There was enormous commotion in the stadium when we entered. Boxing fans are as excitable as the fiercest of soccer fans. People had traveled from all over the globe. Some fans were dressed in attention-getting attire, all sorts of tacky glitz intermingled with real glittering jewelry—African diamonds and gold.

As I moved toward my seat in the eighth row, I reflected what it must have been like in the early days of the Roman Empire when citizens would come to a stadium to watch gladiators fight and kill one another or runaway slaves and Christians tried to fight off lions.

Officials estimated attendance at 60,000. Mobutu wasn't among them though: He watched the match on TV from his compound, while rumors swirled that he did this out of a fear of a possible assassination attempt.

The fighters entered the ring at 4:00 a.m., which translated to U.S. primetime and was baked into Hemdale's plan to maximize pay-per-view revenues. When the fight began, my heart was in my throat. I thought this really might be Ali's last fight. I was praying and hoping he would win, but thought that if he did, it would be a miracle. Foreman looked so big and menacing to me. There were moments, watching from ringside, where it looked like Foreman was throwing more punches than Ali. In some of the early rounds, Foreman would back Ali against the ropes of the ring and throw just one punch after another.

Yet, as I watched Ali, I had a once-in-a-lifetime view of the most extraordinary grace, elegance, and artistry in boxing. I was spellbound. I watched Ali repeatedly go to the ropes, deliberately. I began to wonder if I were witnessing some grand new boxing strategy unfolding that no one had attempted before. I was—it was Ali's soon-to-be-famous "rope-a-dope."

In the eighth round it seemed Ali was using the ropes to absorb punches and during that process Foreman was slowing down, showing signs of fatigue. The younger man seemed almost lightheaded, as if he were boxing in slow motion. Then, suddenly, a flurry of punches by Ali... Foreman dropped to the canvas. He was unable to get up under the count. The referee called "knock out" and declared Ali the winner.

Pandemonium broke out. My group ringside jumped out of our seats and ran into the ring to hug and congratulate Ali.

On the way back to the hotel on the bus, dawn was breaking. Thousands of people were lined up along the route, shouting "*Ali Boma Ye,*" and cheering. It seemed as if all of Kinshasa was celebrating Ali's victory.

But I couldn't celebrate quite yet. Even in the midst of the sporting world's greatest spectacles, there are still *i*'s to be dotted, *t*'s to be crossed. So, there I was in the African morning, telexing forms to Europe. This is why, sometimes, you want a lawyer with eyes on the fine print.

A condition precedent: President Mobutu's Risnelia Trust personal payment guarantee only activated *after* there has been formal confirmation that the fight has occurred as proposed. Though more than two million people had just seen the event live half a world away, a "certified copy" of a Reuters news dispatch was required to be telexed to Hemdale's and Mobutu's banks confirming that the fight had actually taken place and that the match had been concluded. Otherwise, someone would have to tell Ali and Foreman their paychecks weren't available.

I didn't want to be the one to have to do that. Because if you watch the documentary *When We Were Kings,* you know they worked for it.

They earned it.

I caught up with Don King in person 42 years later, in 2016. We gathered in Louisville with thousands of boxing enthusiasts and people who loved and admired Muhammad Ali as much as I did. The occasion was his funeral. Ali was only 74 years old at the time.

Even the great ones fall and can't get up off the canvas. Even the greatest.

CHAPTER 26 | INSTITUTIONAL MEMORY

In 1980, an acquaintance of mine, Ms. Marian Gibson, was working as John DeLorean's executive secretary.

DeLorean was a somewhat swashbuckling entrepreneur. He lived on Fifth Avenue with his wife, a personality on ABC morning television. He was a celebrity from a business that didn't have any: The automotive industry. DeLorean appeared to be living the American dream. He was both highly regarded and suspiciously envied in the car business.

He had been both fired and rehired by the big three automobile companies in the United States multiple times. He was a wunderkind who loved the spotlight and was busy bringing his dream to life with the insanely innovative DeLorean Motor Company. The man had developed and designed his namesake stainless steel car and set up a state-of-the-art manufacturing facility in Northern Ireland.

The UK government, then under the political leadership of Conservative Party Prime Minister Margaret Thatcher, had invested more than $150 million (over half a billion in today's dollars) in DeLorean's manufacturing plant in Belfast, under the belief that DeLorean and his pool of investors were supplying an equivalent sum.

Coincidently, Miss Gibson, his secretary, was from the UK.[48] While she was certainly loyal to the crown and to her employer, she was loyal to the truth above all else. When documents came across her desk that suggested DeLorean was going to take the company public to raise capital, Marian felt it an irresponsible way to treat the government invest-

---

48 Miss Gibson has dual citizenship. Even after decades in America, she still speaks as if she just stepped off the Queen Mary after a transatlantic journey.

ment and planned a trip to her home country to inform the Thatcher government about the situation.

To this day, Marian believes her concerns were buried by the Conservative Party for political reasons. However, when the *Daily Mirror*, a British tabloid, ran the story about improprieties with the UK/DeLorean deal (slandering Marian in the process), the Thatcher government sought to take over the DeLorean Motor Company's facilities in Ireland and reclaim the balance of its investment. President Reagan was close with Thatcher, and the United States authorities supported Britain's claims. Still, the investigation went nowhere: DeLorean and his partners' investments in the car company through tax shelters were validated. Eventually, DeLorean sued the *Mirror* and the BBC, as well as one of the lawmakers who leaked the story.

But that wasn't the end of the trauma. Within the year, DeLorean was made the target of an FBI sting operation focused on drug trafficking. The entrepreneur was caught by undercover agents on videotape agreeing to smuggle millions of dollars' worth of cocaine into the country and was charged with distributing cocaine, a situation that many believe was a U.S. government "make good" on behalf of the UK's DeLorean Motor Company affair.[49] Though DeLorean was acquitted, it was too little too late. By the end of the trial, his avant-garde car company was finished.

Marian today, at age 84, will tell you the drug bust was a set-up, that the British government wanted the state-of-the-art Belfast factory for production on a Saudi arms deal they had in the works, and that John DeLorean was a patsy for the political machinery.

I wouldn't bet against her.

• • •

---

49 Worth noting is the fact that the DEA agents approached DeLorean as potential investors in his struggling company and then proceeded to coerce the smuggling as a condition of their investment.

Like DeLorean, in the early '80s I too was brought up on federal charges fueled by the FBI's internal agenda. The circumstances surrounding this indictment were complex, and I believed then (and still do) that the charges reflected the federal government's extralegal activities, not mine. In fact, if it was an indictment of anything, it was one of the FBI's tendency to hold a grudge. Nevertheless, it forced me into a kind of Sophie's choice.

To understand the alleged crime and punishment, I need to take you on a detour down the winding side street of what the armed services would call "mental hygiene." The shadow of depression and its possible cure, psychotherapy, played a part in some of my most challenging moments.

In 1964, in the aftermath of the March and during the escalating, aggressive, and vicious attempts to stop Martin Luther King, Jr. from spreading his message (remember, he was the "most dangerous Negro of the future in this nation" according to the FBI), Coretta received a package with an audio tape accompanied by a letter. The tape was alleged to be surreptitious recordings from hotel rooms of illicit affairs of his, while the letter was explicit, threatening, and not at all subtle. The upshot: Kill yourself or we'll send a copy of the tape to the media. Your followers will know the truth.

Martin received the same package at his office.

I had my suspicions as to the origin of these letters and tapes, but I wouldn't have proof that I was right for some years. Nevertheless, regardless of the veracity of the audio or who sent them, the threats were obviously extremely upsetting to Martin. He began to exhibit the behavior consistent with a depressive episode. At the time, Stanley and I began to discuss it as a "nervous breakdown."

The question we asked ourselves was this: How should we best help him? We of course were staring the obvious right in the eye; the answer was to find him a doctor—a psychologist or perhaps even a psychiatrist who could prescribe medication to ease our friend's anxiety. Martin's physician told us directly: Find him a mental health professional. There was a catch to that, however.

KING,

     In view of your low grade, abnormal personal behavoir I will not dignify your name with either a Mr. or a Reverend or a Dr. And, your last name calls to mind only the type of King such as King Henry the VIII and his countless acts of adultery and immoral conduct lower than that of a beast.

     King, look into your heart. You know you are a complete fraud and a great liability to all of us Negroes. White people in this country have enough frauds of their own but I am sure they don't have one at this time that is any where near your equal. You are no clergyman and you know it. I repeat you are a colossal fraud and an evil, vicious one at that. You could not believe in God and act as you do. Clearly you don't believe in any personal moral principles.

     King, like all frauds your end is approaching. You could have been our greatest leader. You, even at an early age have turned out to be not a leader but a dissolute, abnormal moral imbecile. We will now have to depend on our older leaders like Wilkins a man of character and thank God we have others like him. But you are done. Your "honorary" degrees, your Nobel Prize (what a grim farce) and other awards will not save you. King, I repeat you are done.

     No person can overcome facts, not even a fraud like yourself. Lend your sexually psychotic ear to the enclosure. You will find yourself and in all your dirt, filth, evil and moronic talk exposed on the record for all time. I repeat - no person can argue successfully against facts. You are finished. You will find on the record for all time your filthy, dirty, evil companions, male and females giving expression with you to your hidious abnormalities. And some of them to pretend to be ministers of the Gospel. Satan could not do more. What incredible evilness. It is all there on the record, your sexual orgies. Listen to yourself you filthy, abnormal animal. You are on the record. You have been on the record - all your adulterous acts, your sexual orgies extending far into the past. This one is but a tiny sample. You will understand this. Yes, from your various evil playmates on the east coast to   and others on the west coast and outside the country you are on the record. King you are done.

     The American public, the church organizations that have been helping - Prostestant, Catholic and Jews will know you for what you are - an evil, abnormal beast. So will others who have backed you. You are done.

     King, there is only one thing left for you to do. You know what it is. You have just 34 days in which to do (this exact number has been selected for a specific reason, it has definite practical signfficant. You are done. There is but one way out for you. You better take it before your filthy,abnormal fraudulent self is bared to the nation.

From the FBI files at the National Archive

    Both Stanley and I felt strongly that news of Martin's visiting a mental health professional, if ever leaked, could be weaponized against him. We could imagine the headlines:

Civil Rights Leader Mentally Ill, MLK Sees Doctor for Brain Disorder, King Is Crazy.

We knew Martin had enemies that would go to great lengths to discredit him, and the stigma associated with psychotherapy at that time was powerful. This was a dangerous combination.[50]

The more Stanley and I talked, the clearer it became. In our duties to keep Martin's mission on track, we couldn't in good conscience make arrangements or recommendations that he seek therapy. Of course, we had moral obligations to our friend Martin as well, and this is where we clearly fell down. What was best for Martin was worse for Martin's work (and vice-versa). Stanley and I took a side. We let him suffer alone, for the good of the Movement.

Of all the regrets I have after all this time on earth, that may be the one that hurts the most. I think Stanley may have said the same if he were still around.

I had a second chance to get it right on psychotherapy almost twenty years later. It turned out even worse. My daughter Alexia was in college in 1981, and she was struggling with some emotional issues. Meanwhile, I was continuing my busy deal-making and consulting, and I didn't interpret the warning signs or register the cries for help until it was too late.

Alexia attempted suicide.

That was an ice-water-in-the-face wake-up call. I dropped everything and scrambled to get her care. The best hospital I could find was north of the city in White Plains, a mental health facility now called the New York–Presbyterian Westchester Behavioral Health Center.

Alexia spent the next twenty months as a patient there, and I essentially stopped working so that I could focus on her. I visited constantly, so often in fact that I became friendly with a female commuter who often saw me on the train from Grand

---

50 Only seven years later, when Daniel Ellsberg leaked the Pentagon Papers, Nixon's White House "plumbers" would break into Ellsberg's psychologist office in hopes of finding embarrassing information about Ellsberg with which to smear the whistleblower.

Central to White Plains. Years later the woman, Elise Caputo, and I were in contact again, and she told me mostly what she remembered was me, head in hands, sobbing on the train.

Life was intensely stressful. Charlotte did her best, but after many months of having little of my attention, she started suggesting, accurately, that the hospitalization was having adverse effects on our marriage. My alcohol consumption skyrocketed, and I often found myself having drinks near the train stations at both ends of the White Plains commute.

It was against this background that I met Hoyt Torrey and eventually became involved with his company, the RA Financial Corporation of Chicago. It would prove to be a turning point in my career, to say the least.

Torrey, RA's President and CEO, was a Black real estate agent and developer. Shortly after the two of us met, he wanted to retain me to act his company's general counsel. Among other things, he specialized in soliciting members of Chicago area Black churches in need of second mortgage financing. It seemed like their need for actual legal services would be minimal, but he wanted me. To me, it sounded like a check every month for doing little or nothing. That sounded just right.

What I didn't know at the time was that Torrey wanted me because of my association with an icon. Without divulging his plan, once I'd agreed to be of counsel, Torrey's new approach to business solicitation included pamphlets with a photo of me and a summary of my educational and professional qualifications, including my earlier work with Martin. He was using my connection with Martin to build a brand and impart a sheen of respectability on an enterprise that, in fact, wasn't respectable at all. The targets were primarily Black and had limited financial resources. Torrey's company promised these people loans or mortgages at favorable rates. There were, as befitting a fraudulent enterprise, certain non-refundable "upfront deposit and application fees." Torrey was then taking the fees and denying the loans. That was the business model. I was the bait used to lure in the suckers on the too-good-to-be-true offer. But the flyer sure looked legit, with the picture of Clarence B. Jones and his impressive credentials.

If I'd taken any time at all to vet the company, I would've seen it. But I didn't have my eye on the ball. My mother, with her pencil-and-a-dollar-bill worldview, would've been appalled. But my life had essentially become about helping my daughter; everything else that I let slide was just collateral damage.

Upon learning what Torrey did with my likeness, of course I immediately insisted that he cease and desist, but it was too late. Complaints had been lodged against RA Financial, and local authorities looking into the matter found a cancelled check written to me.

It was true that I'd been handed an initial payment of $9,000 in Illinois, and I'd then flown halfway across the country to deposit it into my New York business account. Which meant I'd traveled across state lines with what could be considered the proceeds of a fraudulent enterprise.

That opened up this low-grade Chicago scam to a potential federal crime, if the authorities wanted to pursue that avenue.

The FBI was certainly interested. Because of *who* had cashed that check.

Before indictments were handed down, if any were, the FBI asked to interview me. I flew to Chicago and sat down with them.[51] While the FBI can be involved in any federal crime, mail fraud by and large falls under the purview of the Treasury Department. But the Bureau was interested in this case. As I was being interviewed by two FBI agents, I protested my innocence and told them I had no knowledge of what Hoyt Torrey was doing.

One agent looked at the other. "Oh, Clarence here would never take advantage of the saintly poor." Then he turned back to me, sighting down his finger with one eye—like he

---

51 At the time, one of my closest friends, Bennett Johnson, Jr., lived in Evanston, Illinois. I rarely stayed at a hotel when I visited the Chicago area. I frequently stayed with Bennett and his wife Cathy. The Johnsons' had a giant Siamese cat—Tony the Tiger. My use of the pull-out sofa bed in the Johnson living room was an invasion of the cat's "space" and Tony wasn't shy about pointing out that I was an unwelcomed invader.

was taking aim. "'Cause you're... Martin Luther King's boy, aren't you? We know all about you."

They tipped their hand. It's what I'd always suspected. What I'd always told Martin. They've been watching. They've been keeping score.

On my way out of the building, a Black administrative assistant stopped me and whispered, "Mr. Jones, you've got to look out. I heard some of those FBI agents talking in the hall before, and one of 'em said, 'We're finally gonna get that King nigger lawyer!'"

Hoyt Torrey was indicted on fraud charges, and I was also indicted as a "party defendant." Now, I was a guy who was used to fighting, used to arguing, used to defending myself. However, as I was trying to figure out my approach, Torrey was convicted and sentenced to five years in prison. This sent a message to me loud and clear: The stakes were real. I knew I couldn't go to prison, not with Alexia under the pressure she faced.

The first person I discussed the Chicago indictment with was my dear friend Martin "Mickey" Horowitz. He called the U.S. Attorney for the Northern District of Illinois to see how serious the matter was. On my behalf, he retained a former U.S. Attorney from that district to be my defense counsel and gave me $15,000 to send as an initial retainer fee.

I told my new lawyer I wouldn't risk going to trial.

"Find out how far a guilty plea gets me," I instructed him.

He wanted to fight, though. "We can win this, Clarence. it's a slam-dunk."

I understood his eagerness. I felt it, too. "Can you guarantee a trial where I don't get any jail time?"

"Practically."

"I didn't ask about practically."

"You know as well as I do trials don't come with warranties. But if you plead guilty to a felony, you're disbarred."

I knew that, and I knew if I went to jail, Alexia may well not be alive when I got out.

"All you've been through, all the fights, you've never backed away from one," my lawyer said. "Now you roll over? Take injustice lying down? I'd think long and hard about that."

I already had.

The deal was for my plea of *nollo contendre* to two felony counts, in exchange for three years' probation and no incarceration.[52] It was the best deal I ever made.

In the customary "Presentence Report," I presented Letters of Commendation attesting to my character and trustworthiness from people like Arthur Levitt, Jr., my former Wall Street partner, then Chairman of the Securities Exchange Commission, Bennett Johnson, several prominent clergymen, a Judge of the Supreme Court of the State of New York, and of course Mickey Horowitz in his capacity as Chairman of UV Industries, a successful company on the New York Stock Exchange.

In my statement to the court at the sentencing hearing, I made the point that in the event the Judge felt that some period of incarceration was necessary to set an example, it might bend me but would not break me. However, if I my daughter harmed herself or died during any such imprisonment, that this event would absolutely break me.

The Judge listened intently, with tears rolling down his cheeks, and he accepted the negotiated plea of probation with community service.

The resolution of the Chicago criminal proceeding enabled me to continue visiting Alexia regularly while she was in the hospital and to perform my community service.

I remain proud of the compromise I made principally on behalf of my daughter. I look back on this "a badge of honor" and a belief in and commitment to the principle that "the

---

52 Amazingly, in a real Forrest Gump moment, the prosecutor in the case was Scott Turow, who would turn out a decade later to be the best-selling author of garish legal thriller fiction, a kind of John Grisham-lite who coughed out titles like *Presumed Innocent* and *Burden of Proof*.

strongest steel is tempered by the hottest fire." The only thing close to my feelings of protection for Alexia is my memory of my mother at home dying of colorectal cancer and how I, as a nineteen-year-old, had to carry my formerly 160-pound, now 99-pound, mother to the bathroom for weeks leading up to her death.

These experiences bent me, but they did not break me. Even the mighty FBI fell short of that, no matter how badly they wanted it.

We know all about you.

We're finally gonna get that King nigger lawyer.

It was those comments (one for my ears and the other not) that got me thinking—it's about time I found out what the FBI files on me contained.

As paranoid as he was, no one has ever been surprised by the fact that Nixon famously kept an "Enemies List." I would argue that the former president's concept is a kind of metaphor for the U.S. government: it jots things down, it has a long memory, and it holds grudges.

One such grudge included casting a wide snare for Martin Luther King, wide enough to catch me up in it. Those FBI men chasing me down for something I clearly had nothing to do with illustrates that.

In a way perhaps not so different from (and pre-dating) the Nixon era, many of my associates in the Movement used to refer to me as paranoid. To my face, mind you, jokingly, with a wink and an elbow to the ribs. But still, not without some message there. Let's not lose our heads, Clarence. Let's not believe crazy things.

But you know the saying: Just because you're paranoid doesn't mean they're not out to get you.

I alone in the group had previously had the profoundly disturbing experience of directly learning I'd been spied upon. The spying happened to the others, notably Stanley Levison, but at the time they were unaware of it. Not me. I told all my SCLC friends about the man in the Army who had gained my confidence and friendship purposefully, simply because that was his assignment. To me he was just the talkative, likeable guy who happened to occupy the bunk above mine, I said. But that likeable guy spent nearly two years on the U.S. government's payroll with only one job: Get Private Clarence B. Jones to confess what he's up to, what he's thinking. Spying was their best option, an approach to a perceived problem. If that bunkmate hadn't confessed to me, I never would have known a thing about it... but it *still would've happened to me.*

But he did confess. So, I'd had a taste of betrayal and deception, and I'd developed a keen eye for the little clues that might point to such goings-on. It's not that I had evidence that the FBI was watching, it's that I knew they could if they wanted to, so I presumed they did. It wasn't difficult at all. To me, the only question was, did they want to watch me, Dr. King, and others in the SCLC? And every indication I'd ever gotten from the government suggested that they did.

So, nearly twenty years later, after my disbarment, when I submitted a Freedom of Information request to get FBI files regarding me, it wasn't with much sense of surprise to find it yielded results. The only surprise was in the sheer volume. The files that were delivered to my office reminded me of the newsprint delivery at the *Amsterdam News* loading docks in Westchester County. Only these pages were already covered with my editorials and photo-illustrations. Whatever issue I'd pontificated on during our conference calls, our one-on-one calls, our meetings in restaurants and coffee shops and boarding areas, there it was.

The FBI had watched me everywhere I went for five straight years. From 1963 though 1968, they had taped almost every phone call I'd made and received from my home or office and conducted photographic surveillance of my meetings, travels, and dining with Martin, Stanley Levison, and whomever else was associated with me or in my company at the time.

My tax dollars at work.

Before the FBI had declassified these documents, the telephone wiretaps and photo surveillance records of my time with Martin and Stanley were classified as "Top Secret" or "Secret." Even more chilling was the realization that, because of my associations and political activities, the FBI had maintained files on me as far back as 1950 when I was a student at Columbia. I can't imagine many readers have actually had the experience of seeing transcripts of their *illegally* wiretapped phone conversations or seen themselves captured in surveillance photos. It is *1984*-level eerie, and it throws everything you think you know about our republic into a dizzying new perspective. When the Bush White House tried to shrug off the "warrantless wiretap" domestic surveillance project uncovered by Eric Lichtblau at the *New York Times* as a minor price to pay for our safety, I saw that in a completely different light. No government ever asks if you want to trade freedom for safety... or anything else. They just take your freedom without telling you and if you happen to notice, they tell you you've traded it for something more valuable.

I would argue that: 1) you haven't traded it, you've had it taken from you; and 2) there isn't anything more valuable than your freedom.

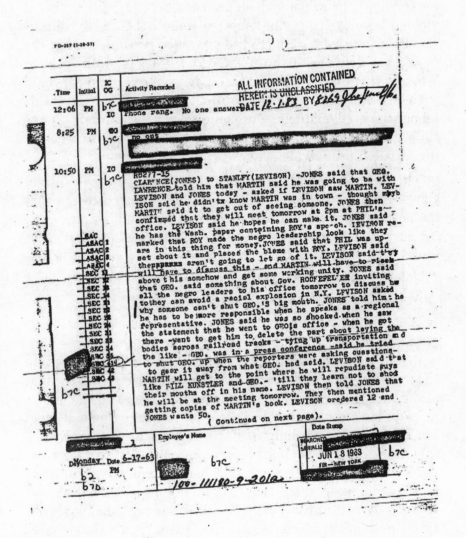

FD-287 (1-28-57)

Time	Initial	IC CG	Activity Recorded
5:59	PM	TC	W-6036-42

(CLARENCE JONES) to (STANLEY LEVISON). JONES tells LEVISON
that after "about 17,000 phone calls" he has finally arranged
to get "the additional material" but he says he won't be able
to get it until tomorrow afternoon. LEVISON says that's all
right. He asks if JONES went over "that other stuff". JONES
replies that he did. LEVISON then asks JONES how it seemed
to him. JONES replies that he thought it was very good and
adds that he thinks it "just... needed to go on". LEVISON
agrees and JONES says that's the only problem. LEVISON laughs
and comments, "Not enough", with which JONES agrees. LEVISON
then says he knows. He then tells JONES that it's all right;
that "it'll go on". JONES agrees and adds that he is just
being pressed by everybody, remarking that LEVISON knows.
LEVISON confirms that he does.
JONES then swears about "this-... march", calling it "something". LEVISON agrees and tells JONES that the stories (on
the march) are now getting very conflicting. JONES asks him
what the conflicting stories are now. LEVISON replies that
there's a story from Washington that 37,000 are expected to
come from New York and 30,000 from elsewhere, etc.; that
there was another story that "they" had 800 buses. LEVISON
says he was wondering which is close to the fact. JONES
tells LEVISON that he will find out tomorrow as he says they
are going to have "a reviewing meeting". JONES remarks that
he will find out tomorrow "whether they're planning civil
rights by public relations or planning it by plans". LEVISON
agrees but then adds, "by transportation". He tells JONES
that when "BEA" called "BAYARD" to ask him if the LEVISONs
could get some tickets on a train BAYARD said he didn't know
anything about transportation; that BEA would have to talk
to ROCHELLE (ph). JONES laughs at this. LEVISON then comments
that BAYARD doesn't know anything about transportation but
that that's only the most important thing. JONES asks if
this is really true (story about BAYARD). LEVISON confirms
that it is and tells JONES that BAYARD didn't know what trains
or buses or anything were going. JONES interjects that "the
C.D.V. has trains". LEVISON confirms this but tells JONES
that "they" don't have any tickets left; that they are trying
to add a car. JONES then says he knows "ANN" is charge of
trains at C.D.V. He then remarks that he thinks LEVISON is
right because ANN organized a new train today, but he says he
thinks it was quickly filled. LEVISON asks if JONES doesn't

SAC	
ASAC 1	
ASAC 2	
ASAC 3	
ASAC 4	
SEC 11	
SEC 12	
SEC 13	
SEC 14	
SEC 21	
SEC 22	
SEC 23	
SEC 24	
SEC 31	
SEC 33	
SEC 34	
SEC 35	
SEC 41	
SEC 42	
SEC 43	

THUR PM   Date 8-22-63

100-111180-9-2672

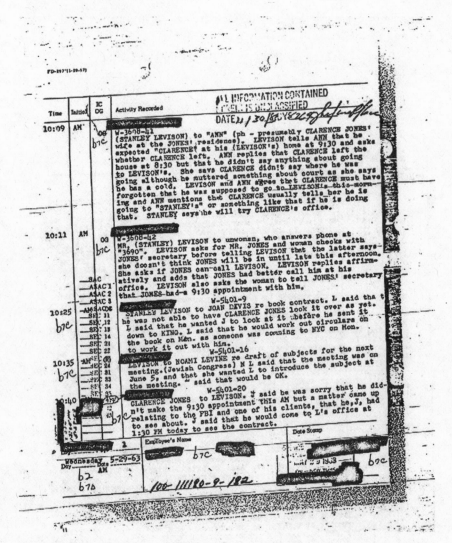

Samples of the thousands of pages of wiretap surveillance in the Clarence B. Jones FBI file

All right then, just how "bad" a brother was I? What was I doing and with whom was I associating that the most powerful investigative agency of the most powerful government felt it necessary to keep a watch on my friends and me? Exactly what was I up to that Washington thought constituted or might constitute a threat to the safety and national security of the United States? I tried to think back and reconstruct a list of names of persons or events and activities that might have triggered the FBI's interest in me—the memos and transcripts offered no illumination in that regard.

My refusal to sign that so-called "Loyalty Oath" swearing I didn't belong to (or associate with anyone who belonged to) some 400 listed "subversive" organizations. That could've been a red flag, but it happened in August 1953, *after* I finished at Columbia. By the same logic, it couldn't have been my marriage to Anne Norton, though she certainly had her own left-wing student activist background perhaps worthy of J. Edgar Hoover's attention. We married in 1956. So... before that, before the Whitehall Street Induction Center, what was it I'd done? It's unclear. Were they watching because I'd spent a summer working as a counselor at Camp Wichita (where many Communist Party parents sent their children and whose name, I came to learn, was a variation of "Wochica," a contraction of Workers' Children's Camp)? Or because I was politically active with Charlotte Goldberg (an outspoken student leader at Brooklyn College), the Labor Youth League's Mel Williamson and Roosevelt Turner Ward (subsequently a co-founder of the National Negro Theatre), Robert Nemiroff and Lorraine Hansberry?

It may have been my association with these people that brought me to the attention of the FBI. Or perhaps it was because I organized a national student protest movement out of my Columbia dorm room? I can't even remember the issues we were protesting, but the government may well have a longer memory than I do.

Sifting through the materials in 1982, I made a sudden connection. There was a standout from my court-martial charges I had all but forgotten: The allegation that I was a national security risk in part due to my friendship with Halsted Holman. My life-long friend (currently a doctor at Stanford University, where I recently have been a Scholar in Residence at the Martin Luther King, Jr. Research & Education Institute) was an "International Vice-President" of the International Union of Students in those years. The I.U.S. was one of the four hundred organizations listed on the Loyalty Oath paperwork, so in retrospect had I signed it, I would've done so fraudulently.

At the Pentagon hearing, we had argued my pre-draft civilian political activities had no bearing on my subsequent military service, but I had never really stopped to consider where the information came from. The conclusion seems definitive: I was on the FBI's radar because Hal Holman was.

But that was just amateur hour. The record on me is scatter-shot until 1960, because that was the year I started my work with Martin King and, through him, began forging my close friendship with Stanley Levison. Stanley had been in the cross-hairs of the FBI, and they never let him out of their sights.

It seemed to Dr. Janet Kennedy that her new husband's work was hard on him. At the time, Jay Richard Kennedy was Harry Belafonte's business manager, but there was other, more mysterious work. As a psychologist, Janet knew that people who harbored secrets or led double lives were corked up, always on the precipice of blowing out from the pressure. Fifty-minute twice-weekly sessions on the couch acted as a kind of release valve, and she encouraged her husband Jay to seek professional help, just someone to talk to about his mood. It would've been in his best interest if he'd taken Janet's advice, because under those circumstances, what he had to share would've been protected by doctor-patient confidentiality. But he wouldn't dare see a shrink.

Yet, as his wife predicted, the pressure had to be relieved somehow. Confession must be good for the soul, even if it isn't good for the career. So, Jay Richard Kennedy began talking, telling his wife his secrets. For years he'd been a high-ranking member of the U.S. Communist Party, and recently, along with a pair of brothers named Jack and Morris Childs, he'd become a secret informant for the FBI. It was stressful, the working undercover and second-guessing and the sharp fear of being revealed. Janet understood and continued doing what she did best—listening. Until she finally heard something she couldn't stay silent about. It came out that the FBI had asked Jay to set up Stanley Levison.

And Stanley Levison was Janet Kennedy's ex-husband.

Not catch, mind you; set up.

The single most damning piece of evidence I can point to that proves J. Edgar Hoover used his agency to further his own goals was the fact that the weasel purposely withheld conclusive exonerating evidence about Stanley's interest in communism from everyone during the Kennedy Administration, including JFK himself. He served only at the pleasure of the President, the leader of the free world, but he acted like he answered to no one. As is clear from this era's current and seemingly unending "War on Terror," our intelligence community has often believed that giving the White House evidence that leads to their pre-designed conclusions is much more useful to them than providing gray-area information and conflicting data points for an honest debate on the next steps.

Setting-up a person is different than catching them. It's not what the good guys are supposed to do. But where in this book did I ever suggest the leaders of my government were the good guys?

To gain some insight into the political impact and ramifications of this strategy by the FBI requires more background on Stanley, my beloved friend, co-speechwriter, and sometime mentor. It was our friendship and close working relationship with Martin Luther King, and our respective, but independent, history of political activity that provided the FBI with the rationale for 24/7 surveillance of all three of us.

In my view, Stanley is worthy of our country's highest civilian presidential award for his extraordinary public service to our country. Stanley's contribution to the work of Martin and to the Civil Rights Movement overall was monumental. It cannot be overstated—not that many of people who should have been touting his accomplishments have tried very hard to do that. While much has been written about his relationship with Martin and his role in SCLC and the Civil Rights Movement. In the years following Martin's assassination, and particularly after Stanley's death in 1979, I detected what appeared to be a concerted effort to diminish Stanley's pivotal role with Martin and his important work with SCLC.

Pulitzer Prize-winning authors David Garrow and Taylor Branch both have written extensively about Stanley. Their writings were based on research and reading of FBI files available to them under the Freedom of Information Act, personal interviews with those around Martin who knew and/or worked with Stanley, and conversations with Stanley's son, Andy. It's a lot, but it's not the whole story.

To my knowledge neither Garrow, Branch, nor anyone else who has written about Stanley's relationship with Martin actually interviewed Stanley. I, on the other hand, talked with him on a daily basis and saw him nearly as frequently. Consequently, I'm confident that my remarks constitute the most accurate commentary possible, the only firsthand account left to tell, and presumably the final word on the relationship between Stanley Levison and Martin Luther King, Jr.

Neither Andy nor I ever disclosed to Garrow, Branch, or anyone else things Stanley said that we felt were truly private. Andy and I have spoken, and together we've determined that now is the time to share this information with the world. Some issues that might have been muddled were further clarified recently by his son, to the extent that he knew about the matters I shared with him. In other instances, amazingly, even Andy was in the dark and I was able to illuminate a bit more about his father for him. This information, which I am revealing here the first time, is based on my personal knowledge during those years Stanley and I worked together. We shared so much, and except on one point indicated where the record is slightly murky, what I say here is not speculation. Rather, it is based on what Stanley disclosed personally to me as well as my own observations.

Stanley Levison's strategic importance to the FBI was principally, if not only, a direct result of his association and relationship with Dr. King. Stanley was also the target of attention by the United States Communist Party, for the exact same reason. These are not revelations. But there is some new information that does feel revelatory: Like something out of a le Carré novel, Stanley was also, unbelievably, a strategically critical element in the plans of the Communist Party of the Soviet Union. Within the context of our tense Cold War with Russia, Stanley was like a college football Heisman Trophy winner the eve before the NFL draft. A valuable, rare, and sought-after commodity. Stanley was "hot." Because of his prior association with the CPUSA, his often round-the-clock contact with Martin (and me secondarily, also because of my relationship with Martin), he came to be considered the indispensable means of reaching and possibly "influencing" the actions of Dr. King for several competing parties. It seemed to those invested in the situation that one had to go through Stanley to really to get Dr. King's attention and try to affect a particular course of his action. Martin was not only, *de facto*, the most influential leader of the largest minority group in America at the time (13.4%) but also represented a philosophical touchstone to a significant segment of the majority white population on the issue of race relations and, subsequently, on the national issues of poverty and the war in Vietnam. He was assessed and courted, followed and flattered. Invaded, dissected, and hunted.

I believe that to accurately evaluate the importance of Stanley *in relation to King*, the following question must be considered: Would the FBI have been interested in Stanley if he decided to devote his commitment to social change by working the same amount of time with the American Jewish Congress instead of Martin during the same years? Or, to look at it another way: Why wasn't the FBI, President Kennedy and his brother, the U.S. Communist Party, and Moscow interested in Roy Wilkins, leader of the NAACP, James Farmer of the Congress for Racial Equality, Whitney Young of the National Urban League, or John Lewis of the Student Non-Violent Coordinating Committee or the leaders of Students for a Democratic Society?

It has everything to do with access to Martin.

The FBI, CPUSA, Moscow, and the Kennedys were only interested in Stanley, Jack O'Dell, and me because of our direct relationship with Martin Luther King, Jr., albeit for different (in some cases parallel) reasons. However, even though they followed different agendas, all of the contending parties shared a common, accurate idea: That Martin Luther King, Jr., although not an elected or appointed politician, was

the most powerful leader in America. This was a tacit conclusion; it was never spoken in circles of power, but it was
understood as a fundamental underpinning of global politics
at the time.

The simple and stunning reason is suggested by the speech
given by Gunnar Jahn, Chairman of the Nobel Committee, in
presenting the 1964 Nobel Peace Prize to Dr. King in Oslo,
Norway:

> (Martin) is the first person in the Western world to
> have shown us that a struggle can be waged without
> violence. He is the first to make the message of broth-
> erly love a reality in the course of his struggle, and he
> has brought this message to all men, to all nations and
> races.
>
> Martin Luther King's belief is rooted first and fore-
> most in the teaching of Christ, but no one can really
> understand him unless aware that he has been influ-
> enced also by the great thinkers of the past and the
> present. He has been inspired above all by Mahatma
> Gandhi, whose example convinced him that it is possi-
> ble to achieve victory in an unarmed struggle.
>
> Today, we pay tribute to Martin Luther King, the
> man who has never abandoned his faith in the unarmed
> struggle he is waging, who has suffered for his faith,
> who has been imprisoned on many occasions, whose
> home has been subject to bomb attacks, whose life and
> the lives of his family have been threatened, and who
> nevertheless has never faltered.

From this perspective, the key to America was the Civil Rights
Movement, and the key to that was King. So, if Stanley Levison
was the key to King, how best to turn that key? Each of the
contenders for Stanley's loyalty asked themselves that question.

Understand, when I discuss Stanley Levison's relationship
with Martin, or with the CPUSA (before and concurrent with
his relationship with Martin) and his attitude toward the
Politburo in Moscow, I am doing so with authority. Everything here is based on my own personal recollections and rela-

tionship with Stanley as well as my recent conversations with his son, Andy. Do my conclusions differ from the "objective" findings in the FBI files? Well, by and large I don't dispute the accuracy of the information transcribed from wiretapped conversations between Stanley and Martin, Martin and me, Stanley and me, or conference calls among the three of us or with other parties. Nor do I dispute the contents of internal FBI memos or those between the Kennedy Justice Department and Hoover. What I do dispute is the FBI's oft-erroneous interpretation or ascribed relevance of conversations recorded and transcribed about events or persons who may have been the subject of such conversations. In many instances they had only limited knowledge about the context of taped conversations, yet they went on to extrapolate a great deal.

Moreover, there were plenty of conversations between Stanley and me that were not overheard and transcribed. Though at times he thought I was slightly paranoid, often in the middle of a discussion in his home, his office, or in my home, I would jot a note to tell him I didn't want to continue a particular conversation at that location. We would then go for a walk in the neighborhood or head for a restaurant, where the likelihood of our conversation being recorded by the FBI was remote.

So, the knock against the FBI record on Stanley is that it's less than complete, and where it is wrong, that's due almost exclusively to bad guesswork on the agency's part. With one glaring exception: J. Edgar Hoover's purposeful withholding of a vital piece of information from the president; that he had grown tired of waiting for proof that Stanley was a Communist agent and so they planned on setting him up.

For years I had derided the FBI assertions that the Kremlin was trying to direct the Civil Rights Movement in the United States, seeing them as nothing but scare tactics to sway public opinion against us at the height of the Cold War. Regrettably and ironically, after all these years of saying this was simply not so, in fact, it *was* so. In this limited instance, intellectual honesty and political integrity compel me to acknowledge that Hoover was right, and I was wrong.

Stanley told me these stories personally, and I never imagined I'd repeat them. I certainly never broke my friend's confidence when talking with David Garrow or Taylor Branch.

In reviewing Stanley's own massive pile of Freedom of Information releases recently, his son Andy learned of the efforts from 1957 to at least 1963 by the Communist Party Central Committee in Moscow to influence Dr. King through repeated efforts to contact and persuade Stanley to meet with their KGB designee. Many of these efforts were on the surveillance radar of the FBI. When the two of us spoke recently, we compared information and Andy quickly realized we had a story he felt his father would want the world to hear. With Andy's blessing, I've decided to shed light on an unknown chapter of the SCLC.

FBI files reveal that Victor Lesiovsky, a special assistant to then-U.N. Secretary General U Thant, was allegedly a KGB officer. Lesiovsky developed a friendship with Stanley Levison because of Stanley's direct relationship with Martin. It's hard to imagine, but apparently leaders in Moscow believed they could dictate their ideas to Stanley, who in turn would direct Martin. They didn't understand the relationship there at all.

When an intermediary allegedly between Moscow and Gus Hall, Secretary General of the CPUSA, tried to get Stanley to agree to meet and "Hear them out," Stanley indicated to me that he told them to "Go shove it, and tell their friends in Moscow the same!" He was appalled at how out of touch with reality they were in connection with Martin, and Stanley's devotion to him.

All of this is yet another indication of the power of Martin's role in America during those years. Imagine a group of old Russian men in the Kremlin seriously considering how they could direct or influence the internal policies of the U.S. and landing on a Black clergyman. The mental picture of Politburo cronies muttering in Russian with the only English the occasional Slavic-tinged "Martin Luther King" is surreal. Yet reality can truly be stranger than fiction.

It was a fool's errand. Except for the consistency in his intellectual acumen and business skill, whoever Stanley may have been on the drive to Baltimore that day in 1956 to hear Martin speak was an entirely different man than the one driving home. He was a member of the U.S. Communist Party pre-Martin, but that man no longer existed. Stanley became a converted disciple of Martin Luther King, Jr., and never looked back.

Stanley confided in me that he had heard through the CPUSA that the CPUSSR was angry with him because they held him "responsible" for Martin's public statements of anti-communism. Stanley and I knew that philosophically Martin was a classic Marxist, but so deeply committed to his religious belief in the Lord Jesus Christ there was no possible way to support a godless political philosophy.

It was Stanley's prior Party association, and my prior associations and friendships with folks like Charlotte Goldberg, Mel Williamson, and Bobby Nemiroff that became the ammunition used by the FBI's repeated attempts to discredit Dr. King by linking him to Communism. The centerpiece of their campaign was the charge that he was a "tool of" or was being "manipulated by" communists who were his principal advisors and speechwriters (presumably Stanley and me). And as I've noted, Hoover was right that Moscow was trying. But the horrible part of this web of deceit is that the FBI knew the truth: They knew that every time Stanley was approached by an agent of Moscow, he would flatly refuse any involvement. It wasn't enough for the FBI to see him turn down genuine attempts at communist recruitment, Hoover still felt compelled to take the word of an informant over this record. Any cop will tell you informants have a vested interest in constantly offering information and that the reliability of that kind of tip must be determined though follow-up investigation. But the Federal Bureau of Investigation had their own reasons for trying to bring Martin Luther King, Jr. down, and tying Stanley Levison to the red menace was only one of the angles.

We know where Stanley stood. What about my role as a "red agent?" Did I occasionally buy and read the *Daily Worker,* a newspaper published by the U.S. Communist Party? Yes. Did I express public admiration for certain people like former communist New York City Councilman Benjamin Davis? Yes. Did I meet and admire Louis Burnham, Paul Robeson, Ewart Guinier (father of Professor Lani Guinier, who was President Clinton's nominee to be Assistant Attorney General for Civil Rights before he forced her to withdraw after she was falsely accused of being a "quota queen") William Patterson, Ada B. Jackson and other people deemed left wing, communist or who associated with communists? Yes.

I had never been a member of the Communist Party, but I didn't think it was the government's business if I had been. My attitude was that if the FBI's "approval" of my activities and friendships meant anything, there was something seriously wrong with this country. Simply stated: Who the fuck did the FBI think it was to proscribe my private political conduct or associations?

When Ramsey Clark became Attorney General in 1967, he ordered the FBI to halt wiretaps of Martin, Stanley, and me. However, as Senator Frank Church's U.S. Senate Select Committee to Study Governmental Operations with Respect to Intelligence Activities unveiled in 1976, the activity continued past the dates when Clark served. Once again, no one could reign in J. Edgar Hoover. My friend Martin had unleashed the power of non-violent change, a concept so fundamentally game-changing it terrified those invested in the status quo. They struck back with all they had, legal or not.

Witness what was found upon close inspection. This excerpt is from the Church Committee's special case study of Dr. King, something I believe should be required reading in America today:

> The FBI's program to destroy Dr. King as the leader of the Civil Rights Movement entailed attempts to discredit him with churches, universities, and the press. Steps were taken to attempt to convince the National Council of Churches, the Baptist World Alliance, and leading Protestant ministers to halt financial support of the Southern Christian Leadership Conference (SCLC), and to persuade them that "Negro leaders should completely isolate King and remove him from the role he is now occupying in Civil Rights activities." When the FBI learned that Dr. King intended to visit

*the Pope, an agent was dispatched to persuade Francis
Cardinal Spellman to warn the Pope about "the likely
embarrassment that may result to the Pope should he
grant King an audience." The FBI sought to influence
universities to withhold honorary degrees from Dr.
King. Attempts were made to prevent the publication
of articles favorable to Dr. King and to find "friendly"
news sources that would print unfavorable articles.
The FBI offered to play for reporters' tape recordings
allegedly made from microphone surveillance of Dr.
King's hotel rooms.*

*The FBI mailed Dr. King a tape recording made from its
microphone coverage. According to the Chief of the FBI's
Domestic Intelligence Division, the tape was intended to
precipitate a separation between Dr. King and his wife
in the belief that the separation would reduce Dr. King's
stature. The tape recording was accompanied by a note
which Dr. King and his advisers interpreted as a threat
to release the tape recording unless Dr. King committed
suicide. The FBI also made preparations to promote
someone "to assume the role of leadership of the Negro
people when King has been completely discredited."*

In any other context, this would be a list of charges of a
criminal conspiracy.

Between Watergate and the 1976 Church Committee Senate
Report, 9/11 and today, my observations suggest that our constitutional Bill of Rights have been under an extended state
of siege. By and large our judiciary, with notable exceptions,
has been the protector of our rights to freedom of speech, religion, association, and public assembly. The greatest threat
of a resurgence of the FBI as a rogue agency, threatening or
violating our civil and political rights, has come in the wake
of terrorist attacks against the United States. The challenge
confronting us is the urgency to develop the appropriate balance between domestic liberties and steps necessary for our
government to initiate to protect our country against legitimate threats to our national security.

ELDER STATESMAN

CHAPTER 28 | THE PROGNOSIS

Writing a memoir has been a unique challenge for me. What to write about, what to omit, how detailed to be with the recollections of experiences and interactions with people which occurred across nine decades.

Limitations of space and holding a reader's attention are challenges as I near the end of my journey. The "self-selected" editing of certain threads of events and the people involved will haunt me after the conclusion of this book. Immediate admission: Some things that I observed or experienced during my journey are simply beyond my capability to discuss with any balanced objective recollection. So, I leave to others who experienced similar events or relationships to tell of those experiences I have omitted from these memoirs. And I ask your forbearance—if not forgiveness—for writing about people or experiences that you may have also known or shared.

There has been much more in my life to celebrate and share than the stories from these pages. My time in the '90s and the first part of the 21st century were also exciting and dynamic. There was my honor at the Kennedy Center with Bobby McFerrin, my one-on-one time in the Oval Office with President Obama, the two documentaries competing to tell my life story, my time working with Bryan Stevenson and John Lewis, my appointments as a visiting scholar at Stanford and the University of San Francisco, and more.

However, to avoid the risk of overstaying my welcome, I feel that the stories shared in this memoir should come to a dignified end with a very simple metaphor: Health.

. . .

It was 1995. I was at the office of my doctor Jay Meltzer for a medical examination. At the time I was living in Putnam County, north of New York City in a town called Paterson. The exam had been requested and required for insurance coverage in connection with some business matter I was involved in. I do not recall what it was, but it was all very routine.

Until it wasn't.

Among the series of tests which were conducted was the test described as a prostate specific antigen or PSA. Dr. Meltzer had blood laboratory facilities on the premises with his office. My blood test returned showing a PSA of P38.

Dr. Meltzer looked troubled. He told me I had to go immediately to Memorial Sloan Kettering hospital a few blocks from his office. He explained to me that PSA level required immediate medical attention. In spite of my protestations, he called the hospital, and a few hours later I was at admitted as a cancer patient.

There I met with medical personnel from the office of Chief radiologist and surgeon Dr. Zvi Fuchs. After some conversation about my overall medical and health condition, he said I needed to have an operation on my prostate to remove the cancerous tissue. I listened carefully. But I also vividly remembered my mother having an operation to remove ovarian cancer on January 8th, 1952, (on my nineteenth birthday) and dying on May 4th, 1952. I advised Dr. Fuchs that I would not agree to have an operation on my prostate. While he thought I was a crazy and considered me a difficult patient, he sat down and patiently explained to me what my option would be if I did not have surgery.

This would involve twelve weeks of radiation therapy after a customized lead shield had been designed with designated holes for radiation beams to be directed at my prostate. I was further advised that they would make a 3D image of my prostate enabling them to direct radiation beams through the holes in the shield. I would be strapped to a board and they would shoot the radiation at the right spots in an effort to destroy the cancer. I liked the sound of that better than the surgery.

I was 64 years old; one year short of eligibility for Medicare. Radiation treatment was insanely expensive. I was involved in business matters with Percy Sutton at the time and discussed my medical and financial situation with him.

"Clarence," he said, "you need to focus on dealing with this." Percy told me he would call Memorial Sloan Kettering and guarantee the payment of all medical costs associated with my treatment.

At Memorial Sloan Kettering, I had been part of a research project exploring new treatments for prostate cancer. In one, they took healthy cells from a mouse and injected them into patients in the hope they would spur the development of cells to destroy the cancer.

It turns out that I was in the control group of 75 patients, meaning I wasn't getting the experimental treatment (though of course I was getting the radiation). Years later, I learned that I ended up the only surviving patient from the control group.

I vividly remember the last day of the twelve week, five-days-a-week treatment. It occurred on December 19th, 1995, a gray and snowy day. Frank Biondi, Jr., the major player in the entertainment industry, had asked me to stop by his office and see him on the last day of my treatment.

After some pleasantries when I visited Frank in his office, he asked his secretary Norma to come in and look at me because he "had never seen a Black man turn pale." He said I looked gray like a mouse, which was from the cumulative effect of the radiation.

Frank asked what I was going to do with my children because it was Christmastime. I hadn't given any thought to it since I was so weak from the radiation. Norma gave Frank an envelope which he passed over to me. Apparently, she'd gone to the bank on his behalf. Nestled in the envelope he handed to me was $5,000 in cash. He said he wanted to assure that my family would be all right for the holidays.

Another human dimension of my cancer treatment was my relationship with Carl Dickerson, who is a Black man, now in his eighties. Carl would call me at Sloan Kettering almost every day while I sat in the waiting room preparing to be zapped by radiation. Afterwards, he would call again just to see how I was doing.

At the time, Carl was at the height of his business success. He was the 24/7, take no prisoners head of one of the most successful insurance agencies in Southern California. I knew he had better things to do than check in on me.

People like Carl Dickerson, Percy Sutton, and Frank Bondi, Jr. are what has helped make my life special. Carl and I remain close, and it still pains me that Frank died in 2019. He was an extraordinarily decent and good person, and hardly a day goes by that I don't think of him and miss him, often tearing up (as I am now writing about him). Life is indeed unfair.

There are some lessons to be learned here. Each of us has to decide at what we can endure. What will "bend" them versus what will "break" them. For example, the death of my mother at the age of nineteen broke me. But I was able to put myself back together. I frequently remind people, even today, that I can really be hurt, but I cannot be broken because I know what it feels like to be at the mountaintop of pain.

Any pain less than the pain of losing my mother struck me as no big thing. As James McMurtry sings, "It don't mean that much if it don't bleed."

I've learned from years of medical discussions, examinations, and treatments that there is a vast difference between what the fit human and what the out-of-shape person can endure during moments of medical crisis.

I had never smoked cigarettes. Occasionally, I puffed on a cigar. I'd never engaged in drug use, except for the occasional hit of marijuana. I exercised frequently for years jogging between four and six miles a day, six days a week, rain, snow, or shine. When I wasn't running, I would be working out in a gym. I ate mostly fish and vegetables.

This healthy lifestyle has helped me conquer the medical issues I faced later, such as having an aorta heart valve implanted and an unexpectedly metastasized cancer in my lower back, neck, and ribs. This too was treated by radiation before it could spread.

But I'm not stupid. I know I'm living an actuarial outlier. The reaper is breathing down my neck, as it does for us all—I just happen to have had a closer look at the dude than most.

The prognosis for my beating the prostate cancer in 1995 was not great. But I persevered, and I prevailed. It took an arsenal of determination, focus, patience, tolerance for pain, and willingness to change fundamental behaviors in order to do so.

I bring up my cancer story not for any lessons it taught me about physiology, medicine, or the human survival instinct, but for its value as a living metaphor. Which brings me, somewhat unceremoniously, to the broader point here: I believe our country suffers from a kind of cancer that is based in— and driven by—racism.

Let me repeat so we're clear: America has a cancer, and it is racism.

It is at the heart of gang violence, the exploding prison population, police brutality, gerrymandering and redlining, the criminal justice code, the public school system, the political machine, the war on drugs, and a longer list of social ills than I have time to type.

But to cite one simple example to stand in for so many others, consider the legislative agenda of Florida's Republican Governor Ron DeSantis. Not content to let his state's Department of Education simply reject a proposed AP African American studies course for "lacking educational value and being "contrary to Florida law," which was preposterous enough. DeSantis had to weigh in personally.

"We want education, not indoctrination," the Governor said at a press conference. "We believe in teaching kids facts and how to think, but we don't believe they should have an agenda imposed on them."

I would suggest there is a touch of the Orwellian in such language. There is no doubt an agenda is being imposed on Florida students, but it's the version of which DeSantis approves. Make no mistake, a white-washed curriculum that avoids critical discussions of race is part of an agenda.

Now, I can agree with the Governor that no one alive today, white, Black, or any other race, is responsible for slavery. Nor are we responsible for the Declaration of Independence. We nonetheless exist in their shadow and under their effects. We all live with the after effects of our nation's entire original sin, an arc of injustice ranging from the first slave trade to Jim Crow to modern policing. Avoiding heavy discussions of race won't make the racial problem disappear. To the contrary, it will fester. I would suggest to Governor DeSantis that flood-light is the best disinfectant.

There is a question. For me, it is easily anticipated. Actually, I rarely meet someone new and not end up fielding the question within the first half hour. Because of my history, my status, my age and, of course, the color of my skin, the question always surfaces.

"Dr. Jones, how do we fix the problem of racism in America?"

Well meaning, certainly... but in many ways this is the wrong question. Trial attorneys have a rhetorical technique referred to as "the theory of the case," which is designed to lay out clearly for a jury a kind of realistic and plausible explanation for how events unfolded to point either to a prosecutor's conclusion of guilt or the defense lawyer's claim of innocence.

In this spirit, allow me to present my theory of the case for racism in the United States:

> Racial injustice is here by design; it is fully, meticulously, and purposefully baked into our institutions, our sacred texts, our laws, our infrastructure. It is beneficial in some ways to the majority class. Therefore, it won't go away through the good will of many eager, well-meaning, and compassionate citizens. Ever.
>
> It is codified.

. . .

If so, if I am right about this, the benefits of racist behavior accrue not by accident, not as anomaly. It is not meant to get fixed but rather to go unnoticed. Further, if it is to be fixed, it must be at a foundational level. As a starting point, consider that the phrase "All men are created equal" cannot be found in the Constitution. However, this phrase can:

> *Representatives and direct Taxes shall be apportioned among the several States... which shall be determined by adding to the whole Number of free Persons, including those bound to Service for a Term of Years, and excluding Indians not taxed, three fifths of all other Persons.*

That is Section I, Article 2, the so called "Three-Fifths Compromise" enshrined in our beloved Constitution, pointing out right off the bat that the Founding Fathers considered some individuals less than whole people. While it's likely the majority of Americans (possibly the *vast* majority), make little or no distinction between the Declaration of Independence and the Constitution, such context is critical, because the Declaration of Independence is the billboard, the movie trailer, the glossy magazine ad. It is aspirational, and it sold the sizzle. But the Constitution is the steak, the blueprint design for the gears and levers and flywheels of actual power. And for hundreds of years, white America has conflated the two. This is the primary reason that the wounds of race are not yet healed; the mythology this country regurgitates about herself clouds the reality of her history to her own citizenry. White America tells itself a story of independence, freedom, and self-determination, and wants it to be true. Further, it shouts the story to the world. It exports it as ideology and holds it up as a model. It believes its own bullshit deeply.

And mind you, I do not say historical record here, I say history. There is a difference. The historical record has been nearly scrubbed free of the truth of the systematic oppression and suppression of the will and rights of Black Americans. But the history is still there to be discovered... if one is willing to dig.

Yet the whitewashing continues. Interestingly, those who claim there is no such thing as institutional racism really mean they would like to hide that fact from view. Consider Donald Trump's September 2020 Executive Order. The Department of Labor at the time called it "a key civil rights priority of the Trump Administration." The driving idea was to fight "offensive and anti-American race and sex stereotyping and scapegoating" but—here's a twist—through a pro-white lens.

As *USA Today* reported:

> *Asked about his executive order during the first presidential debate, Trump said: "They were teaching people that our country is a horrible place, it's a racist place. And they were teaching people to hate our country. And I'm not gonna allow that to happen."*

The idea of an America as inherently racist would be legislated. Any company that had diversity training materials or instructors that even dared to mention concepts such as *white privilege, unconscious bias,* or *systemic racism* would lose the opportunity to gulp from the deep government trough of contracts. These are huge organizations, like Boeing, Microsoft, Apple, and 3M, as well as small companies that would collapse without government work. Talk about a chilling effect. It's almost like a direct pushback on the Civil Rights Act of '64, but without even bothering with Congress to get it underway.

I ask you, are these the words—the legal strategies—of a person interested in a true accounting and reckoning of racism in America? And make no mistake, that person represents a political party, and that party's point of view. And it may be the minority party (not since George W. Bush's post 9/11 reelection has the Republican Party won the presidential popular vote) but its ideology does align with a significant portion of our citizenry. And wherever Republicans are in control, there is considered effort at political redistricting and voter suppression. As a practical matter, these are tools of a ruling minority that do not benefit from continued discussion of intrinsic racism woven into our society. At this point there is much debate surrounding Trump's Executive Order, including litigation.

But had the man won a second term or wrestled the job away from the winner in another way (both reasonable scenarios), America would be further down the fascist memory hole technique of changing the historic facts. It is sobering.

In the roughly four hundred years of European control over what's now known as the United States of America, there have been only a handful of seismic upheavals with respect to the journey of Black people from chattel to citizens. And the journey wasn't always a straight path forward, either. In addition to the Three-Fifths Compromise, we've had the dual Virginia crucibles of Nat Turner's rebellion and John Brown's Harpers Ferry raid, the Civil War and its resultant Emancipation Proclamation, the passage of the 14th, 15th, and 16th Amendments to the Constitution. Tulsa. Tuskegee.

I was alive for—and a part of—the most recent and most positive of these upheavals: The Civil Rights Movement of the 1960s (and with it, the Voting Rights and Civil Rights Acts of 1964 and 1965). But at ninety-two, I'm getting the sinking feeling that I won't be around for the next incarnation. The basic question that confronts the world's oppressed people is: How is the struggle against the forces of injustice to be waged? There are two possible answers. One is resorting to corrosive hatred and all methods of physical violence. The other is non-violent protest. Political history and my own life experiences have persuaded me that power concedes nothing without a demand and that with notable exceptions, the power of nonviolence uniquely transforms all other forms and rhetoric of struggle.[53]

More than fifty years have passed since Dr. King's assassination, and by my clock the next phase should have happened by now. But it hasn't. After the murder of George Floyd, we saw the Black Lives Matter protests throughout the nation and the accompanying media attention (particularly focused on the looting, property damage, rioting). But a sustained shift in the tone and attitudes around racial inequity has yet

---

53 One notable exception—the exception that proves the rule, perhaps—was the war for independence in Algeria. However, in America, the power of violent conflict has never even come close to the power of non-violent protest.

to take root. We have yet to alter the mood or temperature of the country in a wholesale fashion. To be clear, I am not claiming that the vast majority of our country's citizens are actively racist. (And remember that not being actively racist is significantly different from being anti-racist.) Rather, I believe our current mix of true racists, anti-racists, and passive acceptors have tilted our social/legal foundation on a white European-centric axis. That has made for a country that struggles with fundamental equality.

Similarly, if we ignore them, I believe the backslide we witnessed with the whiplash transition from Barack Obama to Donald Trump was just the beginning.

The silver lining in all this? Our government is—also by design—of, by, and for the people. We can change as a country, and there is a system in place to do so, although it is brittle and slow. It is through the change in the laws of the land that constrain and proscribe our behaviors.

Consider as one example the disproportionate prison sentencing guidelines for crack and powder cocaine possession. Two forms of the same drug that nevertheless carried with them vastly different penalties. It should come as no surprise that the version of the drug that was low-priced and primarily found in communities of color was the one with the harsher penalty. Before 2010, the disparity was 100:1. The Fair Sentencing Act compressed the ratio down to 18:1. I'll ignore for now that the only accurate use of the word "fair" would be a ratio of 1:1 and instead focus on the positive aspects here: A bias that was baked into the nation's drug laws was noticed, called out, debated, and eventually improved. Not entirely corrected, clearly... but improved upon.

In this fashion, I see the job ahead as specific: Shining a light on the roots of our institutions that come out of the racist/Eurocentric ideology of our country's founding. In essence, the polar opposite of Trump's Executive Order. By teaching the reality of our history clearly and without hysteria, we will gain some degree of critical mass; agreement on which rules are rigged and how. Once the state of play becomes understood, the game can be rebalanced using changes in the law, which is really the only structure we have to compensate for inequity. We are a nation of laws; when the laws are fair, then the people are treated fairly. When they are not, the unfairness needs to be processed by those under rule, acknowledged.

The United States of America is dancing on a razor's edge. *We will tip one way or the other very soon.* There are leaders of ill will out there, like Trump and DeSantis. But we also have remarkable talents like Barack Obama, who has been uniquely endowed with skills and experiences that transcend just being a former two-term U.S. President.

With a leader like Obama on-board for the long haul, we can then begin the work of deep education on inequity, followed by an organized campaign at the ballot box to bring new representation to power with the mandate to start changing the system legally and from within. A simple two-step process that only requires the will to do right, open hearts and minds, and a deliberate dedication to justice for all.

This is how you remake the Land of the Free in order to form a more perfect union. Better four hundred and fifty years too late than never.

I ain't gone yet. The next book you get from me won't be about the past but the future. Even at ninety-two years, the road ahead calls, littered with pencils and dollar bill to pick up.

I hope you'll walk it with me.

ACKNOWLEDGEMENTS

ACKNOWLEDGMENTS

The authors offer grateful thanks to: Matt Bennett for his good advice, sharp eye, and sense of urgency; Sonya Denyse of DreamDevelopment.com for steering the project through the stormy waters and guiding us to our publishing home; the team at Redhawk—Patty Thompson, Richard Eller, Robert Canipe, Shelly Benoit, Tim Peeler and Melanie Zimmermann— for going the extra editorial mile with patience and Southern ease; Johnathan Greenberg, our *aide de camp* for this book; and to P.J. van Sandwijk, for staying the course, even if it means tacking into the wind.

We honor those no longer with us who fought the good fight (non-violent and otherwise): Percy E. Sutton, Malcolm X, Lorraine Hansberry, Arthur Liman, Robert Nemiroff, Art D'Lugoff, Charlie Chaplin, Fannie Lou Hamer, John Daly, Jack Odell, Shirley Chisholm, Ralph Abernathy, William Kunstler, Grace & John Killens, C.T. Vivian, Johnathan Lubell, David Lubell, Viola Liuzzo, George Douglas & Clementine Pugh, Bella Abzug, Sol Linowitz, Lainie Cook, Dan & Myra Addison, Frank Biondi, Jonathan Edelstein, Betty Olnick, Arthur Kinoy, Morty Stavis, Tony Brown, Mersh Greenberg, Scotty Scott, Harry Wachtel, James Baldwin, Burt D'Ludoff, Adam Clayton Powell, Sr., W.E.B. Du Bois, Hon. John Lewis, Muhammad Ali, Frederick Shuttlesworth, Rip Torn, Steven Ungerleider, Stanley Levison, and Martin Luther King, Jr.

As this book was going to press, we learned of Harry Belafonte's death. Future editions will contain a more thorough remembrance, but for now it will have to suffice for us to say: in a way no other Civil Rights leader possibly could, Harry put everything on the line and had everything to lose for the cause of equality in this country and throughout the world. He put his money where his mouth was; he walked the walk; he righteously championed of the Black man and woman anywhere and everywhere; he was a hero in every conceivable sense of the word.

STUART CONNELLY

As always, I remain indescribably grateful for the loving support of my family—Mary Jo, Wesley, and Callie. Living with a writer isn't easy, but you make it feel that way.

Thanks also to Joe D'Agnese, Denise Kiernan, and Jay O'Connell for being there when it counts.

Of course I raise a glass to the late, great other John Keats, whose ghost consistently gives me traction by asking: *What, in twenty-five words or less, is all this nonsense about?*

And then there's the man himself, Clarence B. Jones. Writers write; what really matters is the story they choose to tell. And you've got some good stories. Eternal gratitude for letting me help tell them, for pointing me in the direction of meaning, for allowing me to do what I do in the service of something that matters.

I thought I was awake before I started working with you, but I wasn't. I'm sure as hell awake now.

CLARENCE B. JONES

At 92 I remember a great deal, but people in my life...please forgive me if I've accidentally left you off this list. For their support and assistance on this project and throughout the years, I would like to thank: President Barack Obama, Andy Levison, Raymond McGuire, C.B. Atkins, John L. Edmonds, Clarence Avant, Jim Baer, Michael & Annette Flicker, Steve Baum, Roger Berlind, Herb Berman, Jerry Kupfer, Michelle Bernard, Carl Robinson, Robert Boehm, Dr. Alfred Cannon,

Joyce Johnson-Miller, Jonathan Capehart, Clay & Susan Carson, Denise D'Rosario, Arthur Carter, Hon. Charles Rangel, Kenneth & Kathy Chenault, June & Walter Christmas, Hosea Williams, Marshall Coggin, Paul Meltzer, Elaine Berman, Sandy & Joan Weill, Jerome Deutsche, Edie Lutnik, Don & Doris Elliot, Marian Gibson, Charlie Sutton, Ron Gillyard, Dr. John Henry Clark, Bonnie Greenberg, Carl & Jean Dickerson, Ewart Guinier, Ben Hill, Alyssa Solomon, Harry Hirshman, Voza Rivers, Bennett Johnson, Sr., Jamie Mount, Jamel Joseph, C.B. King, Robert Levin, Dr. Shari Rogers, Theodore Wells, Jr., Beatrice Levison, Malveaux Marva Jr., Bernard Fishman, Martin Horowitz, Roderick Robert McKay, Steve Ross, John Johnson, Sr., Tenesha Armstrong, Herbert Mohammed, Abe Thompson, Hugh Morrow, Carol Biondi, Constance Baker Motley, James Comey, Gloria Cantor, Michele Norris & Broderick Johnson, James Orange, Frank Mercado Valdes, Joseph Filner, Bert Pearce, Sean Gibbons, Chester & Gladys Redhead, Norman & Arline Rodman, Shelley Archambeau, Robert Ryan, Charlotte Schiff-Booker, Andrea & Jason Spero, Bryan Stevenson, Bennett Johnson III, Charlotte Sutton, Lisa Weitzman, Howard Edelstein, Joe Palermo, Livingston Roy Wingate, Joseph Vadapalas, Enrique Borja Bohorquez, Jeffrey Seller, Soledad O'Brien, Joe Marshall, Natsuko Greenberg, Helen Jacobson, Judy Treistman, Rev. Eugene Rivers, David & Sylvia Goodman, Philip & Peggy Pizzo, Margo Davis, Marty & Andrea Kalin, Ella Baker, Craig Menin, Father Paul Fitzgerald, Stevie Wonder, Budd Mishkin, Damian Woetzel, Galen McKinzie, Michele & Roderick Johnson, Richard Callahan, Stuart D'Rosario, and Father Stephen Privett.

To my family: Christine Jones Tucker, Ed Tucker, Alexia Norton Jones, Clarence Benjamin Jones Jr., Dana Nicholas Goldsboro Jones, Felicia Elizabeth Jones, and my beloved Lin Schaefer Walters.

I offer my highest admiration to his medical enablers for this 92-year-and-counting journey: Drs. Halstead Holman, Jay I.

Meltzer, Zvi Fuks, Howard I. Scher, Edward Anderson, Barry Eisenberg, Natalia Colocci, Valentin Fuster, and Robert Harrington.

And finally, constraint of both space the language itself makes it difficult to express the gratitude I have for Stuart Connelly and his years of 24/7 daily dedication to me (and his wife and children for making room for it). They have become extended family.

In a unique and surreal role-reversal, it seems he has at times become for me the kind of idea-man and wordsmith that I became for Martin Luther King, Jr. I am not nor could ever be a "Dr King," but Stuart Connelly not only has become my Godson, but more importantly, the "Clarence B. Jones" to me that I needed.

This acknowledgment is the highest form of gratitude and deserved tribute that I can think of.

ABOUT THE AUTHOR

ABOUT THE AUTHOR

Dr. Clarence B. Jones served as legal counsel, advisor, and draft speechwriter to Dr. Martin Luther King, Jr. from 1960 until Dr. King's assassination in 1968. During that time, Dr. King depended on Dr. Jones for assistance in drafting landmark speeches and public testimony. He is credited with writing the first seven paragraphs of the iconic I Have a Dream speech.

Vanity Fair called him "The man who kept King's secrets."

He has authored two acclaimed books *What Would Martin Say?* and *Behind the Dream: The Making of the Speech that Transformed a Nation,* and countless articles and essays for many national publications.

Across the decades following Dr. King's death, Dr. Jones worked to carry on Dr. King's legacy. As a lawyer, Civil Rights leader, and businessman, Dr. Jones maintained close friendships and working relationships with influential artists, writers, athletes, and social justice activists.

Jones currently serves as the Chairman of the Spill the Honey Foundation, an organization dedicated to Black-Jewish relations. He also founded the Dr. Clarence B. Jones Institute for Social Advocacy and also serves as the Founding Director Emeritus of the Institute for Nonviolence and Social Justice at the University of San Francisco.

Dr. Jones has been honored at events at Columbia University, where he was an undergraduate, and the Julliard School of Performing Arts, where he studied music. In 2021, he received the Thurgood Marshall Award from the American Bar Association, the highest recognition given by the ABA, awarded in a ceremony in August 2021 with a keynote address from President Barack Obama.

He has been passionately engaged as a writer, public speaker, and teacher, dedicated to furthering the legacy of Martin Luther King, Jr. among a broad public audience and from generation to generation.

Dr. Jones served as a Scholar in Residence at Stanford University's Martin Luther King, Jr. Research and Education Institute and Diversity Professor at the University of San Francisco. A popular course he developed and taught at USF ("From Slavery to Obama: Renewing the Promise of Reconstruction") is now taught online in many historically Black colleges.

EPILOGUE

INDEX

INDEX

Symbols

A

D

L

T

About the Font

Century Schoolbook is a transitional serif typeface designed by Morris Fuller Benton in 1919 for the American Type Founders (ATF) at the request of Ginn & Co., a textbook publisher, which wanted an especially easy-to-read face for textbooks. Century Schoolbook has elements similar to the Didone classification.